"I have admired and learned from Sara Moulton for years. She is first and foremost a teacher, and expert in balancing concrete advice with inspiration and encouragement. Without ever talking down to the home cook, Sara imparts her imitable wisdom, and makes readers say, 'YES. I want to do this, too!' In short, if you want to become a smarter, better, more confident cook, you need to buy this book."

—Katie Workman author of *Dinner Solved!: The Mom 100 Cookbook,* and creator of TheMom100.com blog

SARA MOULTON'S
HOME COOKING 101
How to Make Everything Taste Better

SARA MOULTON'S
HOME COOKING 101
How to Make Everything Taste Better

SARA MOULTON

Oxmoor
House®

Dedication
To my home team—Bill, Ruthie, and Sam.

Special Thanks to
Leah McLaughlin, who dreamt up this book.

Anja Schmidt, of Oxmoor House, for shepherding the project.

Rachel West, of Oxmoor House, who took Leah's idea and made it real.

Marisa Bulzone, the most extraordinary independent editor on the planet.

Grace Parisi, who set the vision for the food styling.

Lucy Schaeffer, for all the excellent field shots.

My very talented guest authors for contributing their recipes and wisdom.

Judith Weber, my intrepid agent.

Jill Levy and Claire Lewis, the hard-working and talented
interns from the International Culinary Center who cheerfully
tested and re-tested all the recipes in this book.

The whole Oxmoor House team for their hard work.

Grateful Appreciation to
Chantal, for donating the cookware used in this book.

Eileen Fisher, for wardrobe.

Broadway Panhandler, for lending kitchen equipment.

The Brooklyn Kitchen, The Meat Hook, Union Square Greenmarket,
and Sobel Weber Associates for serving as photography locations.

GOOD COOKING:
IT'S ALL ABOUT THE DETAILS

If you selected 10 people and handed them the same recipe to prepare, you'd end up with 10 different dishes. And if you asked a panel of everyday people to taste these dishes, they'd declare that some tasted much better than the others. How is that possible?

It's because good cooking is all about the details: having the pan hot enough, salting at the right moment, using certain techniques to maximize flavor, and balancing the five components of taste (sweet, salty, bitter, sour, and umami)—or even knowing that there *are* five components of taste. These are things that most home cooks don't often stop to consider.

The goal of this book, then, is two-fold: to sharpen your sense of taste and to provide you with a raft of time-tested techniques that I hope will become second nature to you. The recipes in this book are very good—I'm proud of them and hope you'll enjoy them, but that's not why I want you to prepare them. More important is that each one specifically demonstrates a tip or method that can make you a better and more confident cook while also teaching you how to make your dishes taste better.

What emboldens me to attempt such an ambitious agenda? A lifetime in the trenches. I studied at cooking school in America, and then studied some more in France. I worked in restaurants for seven years, tested and developed recipes for *Gourmet* for four years, ran *Gourmet*'s dining room for 21 years, and hosted my own cooking shows on the Food Network for almost 10 years. These days I host a show on PBS and write a weekly food column for the Associated Press.

But whatever I was doing out in the working world, I was still Mom at home. And it was still somehow my job to put dinner on the table—a *tasty* dinner—at the end of every day. It wasn't easy. It's not easy. But the solution for me has never been to grab a bucket of McNuggets on the way home. I am a student of Julia Child, who understood that cooking and dining is not at all like pumping gas into a car. She took her cues from the French, for whom the family meal is absolutely central. I sometimes cooked with Julia at her home in Cambridge, Massachusetts, in advance of dinner parties she and Paul, her husband, often hosted. A whole gang of us would be bustling around in the kitchen, when Julia would invariably pipe up, "Aren't we having *fun!*". And, suddenly thinking about it, we realized that the answer was yes, we were indeed having fun. Here's the best recipe I can give you: Cooking and dining together with your loved ones is the recipe for a good life.

1 | *the 10 basics of great home* COOKING

I believe that most folks would love to put a home-cooked meal on the table every night. I also understand that a sizable number of those folks figure that doing so is an impossible dream. They tell themselves that they lack the time, the money, and the know-how.

This book is dedicated to the proposition that none of those hurdles is too high to jump. In fact, chances are they're higher in your imagination than in reality: Making dinner takes less time than you think, it costs less than you think (indeed, it's cheaper than fast food), and it's easier than you think.

As a professional chef, teacher, and home cook, I've spent the last 40 years refining my thinking on these very subjects. In truth, it happens naturally. Anyone who does something—or anything— over and over again finds that the shortcuts begin to make themselves pretty obvious after awhile. (People always ask me, "How do I learn to cook?" My standard answer is, "Just cook.")

The list that follows—the basics of great home cooking—crystallizes my lifetime of experience in the kitchen. I pass it on as an end in itself—good cooking is its own reward—and as a means to an end: Cooking leads to dining, and dining together strengthens the bonds of family and friends.

I. SHAKE HANDS WITH YOUR STOVE.

"Shake hands with your racket" is what they used to tell me as a kid taking tennis lessons. (Although I never really excelled at the sport—I was always too distracted by the thought of what was for lunch.) Essentially, what they were saying was feel comfortable with this tool first before you start playing. I think the basic advice is sound enough to be transferrable. The equivalent for our purposes is "Shake hands with your stove."

You may be shocked to learn that I work with an *electric* stove and oven. Most chefs prefer gas stovetops. I'd probably choose gas myself if the New York City building where we live was zoned for it, but I've been stuck with electric for years, and not just in the city, but at my parent's farmhouse in the country, too. These days I don't mind cooking on an electric stove because I've become familiar with it. I know to move the pan from a high burner to a low burner when I need to reduce the heat quickly. I know on exactly which oven rack I should place that pan when I want to put some color on my food. You should do the same. Whether you cook with gas or electric, get to know your stove.

2. BUY A GOOD KNIFE.

A good knife is an investment for life; if you spend real money on only one piece of kitchen equipment, let it be for that knife. And it should be a 10-inch chef's knife. Seems like a mismatch, you say? What's a woman so small doing with a knife so large? Making it easy for herself.

Let me explain. When you're chopping, the knife should do all the work, not you. You're there to guide the knife, not muscle it. The weight of a chef's knife is greatest at the point where the blade meets the handle. (This is called the bolster.) I refer to the part of the blade that starts at the bolster and extends for several inches toward the tip of the knife as "the guillotine." It's the section of the knife under which you should position your victim, whether it's an onion, a carrot, or a bunch of herbs.

On an 8-inch knife, the guillotine is only about 2 inches long. On a 10-inch knife it's more like 4 inches long. The longer knife's additional real estate allows you to do twice the amount of work in the same amount of time and using the same amount of energy you'd expend with the smaller knife. I rest my case.

It's also crucial to keep the blade sharp. Do so by using a whetstone. A whetstone puts an edge back on a knife that has become dull. It's affordable and effective. Just be sure to read the instructions regarding the correct angle at which to hold the knife when you pull it across the whetstone. (It differs depending on where the knife was manufactured.) Or you can use an electric sharpener. As long as you don't overdo it and grind down the blade until it resembles a boning knife, an electric sharpener will do a fine job. (Chef's Choice makes a good one.)

After you sharpen your knife, you need to hone it on a steel (a long, thin rod made of high-carbon steel), which helps to maintain the edge. And if you run your knife several times down the steel every day, it will stay sharp much longer. There is a terrific gadget from Messermeister called a Taylor's Eye Chantry knife sharpener, which is actually just two short steels crossed at exactly the right angle. All you have to do is pull your knife through it several times and the gadget will maintain the edge on the knife. I have one on my counter and use it every day.

Finally, if you have the time and funds, take a knife skills class; it will improve your performance in the kitchen enormously.

3. PLAN AHEAD FOR SHOPPING.

Planning a menu, or having at least a vague game plan, should happen before you set out for the grocery store. Trying to improvise it on the way home from work—What am I cooking and which ingredients do I need?—is not a recipe for success. Often you'll end up buying all sorts of things you don't truly need just because you're too hungry to think straight.

I try to plan for the week ahead during the weekend, when life is a little less hectic. If I don't select specific recipes, I nonetheless make sure that I've chosen five items in each of three categories: protein, starch, and vegetable. Having those items at hand before the week starts makes it much easier to get dinner on the table. Each night I pick a single item from Column A, Column B, and Column C and start cooking.

All the recipes in this book are based on raw ingredients. (The trouble with prepared food is that much of it's filled with unnecessary and unhealthy additives, especially extra sugar, salt, and fat.) A good meal is based on **good ingredients,** so pay attention when you're shopping.

4. FOLLOW THE RECIPE EXACTLY THE FIRST TIME YOU MAKE IT.

Once you have your groceries in-house, it's time to start cooking. **When making a recipe for the first time, be sure to read it from start to finish *before* you start cooking.** (You don't want your guests anxiously waiting for dinner in the other room when you finally get to the part of the recipe that says, "Chill overnight.") And follow the recipe exactly even if you think you know how to do it better. Usually the person who wrote it had a good reason for writing it that way. You might learn something.

BUYING FRESH PRODUCE

▶ **What about organic fruits and vegetables?** The great thing about organic produce is that it's grown without pesticides, which is much better for the environment. The less great thing about organic produce is that it takes a lot more work to grow than conventional agriculture, which means that it's usually more pricey.

▶ **When you buy nonorganic fruits and vegetables,** just be sure to wash them well with plain old water, which will remove much of the pesticides.

▶ Another option for fresh produce is **buying local** from farm stands, farmers' markets, and food co-ops. Locally grown food has not been engineered to withstand traveling huge distances. Generally, then, it is less contaminated than the stuff that comes from far out of your area.

▶ **Or you can join a CSA,** which stands for community-supported agriculture. CSAs require a group of folks to buy shares in what a farmer will grow in the coming year. That money allows the farmer to buy and plant seeds and to maintain the farm throughout the growing season. In exchange, each shareholder picks up a box of vegetables every week at an affordable price. (To find a CSA near you, visit localharvest.org.)

There are many different kinds of salt available at the store; but broadly there are two kinds: mined salt and sea salt. Here are some of your choices and their properties:

Table salt is comprised of tiny, regularly-shaped grains. It contains an additive to keep it free flowing. It's my salt of choice in dessert recipes because it dissolves quickly.

Kosher salt is comprised of large, irregular flakes. Usually there are no additives, although some brands contain an additive to make them free flowing. Chef's love kosher salt because, unlike table salt, it's very easy to pick up with your fingers and sprinkle onto your ingredients, it falls evenly on top of the food you're seasoning, and it's easier to gauge how much you are adding. Kosher salt is less dense than table salt, so if a recipe calls for 1 teaspoon of table salt, add 2 teaspoons of Diamond Crystal kosher salt or 1½ teaspoons of Morton coarse kosher salt (two of the most readily available brands).

5. DISPENSE WITH *MISE EN PLACE.*

Mise en place, a cornerstone of classic French cooking technique, is one of the first things taught at cooking school. It means "put in place." The rule is to prep and measure all your ingredients *before* you start cooking.

I don't bother with it anymore, except in a few rare cases. Why not? Because I realized that I was spending a lot of time preparing all the ingredients in advance instead of taking advantage of lulls in the cooking time of one ingredient to prep the next ingredient. Say I'm making a pasta dish. I start by pulling all the ingredients out and laying them on the counter. (In fact, I start every recipe this way.) I put on a pot of water, and then chop the onion and start cooking it in a pan with oil. Then, *while the onion is cooking,* I mince the garlic. When the onion is softened, I add the garlic. Then, *while the garlic is cooking,* I start chopping the tomatoes for the tomato sauce, etc. You see what I mean? It's another good reason to read the recipe from start to finish first before you start cooking—you can plan your prep to take advantage of cooking times.

My one exception to the No *Mise en Place* Rule? Stir fries, the Asian dishes in which ingredients are added rapid fire to the pan, one after another. Without *mise en place* you will have burned the first ingredient before you've prepped the second ingredient. That's how fast the action is. With stir-fries, all the ingredients must be prepped and laid out in advance. (See Grace Young's Stir-Fried Beef with Broccoli and Red Peppers, page 194.)

6. REACH FOR THE SALT.

No ingredient is more crucial to making food taste good than salt. Added in the right amounts at the right time, salt not only contributes saltiness, it also enhances the flavor of any ingredient to which it's added. With salt, steaks taste more steak-y, tomatoes more tomato-y. Salt lightly, but regularly, as you go, adding a pinch at the beginning, middle, and end. Folks who add no salt to a recipe until the very end are denying this super seasoning the chance to work its magic in full.

In practice, salt doesn't really amplify flavor as much as it tamps down bitterness, thus allowing a food's other flavors—notably its sweetness or sourness—freer rein. Studies have also suggested that salt helps to increase the aroma of food, which also makes it taste better.

Here's an experiment to illustrate my point: Cut a steak in half. Season the first half *before* you cook it and the second half *after* you cook it. The first half will taste nicely steak-y. The second half will taste like steak with salt on top. Better yet, take a third steak, season it a few hours ahead of time, pat it dry, cook it, and then give it a taste. Now you're talking *extra* steak-y.

Salt also rids vegetables of excess water—and the less your veggies taste like water, the more they taste like themselves. Even the ripest tomatoes benefit from presalting. Depending on how you plan to use them, cut or slice fresh tomatoes, lay them out on a plate, and sprinkle them with salt. Let them stand for 20 to 30 minutes, pour off any liquid, and proceed to add the tomatoes to your sandwich or salad (see Tomato-Avocado Salad with Gingered Tomato Vinaigrette, page 284). I also salt my zucchini ahead of time, transforming a notoriously bland and watery squash into something sweet and shining (see Zucchini Patties with Garlicky Yogurt Sauce, page 227).

Similarly, if you salt, drain (for at least 20 minutes), rinse, and pat dry your shredded cabbage or sliced cucumbers (for at least 30 minutes), they won't water down your salad dressing. Eggplant also benefits from a presalting: This will not only tamp down any possible bitterness, but also eliminate excess water and collapse the cells; after salting, eggplant does not soak up as much oil when fried.

Starchy foods cry out for salt. If you don't add salt to the cooking water for potatoes, pasta, or grains—that is, at the beginning of the process—then adding it at the end won't make any difference. Dried beans don't come alive until they're soaked in salt water overnight, which not only deeply seasons and tenderizes them, but also keeps the skins from bursting when the beans are cooked (see Beans Primer, page 36).

When turkey, white meat chicken, and pork loin are soaked in salt water, it's called brining, and it's a surefire way to improve the flavor and texture of these leaner meats. Without going into the science of brining, the basics are that soaking lean meat in salted water increases the amount of liquid inside the meat cells, which makes the cooked meat juicier and more deeply seasoned.

My preference, though, is not to brine meat, but to salt it heavily, which jacks up the juiciness without having to soak the piece of meat in a bowl of liquid or, in the case of turkey, submerge it in the bathtub. Also, salted chicken or turkey skin becomes much crispier than brined chicken or turkey skin because it's not water-logged. As a huge fan of crispy skin, I consider this is a big plus.

So, if you have the time, salt your meat ahead of time and let it stand for at least an hour (in the case of pork tenderloin, pork chops, chicken breasts, steaks, and so on) or up to 36 hours if it is a large piece of meat like a whole turkey.

There are many different kinds of salt available, and each has its own best purpose. See What Kind of Salt? (page 12 and above right) for a guide.

WHAT KIND OF SALT? (PART 2)

Sea salt is available in many varieties boasting different shapes, colors, and flavors. This variety reflects the minerals in each kind of sea salt, which in turn reflects the place where it was harvested. Sea salts can be wonderful, but they're very pricey.

When I use one, it's usually as a finishing salt, added for its crunch at the end of the recipe, almost like a tiny salt crouton. There's no point in adding sea salt to food as it's cooking because its subtle flavor and color disappear when it dissolves. My favorite sea salts are **fleur de sel** and **sel gris** from France, and **Maldon** from England.

7. BALANCE FLAVORS.

7. BALANCE FLAVORS.

There are five flavors that combine to make up our sense of taste. Salt is only one. The other four are sweet, sour, bitter, and umami. (I address the last of these on page 15). Striking a harmonious balance of these flavors is key to making delicious food.

If a dish is:

Too bitter? Add salt. As mentioned on pages 12–13, salt suppresses bitterness, allowing the other flavors in the dish to emerge. Or add fat—butter, oil, cream, cheese, or animal fat (duck, beef, chicken, pork)—which also can take the edge off bitterness.

Too sweet? Add something sour, such as lemon, lime, or grapefruit juice, vinegar, or wine. Or add a hot spice—some form of chile, either chopped fresh chile, red pepper flakes, cayenne, or hot sauce. Salt can also balance too much sweetness.

Too acidic? Add something sweet, such as sugar or honey, or some fat—butter, oil, cream, cheese, or animal fat (duck, beef, chicken, pork).

Too salty? If you taste what you're cooking often, as it's cooking, this shouldn't be a common problem. But if for some reason it ends up too salty anyway, there's only one solution: dilute it by adding more water or unsalted liquid. There was a myth, perpetuated for years (and I believed it too) that adding starch in the form of potatoes, pasta, or rice would reduce the saltiness of a dish. There is no truth to that.

Here are some other possible scenarios:

What if a dish is too spicy? Add a little sugar or honey and/or some dairy—heavy cream, sour cream, yogurt, or butter.

What if a dish tastes lackluster? I'd always start by adding salt, then reach for any of these others depending on the dish in question: acid (lemon or lime juice, vinegar, wine), sugar (but just a pinch—sugar shouldn't dominate savory dishes), chiles or hot sauce, or chopped fresh herbs (which do wonders to brighten up a stew or soup).

Sometimes the solution is simply to simmer the dish a little longer, causing the excess water to evaporate and the flavor to become more concentrated. For example, I always cook down my strained homemade chicken stock. Likewise, if your stew has finished cooking, but the broth is boring, remove the meat (so that it doesn't boil and become tough) and reduce the broth to intensify its flavor.

8. BUILD UMAMI.

Discovered in 1909 by a Japanese chemistry professor, umami was officially declared the fifth taste in 2000. The word is generally translated as "meaty" or "savory." Our umami receptors are lit up by a common amino acid known as glutamate. Any time you add umami to your dish, you're boosting its depth of flavor. Seaweed (kombu and nori) is very high in glutamates, as are such fermented sauces as:

Soy sauce

Fish sauce

Oyster sauce

Miso

Worcestershire sauce

You can also find umami in:

Aged cheeses such as Parmigiano-Reggiano

Anchovies

Fresh and dried mushrooms

Tomatoes and tomato paste

Cured pork (prosciutto and bacon)

Onion

Garlic

Olives

When it comes to actual meat and seafood (all of which will add umami), aged and cured meats have higher umami, while clams, scallops, mussels, squid, and sardines are the seafood with the highest umami.

9. USE ALL YOUR SENSES.

We have five of them, and they should all come into play when we cook. **Taste** is obviously number one. You should be tasting as often as you can, not just when the recipe is complete. As mentioned earlier, if you wait until the end, it may be too late to adjust the seasoning.

But the sense of **touch** is also big. Is your steak done? Give it a poke. If it feels soft, it is rare. If it feels very firm, it is well done. (Medium-rare and medium are in between.) Get in the habit of touching your steaks, chops, and smaller pieces of chicken so that you can better understand the correlation between their firmness and doneness.

HERB PAIRINGS: PROTEIN

When it comes to pairing herbs with protein, these are some of my favorites (see my pairing suggestions for vegetables on page 14):

Beef: Marjoram, oregano, rosemary, thyme

Chicken and Turkey: Basil, cilantro, dill, marjoram, oregano, rosemary, sage, tarragon, thyme

Duck: Sage, thyme

Eggs: Chives, dill, tarragon

Fish: Basil, chives, cilantro, dill, tarragon

Lamb: Cilantro, dill, marjoram, mint, oregano, rosemary, thyme

Lobster and Shrimp: Basil, chives, dill, tarragon

Pork: Cilantro, marjoram, oregano, rosemary, sage, thyme

Veal: Dill, sage

Have you added enough liquid to your pastry or biscuit dough? Pinch together a small handful of the stuff and see if it sticks together or falls apart. And how else are you going to be sure that an avocado or peach is ripe if you don't press the flesh to see whether it gives a bit?

Then there's **smell.** When buying fresh fruit, aroma is an indication of ripeness. If you sniff the stem end of a tomato or melon, it should smell like essence of tomato or melon.

Julia Child used to say if you can smell it, it's done or close to done. She was referring to baked items, but I've found it to be equally true for roasted vegetables and steamed broccoli. Of course, when it's beyond done (or, uh, burned), the nose knows that, too.

What about the role of **hearing?** If you place a steak or a cutlet in a pan and don't hear it sizzle as soon as it hits the skillet, you know your skillet's not hot enough. Pull that steak out of the pan immediately and heat the skillet some more. If the stew you're cooking starts to boil (a no-no because the meat will be tough), you'll hear that boiling gurgling noise from across the room.

Last, not but least, there is **sight.** Eyeballing your ingredients before you buy them helps you to figure out if they're fresh. And, once you get them home and cook them, you need to be observant—Is the oil in the pan shimmering, indicating that it is hot enough to sear a steak? Are the ingredients in the recipe properly browned, puffed, reduced, whipped, smooth?

10. DON'T WASTE FOOD.

This won't necessarily make you a better cook, but it will make you a more thoughtful cook (and a better citizen) and save you some money in the process.

According to recent statistics, as a nation we waste between 30 and 40 percent of our food supply. This organic waste is the second highest component of landfills, which are, in turn, the largest source of methane emissions. Methane is a greenhouse gas 21 times more damaging to the environment than carbon dioxide. On the individual level, this translates to more than 20 pounds of wasted food per person per month. Money-wise, it translates to between $1,350 and $2,275 annually for a family of four.

Shocking, isn't it? I'll bet you had no idea we were wasting so much food. I certainly never gave it a thought until I started working in restaurants, where "food cost" was crucial. As a chef, I had to keep an eagle eye on how much we spent for food and how much we charged for it, as well as on how much we used of the food we bought versus how much we threw out—and if I didn't pay strict attention, I was out of a job. My early stint as an apprentice at a very good restaurant in France also taught me a lot along these lines. The chef there, like many French folks, was studiously frugal; one way or another we used *every part* of the meats, produce, and other ingredients that comprised the daily menu. A new generation of chefs has become conscious of food waste, too. Amanda Cohen offers a delicious use for broccoli stalks in her Broccoli Carpaccio with Broccoli Stalk Salad (page 231).

How can the home cook get in on this act? Here are a few tips:

▶ **Save all your vegetable scraps** (including things like tough shiitake stems) in a bag in the freezer. Once you've gathered enough, add the scraps to water to make a vegetable stock (see page 29).

▶ **Don't throw out beet, carrot, turnip, or radish tops.** These little ragamuffins are perfectly edible. Sauté them in olive oil, add a squeeze of lemon and some salt and pepper, and enjoy.

▶ **Save your chicken bones from cooked chicken** (including rotisserie chicken) in a bag in the freezer. When the bag is full, use them instead of the chicken wings to make a chicken stock (see page 26). (The French call this practice *remouillage*. It translates as "re-wetting.")

▶ **Save all the fat rendered from the meats you cook**—beef, pork, duck, and chicken. All of them are full of flavor and freeze well; just keep them separate from one another. Then pull them out of the freezer when you want some tasty oil in which to cook potatoes or vegetables. (Chicken fat is a signature ingredient in Jewish cooking. The Yiddish word for it is *schmaltz*.)

▶ **If a raw piece of meat/fish/chicken is in danger of going bad** after several days in the fridge, don't wait to use it in a specific recipe. **Just cook it.** Drizzle it with oil or butter, sprinkle with salt and pepper, and bake it until it's just cooked through. Then freeze it if you don't eat it right away. It'll have a longer shelf life cooked than raw.

▶ **Don't toss out your leftover cooked pasta, rice, or grains.** Save them in the freezer. Reheat them by combining them with a little stock or water in a saucepan, adding some butter or Parmigiano-Reggiano to finish.

▶ **Leftover artisanal bread,** which stales after 1 day, can be sliced, double wrapped, and stored in the freezer. Pull out the slices and toast them as the spirit moves you.

▶ **Unused vegetables heading south?** You can chop and throw them into a one-size-fits-all soup, or blanch and freeze them.

▶ **Love your leftovers.** Put on your chef's hat and combine your leftovers with fresh ingredients for a second meal.

DON'T LEAVE OUT THE FAT

For so many years, the presence of fat in recipes was maligned. All fat. You were commanded by the food police to cut way back. The trouble with that is fat doesn't just add its own flavor and texture to a dish, it also plays a more profoundly important role in cooking: Fat is a conductor of flavor. So anytime you add fat to a dish, even if you don't taste the fat, the dish will just taste better.

When food companies removed all the fat from their crackers, cookies, and prepared food, the public responded by consuming boxes of fat-free products that had simply replaced the fat with sugar. American consumers desperate for flavor became addicted to this replacement, namely sugar. I believe that was the beginning of the obesity era.

I am so glad that the anti-fat era has passed and now all kinds of fat, including nuts, seeds, and avocados, are being embraced by nutritionists. So please don't leave the fat out of your recipes. Not only is it good for you (in measured amounts), it's also key to the good taste of your food.

A LIST OF MY FAVORITE TOOLS—BIG AND SMALL

1. **Food processor** (including its slicing and grating disks). The right machine for quickly grating and slicing vegetables, which significantly lowers their cooking time. (Beets cooked in 15 minutes anyone? See page 300.)

2. **Graters.** A traditional Microplane (for cheese, ginger, chocolate, garlic) and a KitchenIQ Better Zester (for citrus). Also, a grater with large holes for coarsely grating cheese.

3. **Spaetzle maker.** A handy tool for making homemade German pasta (see page 68).

4. **Pots and pans.** An assortment, including a stockpot (8- or 10-quart), large (4-quart) and small (1-quart) saucepan, large (12-inch) and small (7-inch) skillet, and a large stick-resistant (11- to 12-inch) skillet. (I am not a fan of nonstick.) I *am* a big fan of Chantal copper fusion, as well as the Chantal 21 Steel Induction ceramic line of pans, both of which are stick-resistant without being toxic.

5. **Tongs.** You will need a short pair for turning over ingredients in a skillet and a long pair for grilling and for sautéing ingredients that spit fat, like chicken, chicken livers, and soft-shell crabs.

6. **Spider.** Works well for turning and lifting fried items in hot fat but also useful for lifting small amounts of cooked pasta or boiled vegetables out of hot liquid.

7. **Kitchen spoons.** Large ones, both with and without slots.

8. **Whisks.** A flat whisk is the perfect tool for getting out roux wedged in the corners of a saucepan. You should also have a small whisk for cold sauces, a medium whisk for hot sauces, and a balloon whisk for whipping cream and egg whites.

9. **Cutting boards.** One for chopping ingredients to be used in savory recipes and one for chopping ingredients to be used in desserts. I prefer wood because plastic can get nasty smelling.

10. **Blender.** Preferably one of the super blenders, such as a Vitamix (excellent but pricey), or Ninja (a very good blender at an affordable price).

11. **Mandoline.** Necessary for slicing very thin, even pieces of potatoes (see Foolproof Scalloped Potatoes, page 308) or shaving fennel or other vegetables, but please use the guard that comes with it!

12. **Digital scale.** For weighing all ingredients, including flour.

13. **Knives.** For the merits of a 10-inch chef's knife, see page 10, but I also recommend that you purchase a large serrated knife for slicing bread and tomatoes and chopping chocolate and a paring knife for small tasks. A boning knife would be a nice bonus for boning chicken (see page 184) or meat or removing silverskin from a rack of lamb (see page 278). I like the European knives, which are a combination of carbon and stainless steel. Japanese knives are excellent too, but expensive and designed for right-handed people (but you can order a left-handed knife at extra cost).

14. **Stand mixer.** Indispensable for making cakes, cookies, and beating egg whites.

15. **Thermometers.** An infrared digital laser thermometer for frying and making candy. An instant-read thermometer for meat.

16. **Onion goggles.** A very useful tool when you are slicing many onions, they are the only thing that will keep you from crying, although a sharp knife helps, too. (Believe me, I have tried all the tricks.)

17. **Giant cake lifter.** Originally designed to lift and transport cakes layers, I use this tool for transporting huge quantities of chopped vegetables from cutting board to pan.

18. **Bench scraper, metal and plastic.** I use these tools both for baking (which is what they were designed for) and also for transporting chopped onions, garlic, herbs, and the like from counter to skillet.

19. **Fish spatula.** Designed to be flexible for the gentle handling of delicate fish, I use it for everything, including pancakes.

20. **Grapefruit spoon.** I rarely employ a grapefruit spoon to cut out grapefruit sections, but have found so many other applications for it: loosening the skin on a turkey (see page 252), lifting capers from a jar, removing the ribs and seeds from a chile, digging out a stem from a fresh white mushroom, scraping out the gills from a portobello, and I'm sure I will discover more.

21. **Skimmer.** Does the best job of removing scum from a stock or simmering beans.

22. **Ladle.** For serving soups and stews.

23. **Can opener.** The key is to use one that cuts safely. Kuhn Rikon makes one that does not leave a sharp edge on the can.

24. **Vegetable peelers.** Either a sturdy straight or Y-shaped peeler. I have both: I like to use the Y-shaped for peeling broccoli and asparagus stems, and use a serrated straight peeler for peeling peaches, plums, nectarines, and tomatoes. (They are usually labeled as peach or tomato peelers.)

25. **Citrus juicer.** I prefer the colorful Mexican-style citrus squeezers.

26. **Measuring cups.** A set of dry and wet, plus an Oxo Good Grips mini angled liquid measuring cup as a substitute for measuring spoons. (This comes in very handy when you need to measure more than 1 tablespoon of liquid. You are less likely to spill the liquid when you transport it to the pan in this little cup.)

27. **Chantry knife sharpener.** This is not really a knife sharpener— essentially it is two steels crossed at exactly the right angle so when you pull your knife through, it hones your knife. If you run your knife through it ten times every time before you start slicing and dicing, it will keep a nice edge.

28. **Fat separator.** Indispensable for removing fat from stocks or pan juices. (But save that fat and use it for cooking vegetables.)

29. **Egg slicer.** Not just for slicing eggs, but also cooked beets, raw mushrooms, mozzarella, strawberries, and boiled potatoes.

30. **Dental floss, unflavored.** The best tool for slicing cheesecake, goat cheese, and some fetas.

31. **Rubber spatulas.** The flexible silicone versions, in several sizes. They are indispensable for getting those last bits of batter and sauce out of the bowl or pan.

A GUIDE TO THE RECIPES AND INGREDIENTS USED IN THIS BOOK

All the recipes in this book were tested on electric burners and with an electric oven that has the heat element at the top. You might need to adjust the cooking times and temperatures slightly if you have a different kind of stove (see page 10).

> Avocados are Hass avocados.

> Bay leaves are from Turkey.

> Black pepper is freshly ground.

> Butter is unsalted.

> Cheeses are freshly grated. I prefer to use a Microplane to grate Parmigiano-Reggiano. Please note that this produces double the volume of cheese grated on the fine side of a four-sided grater, so follow the weight indicated in the recipe—1 ounce of cheese grated on a Microplane will measure a firmly packed $1/2$ cup; 1 ounce of cheese grated on the fine side of a 4-sided grater will measure about $1/4$ cup.

> Chorizo is Spanish-style, meaning cured, not fresh. You can buy excellent chorizo imported from Spain, but there are also some wonderful Spanish-style chorizos made in this country (see Sources, page 350).

> Cream cheese is neufchatel ($1/3$ less fat) or full fat. Please do not use fat-free cream cheese.

> Eggs are large.

> Fish are not endangered. Visit seafoodwatch.org to find sustainable choices. I used fish that are sustainable and available nationally, but there might be other local sustainable choices near you.

> Flour is unbleached all-purpose, unless otherwise noted.

> Herbs: use fresh whenever possible (see the boxes on pages 14–15); if fresh are not available, 1 teaspoon dried herb is the equivalent of 1 tablespoon fresh. Fresh herbs reduce in volume by half when you chop them, so $1/4$ cup fresh oregano leaves, chopped, will yield about 2 tablespoons.

> Jalapeños should have heat. (They are growing some in Texas that are designed to have no heat. I don't get it: Who needs a little green pepper?) Test the chile before you add it to a recipe. Just cut off a thin slice, rub your finger over it, and lick your finger to see what kind of heat it has.

> Lemon and lime juice is freshly squeezed.

> Lemon, lime, and orange zest are freshly grated. (See Graters on page 18 for the best tool for grating.)

> Mayonnaise is full fat or low fat. Please do not use fat free.

READ THE INTROS

Please read the side introduction to each recipe before you start to cook. This text contains valuable information regarding the preparation of each particular recipe and sometimes useful general tips as well.

> Meat is grass fed or organic, or minimally processed and raised without antibiotics and hormones.

> Milk is whole. If you want to slim down the recipe, you can use 2% or 1%. Please do not use fat-free milk in these recipes; it has no flavor.

> Olive oil is extra virgin.

> Poultry is organic or minimally processed and raised without antibiotics and hormones.

> Rice vinegar comes in two varieties: seasoned and unseasoned. Seasoned has sugar and salt added to it. If all you have in-house is unseasoned, and a recipe calls for seasoned, just add a pinch of sugar and salt to it.

> Salt is Diamond kosher salt, except where otherwise indicated. (See the box on page 12 for equivalent measures if using other brands of kosher salt.)

> Sour cream is full fat, although low fat is an acceptable substitution. Do not substitute fat-free sour cream.

> Vanilla extract is pure.

> Vegetable oil is grapeseed, safflower, or sunflower.

> Wine must be drinkable. Don't ever use "cooking wine."

2 *the good cook's* PANTRY

A well-stocked pantry is the good home cook's secret weapon. Many of the ingredients you'd otherwise have to run out and buy at the last minute are much better when made at home—and it's not only much easier to make them yourself than you might've imagined, the payoff in flavor and freshness is huge.

This chapter includes my favorite chicken and vegetable stocks; a good, quick tomato sauce; several variations on a basic vinaigrette salad dressing; and foolproof instructions for homemade mayonnaise. Grains and beans can be cooked ahead and frozen when you have the time (as can pizza and pie doughs), and then unfrozen when time is at a premium. What about whipping up your own butter and cheese? You can do it. It's basic kitchen science, but feels like a magic trick and will really impress your family and friends. Freshly made or store-bought butter can be the base of flavored butters, clarified butter, and ghee, too.

All the recipes in this chapter are employed as components in other recipes in this book, but they're also versatile enough to be incorporated into recipes of your own invention. Here's the point: With a stockpile of these basics at hand, you're much better prepared to throw together a meal that's delicious and nourishing, even if you begin without a plan. Think of them as head starts.

HOMEMADE CHICKEN STOCK

Why bother making chicken stock at home when there are so many respectable versions at the supermarket? Because it's so much better than the stock you pour out of a can or a box.

The difference is in the flavor and the texture—the rich texture that comes from the long, slow simmering of bones. Homemade has it; store-bought doesn't. You can see for yourself if you ever boil a sample of each side-by-side. A homemade stock thickens and becomes concentrated. A store-bought stock, completely lacking in collagen, simply evaporates into thin air. Poof!

Wait a minute, you say. Making stock at home sure takes a lot of time! Indeed, it does. There's four hours of simmering, but it's not hands-on time. I see it as a great weekend project. To me, homemade chicken stock is like liquid gold; it makes any soup (such as my Speedy Korean Chicken Noodle Soup, page 71) or sauce that much tastier.

START TO FINISH: 5 HOURS / **HANDS-ON TIME:** 10 MINUTES / **SERVINGS:** MAKES ABOUT 8 CUPS

5 pounds chicken wings	2 thyme sprigs
2 medium onions	1 Turkish bay leaf
2 small carrots	1 teaspoon black peppercorns
2 medium celery stalks	Kosher salt and freshly ground black pepper
6 parsley stems	

> Put the chicken wings in a large stockpot and add enough cold water to cover them by 2 inches. Bring the mixture just to a simmer, frequently skimming the surface scum with a slotted spoon or skimmer, until no more scum floats to the surface, about 20 minutes.

> Meanwhile, quarter the onions and halve the carrots and celery; add the vegetables to the stockpot with the herbs and peppercorns. Return the mixture to a simmer and cook for 4 hours. Add additional water, if necessary, to keep the bones covered.

> Strain the stock and skim off all the fat that rises to the surface (see box, left). Return the stock to the pot and simmer until reduced by one-third, about 30 minutes. Add salt and ground pepper to taste.

SKIMMING AND SAVING THE FAT

If you have time, cool the stock and refrigerate it, covered, overnight. The fat will harden on top of the stock, making it much easier to remove.

Chicken fat freezes nicely, so always save the fat to use in future recipes, like matzo balls. Just replace the vegetable oil in the recipe on the back of the package with melted chicken fat.

HOMEMADE BROWN CHICKEN STOCK AND GLACE

START TO FINISH: 5½ HOURS / **HANDS-ON TIME:** 40 MINUTES
SERVINGS: MAKES ABOUT 9 CUPS STOCK OR 4½ CUPS GLACE

5 pounds chicken wings

2 medium onions, coarsely chopped

1 large carrot, coarsely chopped

10 garlic cloves, smashed and peeled

2 tablespoons tomato paste

2 cups dry red or white wine

2 small celery stalks, coarsely chopped

6 parsley stems

2 thyme sprigs

1 teaspoon black peppercorns

Kosher salt and freshly ground black
  pepper

> Preheat the oven to 450°F; set one oven rack in the upper third of the oven and a second rack in the lower third of the oven. Arrange the wings in one layer on two rimmed baking sheets and roast for 20 minutes. Turn the wings over, rotate the baking sheets, return them to the opposite oven shelves, and roast for 15 minutes longer.

> Turn the wings over again, add the onions and carrots and roast for 10 minutes. Add the garlic and tomato paste, rotate the pans again, and roast until the vegetables are nicely browned, 10 to 12 minutes.

> Transfer the wings and vegetables to a stockpot (discarding any bits of onion that have burned) and set aside. Put the baking sheets on top of the burners on the stove over medium heat, and carefully pour 1 cup of wine into each. Simmer, scraping up the brown bits from the bottom of the pan, until the wine has reduced by half. Add the reduced wine to the stockpot with the celery, parsley, thyme, peppercorns, and enough cold water for the liquid to cover the bones by 2 inches.

> Bring the liquid to a simmer and cook, frequently skimming the surface scum with a slotted spoon or skimmer, until no more scum floats to the surface, about 20 minutes. Continue cooking, adding additional water if necessary to keep the bones covered, for 3½ hours. Strain the stock through a strainer and skim off any fat that settles at the top (see page 26). Season with salt and pepper to taste (unless you are going to reduce it further to make chicken *glace,* in which case hold off on the seasoning).

> **To make a brown chicken glace,** simmer the strained and de-fatted stock until it has reduced by half or until it has the consistency of honey. Season with salt and pepper to taste.

> "I haven't made veal or beef stock at home in years. When a dish calls for a more assertively meaty stock than the usual white chicken stock, I make this brown chicken stock. The main difference between this stock and its white cousin is that the chicken bones and the vegetables are browned before they're simmered. I also add some red wine. Otherwise, you prepare this brown chicken stock just as you would regular chicken stock: start with cold water, skim the scum, and reduce the stock after you've strained it to concentrate the flavor. (See Making Flavorful Stock, page 28.)
>
> In fact, if you keep reducing the stock until it becomes thick and syrupy, you'll end up with chicken *glace* (it's French for glaze). This glace is so concentrated that a little goes a long way. Add wine or water to it and it's reconstituted as an instant sauce. (See, for example, Seared Steak with Peppercorn-Cognac Sauce, page 150). It'll last in the fridge for several weeks or in the freezer for a few months—and because it's so concentrated, it takes up very little space."

HOMEMADE TURKEY STOCK

START TO FINISH: 3½ HOURS / **HANDS-ON TIME:** IO MINUTES
SERVINGS: MAKES ABOUT 8 CUPS

"Turkey, like chicken, arrives on your doorstep bearing gifts, namely the giblets and neck. Typically secreted in the cavity of the bird, these flavorful tidbits provide the base for the stock that becomes sauce for the turkey. You can use them on the spot or sock them away for future use—on Thanksgiving, for example, when they're crucial in my Make-Ahead Turkey Gravy (page 255). Save the liver for another use (it will make the stock bitter), such as sautéing and serving on a piece of toast. "

The giblets, neck, and wing tips from one turkey

4 cups Homemade Chicken Stock (page 26) or store-bought chicken broth

1 small onion, coarsely chopped

1 small carrot, cut in half

1 celery stalk, cut in half

1 small parsnip (optional), cut in half

6 parsley stems

2 thyme sprigs

1 Turkish bay leaf

Kosher salt and freshly ground black pepper

> Combine the giblets, neck, and wing tips with the stock in a medium saucepan and bring the mixture to a simmer, frequently skimming the surface scum with a slotted spoon or skimmer, until no more scum floats to the surface, about 20 minutes.

> Add the onion, carrot, celery, parsnip (if using), parsley, thyme, bay leaf, and 4 cups cold water and bring the liquid back to a simmer. Simmer the stock, adding water as necessary to keep all the ingredients submerged in liquid, for 2½ to 3 hours. Strain the stock through a strainer and skim off any fat that settles at the top (see page 26). You can use that fat for pan gravy (see page 255). Add salt and pepper to taste.

MAKING FLAVORFUL STOCK

I make my chicken stock from chicken wings because wings boast equal amounts of the three components you need to make a good stock: meat (which contributes flavor), bones (their gelatin provides body), and lots of skin (its fat amplifies the flavor). Start the wings in cold water to extract the most flavor.

Making a clear stock requires skimming off the scum that rises to the top of the liquid during the initial part of the cooking process. What is that? As the wings boil, the protein solids and the fats coagulate, get trapped by fat, and float to the surface. Do your skimming with a slotted spoon or, better yet, with the tool made just for the job: a skimmer (see page 21).

Keep an eye on the pot so that the **stock doesn't boil.** If it does boil, the protein solids and fat get mixed into the liquid and the stock becomes cloudy. And make sure that the bones are always covered with liquid. (If the bones are not covered you are not extracting any flavor or gelatin from them.) **If the liquid evaporates to below the level of the bones, add more water.**

After removing the fat, you'll need to **boil down the stock to concentrate its flavor.** Season well with salt and pepper. (Don't add any salt or pepper before this final stage or you might end up with a salty stock.) Divide it into 1-cup and 2-cup amounts, or in the amounts that you are likely to use the stock, and freeze it.

HOMEMADE VEGETABLE STOCK

START TO FINISH: I HOUR 55 MINUTES / **HANDS-ON TIME:** 30 MINUTES
SERVINGS: MAKES 6 CUPS

2 tablespoons extra-virgin olive oil

1 pound onions, medium sliced

1 pound carrots, medium sliced

8 garlic cloves, smashed and peeled

4 ounces white mushrooms, coarsely chopped

2 tablespoons tomato paste

1 medium parsnip, coarsely chopped

1 large boiling potato (about 5 ounces), coarsely chopped

4 celery stalks, coarsely chopped

6 parsley stems

2 thyme sprigs

1 Turkish bay leaf

1 teaspoon peppercorns

1/2 teaspoon kosher salt

> Heat the oil in a large Dutch oven over medium heat. Reduce the heat to medium-low and add the onions and the carrots. Cover and cook, stirring occasionally, until the vegetables are softened, about 30 minutes. Uncover and cook until they are nicely browned, 15 to 20 minutes more. Add the garlic and mushrooms and cook, stirring, for 5 minutes or until all the liquid the mushrooms give off is evaporated. Add the tomato paste and cook, stirring, for 3 minutes. Add the parsnip, potato, celery, parsley, thyme, bay leaf, peppercorns, salt, and enough water to cover the vegetables by 2 inches. Bring to a boil, reduce the heat, and simmer gently for 45 minutes. Strain the stock through a strainer, discard the solids, and return the liquid to the pot. Boil until it is reduced to 6 cups.

"Vegetable stock is indispensable for vegetarian soups and sauces, but why stop there? This full-bodied vegetable stock will improve any dish. It gets its depth of flavor from browning the onions and carrots, as well as from the built-in umami of the mushrooms and tomato paste. For a lighter version, just omit the browning stage and toss all the vegetables into the pot with the water. This is also a great use for the bits and scraps of vegetables that you've been saving in the freezer (see page 17)."

SPEEDY MARINARA SAUCE

START TO FINISH: 35 MINUTES / **HANDS-ON TIME:** 10 MINUTES
SERVINGS: MAKES ABOUT 2½ CUPS

The all-day, slow-simmered tomato sauce is an elaborate affair. In contrast, this marinara sauce takes no time at all to prepare, yet it's very flavorful and the perfect ingredient for a quick pasta dinner, Personal Pizzas (page 281), Inside-Out Eggplant Parmesan Rolls (page 201), and Toasted Pasta with Shrimp and Chorizo (page 240).

2 large garlic cloves, smashed and peeled

2 tablespoons extra-virgin olive oil

Hefty pinch or two of red pepper flakes

1 (28-ounce) can plum tomatoes (preferably fire roasted), chopped (see Buying Canned Tomatoes, below)

Kosher salt

> In an unheated medium saucepan, combine the garlic and the oil. Turn the heat to medium and cook, turning over the garlic several times, until it is just golden, 4 to 6 minutes. Add the red pepper flakes and cook, stirring, for 30 seconds. Add the tomatoes and a hefty pinch of salt, bring to a boil, reduce the heat, and cook at a brisk simmer until the sauce is reduced to about 2½ cups, 20 to 25 minutes. Discard the garlic. Season with kosher salt to taste.

BUYING CANNED TOMATOES

You may be tempted to save a step by buying pre-chopped tomatoes in a can. Don't do it. The manufacturers add some kind of preservative to ensure that the chunks hold their shape. You want your tomatoes to break down in the sauce, so always buy whole plum tomatoes. (I prefer the fire-roasted tomatoes, if you can find them.)

There are two simple ways to chop canned whole plum tomatoes: Dip a pair of clean scissors into an open can and start slicing away, or pour the tomatoes from the can into a bowl and break them up with your impeccably clean hands.

Either method is better than trying to chop the tomatoes on a cutting board and watching all the juices run off the edge of the board, onto the counter, and from there, most likely, to the floor. Miserable. You want those juices in the sauce. **And don't worry about the seeds.** The pulp attached to them adds flavor; leave them in.

ONCE-A-WEEK VINAIGRETTE

Pictured on page 9

START TO FINISH: 5 MINUTES / **HANDS-ON TIME:** 5 MINUTES / **SERVINGS:** MAKES ABOUT 1 CUP

> I imagine that most people buy prepared salad dressing because they don't want to whip up yet another dish on a weeknight. After cooking a main course *and* some sides *and* tossing together a salad, who still has the time and energy to make a dressing?
>
> But convenience aside, most supermarket dressings contain a number of unhealthy ingredients. Your homemade dressing will not only be fresher and tastier, but healthier, too. Take a tip from my mom—as I do—and make a big batch once a week. It'll take no more than five minutes, I promise.
>
> By the way, there's no reason to confine vinaigrettes to the salad bar. They can perk up grilled vegetables, chicken, or steaks, and they partner beautifully with fish.

$\frac{1}{4}$ cup acid (see choices below under Cook's Notes)

1 teaspoon kosher salt

2 teaspoons Dijon mustard

$\frac{1}{2}$ teaspoon freshly ground black pepper

$\frac{1}{2}$ to $\frac{3}{4}$ cup oil

> In a 1-cup measuring cup or screw-top jar, combine the acid, salt, mustard, and pepper. Whisk (or shake if using a jar) until the salt is dissolved. Add $\frac{1}{2}$ cup of the oil in a stream whisking constantly (or add the oil to the jar all at once and shake). Dip in a piece of lettuce to taste the vinaigrette. Add more oil if necessary to balance the acid. Store in the fridge but let the vinaigrette come to room temperature before using. (The oil will solidify when chilled but will melt when brought to room temperature.)

Cook's Notes: Customizing Vinaigrette

The standard recipe for a vinegar-based dressing is a ratio of three parts oil to one part vinegar, but really that's just a starting point. Years ago, while teaching a basic techniques class, I asked my students to make dressings of their own. All of them used olive oil, but each one picked a different acid. What an eye-opener! Three tablespoons of oil swamped the rice vinegar, but barely balanced the acidity of sherry vinegar. Bottom line: the acid content in vinegar can vary *a lot* from one kind to the next. Here's step-by-step advice to make a vinaigrette that's balanced to your particular taste:

▶ **Start with the acid.** Here are some suggested acids, listed from the most to the least acidic:

Sherry vinegar (use more oil), red wine vinegar, balsamic vinegar, white wine and Champagne vinegar, cider vinegar, rice vinegar, raspberry vinegar, fresh lemon, lime, orange, or grapefruit juice (use less oil)

▶ **Then choose the oil.** Whether flavorful or neutral, select an oil that will complement the acid.

Good-quality extra-virgin olive oil. This is most often what I choose. Break out the good stuff because you're really going to taste it in a salad dressing.

Grapeseed oil. My favorite when I want a more neutral-flavored oil, but it's expensive.

Safflower and sunflower oils. Less pricey and perfectly acceptable neutral oil alternatives.

Canola oil. I am not a fan. I think its taste is odd and its texture is greasy. Also, most canola oil is genetically modified. If you want to use canola oil for health reasons, reach for the organic version, which cannot by law be genetically modified.

Nut oils, including walnut, hazelnut, pistachio, and pumpkin seed. These flavorful oils pair very well with fruit vinegars, such as raspberry. All of them, however, need to be cut half and half with vegetable oil because they're so strong.

▶ **Add an emulsifier,** if you like. A vinaigrette is a temporary emulsion, meaning that when you whisk or shake it, the oil and vinegar will combine long enough to coat your salad. Eventually, though, these components will separate again. You can make the dressing stay together longer if you add an emulsifier, such as mustard or an egg. I prefer mustard, not only because of its power to emulsify, but because I really like its taste.

▶ **Tasty add-ins?** Your choice: minced shallots (which contribute a pleasant sweet crunch), a cut clove of garlic, chopped fresh herbs, a bit of soy sauce or miso, crumbled cheese, grated fresh citrus zest, or capers all work well.

▶ **Looking for lower fat?** To reduce the vinaigrette's calorie count, cut down the amount of oil. Depending on my mood, I'll swap in chicken broth, pureed fresh tomato, roasted red pepper, or (very ripe) pear, all of which contribute flavor and body. Sugar, too, can replace oil, which is why relatively sweet balsamic vinegar requires relatively less oil for balance in a vinaigrette. But I'm not a fan of sugar in dressings. We already eat way too much of it.

HOW TO PROPERLY TOSS A SALAD

Tossing a salad properly is important: It can make the difference between a bland, wilted mess of greens and a perfectly flavored, crisp and crunchy salad.

To start, the lettuce must be dried well; if it's wet, the dressing won't stick to it. Use a salad spinner to dry your lettuce and if it's still not completely dry, lay the greens out on paper towels or a clean kitchen towel and *gently* pat dry before adding to the mixing bowl.

Sprinkle a little salt and freshly ground pepper on every part of the salad, including the greens. *Then* add the dressing (about 1 tablespoon for every 4 cups of lettuce) and gently toss the salad—not with tongs, but with your impeccably clean hands. (Your hands are absolutely the best tools for the job because they won't bruise the lettuce.) As soon as the dressing has coated all the leaves, stop. You're done.

COOKING GRAINS

The grains that you can cook easily from start to finish on a weeknight in 30 minutes or less are:

▶ White rice

▶ Couscous

▶ Quinoa

▶ Kasha

▶ Millet

▶ Bulgur

▶ Freekeh

▶ Pearled or semi-pearled farro (*semi-perlato* in Italian)

▶ Pearled or semi-pearled barley

▶ Forbidden rice

The grains that take much longer to cook are:

▶ Whole or hulled farro

▶ Hulled or hull-less barley

▶ Rye berries

▶ Wheat berries

▶ Brown rice

Note: The word "whole" or any iteration of the word "hull" on the package indicates a longer cooking grain; the word "semi pearled" or "pearled" indicates a shorter cooking grain.

GRAINS PRIMER

If you want to start incorporating more grains into your diet but find the world of grains confusing, welcome to the club. The good news is that there are so many more grains readily available (stocked at your supermarket, not a dusty ancient health food store; see Sources, page 350) than there were even five years ago.

Since there doesn't seem to be a consensus about how to cook them or for what length of time, my best advice is: **Read the back of the package.** Most boxes and bags of grains will have basic cooking instructions on the back and because there are so many options, even with one grain (for example barley, which you can find hulled, hull-less, pearled, and semi-pearled), it makes sense to just follow the cooking time the manufacturer recommends. For more in-depth reading, I recommend *Ancient Grains for Modern Meals* by Maria Speck (Ten Speed Press, 2011) and *Grain Mains* by Bruce Weinstein and Mark Scarbrough (Rodale, 2012). See the box at left for general guidance on the cooking times for grains.

Here are some other things to consider when preparing grains:

Check for freshness. Keep in mind that if that box of grains has been sitting on the shelf for a year, it might have gone rancid (it's best to store the longer cooking grains in the fridge) and/or might take forever to cook because it has dried out somewhat.

Soak before cooking. The longer cooking grains benefit from a soak (about 8 hours), which not only speeds up the cooking time but also tenderizes the grains and helps them to cook more evenly. (Drain the soaking water and start with fresh when you cook them.)

Make ahead and freeze. I suggest preparing the longer cooking varieties on a weekend, making extra, and freezing the extra in the amounts that you think you might use them: 1-, 2- or 3-cup amounts. All grains freeze well for at least 3 months.

There are three methods for cooking grains:

1. The Measured Method. The grains are combined with a measured amount of liquid (which will be listed on the package), brought to a boil, covered and simmered slowly until tender. I have not had much luck with this method because it's hard to maintain a constant temperature on my electric stove burners; either the liquid evaporates too quickly or not quickly enough.

2. The Pilaf Method. The grains are toasted first like a pilaf in a pan, with or without oil, and then combined with a measured amount of liquid (which will be listed on the package), brought to a boil, covered, and simmered until tender. If you are going to go the measured liquid route, you might as well toast the grains first; the toasting adds great depth of flavor.

After following the methods one and two (see page 34 and above), the cooked grains should be left on the stove, covered, off the heat, for an additional 10 minutes, and then fluffed gently with a fork before serving.

3. The Pasta Method. Add the grains to plenty of simmering salted water (no measuring required). Stir when they are first added to the water; then simmer until tender, and drain. This foolproof procedure is my favorite.

To defrost frozen grains:

Defrost frozen grains overnight in the fridge, or...

Combine them with a little water and microwave them in a microwave-safe container, or...

Float the container or bag that holds the grains, making sure it is airtight, in a bowl of warm water and leave them there, adding additional warm water if necessary, until they are defrosted, or...

Add the frozen grains directly to the recipe if it is a soup or stew, and let the grains defrost in the hot liquid.

To reheat grains:

Heat them in a steamer basket set over 1 inch of boiling water, covered, for 5 minutes, or...

Combine them with a little bit of water or stock, about $\frac{1}{4}$ inch, in the bottom of a saucepan; cover and heat them gently.

FOR TASTY GRAINS

▶ **Season them well.** Make sure the liquid you cook the grains in is well seasoned. They will be more deeply seasoned if they are cooked *with* salt; it you wait until afterward, the salt will not penetrate.

▶ **To test for doneness,** take a grain or two out and taste them. The grain should taste tender but not mushy.

▶ **Dress up reheated grains** with butter, olive oil, Parmigiano-Reggiano, or chopped fresh herbs.

BEANS PRIMER

I didn't appreciate the numerous lovable qualities of dried beans until my college years, when I was living on my own in a house with several other women, all of us strapped for cash. As soon as we discovered that beans are a tasty, economical, and nutrient-rich alternative to animal-based protein, they began turning up in the center of our plates with real regularity.

Today you can buy already cooked dried beans in cans, although canned beans tend to be slightly overcooked, which makes them mushy. Sometimes a mushy texture is not important in a dish (like when you are going to mash the beans) and certainly canned beans are a convenience if you don't have time to cook up a batch of dried beans. But canned beans cost significantly more than their bagged brothers. One 16-ounce bag of dried beans yields roughly 5 or 6 cups of cooked beans, while one 15-ounce can of cooked beans yields roughly 1$\frac{1}{2}$ cups. Cup for cup (and depending on the local price, of course), canned beans are almost twice as expensive as dried.

Still, maybe you worry that cooking dried beans from scratch just takes too darned long. In fact, it does take time to cook them properly, but most of that is not *hands-on* time. If you make it a weekend project, you can cook up a large batch of dried beans and freeze them in 1- or 2-cup amounts. Then, there they are, ready when you need them for any dish of your choosing. The basics for cooking almost all dried beans (except dried lentils and split peas, which cook so quickly you can make them from start to finish in about 20 minutes) are below. I won't offer exact cooking times, because the timing can vary widely depending on how fresh the dried beans are.

However you use them, I think you'll be delighted with the taste, texture, and price of beans cooked from scratch.

Prepping the beans:

Cook a pound of beans at a time (which is the weight of the bag you buy at the store). Sort through the beans to pick out any random little stone or stick among them and rinse them. Dissolve 3 tablespoons of salt in 4 quarts of water, add the beans and soak them overnight at room temperature. Soaking not only pre-seasons the beans, but also ensures tenderer skin, a more evenly cooked bean, and a shorter cooking time.

Cooking the beans on top of the stove:

After the beans have soaked overnight, drain and rinse them, put them in a large pot, add cold water (3 parts water to 1 part dried beans, or 6½ to 7 cups water for 1 pound of beans) and 2 teaspoons salt, bring to a boil and reduce the heat to a simmer. For the first 20 minutes or so the beans will give off a foam (caused by the release of water-soluble proteins from the beans), which collects at the top of the pot. Skim it using a skimmer if you have one, or a slotted spoon if you don't, and discard it. When the beans stop producing foam, add some vegetables if you want, for flavoring, maybe some onion, carrot, and celery stalk (all coarsely chopped), and a few smashed garlic cloves, and simmer the beans until tender. Depending on the bean, this will take anywhere from 35 minutes to 2½ hours more. Start checking them at 35 minutes.

Cooking the beans in a pressure cooker:

It's much speedier to cook dried beans in a pressure cooker, as long as it's not your grandmother's pressure cooker. The new versions are streamlined and—unlike grandma's—not at all inclined to explode. Just read the bean-cooking instructions very carefully. If you pre-soak your beans as I've suggested above, the pressure cooker will finish the job in just a few minutes.

I tested my beans with a stovetop Fagor Duo pressure cooker. Here is the method that worked for me: After presoaking 1 pound of beans, draining and rinsing them, I combined them with 7½ cups water, 1 tablespoon vegetable oil (the oil keeps the foam from the beans from clogging the steam vent), and 2 teaspoons salt. I put the pan on a burner, set the gauge to high pressure, and turned the burner to high. When the pressure had been achieved (the button popped up), I moved the pan immediately to another burner set on low (on my electric stovetop because if I waited for the burner to cool down at its own slow pace, the beans would overcook). If you have a gas stove, just turn the heat down to low.

Once the pressure is reached, the beans will take somewhere between 4 and 7 minutes to cook. Then let the pan cool down and release the pressure, following the instruction manual for your pressure cooker.

Cooking the beans in a slow cooker:

Soak the beans as described above, drain and rinse them, and combine them in a slow cooker with onion, carrot, and celery (all coarsely chopped); a few smashed garlic cloves; and 2 teaspoons salt. Cover the beans by 1 inch with cold water and cook on high for 4 to 6 hours or until completely tender.

BEAN FACTS

▶ 1 pound dried beans equals 2 to 2½ cups

▶ 1 cup dried beans equals 2 to 3 cups cooked beans

▶ 1 (19-ounce) can cooked, drained beans equals 2 cups

▶ 1 (16-ounce) can cooked, drained beans equals 1¾ cups

▶ 1 (15-ounce) can cooked, drained beans equals 1½ cups

10-MINUTE PIZZA DOUGH

START TO FINISH: 1 HOUR 10 MINUTES / **HANDS-ON TIME:** 10 MINUTES
SERVINGS: MAKES ENOUGH FOR 6 PERSONAL PIZZAS, 12 CALZONES, OR 3 FULL-SIZE PIZZAS

> " This recipe should convince you that making homemade pizza dough is a snap.
>
> What makes it so easy is that you mix and "knead" the dough in a food processor rather than by hand. It's quicker and neater that way. And, as long as you measure the ingredients accurately (weighing with a kitchen scale) and don't add very hot water, this dough is foolproof. And it only takes 10 minutes to mix the dough starting from the moment you pull out all the ingredients.
>
> This recipe makes enough dough for six 9- to 10-inch Personal Pizzas (page 281), 12 Dessert Calzones (page 328), or 3 large pizzas. It only takes 1 hour to rise and you can take advantage of that time to prepare the toppings (or in the case of calzones, the stuffing).
>
> If you want to make extra and freeze it, add a little extra yeast as directed in the recipe. Or you can roll out the dough, prebake it (for 3 minutes on the bottom rack of a preheated 500°F oven), cool it completely, wrap it well and freeze the shells. To make pizza with the prebaked shells, defrost the shells, spread them with the toppings and bake until the cheese is melted, about 5 minutes. "

360 grams (about 3 cups) unbleached all-purpose flour

1 (¼-ounce) package instant yeast (about 2¼ teaspoons, see Note)

1 teaspoon sugar

1 teaspoon table salt

1½ tablespoons extra-virgin olive oil (or vegetable oil if making dough for calzones), plus more for oiling the bowl and rolling out the dough

> Combine the flour, yeast, sugar, and salt in the bowl of a food processor fitted with the metal blade and pulse once or twice. Add 1 cup very warm (120° to 130°F) water and the oil; process until a dough forms. It should be soft and slightly sticky. If it is too sticky, add more flour, 1 tablespoon at a time. If it is too stiff, add more warm water, 1 tablespoon at a time.

> Shape the dough into a ball and place in an oiled bowl, turning the dough so the surface is completely coated. Cover with plastic wrap and let rise in a warm place until double in bulk, about 1 hour. Divide as directed in your recipe or as needed.

Note: Add ⅛ teaspoon more yeast if you are going to freeze the dough.

ALL ABOUT YEAST

What is the difference between active dry yeast and instant yeast (quick rise, SAF instant, and rapid-rise)?

Active dry yeast needs to be hydrated, or "proofed," meaning dissolved in warm (not hot, about 110°F) water with a pinch of sugar or flour for about 10 minutes before using. It requires this jump start before adding it to the dough because it has been dehydrated into tiny granules, which take time to dissolve. Also, this is a way to determine if the yeast is still alive; if it doesn't bubble up and get foamy after 10 minutes, you will know that it has lost its oomph.

Instant yeasts, all of which make the dough rise faster than regular active dry yeast, are more porous than active dry and do not need to be hydrated before adding them to the rest of the ingredients. They are mixed with the dry ingredients, and then the liquid (in this case, water) is added. The liquid added to these quick-rising yeasts needs to be quite warm, 120° to 130°F.

Any of these yeasts will work in my pizza dough recipe. If all you can find is active dry, proof it as described above in ¼ cup of the water (barely warm, about 110°F), and then add the proofed yeast with the remaining water (again warm) to the dry ingredients in the food processor. Dough made with active dry yeast will take a little longer to double in bulk.

THE BEST WAY TO ROLL OUT PIZZA DOUGH

1. When you roll out pizza dough on a lightly floured counter...

2. ...it shrinks back after every roll.

3. Note the flour line from where the dough retracted.

4. But if you roll it out instead on a lightly oiled counter with a lightly oiled rolling pin...

5. ...the dough sticks to the counter...

6. ...and does not shrink back.

PIE DOUGH

START TO FINISH: 1 HOUR 15 MINUTES / **HANDS-ON TIME:** 15 MINUTES
SERVINGS: MAKES ENOUGH DOUGH FOR A LARGE (10-INCH) SINGLE-CRUST PIE

180 grams (about 1½ cups) unbleached all-purpose flour

¼ teaspoon table salt

10 tablespoons cold unsalted butter, cut into ½-inch cubes

2 to 4 tablespoons ice water

> Stir together the flour and salt in a large bowl, add the butter, and, working quickly with your fingertips or a pastry blender, mix the dough until most of mixture resembles coarse meal, with the rest in small (roughly pea-sized) lumps. Drizzle 2 tablespoons ice water evenly over the mixture and gently stir with a fork until incorporated. Gently squeeze a small handful: it should hold together without crumbling apart. If it doesn't, add more ice water, ½ tablespoon at a time, stirring 2 or 3 times after each addition until it comes together. (If you overwork the mixture or add too much water, the pastry will be tough.)

> Turn the dough out onto a clean work surface and divide into several portions. With the heel of your hand, smear each portion once in a forward motion on the work surface to help distribute fat. Gather the smeared dough together and form it, rotating it on the work surface, into a disk. Wrap in plastic wrap and chill until firm, at least 1 hour.

Cook's Notes: Weigh, Don't Measure, Your Flour

> Years ago, when I took a bread-making class at the King Arthur Flour Baking Education Center in Norwich, Vermont, we students were asked to measure out 2 cups of all-purpose flour, and then to bring them to the front of the room to be weighed. There were 20 of us in the class and 20 different weights of the flour, ranging from 7 to 10 ounces. The punch line was that 2 cups of flour *should* weigh 8.5 ounces. Can you imagine how much difference that variance would make in a loaf of bread? That's why you should weigh, not measure, your flour.

> My recipes list the cup measures for the flour alongside the weights, as a courtesy for folks who don't have a scale, but I do recommend purchasing one (see Sources, page 350). They come in handy for measuring all sorts of things, not just flour. I've used the King Arthur Flour conversion chart for the measurements in this book.

> By the way, King Arthur Flour baking classes are fantastic. You'll learn a ton, plus there you are in beautiful Vermont. See kingarthurflour.com/school for more information.

❝ I tried out several variations of pie dough and settled on this one as my favorite. No surprise, really. I've always preferred the taste of butter to lard or shortening. Yes, those other fats produce a flaky crust, but I found that by going with a high percentage of butter to flour, my butter-based dough was plenty flaky. ❞

FOR BETTER PIE DOUGH

▶ Be sure the butter is very cold.

▶ Don't mix the butter into the flour too thoroughly (some pea-sized lumps are okay).

▶ If the dough gets soft when you're rolling it out, chill it briefly.

▶ After you add the water, try to mix the dough as little as possible. Water plus kneading stimulates the production of gluten strands in the flour, which will make your dough tough.

▶ Be sure you allow time for the dough to rest in the fridge, both after you make it and again after you roll it out and put it in the pan.

HOW TO MIX PIE DOUGH

1. Toss the flour with the salt in a bowl and top it with the well-chilled butter chunks. Break up the butter chunks with your fingers, mixing them with the flour.

2. Continue to mix until the dough is mostly combined, with a few larger chunks of butter remaining.

3. Add 2 tablespoons of ice water. Mix, adding additional water in ½-tablespoon amounts if the mixture still seems dry, until the dough comes together when you press it.

4. Dump the dough onto the counter.

5. Divide it into several mounds and smear each mound across the counter with the palm of your hand to finish mixing the dough (some small lumps of butter should remain).

6. With the help of a bench scraper, scrape the dough off the counter and shape it into a round.

HOMEMADE BUTTER

One of the perks of working at La Tulipe in the early 1980s were the occasions when Jacques Pépin joined us in the kitchen as guest chef. I learned so much from him on those visits. He's not only *the* maestro of French culinary technique (who else can cut up a whole chicken in 29 seconds?), he's a great teacher.

One of his most memorable lessons had to do with butter. Entering the kitchen at the start of one of his stints, he'd make a beeline for the walk-in refrigerator to check out the butter. Inevitably, he'd end up tossing out several pounds of it, declaring it to be past its prime. The point? Butter is very perishable; its fresh, pure taste heads downhill quickly if it's not well chilled—and there's just no counting on proper storage while butter is being transported and unloaded.

All the more reason, then, to make your own butter. It's super easy and it tastes better than anything you can bring home from the market. Serve the finished product, topped with sea salt, with a nice, crusty bread. Or flavor it and freeze it for future recipes. You'll wow your family and friends, and you might just end up adding it to your weekly prep schedule.

START TO FINISH: 20 MINUTES / **HANDS-ON TIME:** 20 MINUTES
SERVINGS: MAKES ABOUT ¾ POUND (THE EQUIVALENT OF 3 STICKS)

1 quart heavy cream (if you can get it
   fresh at the farmers' market that
   would be preferable)

> As shown in the photos on pages 44–45, beat the cream in a stand mixer fitted with the whisk on medium speed, scraping down the sides with a rubber spatula every so often, until the cream has separated into something that looks like butter (mostly clinging to the tines of the whisk) with a milky liquid at the bottom of the bowl, 12 to 15 minutes.

> Transfer the butter from the whisk to a bowl of ice and cold water. Squeeze the butter with your hands for several minutes under the water, being careful not to get any ice cubes embedded in the butter. Dump off the water, add fresh water, and repeat the procedure until the liquid you squeeze out of the butter is clear. Lift the butter out of the water and squeeze it to remove any excess liquid. Divide into three equal parts, wrap well with plastic wrap, and chill.

> Use the butter within the week, freeze it for up to a month, or turn it into a flavored butter (see page 43).

HERB BUTTER

START TO FINISH: 10 MINUTES / **HANDS-ON TIME:** 10 MINUTES
SERVINGS: MAKES ABOUT 16 TABLESPOONS (½ POUND)

½ pound Homemade Butter (page 42) or store-bought unsalted butter, cut into tablespoons and softened to room temperature

2 teaspoons minced shallots

3 tablespoons chopped fresh tarragon, dill, chives, parsley, basil, or a mix

1 teaspoon kosher salt

¼ teaspoon freshly ground black pepper

› Using an electric hand mixer, combine the butter, shallots, herbs, salt, and pepper and mix well. Divide the butter in half, roll up each half of the butter in a log shape in plastic wrap or parchment paper (see page 44) and chill or freeze.

CITRUS BUTTER

› Follow the procedure above as directed, combining ½ pound butter, with 1 teaspoon freshly grated lemon zest, 1 teaspoon freshly grated lime zest, 2 teaspoons fresh lemon juice, 2 teaspoons fresh lime juice, and ½ teaspoon kosher salt.

STEAK BUTTER

› Follow the procedure above as directed, combining ½ pound butter with 2 tablespoons Worcestershire sauce, 1 tablespoon Dijon mustard, 1 finely minced garlic clove, and ½ teaspoon kosher salt.

"Flavored butters, stashed in the fridge or the freezer, can be a godsend on a weeknight, turning a plain-Jane entrée or naked vegetable into something uniquely delicious. Using it as a sauce is no more complicated than dropping a spoonful of the butter on top of the hot food and letting it melt.

The Herb Butter is the ideal complement to fish (see Baked Char with Asparagus, Potatoes, and Herb Butter, page 177), poultry, meats, and vegetables. The Citrus Butter plays nicely with fish and vegetables. And the Steak Butter is the perfect partner for, well, steak, as well as for mushrooms, especially portobellos.

You can make these flavored butters with supermarket butter, but they're even better if you start with your own Homemade Butter (page 42 and technique pages 44–45). I recommend rolling each one into a cylinder with the help of plastic wrap or parchment paper, followed by foil so it doesn't pick up the aromas of its neighbors in the fridge or the freezer. When the moment's right, just slice off as much as you want."

HOW TO MAKE BUTTER AT HOME

MAKING BUTTER

1. Add heavy cream to a stand mixer fitted with a whisk. Beat on medium until the cream turns to whipped cream.

2. Keep beating the mixture until it becomes quite stiff.

3. Continue until the mixture separates completely into butter and a milky liquid. It will take 12 to 15 minutes for this to happen.

4. Remove the butter from the whisk and the bowl and drop it into a bowl of ice and water.

5. Knead the butter in the water (the water will become cloudy).

6. Change the water several times until it is completely clear. Now the butter is cleaned and ready to be eaten straight up or added to recipes.

MAKING AND SHAPING FLAVORED BUTTER

7. Cut the butter into cubes, place in a bowl, and leave at room temperature to soften (but don't let it get too warm). Add all the flavorings to the butter. Using an electric mixer or a spoon, mix the butter with the flavorings until they are incorporated.

8. Spoon half the butter onto a piece of plastic wrap, and with the help of a rubber spatula, shape it into a log (the length and thickness of the log is up to you). Fold one half of the wrap over the butter and pull back to smooth out the log. Repeat with the remaining butter.

9. Twist the ends to compress the butter. Refrigerate or freeze the finished compound butter.

CLARIFIED BUTTER

START TO FINISH: 10 MINUTES / **HANDS-ON TIME:** 10 MINUTES
SERVINGS: MAKES ABOUT ¾ CUP

1 pound unsalted butter, cut into
    tablespoons

› Heat the butter in a small saucepan over medium-low heat until it is completely melted. Skim off the scum that settles at the top, using a spoon, and discard it. Gently pour or ladle the butter oil (the clear yellow part of the mixture) into a jar, and discard the watery milk solids left behind.

GHEE

START TO FINISH: ABOUT 50 MINUTES / **HANDS-ON TIME:** 5 MINUTES
SERVINGS: MAKES 1⅓ TO 1½ CUPS

1 pound unsalted butter, cut into
    tablespoons

› Place the butter in a heavy-bottom 3-quart saucepan (do not use one with a gray or black interior because you will not be able to see when the butter is browned) and cook over low heat until the butter has melted completely, about 20 minutes. Increase the heat to medium and bring the butter to a simmer. Let it simmer until the crackling noise has stopped and the foam has subsided, 15 to 20 minutes. Continue simmering, stirring and watching the butter carefully to make sure it does not burn, until the solids at the bottom of the pan just turn brown, about 10 minutes. Turn off the heat and let the ghee stand for 5 minutes before straining it through a double layer of cheesecloth. Transfer to a glass jar with a lid and store in the fridge.

"Have you ever tried to sauté a piece of meat in butter and discovered to your dismay that the butter was burning up before the meat was properly seared? That's because butter isn't pure fat, and the parts that aren't fat burn quickly.

Melted butter separates into three layers. On the bottom are the milk solids. On the top is a thin film of scum (protein solids). In the middle is butter oil or pure butterfat. Clarified butter is that middle part. Clarified butter has a much higher smoke point (350° to 375°F) than whole butter (250° to 300°F) and you can use it to sauté meat or whatever else you want to cook over high heat.

A bonus is that clarified butter doesn't spoil as quickly as regular butter; it will keep for several months in the fridge."

"Every cuisine has its fat of choice. The French use clarified butter, Americans use vegetable oil, Italians use olive oil, and Mexicans use lard. Throughout the Indian subcontinent, the preference is for ghee. It's a kind of clarified butter, although the process of making it differs from the French classical style. For ghee, the butter is simmered until all the liquid from the milk solids evaporates and the milk solids themselves stick to the pan and brown lightly. The finished product boasts a signature nuttiness. Several recipes in this book call for ghee."

QUICK PRESERVED LEMON SLICES

START TO FINISH: 24 HOURS / **HANDS-ON TIME:** IO MINUTES
SERVINGS: MAKES I½ CUPS

2¹/₂ thin-skinned lemons cut into ¹/₈-inch thick slices

¹/₄ cup kosher salt

> Arrange half the lemons on the bottom of a nonreactive 8- or 9-inch square pan in a single layer and sprinkle 2 tablespoons of the salt evenly over them. Arrange the remaining lemon slices on top in a single layer and sprinkle evenly with the remaining salt. Cover with plastic wrap, pressing down so it covers the surface of the top layer of lemons. Leave at room temperature for 24 hours and up to 48 hours. Rinse the lemons, remove the seeds and pat dry before using. Store in a glass jar in the fridge for up to 1 week or, if you are going to freeze them, wrap them tightly in several layers of plastic wrap. They will keep for a few months in the freezer.

"Preserved lemons (actually pickled lemons) are one of the signature treats of Moroccan cuisine. The traditional way of making them is to combine scored lemons, lemon juice, and salt, and then let the mixture cure for three to four weeks.

Working with lemon slices, not whole lemons, this short-cut version requires only 24 to 48 hours to cure. Marie Ostrosky introduced me to this method back when she and I worked together on *Cooking Live*. It's a wonderful keepsake from Marie's days as a caterer.

There's scarcely a fish dish you could name that wouldn't benefit from the tangy counterpoint provided by the salt and acid in these little charmers. (For example, Baked Arctic Char with Chermoula, page 239.) But they also make a terrific garnish for salads, sandwiches, and meat stews. And they freeze beautifully."

HOMEMADE RICOTTA-STYLE CHEESE
WITH BUTTERMILK

START TO FINISH: 45 MINUTES / **HANDS-ON TIME:** 10 MINUTES / **SERVINGS:** MAKES A SCANT CUP

1 quart whole milk
1 cup low-fat buttermilk

$1/2$ teaspoon table salt

> Combine the milk, buttermilk, and salt in a medium heavy saucepan and heat the mixture over medium heat, stirring often, until it reaches 190°F. Remove from the heat and let it stand for 15 minutes. Using a small strainer gently transfer the curds to a colander lined with cheesecloth or a damp paper towel.

> Let the cheese drain for 20 minutes, transfer to a bowl, and refrigerate until ready to use.

WITH VINEGAR

START TO FINISH: 45 MINUTES / **HANDS-ON TIME:** 10 MINUTES / **SERVINGS:** MAKES ABOUT ¾ CUP

1 quart whole milk
$1/2$ cup heavy cream
$1/2$ teaspoon table salt

2 to 3 tablespoons white distilled vinegar

> Combine the milk, heavy cream, and salt in a medium heavy saucepan and heat the mixture over medium heat, stirring often, until it reaches 190°F. Remove from the heat, stir in 2 tablespoons of the vinegar, and let the mixture stand for 15 minutes. (If the mixture does not look like it curdled significantly after you add the vinegar, add the additional tablespoon.) Using a small strainer gently transfer the curds to a colander lined with a damp paper towel.

> Let the cheese drain for 20 minutes, transfer to a bowl, and refrigerate until ready to use.

"I call this recipe "ricotta-style" because it isn't true ricotta cheese. (True ricotta is made by heating the whey left over when making mozzarella, and then adding acid.) Whatever it's called, this homemade fresh cheese is delicious—much more tasty than what you buy at the store—and it's easy to make, requiring no special ingredients or equipment.

Over many years of making this cheese in the *Gourmet* dining room, I learned that heating the milk and cream to a specific temperature helps to yield consistent results.

Here are recipes for two versions: one made with buttermilk and one with vinegar. They're similar, but each has its own unique appeal. The buttermilk version is creamy and the vinegar version is tangy."

MAKING HOMEMADE RICOTTA-STYLE CHEESE

1. Pour the milk and heavy cream (or buttermilk, if making the buttermilk version) into a heavy saucepan and add the salt. Heat the mixture over medium heat, stirring occasionally, until the temperature reaches 190°F. Add the vinegar if making the vinegar version.

2. Let the mixture stand for 15 minutes.

3. Lift out the curds using a small strainer. (If you just dump the curds out they tend to break up.)

4. Transfer them to a large strainer lined with cheesecloth (or a damp paper towel). Let the curds drain for 20 minutes. (The longer you leave them, the firmer the ricotta will be; I like a creamy, soft ricotta.)

5. Leaving the whey behind...

6. ...transfer to a bowl, and refrigerate until ready to use, or drain and press to make paneer (see page 50).

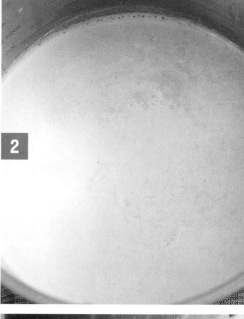

HOMEMADE SEMISOFT CHEESE (PANEER)

START TO FINISH: I HOUR 55 MINUTES / **HANDS-ON TIME:** IO MINUTES
SERVINGS: MAKES A SCANT ½ POUND

Two thousand years after it originated in ancient India, paneer remains a staple not only of Indian cuisine, but also of the traditional cuisines of Nepal, Pakistan, and Bangladesh. The first time I made paneer, in the test kitchen at *Gourmet,* I just about did a happy dance around the room. I couldn't believe there was a way to make fresh cheese in your own kitchen without any special equipment. And it tasted *very* fresh, with no additives or random flavors absorbed from the fridge.

Paneer's DNA is very similar to that of ricotta. It's just that paneer is eventually pressed and weighted, which allows it to hold its shape and allows it to be cubed or sliced. I'm a big fan of paneer's texture. It's reminiscent of tofu and, like tofu, it's a great foil for the sauce of your choice.

Paneer is featured, as advertised, in Saag Paneer with Cauliflower (page 209), but feel free to add it to any recipe that calls for semi-soft cheese. Just keep in mind that paneer is not a melting cheese. It holds its texture when heated.

2 quarts whole milk
1 teaspoon table salt

¹/₄ cup distilled white vinegar

> Combine the milk and salt in a medium heavy saucepan and heat the mixture over medium heat, stirring often, until it reaches 190°F. Remove from heat, stir in the vinegar, and let the mixture stand for 15 minutes. Using a skimmer or slotted spoon, gently transfer the curds to a colander lined with a double layer of cheesecloth and let the cheese drain for 20 minutes.

> Twist the cloth around the cheese, transfer it to a plate with the twisted cheesecloth knot on the side, and top it with another plate followed by some heavy cans or a saucepan to weigh it down. Let the cheese drain, discarding the whey that pools on the plate several times, until it is very firm, about 1 hour.

USES FOR PANEER

▶ Saag Paneer (page 209)

▶ Slice it into "cutlets," sauté it in olive oil until golden on both sides, and then add thin lemon slices (Quick Preserved Lemon Slices, if you want, page 47), capers, fresh herbs, and red pepper flakes and a few tablespoons of butter.

▶ Or top the browned cutlets with sautéed peppers and onions, a mix of sautéed wild mushrooms, or fresh tomato sauce.

MAKING PANEER

1. Lift up the cheesecloth in which you have drained the cheese for 20 minutes.

2. Twist the cheesecloth tightly around the cheese.

3. Lay the cheese down on a plate with the cheesecloth knot placed on the side.

4. Top with a plate and a heavy object such as a cast-iron skillet.

5. After 1 hour the cheese will be quite firm.

6. Remove the cheesecloth. The paneer is ready to be cut and used in recipes.

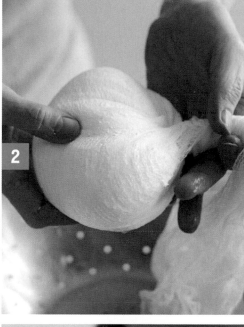

AIRY MAYONNAISE

START TO FINISH: 10 MINUTES / **HANDS-ON TIME:** 10 MINUTES
SERVINGS: MAKES ABOUT 2 CUPS

2 large egg yolks, at room temperature (see Note in Tips for Making Mayo, page 53)

Pinch of cayenne

¼ teaspoon table salt

⅛ teaspoon dry mustard

3 tablespoons cider vinegar

2 cups vegetable oil, preferably grapeseed, divided

Freshly ground black pepper

> Combine the yolks, cayenne, salt, mustard, vinegar, 1 teaspoon water, and ½ cup oil in a blender or food processor and pulse briefly, just until combined. With the blender on low, or the food processor running, add the remaining oil in a slow, steady stream (see Tips for Making Mayo, page 53), stopping midway to scrape down the sides. If the mixture starts to look oily around the edges, add 2 tablespoons water. When all the oil has been added, turn off the machine and scrape down the sides. Turn it on again if the mayonnaise is not completely mixed and thickened, and pulse two or three times briefly on high, scraping down the sides as necessary, until thick. Season with pepper to taste. The mayonnaise will keep for 1 week in the fridge.

Note: You may not have noticed it, but your food processor probably has a very small hole in the bottom of the "pusher" that sits inside the feed tube. You can pour the oil into the "pusher" and it will let the oil drip out at the pace needed. I've never had the mayonnaise split when using this feature.

> "I like these recipes for basic mayonnaise equally well, so I decided to share both of them. The Airy Mayonnaise is my Aunt Jean's. I'm a big fan because it's so much lighter in texture than traditional mayo, whether homemade or store-bought. But I'm also partial to the Lemony Mayonnaise, which is denser and flavored with citrus. I'll leave it to you to choose your favorite.
>
> Mayonnaise requires oil. My preference is for grapeseed oil because of its pure, clean taste, but it's pricey. You can use vegetable oil instead, and perhaps enrich it with a little bit of extra-virgin olive oil. Just don't add too much olive oil; it takes over and makes the mayonnaise bitter. I also stay away from canola oil. Not only is most of it genetically modified, but it's also too heavy for this purpose.
>
> My Aunt Jean's method is a little unconventional because she adds some of the oil at the beginning. It is a little trickier to make than the lemony version, but if you follow the instructions exactly, you will not have a problem."

LEMONY MAYONNAISE

START TO FINISH: IO MINUTES / **HANDS-ON TIME:** IO MINUTES / **SERVINGS:** MAKES ABOUT I CUP

2 large egg yolks, at room temperature

Pinch of cayenne

¼ teaspoon table salt

1 tablespoon plus 1 teaspoon fresh
  lemon juice

1 teaspoon Dijon mustard

1 cup vegetable oil, preferably
  grapeseed

Freshly ground black pepper

> Combine the yolks, cayenne, salt, lemon juice, and mustard in a blender or a food processor and pulse briefly, just until combined. With the blender on low, or the food processor running, add the oil in a slow, steady stream (see Note, page 52), stopping mid way to scrape down the sides. If the mixture starts to look oily around the edges, add 2 tablespoons water. When all the oil has been added, turn off the machine immediately and scrape down the sides.

> Season the mayonnaise with pepper to taste. The mayonnaise will keep for 1 week in the fridge.

TIPS FOR MAKING MAYO

▶ As soon as the mayo is done, turn off the machine. Too much agitation can make it break down.

▶ Be careful not to add the oil too quickly; you don't want the mayonnaise to split. If it somehow splits anyway, follow the instructions in the box at right for Fixing a Broken Mayonnaise.

▶ **Note:** Although very few eggs are actually contaminated with salmonella, I'd err on the side of caution and refrain from serving mayonnaise to children under the age of five, the elderly, or the immune-impaired.

FIXING A BROKEN MAYONNAISE

1. If you have added the oil too fast, your mayonnaise might split and look like this.

2. To fix it, add 1 tablespoon hot water to a food processor. (A blender will work, too.) With the processor running on low, add the split mayonnaise slowly, in a steady stream, through the feed tube. Continue processing until all the split mayo has been added.

3. The mayo will become emulsified and thick again.

HARD-"BOILED" EGGS

START TO FINISH: 40 MINUTES / **HANDS-ON TIME:** 10 MINUTES
SERVINGS: MAKES 6 HARD-BOILED EGGS

6 large eggs (see Note, at left)

> Fit a collapsible steamer inside a medium saucepan and fill the saucepan with about 1 inch of water or to just below the level of the steamer basket (no water should be touching the eggs). Put the lid on top of the pan and bring the water to a medium-high boil over medium-high heat.

> Using a large, long-handled, slotted spoon, place the eggs in a single layer in the steamer, being carful not to burn your hand with the steam. Steam the eggs for 10 to 12 minutes. (At 10 minutes, the yolks will be slightly undercooked; I prefer them this way.) Transfer the eggs carefully to a bowl of ice and water and let them cool completely.

> When they are cool, crack them all over and peel them under cold running water, starting at the wide end of the egg, and making sure to get under the membrane (which makes it much easier to peel the egg).

FANCY STUFFED EGGS

START TO FINISH: 40 MINUTES / **HANDS-ON TIME:** 10 MINUTES
SERVINGS: MAKES 12 STUFFED EGGS

6 Hard-"Boiled" Eggs (above)

2 tablespoons Homemade Mayonnaise (pages 52–53) or store-bought mayonnaise

2 tablespoons crème fraîche

1 teaspoon Dijon mustard

2 tablespoons finely grated Parmesan

1 tablespoon truffle oil

Kosher salt and freshly ground black pepper

Snipped chives, for garnish

> Cut the eggs in half lengthwise, remove the yolks, and set the whites aside. Push the yolks through a medium sieve into a bowl. Add the mayonnaise, crème fraîche, mustard, Parmesan, and truffle oil to the mashed yolks and mix well with a fork. Add salt and pepper to taste and transfer the mixture to a re-sealable plastic bag. Cut off one of the corners of the bag, pipe the mixture evenly into the hollow of each of the whites, and garnish each egg half with some of the chives. (For a fancier look, transfer the mixture to a pastry bag fitted with a star tip.)

---

66 ~~~~~~

I have been making hard-boiled eggs using Julia Child's method with great success for years. Her method ensures tender whites and no green line. (In a nutshell, she advised to start the eggs in cold water, bring them to a boil, remove them from the heat, and cool them in ice water right away, before peeling.) So I was pretty skeptical when Carol Montag and Jonathan Horwich, fans of my show, reached out to share their method for "boiling" eggs (which was to steam them!). Why fix it if it ain't broke?

Well, I was wrong to be skeptical; their method trumps Julia's. (Sorry, Julia!) Somehow the whites are even more tender and the yolks perfectly cooked. I hope you try it. Eternal student that she was, I know Julia would.

By the way, Carol and Jonathan have written their own cookbook, *Chicago Cooks: 45 Perfect Recipes for the Passionate Palate* which they're hoping to publish soon.

I also have included a very tasty recipe for stuffed eggs to make use of the hard-boiled eggs. Who knew stuffed eggs could be so fancy?

Note: Older eggs are much easier to peel, so this is one time when you might not want farm-fresh eggs.

99

3 | *soups & salads* FOR SUPPER

I
f you find yourself making the same ten dishes for dinner over and over again (and boring yourself silly in the process), it's time to break the mold. At least one night a week you should consider sidelining the tired trio of meat/starch/vegetables in favor of a substantial soup or salad.

I love soups—cooking them and eating them. There are *so* many variations it's hard to go wrong. The menu for this chapter includes two chilled soups for summertime and eight for the colder months, including two vegetarian recipes and one that takes advantage of all those Thanksgiving leftovers. Each is just about a meal in itself, requiring little more to round it out than a simple salad or side dish and some good, crusty bread.

The salad menu also reflects the seasons, running from height-of-summer fare like the Stuffed Red Pepper Salad to stick-to-your ribs winter dishes like Warm Red Cabbage, Potato, and Kielbasa Salad with Creamy Mustard Dressing. Along the way you'll learn the perfect way to poach an egg, reduce the fat in a dressing without losing flavor, and how to cook octopus from my buddy Dave Pasternack.

COLD SOUTHWESTERN GAZPACHO

START TO FINISH: 60 MINUTES PLUS CHILLING TIME / **HANDS-ON TIME:** 60 MINUTES
SERVINGS: 4 (MAKES ABOUT 6½ CUPS)

4 cups coarsely chopped, peeled, English (seedless) cucumbers plus 1 cup diced peeled cucumber

2 cups coarsely chopped plum or beefsteak tomatoes plus 1 cup finely diced tomatoes

3 teaspoons kosher salt, divided

1 cup coarsely chopped avocado plus 1 cup finely diced avocado tossed with 2 teaspoons fresh lime juice

½ cup coarsely chopped roasted peeled poblano peppers or ½ cup drained canned green chiles

¼ cup packed fresh cilantro, leaves and stems

1 garlic clove, smashed and peeled

3 tablespoons fresh lime juice

2 tablespoons vegetable oil, preferably grapeseed

2 cups fresh corn kernels

2 cups Tortilla Strips or crushed store-bought tortilla chips

> Toss the coarsely chopped cucumbers and coarsely chopped tomatoes with 2 teaspoons salt in a bowl and set them aside for 15 minutes. In a separate bowl, toss the finely diced cucumber and finely diced tomato with 1 teaspoon salt and set them aside.

> Working in batches if necessary, blend the coarsely chopped cucumber, coarsely chopped tomato, coarsely chopped avocado, poblano, cilantro, garlic, lime juice, and oil in a blender until very smooth. Transfer to a bowl and stir in three-fourths of the finely diced cucumber and tomato mixture and the juice from the bowl they were in, three-fourths of the diced avocado, and all of the corn.

> Chill until very cold. Ladle into 4 bowls and top each portion with some of the reserved diced vegetables and the tortilla strips.

TORTILLA STRIPS

START TO FINISH: 25 MINUTES / **HANDS-ON TIME:** 15 MINUTES / **SERVINGS:** MAKES 2 CUPS

2 tablespoons vegetable oil, preferably grapeseed

2 teaspoons chili powder

½ teaspoon kosher salt

8 (6-inch) Homemade Corn Tortillas (page 270) or store-bought tortillas

Preheat the oven to 400°F. Combine the oil, chili powder, and salt in a small bowl and brush over 1 side of each tortilla. Cut the tortillas in half and then into ¼-inch strips. Arrange strips on a rimmed baking sheet and bake on the middle shelf of the oven until crisp, about 8 minutes.

> This is a height-of-the-summer soup, a cold and refreshing Southwestern spin on gazpacho. It turns out best when you take advantage of the season's bounty; the fresher your produce, the more delicious the finished product. If your corn is very fresh—picked at the peak of its ripeness and kept chilled until ready to shuck—you can throw it in raw. If not, give it a quick blanch to start. (Use a mandoline to easily strip off the kernels.)

When it comes to the tomatoes, you're welcome to mix up the varieties if (lucky you) you have a variety at hand. Puree beefsteak tomatoes to make the soup itself, and use cherry tomatoes (halved or quartered) for the garnish. Then pre-season the tomatoes and the cukes to concentrate their flavor (see page 13).

And please use a blender to puree it all. A blender is the right tool for this job, as it is any time you want a really smooth texture. You just won't get the same results with a food processor or immersion blender.

The homemade tortilla chips here are baked, not fried, which reduces their fat content with no loss of deliciousness.

PEA VICHYSSOISE
WITH SMOKED SALMON

START TO FINISH: 50 MINUTES PLUS CHILLING TIME / **HANDS-ON TIME:** 40 MINUTES
SERVINGS: 4 (MAKES 7 TO 8 CUPS)

"
I've always loved this chilled potato leek-soup, which the French call *vichyssoise*. It was one of my mom's specialties. Here, I've added buttermilk and peas to the standard recipe, which makes it even more refreshing and filling.

I enlisted two potato varieties for this soup: baking and boiling. The baking potatoes, with their high starch content, absorb flavors really well. The boiling potatoes provide creaminess. Blend the soup just until it becomes smooth, and then stop. If you overwork the starch in the potatoes, your soup will turn to glue.

If you can find fresh peas at a farm stand or market in the summer, by all means snatch them up for this recipe, but only if you can make the soup soon after you have purchased them. The natural sugar in peas starts to turn to starch as soon as they're harvested. As the starch increases, that bright and beautiful fresh pea flavor goes bye-bye. (If you can't find fresh peas, frozen peas are a very acceptable alternative.)

This soup becomes a one-dish meal by adding smoked salmon and goat cheese. Swap in smoked turkey or boiled shrimp for the salmon, if you wish, but please don't skip the wasabi peas: Available as snack food at many check-out counters, their heat and crispiness provide the perfect finishing touch.
"

2 cups medium chopped leeks, white part only

1 cup medium chopped peeled baking (russet) potatoes

1 cup medium chopped peeled boiling potatoes

2 garlic cloves, crushed and peeled

2 cups Homemade Chicken Stock (page 26), Homemade Vegetable Stock (page 29), or store-bought vegetable or chicken broth

2 cups fresh or defrosted frozen peas

2^1/$_2$ cups low-fat buttermilk

Kosher salt and freshly ground black pepper

4 ounces smoked salmon, medium chopped

4 ounces fresh goat cheese or feta cheese, crumbled

^{1}/$_2$ cup wasabi peas

› Combine the leeks, potatoes, and garlic in a medium saucepan. Add 2 cups of water and the stock, bring the liquid to a boil, reduce the heat, and simmer until the potatoes are very tender, about 15 minutes. Add the green peas, bring the liquid back to a boil, and simmer, until the peas are tender, about 2 minutes. Fill a blender one-third full with some of the soup mixture, add some of the buttermilk, and puree until just smooth. Repeat the procedure until completely pureed, transferring each batch to a bowl. Season with salt and pepper to taste and chill well. Ladle the soup into 4 bowls. Top each portion with one-fourth of the salmon, cheese, and wasabi peas.

HOW TO QUICK-CHILL A SOUP (OR A BOTTLE OF BUBBLY)

If you want to chill your soup quickly, just transfer it to a metal bowl, set the bowl into another larger bowl filled with ice and water, and let it chill. (The water part is key, as ice is not as effective by itself.) You can speed up the process by stirring the soup from the edges every so often, as it will chill from the outside in.

This method works equally well when you have a bottle of wine or any other liquid that you want to chill quickly. You can chill a bottle of Champagne in a bucket of ice and water in about 15 minutes flat.

SMOKY BROCCOLI-CHEDDAR SOUP

START TO FINISH: I HOUR I5 MINUTES / **HANDS-ON TIME:** 50 MINUTES
SERVINGS: 4 (MAKES ABOUT 8 CUPS)

4 tablespoons extra-virgin olive oil,
divided

¾ pound Canadian bacon, cut into
small cubes

1 cup sliced onion

2 pounds fresh broccoli (about
2 heads), 6 cups small florets set
aside, the rest of the florets and
stalks peeled of tough skin and
coarsely chopped

1 small Yukon gold potato (about
6 ounces), peeled and thinly sliced

5 cups Homemade Chicken Stock
(page 26) or store-bought chicken
broth

Kosher salt and freshly ground black
pepper

1 teaspoon fresh lemon juice or to taste

2 ounces sharp cheddar cheese,
coarsely grated

> Preheat the oven to 450°F. Heat 1 tablespoon of the oil in a large saucepan over medium heat. Add the bacon and cook, stirring, until lightly browned, 6 to 8 minutes. Use a slotted spoon to transfer the bacon to a bowl and set aside.

> Add another tablespoon of the oil and the onion to the pan and cook until the onion is softened, about 5 minutes. Add the coarsely chopped broccoli (not the small florets), potato, and chicken stock. Bring the stock to a boil, then reduce the heat and simmer, partially covered, for 20 minutes, stirring every so often, or until the broccoli and potatoes are very tender.

> Meanwhile, on a rimmed baking sheet, toss the small florets with the remaining 2 tablespoons oil, season with salt and pepper to taste, and then spread in a single layer. Roast in the top third of the oven until lightly caramelized, about 5 minutes.

> When the vegetables are very tender, fill a blender one-third full with vegetables and liquid and puree until very smooth. Repeat the procedure until the mixture is completely pureed, transferring each batch to a bowl.

> Return the soup to the saucepan, along with the roasted broccoli florets and the Canadian bacon. Add the lemon juice, then season with salt and pepper to taste and heat the soup through. Add water, if necessary, to achieve the desired texture. Ladle the soup into 4 shallow soup bowls and top each portion with some of the cheddar.

I've always loved broccoli (unfortunate aroma and all), and that's why it's the star of this substantial, stick-to-your-ribs soup for fall. There's some Canadian bacon too, but only in a supporting role, as a way of adding smoky flavor.

And just as this soup boasts smokiness without a lot of bacon fat, it boasts creaminess without any butter, cream, or flour. The trick? Any soup with enough vegetables becomes creamy when pureed—and just about any vegetable will work, although I'll confess that I've smuggled in a lone Yukon gold potato to partner up with the broccoli here. A soup without a lot of cream or butter will not only be leaner, it'll also taste that much more vividly of the vegetables with which it's made.

And to save time and money, I've used every part of the broccoli, making the base of the soup from the stalks and roasting the florets (which intensifies their flavor) and tossing them in at the end to add crunch and color.

CREAMY ROOT VEGETABLE SOUP
WITH EVERYTHING PITA CRISPS

" Several times a year I teach a cooking class at the Lake Austin Spa Resort in Texas, which happens to be one of my favorite places on earth. Usually I'm joined by my sister Anne, a doctor, who lectures on women's health. During a recent visit, we ordered the soup of the day, an inspired amalgamation of pureed root vegetables, which was nothing short of sublime. I decided on the spot that I had to invent a version of my own.

I love this soup, but I must confess I love the pita crisps even more. If you happen to become addicted to Everything Pita Crisps (page 63)— a not unlikely possibility—you can make a big batch of the topping and freeze the extra for future use. (Nuts and seeds go rancid quickly.) Or visit King Arthur Flour online to buy their Everything Bagel Topping (see Sources, page 350). "

START TO FINISH: 1 HOUR 20 MINUTES / **HANDS-ON TIME:** 60 MINUTES
SERVINGS: 6 (MAKES ABOUT 10½ CUPS)

2 tablespoons vegetable oil, preferably grapeseed

1½ cups thinly sliced onion

2 teaspoons minced garlic

1½ pounds carrots, peeled, half cut into 1-inch chunks and half cut into ½-inch dice

1½ pounds turnips, peeled, half cut into 1-inch chunks and half cut into ½-inch dice

1½ pounds parsnips, peeled, half cut into 1-inch chunks and half cut into ½-inch dice

1 small Yukon gold potato (4 to 6 ounces), peeled and cut into 1-inch chunks

4 cups Homemade Vegetable Stock (page 29), Homemade Chicken Stock (page 26), or store-bought vegetable or chicken broth

Kosher salt and freshly ground black pepper

1½ tablespoons fresh lemon juice

Crumbled feta cheese for garnish, optional

1 recipe Everything Pita Crisps (page 63) or 3 cups store-bought pita crisps

> Heat the oil in a large saucepan over medium heat, add the onion and cook, stirring occasionally, until it is softened, about 5 minutes. Add the garlic, and cook, stirring, 1 minute. Add the carrot chunks, turnip chunks, parsnip chunks, and all of the potato, along with the stock and 2 cups of water. Bring to a boil, reduce the heat, and simmer, covered, until all the vegetables are very tender, about 15 minutes.

> Fill a blender one-third full with some of the vegetables and liquid and puree until very smooth, transferring it to a bowl. Repeat the procedure until the soup mixture is completely pureed. Return all the soup back to the saucepan, add the diced vegetables, and salt and pepper to taste. Bring the soup back to a boil, reduce the heat, and simmer, covered, until the diced vegetables are just tender, 10 to 12 minutes.

> Add the lemon juice and adjust seasoning, if necessary. Ladle the soup into 6 bowls, sprinkle with the feta cheese, if using. Top with the crisps or serve them on the side.

EVERYTHING PITA CRISPS

START TO FINISH: 20 MINUTES / **HANDS-ON TIME:** 10 MINUTES / **SERVINGS:** MAKES ABOUT 3 CUPS

2 teaspoons poppy seeds
2 teaspoons sesame seeds
2 teaspoons dried garlic flakes
2 teaspoons dried onion flakes
$3/4$ teaspoon kosher salt
4 (6-inch) pitas
$1/4$ cup vegetable oil, preferably grapeseed

Preheat the oven to 375°F. Combine the poppy and sesame seeds, garlic and onion flakes, and salt in a small bowl and stir well. Separate each pita in half to form two rounds and brush the rough side of each pita round with the oil. Cut the pita rounds in half and then into strips, and sprinkle with the seed mixture. Place on rimmed baking sheets and bake on the middle shelf of the oven until crispy, 5 to 8 minutes.

HOW YOU SLICE AND COOK ONIONS MAKES A DIFFERENCE

Years ago we were looking for someone to replace me as the prep person for Julia Child on *Good Morning America*. I invited a friend to come in and cook with us so Julia could decide if she was the right fit. Now, this friend was trained in France and had many years of experience in test kitchens, but she made one *huge* mistake that day: She sliced an onion the wrong way.

How did she slice it? Crosswise, rather than from pole (stem) to pole (root). On the basis of that mistake, Julia would not hire her. I had always sliced an onion pole to pole as I learned at cooking school but I didn't know why it mattered. Now I do.

If you slice an onion crosswise, essentially across the grain, it will have an uneven texture when cooked. Onions sliced with the grain, from pole to pole, break down more evenly.

The temperature at which you cook an onion is also very important. Onions contain several types of sulfur molecules. When you chop or slice an onion you activate an enzyme that transforms the sulfur molecules into compounds that start out pungent but become very sweet as the onion cooks slowly over low heat. Cooking over low heat provides a greater depth of flavor to the onions and any dish to which they are added. High heat, on the other hand, deactivates the enzyme so that fewer of these compounds develop.

HEARTY CABBAGE AND SMOKED FISH CHOWDER

START TO FINISH: 50 MINUTES / **HANDS-ON TIME:** 25 MINUTES
SERVINGS: 4 (MAKES ABOUT 8 CUPS)

2 tablespoons unsalted butter

1 large leek, white and light green parts, medium chopped and rinsed (a scant 2 cups)

Kosher salt

3 tablespoons all-purpose flour

2 cups Homemade Chicken Stock (page 26) or store-bought chicken broth

1 pound Yukon gold potatoes, peeled and cut into $1/2$-inch dice

2 cups milk (whole, 2%, or 1%)

$1/2$ teaspoon dried thyme

4 cups thinly sliced napa or savoy cabbage

$1/2$ pound smoked fish fillets (trout, whitefish, haddock, or mackerel), skin discarded and fish coarsely chopped

1 tablespoon fresh lemon juice

Freshly ground black pepper

Thinly sliced scallions and smoked paprika for garnish

> Melt the butter in a large skillet over medium heat. Reduce the heat to medium-low, add the leeks and a hefty pinch of salt, cover them with a round of parchment paper (see page 265) and a lid and cook, stirring occasionally, until the leeks are very soft but not colored, 12 to 15 minutes. (The parchment traps the moisture given off by the leeks and allows them to soften completely without browning.)

> Add the flour and cook, stirring, 2 minutes. Increase the heat to high, add the chicken stock in a stream while whisking, and bring it to a boil. Add the potatoes, milk, and thyme, and bring the mixture to a simmer.

> Cover partially and simmer, stirring occasionally, until the potatoes are just tender, 10 to 15 minutes. Stir in the cabbage and simmer until it is tender, about 3 minutes.

> Add the fish and the lemon juice and cook just until the fish is heated through. Season with salt and pepper to taste. Ladle into 4 bowls and garnish with the scallions and a sprinkling of paprika.

66

This recipe was inspired by corned beef and cabbage, but swaps out the corned beef in favor of smoked fish and floats the main ingredients in a savory broth.

Smoked fish happens to be one of my favorite "secret" ingredients. Like bacon, it adds outsized oomph to any dish. Unlike bacon, smoked fish has minimal saturated fat.

The liquid is a combination of milk and chicken stock. Why use chicken stock in a fish soup? Because I've never found a commercial fish stock to my taste and because the liquid requires some kind of stock—soups made only with dairy are far too rich.

In the end all the ingredients come together beautifully, if I do say so myself. Add a tossed green salad and the refreshing libation of your choice, and you can call it a meal.

99

EGG-LEMON SOUP
WITH CHICKEN, ARTICHOKE, AND SPAETZLE

START TO FINISH: 50 MINUTES / **HANDS-ON TIME:** 30 MINUTES
SERVINGS: 4 (MAKES ABOUT 9 CUPS)

> This dish combines two cuisines: Greek soup and German *spaetzle*. Traditionally, *avgolemono*, or egg-lemon soup, is a rich chicken broth combined with rice, thickened with eggs, and flavored with lemon. Here, I've bulked up the soup with chicken meat (choose between store-bought rotisserie chicken or leftovers from your own Blasted Chicken, page 242) and roasted artichokes. And I swapped in spaetzle for the rice.
>
> Spaetzle is fresh German pasta. The dough—a thick, pancake-like batter—can be mixed together in minutes, and then simply dropped into boiling water through a spaetzle maker (see page 18) or a colander with large holes. Apart from its role in this recipe, spaetzle is a dependably satisfying side dish, whether it's boiled and tossed with butter and herbs or lightly browned in olive oil in a large skillet.
>
> I hope you'll try making spaetzle, but you can also use Arborio rice in its place, if you prefer. Bring the stock to a boil, add ⅔ cup of Arborio rice, stir, and simmer until al dente, 12 to 14 minutes. Leave the rice in the pot, whisk together the lemon juice and three eggs, and proceed with the recipe as written.

6 to 8 cups Homemade Chicken Stock (page 26) or store-bought chicken broth

1 cup all-purpose flour

$1/2$ teaspoon kosher salt

Pinch of freshly grated nutmeg

4 large eggs, divided

$1/2$ cup plus 2 tablespoons whole milk

$1/4$ cup fresh lemon juice

2 cups shredded or chopped cooked chicken

$1^1/2$ cups Sautéed Artichoke Hearts with Pancetta (page 295) or Roasted Canned Artichoke Hearts

Kosher salt and freshly ground black pepper

Chopped fresh dill for garnish

> Bring the stock to a boil in a large saucepan.

> Whisk together the flour, salt, and nutmeg in a large bowl. In a separate bowl whisk together one of the eggs and the $1/2$ cup milk. Add to the flour and whisk until smooth. Follow the procedure on page 68 to cook the spaetzle. Use a small strainer to transfer the spaetzle to a rimmed baking sheet, spreading it evenly to avoid clumps. Set aside.

> Whisk together the lemon juice and the remaining 3 eggs in a small bowl. To prevent the eggs from scrambling, gradually add 2 cups of the stock to the egg mixture in a stream, whisking. Slowly pour the egg-lemon mixture back into the pot, and cook over medium heat, stirring with a wooden spoon, just until the mixture coats the back of the spoon, 10 to 15 minutes. Do not let the liquid boil.

> Add the spaetzle, chicken, artichoke hearts, and additional stock to thin the soup if desired, and cook just until heated through. Season to taste with salt and pepper, ladle into 4 bowls, and garnish with fresh dill.

ROASTED CANNED ARTICHOKE HEARTS

START TO FINISH: 30 MINUTES / **HANDS-ON TIME:** 5 MINUTES
SERVINGS: MAKES ABOUT 1½ CUPS

1 (13.5 ounce) can artichoke hearts, drained (about $1^1/2$ cups)

2 tablespoons extra-virgin olive oil

Kosher salt and freshly ground black pepper

Preheat the oven to 400°F. Toss the artichokes with the olive oil on a rimmed baking sheet, season them with salt and pepper, and spread them in a single layer. Roast on the middle shelf of the oven until nicely caramelized, 20 to 25 minutes.

Cook's Notes: Getting the Most Out of Lemons

▶ Whenever I have finished making a soup, I taste it to make sure that it is properly seasoned. I often **add fresh lemon juice to point up, or brighten, the flavor.** Lemon juice is one of the star tools in my fix-it kit, along with salt, sugar, various other acids, and chiles (see Balance Flavors, page 14).

▶ **To get the most juice from lemons, start at the store:** Squeeze the lemons gently with your hand to make sure they're juicy. As you squeeze, there should be some give, indicating a thinner skin and more pulp. More pulp means more juice.

▶ **My favorite tool for juicing lemons** is one of those old-fashioned Mexican-style squeezers (see the citrus juicer on pages 20–21). But Ming Tsai taught me another great way to juice lemons during his appearance on *Sara's Weeknight Meals* (and Ming said he'd learned it from fellow Bostonian Jasper White, see page 115). After cutting the lemon in half, put the halves, one at a time, between the arms of a set of tongs, up at the top near the point where the arms meet. Squeeze the tongs, which provide an amazing amount of leverage, and out comes tons of juice.

▶ **Pop them in the microwave.** If you nuke lemons on high for 20 seconds, their juice comes out much more readily. (This technique also works with limes, which are notoriously reluctant to give up their juice—quite annoying when it is margarita night.)

HOW TO MAKE SPAETZLE

1. Add the liquid ingredients to the dry ingredients.

2. Whisk until smooth.

3. Set the spaetzle maker over a pot of boiling chicken stock.

4. Pour the batter into the cup part of the spaetzle maker.

5. Much of the dough will fall right through the holes in the maker, but move the cup back and forth to force the last strands of batter through the holes.

6. The spaetzle will float to the top. Taste it after several minutes of cooking; if it is al dente, using a slotted spoon or a small strainer, transfer the spaetzle to a rimmed baking sheet, spreading it evenly to avoid clumps.

SPEEDY KOREAN CHICKEN NOODLE SOUP

START TO FINISH: 60 MINUTES / **HANDS-ON TIME:** 20 MINUTES
SERVINGS: 4 (MAKES ABOUT 6 CUPS)

¹/₄ cup vegetable oil, preferably grapseseed, divided

¹/₂ pound shiitake mushrooms, stems discarded and caps cut into halves or quarters if large

Kosher salt

3 (¹/₄-inch-thick by 1¹/₂-inches-long) pieces ginger, smashed with the side of a knife

2 garlic cloves, smashed and peeled

6 scallion greens left whole, plus ¹/₃ cup chopped white parts

6 cups Homemade Chicken Stock (page 26) or store-bought chicken broth

¹/₂ pound fettuccine, broken in half crosswise

2 cups shredded cooked chicken

3 tablespoons white or yellow miso paste (see page 131)

1 cup drained Vegan Kimchi (page 235) or store-bought spicy kimchi (my favorite is Mother-in-Law's Kimchi, see Sources, page 351)

4 large eggs

Freshly ground black pepper

This is a perfect "cook from the pantry" recipe. If you happen to have some cooked chicken, dry noodles, miso, and kimchi in the house, your dinner is calling. All the flavor you could ask for is right there in the miso and the kimchi. (And you'd make your life even easier, prep-wise, by buying pre-sliced shiitakes.) The final touch—a fried egg on top—turns this dish into the ultimate comfort food.

> Heat 2 tablespoons of the oil in a large saucepan over medium heat, add the mushrooms and a hefty pinch of salt, and cook, stirring, until the mushrooms are starting to brown, 3 to 5 minutes. Add the ginger, garlic, scallion greens, chicken stock, and 2 cups water. Bring to a boil, reduce the heat, and simmer for 20 minutes. Remove and discard the ginger, garlic, and scallions.

> Bring the stock back to a boil, add the fettuccine, and gently boil until the fettuccine is almost al dente (following the timing on the package). Add the chicken, miso, and kimchi and simmer until just heated through.

> Heat the remaining 2 tablespoons of oil in a large nonstick or stick-resistant skillet over medium-high heat. Reduce the heat to medium, add the eggs, and fry them to the desired doneness. Season with kosher salt and black pepper to taste.

> When the chicken is hot, ladle the soup into 4 bowls and top each portion with a fried egg and some of the chopped scallions.

ITALIAN-STYLE POTATO AND TURKEY SOUP
WITH PARMESAN STUFFING DUMPLINGS

START TO FINISH: 55 MINUTES / **HANDS-ON TIME:** 35 MINUTES
SERVINGS: 6 (MAKES ABOUT 10 CUPS)

> What to do with all those Thanksgiving leftovers? You can pick away at them for days, one by one, or you can try this recipe, which combines a bunch of individual dishes into a super-hearty and flavorful soup.
>
> To start, thicken the leftover turkey or chicken stock with mashed potatoes. You can even use sweet potatoes, as long as there was no extra sugar added to them in the first place. (This may seem like an odd combo, but if you've ever tasted butternut squash or pumpkin ravioli in a chicken broth topped with Parmigiano-Reggiano, you know how delicious it can be.) Then add some leftover turkey and green beans to the soup—and top it all off with dumplings made from leftover stuffing spiked with Parmigiano-Reggiano.

1½ cups Basic Turkey Stuffing (page 253) or your own leftover stuffing

1½ cups fresh white breadcrumbs

3 large eggs, lightly beaten

1½ ounces freshly grated Parmigiano-Reggiano

½ to 1 teaspoon hot red pepper flakes, optional

3 cups Homemade Turkey Stock (page 28), Homemade Chicken Stock (page 26), or store-bought chicken broth

2 ounces thinly sliced prosciutto

3 cups mashed white potatoes or mashed unsweetened sweet potatoes

2 cups chopped green beans

2 cups chopped cooked turkey or chicken

> Preheat the oven to 400°F. Combine the stuffing, breadcrumbs, eggs, Parmigiano-Reggiano, and red pepper flakes, if using, in a large bowl, and roll the mixture into balls about the size of a walnut (you should get about 20). This dumpling "dough" should be firm enough to form a ball. If it's too stiff, add a little broth. If it's too wet, add more breadcrumbs.

> Combine the stock with 3 cups water in a large saucepan and bring just to a boil. Add the dumplings, reduce the heat, and simmer, covered, turning them over every so often, until tender and cooked through, 15 minutes.

> Meanwhile, set a wire rack over a rimmed baking sheet. Arrange the prosciutto slices in a single layer on the rack, and then bake on the middle shelf of the oven for 6 to 8 minutes or until they are crisp. Let the prosciutto cool and then crumble it.

> When the dumplings are cooked, use a slotted spoon to carefully transfer them to a shallow bowl. Add 2 cups of the cooking liquid to the mashed potatoes in a medium bowl and stir until the mixture is smooth. Add the potato mixture back to the saucepan and bring the soup to a boil, stirring.

> Add the green beans and turkey to the soup and simmer just until they are heated through. To serve, arrange several dumplings in each of 6 bowls, ladle some of the soup over them and top with a sprinkle of the prosciutto.

TOMATO PAELLA SOUP

START TO FINISH: I HOUR 30 MINUTES / **HANDS-ON TIME:** 40 MINUTES
SERVINGS: 4 TO 6 (MAKES ABOUT 7¾ CUPS)

¼ teaspoon saffron, optional

½ cup dry white wine

¼ cup extra-virgin olive oil

6 ounces Spanish chorizo (see Sources, page 350), finely chopped

1 cup finely chopped onion

1 red bell pepper, finely chopped

2 tablespoons minced garlic

½ teaspoon smoked paprika

1 (15½-ounce) can crushed tomatoes (preferably fire-roasted)

4 to 5 cups Homemade Chicken Stock (page 26) or store-bought chicken broth

1 Turkish bay leaf

½ cup medium-grain rice such as Valencia, Arborio, carnaroli, or vialone nano (see Sources, page 351)

½ pound medium shrimp (31/40), peeled and deveined (see page 81) and cut in half crosswise

½ pound boneless skinless chicken breast, cut into ½-inch pieces

> Combine the saffron, if using, with the wine in a small saucepan and heat just until hot over medium heat. Remove from the heat and set aside.

> Heat the oil in a large saucepan over medium heat. Reduce the heat to medium-low, add the chorizo, and cook, stirring, 3 minutes. Transfer the chorizo with a slotted spoon to a bowl. Increase the heat to medium, add the onion to the pan, and cook, stirring, until it is golden, about 12 minutes.

> Add the bell pepper, garlic, and paprika, and cook, stirring, 2 minutes. Add white wine (with saffron, if using), the chorizo, tomatoes, 4 cups of the chicken stock, and bay leaf. Bring to a boil, reduce the heat, and simmer, partially covered, 20 minutes.

> Add the rice, bring back to a simmer and cook, covered, until the rice is almost al dente, 10 to 12 minutes. Add the shrimp and chicken and simmer until they are just cooked through, 4 to 5 minutes.

> The soup will thicken as it sits. If you are not eating it right away, thin it down with the additional chicken stock right before serving.

“ As a long-time fan of *paella*, I thought I might be able to transform this delicious Spanish rice dish into a wonderful soup with rice.

Traditional paella is a one-dish meal cooked in a wide, flat-bottomed pan. Besides rice, the original ingredients were whatever the local farmers and laborers had at hand: tomatoes, onions, snails, beans, rabbit, or duck. On special occasions, the line-up might also feature chicken and saffron.

This soup repurposes paella's medium-grain rice, as well as its tomatoes and saffron. I've added a few other classic Spanish ingredients—chorizo and paprika—and turned it into a meal-in-a-bowl with the addition of shrimp and chicken.

Add the ingredients in stages to ensure this soup's success. The last to join the party should be the chicken and the shrimp, a precaution that keeps them from overcooking and becoming rubbery. Serve it with Grill Pan Garlic Bread on page 305. ”

COUNTRY PORK SOUP
WITH CORNMEAL DUMPLINGS

START TO FINISH: 2 HOURS 40 MINUTES / **HANDS-ON TIME:** 60 MINUTES
SERVINGS: 6 (MAKES ABOUT 10 CUPS)

> Here's a soup that will warm you to the core on a wintry night. It requires a chunk of time to prepare, so make it on a weekend or several days in advance (the flavor improves over time). Then, about 40 minutes before you want to serve it, heat up the soup, whip up the dumpling batter, and in no time at all you'll have a cozy dinner on the table.
>
> I use pork shoulder (sometimes called pork butt) for this recipe; it's a cut that benefits from slow cooking. If you have saved rendered pork fat from a prior soup or stew, use it in place of the vegetable oil; it will add to the soup's meaty flavor. The ham hock in the recipe contributes smokiness and body; try to buy one that's split (and if it is not split, score the fat in several places to expose the meat underneath). If you can't find a ham hock at the supermarket, substitute about 4 ounces of chopped Canadian bacon. Finally, you can replace or augment the greens with sliced carrots, potatoes, broccoli, blanched chopped broccoli rabe, or even frozen peas.

¼ cup vegetable oil, preferably grapeseed, divided

1½ pounds pork shoulder, cut into ½-inch cubes

Kosher salt and freshly ground black pepper

1 cup finely chopped onion

1 tablespoon minced garlic

1 ham hock (preferably split)

1½ cups chopped canned plum tomatoes (about 1 [15-ounce] can, see page 30)

⅓ cup cider vinegar

4 cups Homemade Chicken Stock (page 26) or store-bought chicken broth

8 to 10 ounces assorted greens (mustard, collard, kale, chard), tough stems discarded and the leaves cut crosswise ¼-inch thick (about 6 cups)

½ cup (about 60 grams) all-purpose flour

½ cup yellow cornmeal

½ teaspoon baking powder

½ teaspoon baking soda

¼ teaspoon salt

1 large egg, at room temperature, beaten lightly

½ cup low-fat buttermilk, at room temperature

2 tablespoons melted unsalted butter

> In a large wide saucepan, heat 2 tablespoons of the oil over medium-high heat. Reduce the heat to medium and, working in three batches, season the pork with salt and pepper, add it to the saucepan, and cook until it is browned, 6 to 8 minutes, transferring it to a bowl with a slotted spoon as it is done and adding an additional tablespoon of oil when necessary.

> When all of the pork is browned, add the last tablespoon of oil and the onion to the saucepan and cook it, stirring, until golden, about 8 minutes. Add the garlic and cook, stirring, 1 minute. Return the browned pork to the saucepan along with the ham hock, tomatoes, vinegar, chicken stock, and 2 cups water. Bring to a boil, reduce to a simmer, and cook, covered, until the pork is tender, about 1 hour. Remove the hock and pull off the meat. Return the meat to the pan and add the shredded greens. Bring back to a simmer, cover, and cook for 10 minutes.

> While the soup is cooking, combine the flour, cornmeal, baking powder, baking soda, and salt in a large bowl and stir well. In a small bowl, whisk together the egg, buttermilk, and butter; pour into the dry ingredients and mix just until combined. Drop heaping tablespoons of the cornmeal batter over the top of the soup (you should have about 12 dumplings and they will expand and touch), cover and simmer gently until the dumplings are firm and cooked through, about 20 minutes. To serve, divide the soup among 6 bowls and top each portion with some of the dumplings.

STUFFED RED PEPPER SALAD

START TO FINISH: 60 MINUTES / **HANDS-ON TIME:** 40 MINUTES / **SERVINGS:** 4

3 large red bell peppers, or a mix of red, orange, and yellow

2 tablespoons extra-virgin olive oil, plus extra for brushing

³/₄ pound tomatoes, any size, medium diced, reserving about 1 cup of the juices

1¹/₂ tablespoons sherry vinegar

2 teaspoons Dijon mustard

Kosher salt

Freshly ground black pepper

1¹/₄ cups fresh corn kernels (from 2 to 3 ears)

3 ounces feta cheese, crumbled

¹/₃ cup finely shredded fresh basil

4 cups torn lettuce

> Preheat the broiler or the grill to medium. Brush the peppers lightly on all sides with oil and broil them 4 inches from the heat or grill them, turning often, until they are blackened in spots but not too soft, about 10 minutes.

> Transfer the peppers to a bowl and cover the bowl with plastic wrap. Let stand for 20 minutes. Peel the peppers, halve them vertically, and remove and discard the seeds and ribs.

> Medium chop one half of one pepper and set aside. Combine the remaining half in a blender with ¹/₄ cup of the tomatoes, the reserved juices from dicing the tomatoes, the vinegar, mustard, and ³/₄ teaspoon salt. Puree until smooth, transfer to a small bowl, and whisk in the 2 tablespoons oil and pepper to taste.

> Combine the reserved chopped pepper, remaining chopped tomatoes, corn, feta, and basil in a medium bowl with ¹/₂ cup of the dressing and salt and pepper to taste. Toss well. Arrange a half pepper, cut side up, on each of 4 plates on a mound of lettuce and fill with one-fourth of the filling. Serve the remaining dressing on the side.

> "This salad makes the most of peak summer produce. Make sure your vegetables—especially the corn—are fresh fresh fresh. The sugar in corn starts to turn to starch as soon as it's harvested, so buy it early in the morning and keep it chilled until you prepare the salad, preferably on the same day. When corn is really fresh, you can it eat raw, which is what I recommend here. I don't specify a particular size or kind of tomato for this recipe, because the only ones that matter are the ripest and most flavorful.

> I puree ¼ cup of the tomatoes and half of one of the roasted peppers with sherry vinegar and combine them all with oil for the dressing. These pureed vegetables provide the vinaigrette with body as well as flavor, which means less than the usual amount of oil is required."

BUYING, STORING, AND PREPPING FRESH TOMATOES

To find the best tomato, pick it up and smell the stem. It should smell strongly like...a tomato! To tell if it's juicy, pick it up and check its heft. A heavy tomato is a juicy tomato.

Here's how to store tomatoes: Put the extras on a counter away from the sunlight. Do *not* park them on a sunny windowsill, which can make them rot. Likewise, don't put them in the fridge: This will kill their flavor

if they're not already ripe and make them mealy after a few days.

Do not seed tomatoes. Once upon a time we routinely seeded them, a nod to the French ideal of *finesse,* which decreed that seeds were crude. But discarding the seeds is a mistake. Apparently, the jelly surrounding them is the most flavorful part of the tomato. And—bonus!—you save a bunch of prep.

SEARED SCALLOP SALAD
WITH SPICY WATERMELON VINAIGRETTE

START TO FINISH: 40 MINUTES / **HANDS-ON TIME:** 15 MINUTES / **SERVINGS:** 4

I used to think that lemongrass was Thai cuisine's key ingredient—the thing that gave it its Thai-ness. One day, however, I woke up to the wonder of makrut lime leaves (aka kaffir lime leaves), another integral Thai flavor. Wow! So fragrant! They made me want to get married again just so I could carry a bouquet of those leaves down the aisle.

Likewise, I'm newly enamored of watermelon. I wrote it off for years. It was too sweet and too watery. Boring, finally. Now I love watermelon for all the reasons I used to hate it. In this salad, its sweetness is a wonderful counterweight to the heat of the serrano chile in the dressing. Its wateriness is refreshing and it has a flavor all its own.

The watermelon vinaigrette teams up beautifully with the scallops here, but it would also go very well with any number of other proteins, including grilled shrimp, fish, chicken, beef, and even tofu. Likewise, you could swap in the greens of your choice for the napa cabbage, although you don't want to lose the herbs, no matter which direction you go. They help to put the summer in this summertime salad.

1 cup chopped seedless watermelon

2 large makrut lime leaves (aka kaffir lime leaves, see Sources, page 351), or 2 teaspoons freshly grated lime zest

1-inch piece peeled ginger, coarsely chopped

1 small garlic clove, crushed

1/2 to 1 serrano chile, coarsely chopped with the seeds

3 tablespoons fresh lime juice

1 1/2 teaspoons fish sauce (I like the Tiparos and Three Crabs brands)

1 teaspoon sugar

5 tablespoons vegetable oil, preferably grapeseed, divided

Kosher salt

2 cups torn fresh mint or cilantro leaves or a mix of both

2 cups coarsely shredded carrots

4 cups shredded napa cabbage

1 large red bell pepper, medium chopped

1/2 cup chopped toasted cashews, optional

Wondra flour (see page 265) or all-purpose flour for dredging

1 pound medium sea scallops, preferably dry or day boat, cleaned (see page 83)

Freshly ground black pepper

> Combine the watermelon, makrut lime leaves or lime zest, ginger, garlic, serrano chile, lime juice, fish sauce, sugar, and 3 tablespoons of the oil in a blender and puree until smooth. Add salt to taste. Set the dressing aside.

> Combine the mint, carrots, cabbage, bell pepper, and cashews, if using, in a large bowl and set the salad aside.

> Spread out the flour on a piece of parchment on the counter. Season the scallops with salt and pepper. Working in batches, toss the scallops in the flour, lifting the parchment paper on both sides to move the scallops around; transfer the scallops to a strainer and shake off the excess flour.

> Heat the remaining 2 tablespoons oil in a large skillet over high heat. Add the scallops to the skillet, reduce the heat to medium, and sauté for 2 minutes per side or until just cooked through. Transfer with tongs to a plate and set aside to cool slightly.

> Add half the dressing to the salad and toss well. Divide the mixture among 4 plates, top each portion with some of the scallops, and drizzle with extra dressing.

WARM SHRIMP SALAD
WITH CARROT-GINGER DRESSING

START TO FINISH: 35 MINUTES / **HANDS-ON TIME:** 35 MINUTES / **SERVINGS:** 4

"I've always been a big fan of the carrot-ginger dressing served by sushi restaurants with their green salads, which is why I've cast it as the star of this homemade dish. It's a wonderful example of how a raw vegetable can become your secret weapon. The carrot not only flavors the dressing, it thickens it, thereby decreasing the amount of oil needed. But please don't confine this dressing to this recipe. It'll glorify just about any light summer salad you can name, and would work just as well with scallops, salmon, tofu, vegetables, chicken, pork, or even beef.

To cut down on the prep time, buy shrimp that's already been cleaned and cooked. You can usually find them at the fish counter or in the frozen food section, but if you have the time, peel and clean them yourself (see page 81) and save the shells to make Quick Shrimp Stock (see Notes, page 174)."

CRUNCHY SUGAR SNAPS

Sugar snap peas will lose their crunch if cooked too long—so don't let them boil for more than 30 seconds or they'll become almost slimy. To prevent that dreadful possibility, I literally stand over the pot, counting, "One, one thousand, two, one thousand," and so on.

2 medium carrots (about 1 pound), peeled and coarsely chopped

1 (3-inch) piece ginger, peeled and coarsely chopped (about 1 tablespoon)

4 medium scallions, thinly sliced, white and green parts kept separate

1/3 cup plus 2 tablespoons vegetable oil, preferably grapeseed, divided

3 tablespoons seasoned rice vinegar

2 teaspoons sesame oil

2 teaspoons soy sauce

1 to 2 teaspoons hot sauce or to taste

Kosher salt

4 ounces sugar snap peas, tough strings removed

1 pound large (26/30) shrimp, peeled and deveined (see page 81)

Freshly ground black pepper

8 ounces shiitake mushrooms, stems discarded and caps cut into halves or quarters (if the caps are large)

1 firm ripe avocado, pitted and cut into cubes

8 cups packed baby arugula

> Combine the carrots, ginger, and the white parts of the scallions with the 1/3 cup oil, 1/4 cup water, rice vinegar, sesame oil, soy sauce, and hot sauce in a blender and blend until smooth. Season with salt to taste.

> Bring a large saucepan of water to a boil, add the peas, and blanch for 30 seconds. Drain and rinse the peas under cold water. Lay them out on paper towels to dry.

> Heat the 2 tablespoons oil in a large skillet over medium heat. Season the shrimp with salt and pepper and add them to the skillet. Sauté until just cooked through (cut one crosswise; if it is opaque all the way through, it is done), 3 to 5 minutes. Transfer them with tongs to a bowl and cover with foil.

> Add the mushrooms to the skillet, add a pinch of salt and a grind of pepper, and sauté until the mushrooms are just tender, 3 to 5 minutes. Transfer them to the bowl with the shrimp.

> Combine the peas, avocado, and arugula in a large bowl, add several spoonfuls of the dressing, and toss well. Mound one-fourth of the salad on top of 4 plates. Spoon one-fourth of the shrimp and the mushrooms, including any juices from the bowl, on top of each salad and drizzle some of the remaining dressing over the shrimp and mushrooms.

THE BEST WAY TO PEEL AND DEVEIN SHRIMP

Most people peel and devein shrimp one by one, using a paring knife to score the back of the shrimp and pull out the vein. I find this method inefficient and a tad dangerous. I like to work factory style; you save time if you complete one action before moving on to the next.

1. First peel all the shrimp.

2. Leave on the last piece of shell at the tail, if you want: It looks nicer and makes a good handle for shrimp cocktail. Set aside all those shells and freeze them, if you like, for making a future pot of stock.

3. Take one shrimp at a time from the pile of peeled shrimp and run a knife around the curved back of the shrimp, making an incision about ⅛-inch deep.

4. Line the scored shrimp up on the cutting board like the Rockettes, so they're easy to grab one at a time in the next step.

5. Move the cutting board next to the sink and, one by one, run cold water over the shrimp while you pull out the vein.

6. Working under running water is best because it's much easier to remove the sticky vein when the shrimp is wet—and you'll be rinsing the shrimp at the same time, which is something I always do before cooking them.

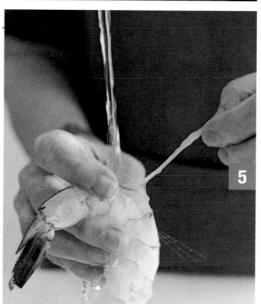

BOUILLABAISSE SALAD
WITH ROUILLE DRESSING

"Bouillabaisse is a famous seafood stew from the Provence region in France. According to Julia Child, 'It originated as a simple Mediterranean fisherman's soup made from the day's catch or its unsalable leftovers, and was flavored with the typical condiments of the region—olive oil, garlic, leeks or onions, tomatoes and herbs.' Here, I have borrowed many of the elements from the stew and turned them into a salad.

Saffron is one of bouillabaisse's signature ingredients. An ancient spice, red-orange in color, saffron is made from the stigma of a variety of crocus grown mainly in Spain, Iran, and India. It must be harvested by hand, which makes it the most expensive spice on earth. Saffron contributes a unique color and flavor, but you can opt to leave it out if you don't feel like splurging.

Typically, bouillabaisse is garnished with rouille, a spicy, rust-colored paste made from peppers and chiles. Here, I've turned the rouille into the mayonnaise that dresses the salad.

This salad takes some time to put together, so save it for a special occasion. Or better yet, make the parts on a weekend, and then toss the salad with the dressing on a weeknight when you want a quick meal."

START TO FINISH: I HOUR IO MINUTES / **HANDS-ON TIME:** 45 MINUTES / **SERVINGS:** 6

For the salad:
1/2 teaspoon saffron, optional
1 1/2 cups dry white wine
2 cups Yukon gold potatoes peeled and cut into 1-inch cubes
1/2 pound haricots verts, trimmed
2 tablespoons extra-virgin olive oil
1/2 cup sliced onion
2 garlic cloves, smashed and peeled
1/2 teaspoon kosher salt
2 pounds mussels (preferably farmed, see page 83), scrubbed and beards removed
1/2 pound medium (31/40) shrimp, peeled and deveined (see page 81)
1/2 pound small sea scallops, preferably dry or day boat (see page 83)
1/2 cup chopped, drained, oil-cured sun-dried tomatoes

For the dressing:
2 tablespoons chopped roasted red pepper, drained
1 teaspoon minced garlic
1 1/2 teaspoons Dijon mustard
1 teaspoon paprika
1/2 teaspoon cayenne
1/4 teaspoon kosher salt
1 large egg yolk
1 tablespoon fresh lemon juice
1/2 cup vegetable oil, preferably grapeseed
2 tablespoons extra-virgin olive oil
Kosher salt and freshly ground black pepper

> **Prepare the salad:** Combine the saffron, if using, with the wine in a small saucepan, heat until just hot over medium heat, remove from the heat, and let the saffron steep while you cook the vegetables.

> Steam the potatoes over water in a vegetable steamer until they are just tender, 20 to 25 minutes, and transfer them to a large bowl. Add the haricots verts to the same steamer and steam them until they are just tender, 2 to 3 minutes. Transfer them to the bowl with the potatoes.

> Heat the oil in a large saucepan over medium heat. Add the onion and cook, stirring, until softened, about 5 minutes. Add the garlic and cook 1 minute more. Add the white wine mixture, the salt, and the mussels; cover and steam until all the mussels have opened, about 5 minutes. Discard any mussels that don't open. Transfer the mussels with a slotted spoon to the large bowl containing the vegetables and let them cool while you cook the rest of the shellfish.

> Add the shrimp to the saucepan and poach at a bare simmer just until they are cooked through, 45 seconds to 1 minute. Transfer them to the large bowl.

> Add the scallops to the saucepan, poach them until they are just cooked, about 2 minutes, and transfer them to the large bowl. Working over the saucepan to catch the juices, remove the mussels from their shells, discarding the shells, and place the mussels back in the bowl with the other fish and vegetables. Strain the cooking liquid and set aside 1 tablespoon for the rouille (freeze the remaining liquid for another use, such as a pasta sauce or fish soup). Add the sun-dried tomatoes to the bowl of seafood and vegetables.

> **Prepare the dressing:** Combine the red pepper, garlic, mustard, paprika, cayenne, salt, egg yolk, lemon juice, and reserved cooking liquid in a blender and blend until smooth. Combine the oils and add them in a slow, steady steam, until all of the oil has been incorporated. Add salt and pepper to taste.

> Pour half the dressing over the fish and vegetables and toss well, adding additional dressing as necessary to completely coat all the elements. Serve at room temperature or chilled. If you chill the salad, you might need to add a little water just before serving to moisten up the salad, as it will absorb most of the dressing while it rests in the fridge.

SHORTCUT ROUILLE DRESSING

> If you don't want to make your own mayonnaise, just add some minced roasted red pepper to ⅔ cup store-bought mayonnaise, along with the garlic, mustard, paprika, cayenne, salt, 1 teaspoon fresh lemon juice, and reserved cooking liquid.

WHAT'S THE DIFFERENCE BETWEEN FARMED AND WILD MUSSELS?

Most of the mussels we find in restaurants, fish markets, and supermarkets are blue mussels from North Atlantic waters. They probably came from Prince Edward Island, Newfoundland, Nova Scotia, or Maine (although recently there is a new mussel, the honey mussel, being farmed in Vancouver, B.C.).

> You can tell right away whether mussels are wild or farmed. Wild mussels have larger, rougher looking shells, often with beards (a hairy string hanging from the side of the shell) and barnacles attached. Farmed mussels have small, smooth, dark shells and negligible beards, if any at all.

> The wild mussels are stronger in flavor, almost gamey. They also contain more grit than the farmed. I prefer the more delicate taste and tender texture of the farmed.

WET VERSUS DRY SCALLOPS

Scallops are sometimes harvested at sea and stored in water with preservatives. These "wet" scallops will steam rather than sauté, so ask your fisherman for "dry" or day boat scallops.

WARM GRILLED OCTOPUS SALAD

Adapted from *The Young Man and the Sea* (Artisan, 2007).

START TO FINISH: 4 HOURS / **HANDS-ON TIME:** 30 MINUTES / **SERVINGS:** 4

6 baby octopus (about 3 ounces each), heads on, cleaned

4 garlic cloves, peeled and divided

1 celery stalk, cut into 3 pieces

1/2 small white onion, roughly chopped

1 carrot, peeled and cut into 3 pieces

1 Turkish bay leaf

3/4 cup dry red wine

Zest and juice of 1 lemon

Leaves of 5 flat-leaf parsley sprigs (about 1/4 cup)

1/3 cup extra-virgin olive oil, plus more for brushing

2 small heads frisée, leaves separated and rinsed

1/2 small red onion, diced

3 cups cooked cannellini beans (see page 36 and Note, page 86), or 2 (15-ounce) cans, rinsed and drained

Sea salt and freshly ground black pepper

Sherry Vinaigrette (page 86)

4 rosemary sprigs

Rosemary Oil (page 86)

> Place the octopus in a large stockpot with 3 garlic cloves, the celery, white onion, carrot, bay leaf, and wine. Add some wine corks (see Dave's Tips on page 87) and fill the pot with water. Bring to a boil over a high heat, and then reduce the heat to a low, gentle simmer. Cook, uncovered, for 45 minutes, adding more water if necessary to keep the octopus covered. The octopus should be completely tender (the tip of a paring knife should easily cut through it) when done. Drain the octopus and set aside to cool.

> Thinly slice the remaining garlic clove. In a large, glass mixing bowl, combine the garlic with the lemon zest and juice, parsley, and the 1/3 cup olive oil. Cut the tentacles from the head and cut the head in half, or slice the baby octopus in half. Add the octopus to the lemon-parsley mixture and toss to coat. Refrigerate for at least 2 hours or overnight.

> Preheat a grill or grill pan to medium-high. Meanwhile, combine the frisée, red onion, and cannelini beans in a large mixing bowl.

> Remove the octopus from the marinade. Brush the octopus with olive oil and season with salt and pepper. Grill the octopus over red-hot coals or on a hot grill pan for 4 to 6 minutes per side, enough time for grill marks to form and the suction cups and the tips to get crispy. Transfer to a plate.

(recipe continues)

Hailed by *The New York Times* as "the fish whisperer," Dave Pasternack has been the chef at Esca, the extraordinary New York City seafood restaurant, for 16 years. I've fished with Dave (exactly one time, off a dock, for 20 minutes, and I didn't catch anything) and I can testify that he's a man who's passionate about fish—so passionate that his idea of the perfect day off is to go fishing.

Needless to say, I completely trust him when it comes to cooking seafood, which is why I asked him for this octopus recipe. Octopus is a delicacy that most folks eat in restaurants, assuming that it must be too complicated to cook at home. But with Dave as your guide, you'll find that it's really quite easy. Note, however, that for this recipe, the octopus is first cooked, and then marinated for at least 2 hours or overnight.

› Dress the frisée and beans with the Sherry Vinaigrette, using your hands to toss. Divide the salad among 4 serving plates. Put the grilled octopus into the mixing bowl and toss to coat with the vinaigrette left in the bowl. Arrange the octopus on top of the salads and garnish with a sprig of rosemary and a drizzle of Rosemary Oil. Serve immediately.

Note: The octopus, after simmering for 45 minutes, has to sit in the marinade for at least 2 hours or overnight. My best advice is to cook the beans (if you are starting with dried beans) and simmer the octopus the day before you serve this.

SHERRY VINAIGRETTE
START TO FINISH: 10 MINUTES / **HANDS-ON TIME:** 10 MINUTES / **SERVINGS:** MAKES ⅜ CUP

1½ tablespoons sherry-wine vinegar
¾ teaspoon fresh lemon juice
1⅛ teaspoons Dijon mustard
¼ teaspoon sea salt
⅛ teaspoon freshly ground black pepper
¼ cup extra-virgin olive oil

In a small mixing bowl, whisk together the sherry-wine vinegar, lemon juice, mustard, salt, and pepper. Add the olive oil in a slow, steady stream while whisking until emulsified. The dressing can be made ahead and refrigerated; whisk before serving.

ROSEMARY OIL
START TO FINISH: 25 MINUTES / **HANDS-ON TIME:** 5 MINUTES / **SERVINGS:** MAKES ¼ CUP

¼ cup extra- virgin olive oil
1 rosemary sprig

Place the olive oil in a small saucepan and add the rosemary. Heat over low until the oil is warm, but not hot. Reserve until the oil is cool. Strain and discard the rosemary sprig.

DAVE'S TIPS FOR PREPARING OCTOPUS

1. Your fishmonger should clean the octopus for you; that's part of the service. Frozen octopus will be cleaned as well. If you should get an octopus with its eyes intact, simply cut them off as shown.

2. When it comes to octopus, suction cups rule. So make sure that when you buy octopus each tentacle has two rows of suckers.

3. When you simmer the octopus, put some (real) wine corks in the pan; they help tenderize the octopus. This is how I was taught in Italy—I don't know why it works, but it does! Don't use any salt when you initially cook the octopus, because the salt toughens it.

4. Cut each octopus in half to create more surface area to get brown and crispy.

5. After braising the octopus until it is tender, it is marinated and then grilled. Brush the octopus with olive oil. This helps caramelize the sugars and crisp the octopus.

6. Grilling the octopus crisps its tips, and crispy is just about always better in my book.

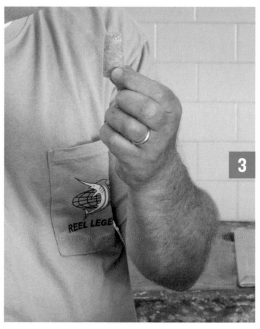

LYONNAIS-STYLE SALAD
WITH SMOKED SALMON

START TO FINISH: 40 MINUTES / **HANDS-ON TIME:** 35 MINUTES / **SERVINGS:** 4

2 cups ½-inch bread cubes cut from country-style bread

3 tablespoons extra-virgin olive oil, divided

3 slices bacon

2 tablespoons minced shallots

3 tablespoons red wine vinegar

1 teaspoon Dijon mustard

Kosher salt and freshly ground black pepper

4 large eggs, preferably very fresh (see page 90)

8 cups torn frisée, baby arugula, or shredded Tuscan kale

4 ounces smoked salmon, cut into 1- by 2-inch pieces

> Preheat the oven to 350°F. Toss the bread cubes with 1 tablespoon of the oil in a large bowl. Spread them in a single layer on a rimmed baking sheet and bake them on the middle shelf of the oven until they are lightly golden, 6 to 8 minutes. Let the croutons cool.

> Meanwhile, cook the bacon in a small skillet over medium heat until crisp, about 5 minutes. Transfer the bacon to paper towels to drain; crumble the bacon when cooled. Discard all but 2 teaspoons of the bacon fat from the pan and add the shallots. Cook over medium heat, scraping up the brown bits, until the shallots have softened, 3 to 4 minutes. Remove from the heat and whisk in the vinegar, mustard, and salt and pepper to taste. Add the remaining 2 tablespoons oil to the pan in a stream, whisking. Stir in the crumbled bacon and set aside.

> Poach the eggs according to the directions on page 90.

> Warm the dressing on low heat. Toss the lettuce with the warm dressing in a large bowl and divide it among 4 plates. Top each portion with one-fourth of the croutons, one-fourth of the salmon, and a poached egg.

"

I was once hired to teach some cooking classes on a riverboat cruise along the Rhône, which allowed The Husband and me to spend a few days in Lyons. (I know, I know. Tough gig.) Lyons is the food capitol of France, so we made it our business to sample as many of the local dishes as we could.

One of my flat-out faves was the aptly named *Salade Lyonnais*. It's built from frisée tossed with bacon lardons and croutons, dressed with a mustardy vinaigrette, then crowned with a poached egg. All of my favorite ingredients in one bowl! This recipe replicates that salad with a little bit of smoked salmon added to make it more substantial.

If you're daunted by the prospect of making a poached egg, don't be. I have a foolproof method (see page 90) that I learned long ago from a cute Australian chef who appeared on my Food Network show, *Cooking Live*. (I remember that he was cute, but I can't remember his name.) It is so much simpler than the method taught in cooking school.

"

Cook's Notes: Are Your Eggs Fresh?

▶ Your egg carton will be stamped with an expiration date, but how can you tell if your eggs are really fresh—and does it matter? In this photo you can see how the egg white has separated into two parts: a viscous center and a thin, watery outer edge. A fresh egg has more of the viscous part as well as a tall, full yolk. Fresh eggs will beat up with more volume (which is especially important in baking).

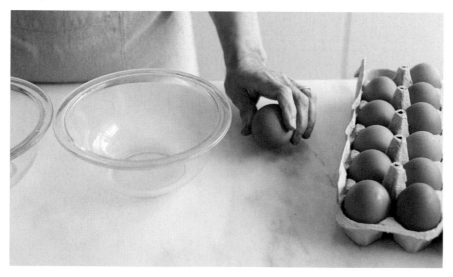

Cook's Notes: Cracking Your Eggs

▶ The best way to crack an egg is on a flat surface. If you crack the egg on the side of a sharp surface (like the rim of a bowl) you risk breaking the yolk.

HOW TO POACH EGGS STRESS FREE

You can poach up to 4 eggs at a time this way. If you need more, or if you want to poach them ahead of time, transfer the poached eggs to a bowl of ice water to stop the cooking. Dip them briefly into barely simmering water to reheat.

1. Break an egg into a fine mesh strainer set over a bowl.

2. Tilt the egg around in the strainer and bang the strainer a few times on top of the bowl to let all the watery part of the egg white fall through the strainer.

3. Bring a large pot of water to a boil, and then turn off the heat. Transfer the drained eggs to individual ramekins.

4. Very gently slide the eggs into the hot water.

5. Cover the pan and poach the eggs in the residual heat for 1½ to 2 minutes, or until they have reached the desired degree of doneness.

6. Transfer the cooked eggs to a shallow bowl with a slotted spoon. Serve right away.

GRILLED CHICKEN
WITH PEACH SALAD
AND BLUE CHEESE DRESSING

START TO FINISH: I HOUR 40 MINUTES / **HANDS-ON TIME:** 40 MINUTES / **SERVINGS:** 4

2 tablespoons fresh lemon juice

2 tablespoons extra-virgin oil, plus more for brushing the chicken

2 teaspoons minced garlic

1 teaspoon kosher salt

Freshly ground black pepper

4 (4-ounce) chicken breast half pieces, pounded until ¼ inch thick (see page 127)

4 cups baby arugula

2 large peaches, thinly sliced

¼ cup nonfat plain Greek yogurt

2 tablespoons low-fat mayonnaise

1 ounce finely crumbled blue cheese

½ cup chopped toasted walnuts

> Combine the lemon juice, olive oil, garlic, salt, and several grindings of black pepper in a resealable plastic bag. Add the chicken, chill and marinate for 1 hour, turning the bag over several times.

> Preheat the grill or grill pan to medium-high.

> Remove the chicken from the marinade and pat it dry. Brush the chicken lightly on both sides with some oil and grill the chicken, covered, until it is just cooked, 1 to 2 minutes per side. Transfer the cooked chicken to a plate, cover it with foil, and let it rest for 5 minutes.

> Meanwhile, in a large bowl, combine the arugula and peaches. In a small bowl, combine the yogurt, mayonnaise, and blue cheese and stir in enough water to achieve the desired consistency. Add the dressing to the salad and toss well.

> To serve, arrange 1 chicken breast piece on each of 4 plates and top with one-fourth of the salad and nuts.

"

Tell the truth, we all tend to overdo it when we grill in the summertime. Ribs, steaks, burgers, and hot dogs? Check, check, check, and check. Vegetables and other light fare? Not so much. The standard routine is like the hot-weather version of Thanksgiving, except that after the meal everyone collapses onto the lawn rather than into a couch in the living room.

Allow me to propose a magical alternative—a dish that's simultaneously light and refreshing *and* substantial: grilled chicken cutlets topped with peach and arugula salad, glorified with a low-fat (but high-flavor) blue cheese dressing.

Chicken breasts come in all sizes these days, with different weights and thicknesses. If you can find thin-sliced cutlets (which are usually about ¼ inch thick), great. If not, you'll need to pound them to the desired thickness (see page 127). If the breasts are very thick, I throw them in the freezer for 30 minutes to firm them up, and then very carefully slice them in half horizontally before pounding.

"

THAI-STYLE CHICKEN SALAD

START TO FINISH: 30 MINUTES / **HANDS-ON TIME:** 30 MINUTES / **SERVINGS:** 4

" I've always loved the green papaya salad in Southeast Asian restaurants. (My favorite version is served at The Slanted Door in San Francisco.) Here, I've taken some of the ingredients in that salad's dressing—the lime juice, the chiles, the fish sauce, the fresh herbs, and the toasted peanuts—and applied them to a mix of crunchy and refreshing vegetables. I also added a little bit of chicken; it transforms the salad into a main dish.

The quickest way to shred the carrots is with the grating disk of a food processor. Of course, it's possible to do the job by hand using the coarse side of a four-sided grater, but I try to keep my distance from that tool because I find it a tad dangerous. (A little bit of you goes into every dish.)

The strings in snap peas can be tough, so be sure to remove them before cooking. As with string beans, you pop off and pull back the tip, losing any of the strings exposed in the process. Sometimes there's a string in the back curve of the pea, sometimes in the inside curve, sometimes on both curves, and sometimes there's no string at all. Blanch the peas for just 30 seconds—not a second longer!—then plunge them into ice water. "

1/4 cup fish sauce

2 tablespoons plus 2 teaspoons sugar

3 tablespoons fresh lime juice

1 teaspoon very finely minced garlic

1 tablespoon cross-cut, finely sliced chile, with seeds, such as serrano, jalapeño, or Thai

2 tablespoons vegetable oil, preferably grapeseed

3 cups thinly sliced napa cabbage

1 1/2 cups shredded cooked chicken (from Blasted Chicken, page 242 or store-bought rotisserie chicken)

1 1/2 cups blanched sugar snap peas, coarsely chopped (about 6 ounces)

1 1/2 cups coarsely shredded carrots

1 cup halved lengthwise and very thinly sliced seedless cucumber

1 1/2 cups coarsely chopped fresh cilantro, basil, mint, or a mix

1/2 cup coarsely chopped toasted peanuts

> Combine the fish sauce, sugar, lime juice, garlic, chile, and oil in a bowl with 1/4 cup water and whisk until the sugar is dissolved.

> Combine the cabbage, chicken, peas, carrots, cucumber, herbs, and peanuts in a salad bowl, add some of the dressing, toss well, and serve with the remaining dressing on the side.

STEAK SALAD
WITH BÉARNAISE DRESSING

START TO FINISH: 1 HOUR 40 MINUTES INCLUDING PRESALTING
HANDS-ON TIME: 20 MINUTES / **SERVINGS:** 4

1 pound ³/₄- to 1-inch-thick steak, such as flat iron, tri tip, or petite tender (see page 153)

Kosher salt

2 cups cherry tomatoes

2 tablespoons vegetable oil, preferably grapeseed

Freshly ground black pepper

Béarnaise Mayonnaise

1¹/₂ cups thinly sliced seedless cucumber

8 ounces firm white mushrooms, trimmed and sliced thin

4 cups butter lettuce, torn into bite-sized pieces

> Sprinkle the steak on all sides with salt. Let stand at room temperature for 1 hour. Halve the cherry tomatoes (see page 181), and sprinkle the cut sides with 1 teaspoon salt. Let stand for 20 minutes then pat dry.

> Heat the oil in a large skillet over medium-high heat. Pat the steak dry and season with black pepper on both sides; cook for 4 to 5 minutes a side for medium-rare. Transfer to a plate, cover with foil, and let rest 10 minutes.

> When ready to serve, add the resting juices from the steak to the Béarnaise Mayonnaise and stir to combine. Combine the tomatoes, cucumber, and mushrooms in a bowl, add half the dressing, and toss well. Slice the steak thin across the grain (see page 152). Arrange a mound of the lettuce on 4 plates. Top each mound with one-fourth of the tossed vegetables and arrange the sliced steak on top. Drizzle the remaining dressing over the steak.

"There are three simple ways to maximize the deliciousness of this salad. First, pre-salt the steak. Second, pre-salt the tomatoes (see page 13). Third, add the meat juices from the resting steak to the béarnaise dressing. (As the great French cooking teacher Madeleine Kamman used to say, 'You must marry the sauce to the protein.')

Of course, starting with good-quality ingredients also makes a huge difference. Be sure to buy ripe cherry tomatoes, firm white mushrooms with no gills showing (mushrooms get flabbier as they get older), and a steak worth cooking. (See New Steaks on the Block, page 153)."

BÉARNAISE MAYONNAISE

START TO FINISH: 15 MINUTES / **HANDS-ON TIME:** 15 MINUTES / **SERVINGS:** MAKES A HEAPING ½ CUP

2 tablespoons finely minced shallots

¹/₄ cup dry white wine

¹/₄ cup white wine vinegar

1 teaspoon dried tarragon

¹/₄ teaspoon kosher salt

¹/₂ cup Homemade Mayonnaise (pages 52–53) or store-bought mayonnaise

1¹/₂ tablespoons chopped fresh tarragon

Freshly ground black pepper

Combine the shallots, wine, vinegar, dried tarragon, and salt in a small saucepan. Bring the mixture to a simmer and simmer very gently until reduced to 3 tablespoons. Transfer to a bowl and let cool. Stir in the mayonnaise, fresh tarragon, and pepper to taste. If not using right away, cover and chill in the fridge for up to 5 days.

WARM RED CABBAGE, POTATO, AND KIELBASA SALAD
WITH CREAMY MUSTARD DRESSING

"This is a hearty, manly dish—sweet-and-sour cabbage topped with warm potato salad and sliced kielbasa. The sweetness comes from the brown sugar and the sourness comes from the vinegar, which also turns the red cabbage a deep, jewel-like pink.

The potatoes are dressed twice: with vinegar and salt while they're still warm, and then with creamy mustard dressing once they've cooled. I always follow these two steps when I make potato salad. Most people just dress the potatoes once with a creamy dressing. But I like what the pre-soak in salt and vinegar does to the potatoes. The result is a more sharply flavored potato salad.

The kielbasa in this recipe is a tribute to Pat Costello, who for years ran the meat counter in the country store near my parents' farmhouse in Massachusetts. Pat not only sold meat, he also made sausages from scratch and smoked his own kielbasa. If we were lucky enough to be there when a batch had just finished, he'd invite us to eat a piece warm, right out of the smoker. It was always impossibly delicious, and woke me up to the wonderfulness of good kielbasa. So hunt around for a superior brand or a Pat-like artisanal producer in your town. (Pat recently left New England for Key West, where he's planning to open a hot dog stand. If you find him, let me know.)"

START TO FINISH: 1 HOUR 35 MINUTES / **HANDS-ON TIME:** 35 MINUTES / **SERVINGS:** 4 TO 6

For the cabbage:
2 tablespoons extra-virgin olive oil
1 cup thinly sliced onion
2 teaspoons minced garlic
2 teaspoons caraway seeds
1/3 cup cider vinegar
2 tablespoons packed brown sugar
1 teaspoon kosher salt
8 cups finely shredded red cabbage (about 1 1/4 pounds)
Freshly ground black pepper

For the potato salad:
1 1/2 pounds small (2-inch) boiling potatoes

3 tablespoons cider vinegar
1 teaspoon kosher salt

For the meat and dressing:
5 tablespoons olive oil, divided
1 pound kielbasa, cut into pieces if necessary to fit in the skillet
2 tablespoons minced shallots
2 tablespoons white wine vinegar
1 tablespoon Dijon mustard
1/2 teaspoon kosher salt
2 tablespoons sour cream
Freshly ground black pepper

> **Make the cabbage:** Heat the oil in a large skillet over medium heat, add the onion, and cook until softened, stirring occasionally, about 5 minutes. Add the garlic and caraway and cook, stirring, 1 minute. Add the cider vinegar, sugar, and salt and cook, stirring, until the sugar is dissolved. Add the cabbage and stir. Reduce the heat to medium-low, cover, and cook, stirring occasionally, until the cabbage is tender, about 25 minutes. Add salt and pepper to taste.

> **Make the potatoes:** Put the potatoes in a small saucepan and cover with cold salted water by 2 inches. Bring to a boil, turn down to a simmer, and simmer until just tender, 18 to 20 minutes. Drain and set aside for 10 minutes, until just cool enough to handle. Slice the potatoes 1/4 inch thick while still warm and in a medium bowl toss them with the cider vinegar and salt.

> **Cook the meat and make the dressing:** Heat 1 tablespoon of the oil in a second large skillet over medium-high heat. Add the kielbasa, reduce the heat to medium and cook, turning often, until browned on all sides and heated through, 8 to 10 minutes. Transfer to a bowl and set the meat aside until it's cool enough to be sliced.

> Deglaze the skillet with 3 tablespoons water, scraping up the brown bits, and transfer the deglazing liquid to a small bowl. Add the shallots, white wine vinegar, mustard, and salt to the bowl, and whisk until the salt is dissolved. Whisk in the remaining 4 tablespoons oil slowly in a stream. Whisk in the sour cream, any juices from the resting kielbasa, and add pepper to taste.

> To serve, slice the kielbasa crosswise, 1/4 inch thick (if it is extra thick, cut it in half lengthwise first). Toss the sliced potatoes with 3 tablespoons of the dressing. Mound some of the cabbage on each plate, top with the potatoes, kielbasa, and a drizzle of the remaining dressing.

WHICH POTATO?

▶ There are two main kinds of potatoes: high starch and waxy. **High starch potatoes,** also known as russets or baking potatoes (the most famous of which is the Idaho), have thick skins and a fluffy texture. They fall apart when cooked in a liquid. If you are looking for a firm texture, such as I was in this potato salad, they should not be your choice. They will break when you toss them with the dressing.

However, they will absorb more of the dressing flavor than waxy potatoes so if you are looking for a more flavored potato, they will work just fine. They are also the potato of choice for baking or mashing because they become very fluffy when cooked and just soak up the butter or sour cream taste.

▶ **Waxy potatoes,** also known as boiling potatoes, have thin skins and a firm texture; they hold their shape when boiled. They also, in my opinion, contribute more of a potato-y taste to whatever dish you add them to.

▶ **Yukon Golds** fall somewhere in between a baking and a boiling potato. They work equally well in mashed potatoes and in potato salad. (I prefer a russet for baking though, because I love its thick skin).

GRILLED JERK PORK
WITH CITRUS SALAD

START TO FINISH: 40 MINUTES PLUS 1 TO 4 HOURS MARINATING TIME
HANDS-ON TIME: 30 MINUTES **SERVINGS:** 4

3 tablespoons vegetable oil, preferably grapeseed, divided

1 tablespoon plus 1 teaspoon Jamaican jerk seasoning (see Sources, page 351) or Homemade Jerk Seasoning

4 ($\frac{1}{2}$-inch-thick) boneless pork chops (1 to 1$\frac{1}{4}$ pounds total)

$\frac{1}{3}$ cup fresh orange juice

$\frac{1}{2}$ teaspoon kosher salt

1 teaspoon Dijon mustard

1$\frac{1}{2}$ tablespoons white wine vinegar

6 cups torn butter lettuce

1 (14-ounce) can hearts of palm, drained and patted dry, sliced crosswise $\frac{1}{2}$ inch thick

1 large Hass avocado, peeled, pitted, and cut into $\frac{1}{2}$ inch chunks

2 medium oranges, peeled and cut into segments

$\frac{1}{2}$ cup toasted sunflower seeds (toasted in a 350°F oven until golden, 5 minutes)

> Stir together 1 tablespoon of the oil and the jerk seasoning in a small bowl and spoon it all over the pork to coat. Marinate for at least 1 hour at room temperature or up to 4 hours covered and chilled.

> Preheat the grill to medium. Put the orange juice in a small saucepan or skillet and simmer until it is reduced to 2 tablespoons. Transfer to a small bowl; add the salt, mustard, and vinegar and whisk until the salt is dissolved. Gradually whisk in the remaining 2 tablespoons oil.

> Grill the pork, turning it over once, about 2 minutes per side for medium.

> Meanwhile, combine the lettuce, hearts of palm, avocado, and orange segments in a large bowl. Add $\frac{1}{4}$ cup of the dressing and toss well.

> Arrange the chops on each of 4 plates, drizzle with a little of the remaining dressing, and top each with one-fourth of the salad and the seeds.

> Jerk refers both to a unique blend of seasonings and to a method of slow cooking. An enduring signature of Jamaican cuisine, jerk originally involved pork cooked in a pit or over a grill. These days any number of proteins are cooked jerk-style, and jerk seasoning is fairly omnipresent.
>
> The seasoning consists of a base blend of scallions, thyme, allspice (known as pimento in Jamaica), Scotch bonnet chiles, salt, and, not infrequently, cinnamon or nutmeg. You're welcome to make your own if you have the time (recipe bottom left), or use your favorite store-bought brand. The Scotch bonnet chiles tend to make jerk seasoning quite spicy, which is why I top these pork chops with a cooling salad of avocado, hearts of palm, and butter lettuce, tossed with a slightly sweet orange dressing. As ever, sugar balances out the chile's heat.
>
> The only lengthy part of this recipe is the time it takes to marinate the chops. Otherwise, you'll be able to whip it up in a jiffy.

HOMEMADE JERK SEASONING

START TO FINISH: 10 MINUTES / **HANDS-ON TIME:** 10 MINUTES / **SERVINGS:** MAKES ABOUT $\frac{1}{2}$ CUP

2 tablespoons vegetable oil

1 cup coarsely chopped scallions, white and green parts

1 Scotch bonnet or habanero chile, coarsely chopped, with the seeds

1$\frac{1}{2}$ tablespoons soy sauce

1$\frac{1}{2}$ tablespoons fresh lime juice

2$\frac{1}{2}$ teaspoons ground allspice

1$\frac{1}{2}$ teaspoons English mustard

1 Turkish bay leaf

1 large garlic clove, crushed

1 teaspoon kosher salt

1 teaspoon sugar

1 teaspoon dried thyme

Combine all the ingredients in a blender and blend until the mixture forms a fine paste.

4 quick & quicker ENTRÉES

This is another opportunity to increase the number of answers to that eternal question, "What's for dinner?" The candidates here include two kinds of recipes: those that are quick to make and those that are *very* quick to make.

How about breakfast for dinner with a souffléed omelet. It's a fancy, fluffy omelet that can be a wrapper for any leftovers from the fridge and the perfect quick dinner for two. I'll show you how to wrap and cook fish in parchment, a low-cal technique that keeps fish moist and creates a tasty sauce at the same time. If you find the prospect of cooking lobster intimidating, Jasper White comes to the rescue with his extraordinary lobster roll.

Also included here are my best tips for cooking pasta and a miso primer to go with Hiroko Shimbo's excellent Spicy Miso Chicken Wings.

You'll learn how to cook duck breasts (a surprisingly healthy protein choice), and grasp the basics of quick sautés and pan sauces, including Sautéed Lemon Chicken with Fried Capers and Sautéed Hungarian Pork Chops. There are recipes featuring several new, very affordable, and flavorful cuts of steak and a how-to about grinding your own meat for burgers.

More than half the recipes in this chapter require 30 minutes or less of hands-on preparation (although there may be added cooking time) and even the most complicated recipe is a done deal in 45 minutes.

GREEK DINER SOUFFLÉED OMELET

START TO FINISH: 30 MINUTES / **HANDS-ON TIME:** 25 MINUTES / **SERVINGS:** 2

1½ tablespoons extra-virgin olive oil, divided

5 ounces baby spinach

Kosher salt

2 ounces feta cheese, finely crumbled

3 large eggs, separated, plus 2 large egg whites (see page 90)

Freshly ground black pepper

2 teaspoons freshly grated lemon zest

Chopped fresh dill for garnish

› Preheat the oven to 450°F. Heat 1 tablespoon of the oil in a large skillet over medium heat. Add the spinach and a pinch of salt and cook, stirring, until the spinach is wilted, 1 to 2 minutes. Sprinkle the feta on top and set aside.

› Whisk the egg yolks with 1 tablespoon of water, a hefty pinch of salt, several grinds of pepper, and the lemon zest in a medium bowl using an electric hand mixer until the mixture is fluffy, about 4 minutes. Clean and dry the beaters well and beat the egg whites with a pinch of salt in a separate bowl until they just hold soft peaks; stir one-fourth of the whites into the egg yolk mixture, then fold in the remaining whites gently but thoroughly (see page 344 for photos of the folding technique).

› Heat the remaining ½ tablespoon oil over medium heat in a 10-inch nonstick or stick-resistant skillet with an ovenproof handle. Pour the egg mixture into the skillet and gently spread it evenly. Bake the omelet on the middle shelf of the oven until it is puffed and almost cooked through, about 3 minutes. Meanwhile, heat the spinach mixture over medium heat, stirring.

› Remove the omelet from the oven and make an indentation down the center with a spatula. Spoon the spinach mixture on one half of the omelet and, using the spatula, fold the other half of the omelet over to cover the filling. Bake the omelet in the center of the oven to heat through for 2 to 3 minutes more. Divide it in half, sprinkle each half with the dill, and serve right away.

❝

I've never met an egg dish I didn't like, but at the tippy top of my list of favorites is the edible magic trick known as the souffléed omelet.

The magic is built into the whites of the egg. A three-egg omelet made the usual way comprises a substantial meal for one person. But a souffléed omelet made with three eggs and two whites makes the traditional omelet look like a runt and is more than enough for two people.

In a nod to the wonderful Greek omelets available in diners from coast to coast, this recipe stars spinach and feta cheese. Of course, you're welcome to swap in the sautéed greens and cheese of your choice. But whatever you do, do not leave out the grated lemon zest. It brightens up the whole dish.

This recipe serves two. To make enough for four people, you'll prepare a double batch, pour it into two medium skillets, and bake them in the oven at the same time.

By the way, when it's time to clean out the fridge, a souffléed omelet (like a plain Jane omelet) is the perfect wrapper for zillions of fillings.

❞

FUSILLI WITH ITALIAN SAUSAGE AND PEAS

START TO FINISH: 60 MINUTES / **HANDS-ON TIME:** 30 MINUTES / **SERVINGS:** 4

2 tablespoons olive oil

1 cup finely chopped onion

1 tablespoon minced garlic

¾ pound sweet or hot Italian sausage, casings removed

1 (28-ounce) can crushed tomatoes (preferably fire-roasted)

2 tablespoons plus 1 teaspoon kosher salt, divided

⅔ cup heavy cream

12 ounces fusilli

2 cups defrosted frozen peas

3 ounces finely grated Parmigiano-Reggiano, divided

Kosher salt and freshly ground black pepper

Shredded fresh basil for garnish

> Bring 6 quarts of water to a boil in a large saucepan or stockpot.

> While the water is coming to a boil, heat the oil over medium heat in a large skillet and add the onion. Cook, stirring occasionally, until the onion is softened, about 5 minutes. Add the garlic and cook, stirring, 1 minute.

> Add the sausage and cook, breaking it up with a spoon and stirring, until the sausage is just cooked through, about 5 minutes. Add the tomatoes and 1 teaspoon salt, bring the mixture to a boil, and simmer, stirring occasionally, 20 minutes. Add the cream to the sauce and simmer for 2 minutes.

> Meanwhile, add 2 tablespoons salt and the pasta to the pot of boiling water, and stir well. Boil the pasta, following the timing instructions on the package, until almost al dente. Reserve 1 cup of the pasta water, and then drain the pasta and add it to the skillet, along with the peas and half of the cheese. Simmer until the pasta is al dente, adding some of the reserved pasta cooking water if necessary to thin the sauce. Add salt and pepper to taste and divide the mixture among 4 bowls. Top each portion with some of the remaining cheese and the basil.

"

For the longest time, I thought all I needed to know about cooking pasta was that boiling it in lots of water would prevent it from ending up gummy. Turns out I was just getting started. This one recipe embodies everything I've learned about the subject in a lifetime of cooking. Please read the Pasta Primer (see page 109) before you plunge in. It'll help you produce a restaurant-worthy entrée for your family. Pair this dish with No-Knead Walnut-Rosemary Bread on page 313 to round out the meal.

"

QUICK TOMATO, GOAT CHEESE, AND FRESH HERB PENNE

"How simple is this tasty recipe? Simple enough that you're done cooking after you've boiled the pasta. It's because the sauce is raw. You combine the ingredients in a bowl while the water's coming to a boil: ripe summertime tomatoes (salted to draw out tomato liquid and concentrate their tomato-y flavor), fresh goat cheese, a bit of Parmesan, and some hot pepper flakes. Then dump the finished pasta along with a little of the pasta cooking water on top, toss it all up, and dive in. The hot pasta will have melted the cheese, turning it into a creamy sauce. Sprinkle your choice of fresh herbs on top of each portion, and you're looking at the ultimate summer supper."

START TO FINISH: 20 MINUTES / **HANDS-ON TIME:** 20 MINUTES / **SERVINGS:** 4

3 cups chopped fresh tomatoes (cut into roughly 1-inch pieces), about 1¼ pounds

Kosher salt

2 teaspoons freshly grated lemon zest

¼ cup extra-virgin olive oil

5 ounces fresh goat cheese, crumbled

2 ounces freshly grated Parmigiano-Reggiano

1 teaspoon red pepper flakes, optional

12 ounces penne or fusilli

1 cup mixed coarsely chopped fresh herbs (such as parsley, basil, oregano, mint, dill, chives, cilantro, and tarragon)

> Bring 6 quarts of water to a boil in a large saucepan or stockpot.

> Meanwhile, toss the tomatoes with 1 teaspoon salt in a large serving bowl and let them stand for 20 minutes. Add the lemon zest, oil, goat cheese, Parmigiano-Reggiano, and hot red pepper flakes, if using, and toss well.

›Add 2 tablespoons salt and the pasta to the boiling water, stir well, and boil the pasta, following the timing instructions on the package, until just al dente. Reserve 1 cup of the pasta cooking liquid, drain the pasta, and add it to the bowl along with ½ cup of the reserved liquid. Toss until the cheese is melted; if desired, add additional pasta cooking liquid to achieve a looser sauce. Add the fresh herbs and salt to taste and toss well. Serve immediately.

PASTA PRIMER

What's the one ingredient you should always have in your cupboard? Dried pasta, of course. It's the base for a zillion easy-to-make weeknight meals and the friendly playmate of two zillion ingredients, including leftovers.

▶ **Pasta shapes.** Pasta comes in all sizes and shapes, each designed with a purpose. Pastas in long strands —including spaghetti and linguine—are best paired with smoother sauces. Tube-shaped pastas—including penne and rigatoni and pasta boasting nooks and crannies, like fusilli, orecchiette, and farfalle—team up well with chunky sauces.

▶ **Use enough water—and salt.** Whichever type you're cooking, 1 pound of pasta should be boiled in 6 quarts of water (although 4 quarts will do if you don't have a pot large enough to hold 6). The water needs to be well salted; every 3 quarts requires 1 tablespoon of kosher salt. (If you add salt after you have cooked the pasta, it will not penetrate and properly season the pasta. It will taste like bland pasta with a salt garnish.) Stir the pasta after adding it to the water to keep the individual pieces from sticking to each other. If you're boiling long strands, push them down gently in the middle to make sure that the ends are submerged, too.

▶ **Skip the oil.** Do *not* add oil to the water. This will only serve to make the pasta oily, and the sauce you want to stick to it will just slide off.

▶ **Pasta should never wait for the sauce, so don't start cooking the pasta until your sauce is either well along or finished.** Follow the cooking times listed on the back of the package, but check the tenderness of the pasta a few minutes before the total cooking time is up. All you have to do is spear a single piece and bite into it. If it's very chewy, keep cooking it. If there's a tiny bit of chewiness, it's ready to be drained. Set aside a little of the cooking liquid, and then quickly drain the rest and add the pasta to the sauce. Do *not* rinse the pasta after you've drained it. That residual starch is what makes sauce cling to it.

▶ **Add the pasta to the sauce, not the sauce to the pasta.** I like to finish cooking the pasta in the sauce, adding some of the reserved cooking liquid if the sauce is too thick. Pasta finished in this fashion is more deeply flavored. The beauty of a pasta dish is that it rarely takes longer to throw together than the time it takes to boil the water and cook the pasta. And a hearty pasta dish is just the thing to warm up a cold and wintry night.

SALMON BAKED IN A BAG
WITH CITRUS, OLIVES, AND CHILES

START TO FINISH: 45 MINUTES / **HAND-ON TIME:** 25 MINUTES / **SERVINGS:** 4

1 small orange, sliced very thin, plus 2 tablespoons fresh juice

1 small lemon, sliced very thin, plus 2 tablespoons fresh juice

4 (4- to 5-ounce) skinless center-cut salmon fillet pieces

Kosher salt and freshly ground black pepper

¼ cup fresh rosemary, chopped

2 tablespoons extra-virgin olive oil

½ cup olives, preferably oil cured, pitted and chopped

1 small serrano chile, sliced thin crosswise

> Preheat the oven to 400°F. Place a large piece of parchment paper, 24 inches long and 13 inches wide, on a baking sheet and fold it in half crosswise. Open the paper, put the right half of the parchment on top of a baking sheet (letting the left half hang off). Arrange half of the citrus on the parchment as shown on page 113.

> Season the salmon on both sides with salt and pepper. Sprinkle half the rosemary on top of the citrus and top the rosemary with the 4 pieces of salmon. Drizzle the citrus juices and olive oil on top. Distribute the chopped olives and sliced chile evenly over the 4 pieces of salmon and top each piece with the remaining rosemary and the remaining orange and lemon slices.

> Bring the left half of the parchment up and over the salmon to completely cover it. Starting at the top left of the parchment package, make ¼-inch folds all around the perimeter and press to crimp and seal, until you have completely encased the salmon (see page 113).

> Bake the wrapped salmon on the baking sheet on the middle shelf of the oven for 12 to 14 minutes, until it is just cooked through. (You can stick a knife through the parchment into the salmon and if it goes in easily that means the fish is done.)

> Cut open the parchment, knock off the citrus slices and transfer the salmon pieces to each of 4 plates. Spoon some of the olives, chile slices, rosemary, and juices from the parchment over each piece and serve right away.

"
Fish *en papillote* is the elegant-sounding name of a staple recipe of classic French cuisine. Translated into English, it becomes the much less elegant-sounding "fish in a bag." By any name, however, this method of baking fish is a smash.

Typically, the fish is combined with some vegetables and herbs, some butter or oil, and often some wine, all of which are then wrapped up in a piece of parchment and baked. The airtight parchment keeps everything sealed in as it cooks, allowing all the juices from the fish and the other ingredients to co-mingle and become a wonderful sauce. The parchment also seals in any cooking odors, so your house won't smell like fish. And because the parchment is stick-resistant, this recipe requires very little fat—the small amount of oil is there for taste and texture only. You can use this method to cook a single serving or a complete meal (see Cook's Notes on page 112).
"

REMOVING THE SKIN FROM SALMON

Removing the skin from fish can be a slippery business. To skin a fillet easily, place it with the thicker end closer to you. Use a sharp knife to separate a corner of the skin at the thicker end.

1. Use a clean kitchen towel to grip the skin.

2. Starting at the end of the fillet—with your knife held at a 20° angle between the flesh and the skin—pull the skin toward you. The knife should not move.

3. The skin comes away in 1 piece.

Cook's Notes: How to Cook in a Bag

▶ **Is It Done?** The only tricky part about cooking *en papillote* is that you can't see when the fish is done. If you slice open the bag, you risk losing some of the delicious sauce that's coming together. My solution is to start with the basic rule of baking fish: In a 400°F oven, bake the fish 10 minutes for every 1 inch of thickness. I stick a very sharp, thin knife right through the parchment and down through the fish as soon as it hits the 12-minute mark. No resistance or very little? The fish is done. Significant resistance? Bake it for a few more minutes. (By the way, this test works well regardless of how you cook the fish.)

▶ **Make a Meal in a Bag.** Let's say you wanted to make a whole meal in a bag, sort of like a high-toned TV dinner. In that case, I would make two bags, each with two pieces of fish, and then add some substantial vegetables, for example sautéed mushrooms, steamed cooked potato cubes, or blanched broccoli or carrots.

If you do add vegetables, they'll need to be pre-cooked. The denser vegetables (like carrots and broccoli) simply won't become tender during the short time the package is in the oven. Similarly, if wetter veggies (mushrooms and spinach, for example) aren't pre-cooked, they'll end up watering down the sauce.

▶ **Premade Bags.** Pre-made culinary parchment paper bags (made by PaperChef, see Sources, page 351) are much more widely available these days than they used to be. This recipe includes instructions on how to fold the paper to make a bag yourself, but if you can find the pre-made ones, grab them. I experimented with a pre-made bag while testing this recipe and discovered that it worked perfectly well. You just layer all the ingredients in the bag, fold the bottom under to seal the package, and bake away.

SEALING THE FISH IN PARCHMENT

1. Arrange half the orange and lemon slices about 2 inches to the right of the center fold in a rectangle shape, about the size of the four pieces of salmon laid next to each other (perpendicular to the crease). Sprinkle with half the rosemary.

2. Place the salmon fillets on top. Top with citrus juices, olive oil, olives, chiles, remaining rosemary, and remaining citrus slices.

3. Start by folding the parchment over to enclose the fish.

4. Then, beginning in the top left corner of the package, make a thin fold, and then another overlapping the first fold. Make sure that the second fold covers the open end of the first fold, so there is no way the moisture from the baking fish can escape.

5. Continue making folds.

6. When you have sealed the whole package, secure the last fold with a paper clip.

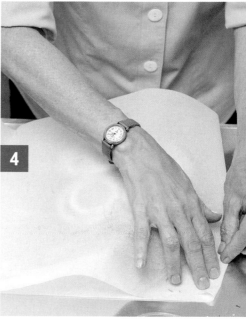

Cover the open end of every fold with the next fold.

SUMMER SHACK LOBSTER ROLLS

Adapted from *The Summer Shack Cookbook: The Complete Guide to Shore Food* (Norton, 2007).

START TO FINISH: 55 MINUTES PLUS LOBSTER COOKING AND SHELLING TIME IF YOU ARE COOKING YOUR OWN / **HANDS-ON TIME:** 25 MINUTES / **SERVES:** 4

1 pound fully cooked lobster meat or 5 pounds live lobsters

1 small to medium cucumber (4 to 5 ounces), peeled, seeded, and cut in ¼-inch dice

½ cup store-bought mayonnaise (Hellman's or Best Foods) or Homemade Mayonnaise (pages 52–53)

2 small scallions, white and light green parts, thinly sliced

Freshly ground black pepper

4 New England–style hot dog buns (see Sources, page 351)

4 tablespoons unsalted butter, softened

4 Boston or Bibb lettuce leaves, washed and dried

4 dill pickle spears, for serving

Potato chips, for serving

> If you are using live lobsters, steam them until fully cooked (see instructions and time chart, pages 116–117), and then let cool to room temperature. Following the steps and photos on pages 118–119, remove the meat from the lobsters. Cut the meat into ½- to ¾-inch dice. You may pick all the meat from the carcass and add it to the meat or freeze the carcass for soup or broth.

> Place the cucumber in a colander for at least 5 minutes to drain the excess liquid.

> Combine the lobster, cucumber, and mayonnaise. If the salad is to be served within the hour, add the scallions. Season with a bit of pepper if needed; it is unlikely that salt will be needed. Cover with plastic wrap and chill for at least 30 minutes or up to 4 hours before serving.

> Heat a 10-inch skillet over medium heat. Spread each of the buns with 1 tablespoon butter (half on each side). Place the buttered buns into the hot, dry pan and toast until golden brown on 1 side, about 1 minute. Turn and cook the other side, about 1 minute more. Remove from the heat.

> Open the buns and place a lettuce leaf on 1 side of the center, inside the bun. Spoon the lobster salad evenly among them. Serve with pickles and chips.

"

I met Jasper White back in my Boston restaurant years and I've been a fan ever since, partly because he's a champion of New England cuisine and that's where my roots lie, but mostly because he's a great chef and one of the nicest guys in the field.

Jasper's original restaurants were devoted to fine dining and white tablecloths. Then, in 2000, he opened Summer Shack, an ideal version of the typical New England clam shack. It's a big, barn-like place in Cambridge, Massachusetts, with picnic tables and lower prices than his more high-toned ventures, but also with a larger menu and better quality food than the typical clam shack. Summer Shack was a smash hit from its first day, and Jasper has opened up four more of them in the years since.

If there's one person who can teach us all how to cook lobster properly, it's Jasper—and the lobster roll he makes with that cooked lobster is out of this world.

"

Cook's Notes: How to Steam Live Lobsters

▶ **Steaming is best.** If you are near the ocean and can boil lobsters in ocean water, then by all means, do so. Other than that exception, steaming is a far superior technique to boiling for fully cooking lobster. Steaming is less messy and more safe and, because it cooks the lobsters more gently, it results in more tender meat, especially with the larger sizes. Steaming also captures the natural flavor of the lobster. Boiling a lobster in tap water dilutes its salty, sweet, wonderful flavor.

▶ **The right pot.** If you do not have a special steamer pot, you will need a pot with a tight-fitting lid large enough to hold the amount and size of the lobsters you have purchased. My rule of thumb is to allow about 3 to 4 quarts of space for each $1^{1}/_{2}$-pound lobster. Place about an inch of ocean water or heavily salted tap water inside the steamer pot (with the rack built in) or other suitable pot. If you are improvising the steamer pot, use a rack to elevate the lobsters over the water. You can also use rockweed (seaweed that you can purchase from most stores that sell lobster) to make a wonderful natural steam rack.

▶ **Arranging the lobsters.** Bring the water to a boil and when the pot fills up with steam, put in the live lobsters, one by one. Hold the lobster with your thumb and fingers on the carapace (the shell covering the body) and arrange them in different directions in a stack on top of each other so the steam can circulate around all the lobsters. Cover the pot and wait until the pot is full of steam again; when you crack the lid a little and see the steam escape, then you can begin timing the lobsters according to the chart (see page 117).

▶ **Timing it right.** The recovery time of the steam that fills the pot will vary with different pots and different ranges, but once the steam is going full blast, start to time the cooking. Halfway through the cooking, use a pair of tongs to quickly rearrange the lobsters in different positions and directions so they cook evenly. Cover the pot again and continue timing them. When they are cooked, remove them with your tongs. If you are removing the meat, let the lobsters cool at room temperature and shuck them before you refrigerate the meat.

STEAMING TIMES FOR LOBSTERS

Lobster Weight (Pounds)	Minutes Male	Minutes Female *	Minutes New Shell**
1	10	12	8 to 9
1¼	12	14	10
1½	14	16	12
1¾	16	18	
2	18	20	
2¼	20	22	
2½	22	24	
2¾	24	26	
3	25 to 30	30 to 35	

*Female lobsters contain roe during the months of June, July, August, and September, and therefore require extra time to steam. Cook them for the same time as the males the rest of the year.

**New Shell (soft shell) lobsters are available in July, August, September, and October. They have less meat inside and therefore require less time to steam.

JASPER'S TIPS FOR LOBSTER ROLLS

The lobster roll, the king of clam shack offerings, is incredibly delicious with its cool fresh lobster salad and warm crisp buttery bun. It is humble, but don't be fooled by the garnish of pickles and potato chips; this dish is like a millionaire driving an old Chevy—understated, but still rich, and typical of New England culture.

▶ Once the lobster salad is ready, this becomes a very easy and fast dish. You may mix the lobster salad up to 4 hours ahead.

▶ The buns must have no crust on the sides—these are real New England buns. If they aren't available, you can trim a top-split hot dog bun with a serrated knife. You'll also find a recipe for them in my book *Lobster at Home* (Scribner, 1998).

▶ A very small amount of fresh tarragon (or better yet fresh chervil) added to the lobster salad is a nice option.

▶ Some seafood markets that sell lobster also sell lobster meat (for a real time-saver), but I only recommend freshly cooked and shucked meat (tail, knuckle, and claw) from a vendor that understands lobster quality and features it regularly. Some only make it when they have weak or even dead lobsters.

▶ The pickle is a very good accompaniment; pickled beets are also excellent with lobster rolls.

HOW TO SHELL A COOKED LOBSTER

1. Working over a bowl to catch the juices, break off the claws by bending them back where they join the body and snapping them off.

2. Grab the tail where is it attached to the body, and twist it off.

3. Remove all the walking legs. Set them aside for biting on and sucking out the meat later, if desired. Separate the claw from the knuckles by snapping them apart where the claw and the knuckles join.

4. Crack the claws and the knuckles using a lobster cracker, and pull out the meat.

5. Use a wooden skewer to remove all the smaller pieces of meat from the shells.

6. Snap off the flaps at the end of the tail.

7. Holding the tail in your hand, stick a fork, curved side up, into the lobster meat at the other end of the tail from where you just snapped off the flaps. Dig the lobster meat out by pressing down on the tines of the fork while pressing the fork handle up and over until it touches the opposite side of the tail. Pull out the tail meat in one piece.

8. Peel off the flap of meat on top of the tail and scrape off and reserve any coral (eggs). Pull up and discard the digestive tract, which you will find in the crevice running down the center of the tail.

9. Here is what you should end up with, clockwise from the right: knuckle meat, small claw meat, large claw meat, tail, walking legs, flap from the tail, and roe (if your lobster had roe).

Dig the tines of the fork into the meat and move the handle up and over to the other side of the tail.

SAUTÉED FISH FILLETS
WITH CREAMY MUSTARD-TARRAGON SAUCE

START TO FINISH: 45 MINUTES / **HANDS-ON TIME:** 35 MINUTES / **SERVINGS:** 4

3 tablespoons extra-virgin olive oil, divided

2 tablespoons minced shallots

1 cup halved cherry tomatoes (see page 181)

$\frac{1}{3}$ cup dry white wine

$\frac{1}{2}$ cup crème fraîche

1 tablespoon Dijon mustard

1 tablespoon fresh tarragon leaves, chopped

Kosher salt and freshly ground black pepper

Wondra flour (see page 265) or all-purpose flour for dredging the fish

4 (6-ounce) boneless, skinless fish fillets such as mahi mahi, tilapia, or catfish

> Heat 1 tablespoon of the oil in a medium skillet over medium-low heat, add the shallots, and cook, stirring, 3 minutes. Increase the heat to medium, add the tomatoes and cook, stirring, until they are softened, about 3 minutes. Add the white wine, bring to a boil, and simmer until most of it is reduced. Add the crème fraîche and simmer until the sauce thickens, about 5 minutes. Add the mustard, tarragon, and salt and pepper to taste, and set aside.

> Spread out the flour on a piece of parchment on the counter. Heat the remaining 2 tablespoons oil over medium-high heat in a large nonstick or stick-resistant skillet. Season the fish fillets on both sides with salt and pepper. Coat them lightly with the flour, lifting the parchment paper on both sides to help coat the fish and shaking off the excess before adding them to the pan, skinned side up. Cook for 3 minutes, turn over, and cook for 3 minutes more on the second side or until just cooked through (see page 239).

> Transfer the fillets to each of 4 plates and top each portion with some of the sauce.

A LOWER-FAT VARIATION

▶ **Replace the crème fraîche** in this recipe with $\frac{1}{2}$ cup nonfat Greek yogurt whisked with 2 teaspoons flour and $\frac{1}{2}$ tablespoon water. Add the yogurt mixture to the skillet at the same point you would have added the crème fraîche and bring the mixture to a boil, whisking. Simmer for 2 minutes and stir in the mustard, tarragon, and salt and pepper to taste.

"

Fish dishes, because fish is so naturally bland, cry out for acid, and this sauce—with its base of cherry tomatoes, wine, and crème fraîche—is all about that tang. It will team up nicely with just about any kind of fish, but do your best to find one that's local and/or sustainable (see page 22). One of the sauce's chief supporting notes is provided by tarragon, but if you're not a fan, you can swap in chives, dill, or basil, all of which are fish-friendly herbs.

Wondra flour creates a coating that's less gummy than regular all-purpose flour, providing this fish with a crust that's crispy and light.

Serve it with the Roasted Radishes and Sautéed Lemony Radish Tops on page 290.

"

PICK THE PRETTY SIDE

A fish fillet has a pretty and an ugly side. Which is which? The skinned side—the side from which the skin has been removed—is considered the ugly side. Given that you're going to flip the fish just once as you cook it, and that you want to serve it with the pretty side up, sauté the pretty side first.

TORTILLA-CRUSTED TILAPIA
WITH PICKLED RED ONIONS AND CREMA

START TO FINISH: 60 MINUTES / **HANDS-ON TIME:** 30 MINUTES / **SERVINGS:** 4

Marinated fish coated with crushed tortilla strips is wonderful all by itself. Adding a topping of *crema* and orange-flavored pickled onions takes it to a whole other level.

Seasoning and marinating the fish for 30 minutes really amps up the flavor. I chose tilapia because it's one of the more sustainable fish to be found at the market these days (just make sure it's from the U.S., see page 22). But because one side of each fillet is much thinner than the other, I cut the fillets down the middle and bake the thinner halves for a shorter amount of time.

This recipe will work with any fish. Simply adjust the cooking time if the fish is thicker than tilapia (see How Do You Know When Fish is Cooked? on page 239).

The pickled onions could grace any number of dishes. Put them on sandwiches or burgers, sprinkle them on soups, or add them to eggs. They'll keep for a few weeks in the fridge, and you'll be happy to have them on hand when some new inspiration strikes.

Serve this with Refried Beans (page 298).

2 (½-pound) tilapia fillets
1 teaspoon kosher salt
2 tablespoons fresh lime or lemon juice
2 tablespoons vegetable oil, preferably grapeseed
1 batch Tortilla Strips (page 59) or 2 cups store-bought tortilla chips and 2 teaspoons chili powder
1 medium red onion, sliced ¼-inch thick (about 1 cup)
¾ cup distilled white vinegar

¼ cup fresh orange juice
1½ tablespoons sugar
¾ teaspoon kosher salt
½ teaspoon cumin seeds
½ teaspoon dried oregano
2 tablespoons chopped pickled jalapeño, optional
1 tablespoon unsalted butter, melted
Crema (see Note) and sliced pickled jalapeños for garnish

> Cut each fish fillet down the seam to separate the thin half from the thick half. Cut each of the pieces in half crosswise (making a total of 8 pieces). Sprinkle the fish pieces evenly all over with the salt, transfer to a resealable bag, and add the lime juice and oil. Chill for 30 minutes.

> While the fish is marinating, finely crush (it should not be a powder) the Tortilla Strips or the store-bought tortilla chips (and toss the store-bought crushed chips with the chili powder).

> Combine the red onion, vinegar, orange juice, sugar, salt, cumin, and oregano in a small saucepan, bring to a boil, and simmer for 5 minutes. Let cool. Drain the mixture and chop the onions. Combine them with the jalapeños, if using, in a small bowl.

> Preheat the oven to 375°F. Arrange the fish in a single layer on a rimmed baking sheet, keeping the thin pieces on one side and the thick pieces on the other. Pack the tortilla crumbs on top of the fillets, drizzle the crumbs with the melted butter, and bake the fish on the middle rack of the oven until it is just cooked through, about 5 minutes for the thinner pieces and 8 minutes for the thicker pieces.

> Transfer a thick and a thin fillet piece to each of 4 plates. Serve each portion topped with some of the crema, pickled onions, and pickled jalapeños.

Note: A kind of Mexican sour cream, crema is increasingly available at American supermarkets. If you can't find it, sour cream or crème fraîche, diluted with a bit of milk, cream, or water, will do.

SAUTÉED LEMON CHICKEN
WITH FRIED CAPERS

START TO FINISH: 45 MINUTES / **HANDS-ON TIME:** 45 MINUTES / **SERVINGS:** 4

1 pound skinless chicken breast cutlets, preferably thin sliced

¼ cup plus 1 tablespoon vegetable oil, preferably grapeseed, divided

3 tablespoons capers, rinsed, drained, and dried very well

Wondra flour (see page 265) or all-purpose flour for dredging

Kosher salt and freshly ground black pepper

1 large lemon, sliced very thin crosswise

2 tablespoons sugar

2 tablespoons minced shallots

1¼ cups Homemade Chicken Stock (page 26) or store-bought chicken broth

This chicken recipe follows a template for how to sauté thin pieces of several different kinds of meat, and then to produce a sauce from the drippings left in the pan. See the Cook's Notes on page 126 to learn the master method, which works just as well with pork and veal. Pair this dish with Sautéed Shredded Zucchini with Lemon and Thyme on page 301.

❯ Working with 1 cutlet at a time, pound the chicken until it is ⅛ inch thick (see page 126) and transfer to a plate. Pat the chicken dry and cut the pieces in half if they are too large to sauté easily.

❯ In a large skillet, combine 2 tablespoons of the oil with the capers and heat the pan to medium-high (capers can pop if added to a hot pan). Cook, stirring, until they are crispy, about 2 minutes. Transfer the capers to a small bowl with a slotted spoon.

❯ Spread out the flour on a piece of parchment on the counter. Heat the skillet over medium-high heat. Working with half the chicken at a time, season the cutlets on both sides with salt and pepper and coat them lightly with the flour, lifting the parchment paper on both sides to help coat the chicken and shaking off the excess. Add the chicken to the oil in the pan and cook until lightly golden, about 2 minutes per side. Transfer to a plate. Add 2 tablespoons oil to the pan. Season and flour the remaining chicken and sauté, transferring it as it is done to the plate.

❯ Dip the lemon slices in the sugar, coating them lightly on both sides, and add them to the skillet. Cook over medium heat until they are lightly caramelized, about 1 minute per side. Transfer to the plate with the chicken. Add the remaining 1 tablespoon oil and the shallots to the pan and cook, stirring, 1 minute. Add the chicken stock and bring to a boil, scraping up the brown bits on the bottom of the pan. Return the chicken and lemon slices to the pan, along with any juices from the plate. Simmer gently, turning the chicken over several times until it is heated through.

❯ Transfer the chicken to 4 plates and simmer the sauce until it has thickened slightly. Spoon the sauce and lemon slices over the chicken and top with the fried capers.

1. After the cutlets have browned on one side and it's time to flip them over, tip the pan to one side. All the oil will pool on one side of the pan, so you can flip the cutlet on the dry (nonoil) side without getting splattered by the hot oil.

2. Repeat the procedure for the second cutlet, tipping the pan in the opposite direction.

Cook's Notes: How to Sauté Any Cutlet and Make a Pan Sauce

Cutlets—be they chicken, pork, or veal—are great for making a quick meal with a flavorful pan sauce. This method will work with whatever meat you choose. Here's the basic procedure:

▶ **Place a cutlet between sheets of plastic wrap** or in a resealable plastic bag sprinkled with water (which prevents the meat from sticking to the bag and shredding), and then pound to an even thickness using a meat pounder or rolling pin (see page 127).

▶ **Season the meat with salt and pepper** before dipping it in flour to coat it lightly on both sides. The flour not only helps to keep the meat from drying out, but also lightly thickens the sauce later on. Don't flour the meat until right before putting it in the pan; as it sits, the meat will sweat and the flour coating will become gummy.

▶ **Lightly brown the cutlets** in oil in a large skillet, and then transfer them to a plate while you make the pan sauce.

▶ **Add shallots or onions** to the fat left in the pan and sauté for a minute or two.

▶ **Deglaze the pan** by adding wine, stock, or water. In the process, be sure to scrape up the brown bits at the bottom of the skillet.

▶ **Reduce the heat to a simmer,** return the cutlets to the pan along with any juices from the plate on which they were resting, and cook them very gently, turning them from one side to the other several times until they're just heated though. (Do not allow the liquid to come to a boil; the cutlets will become tough.) Then transfer them to plates. Further reduce the sauce, if necessary, and spoon over the meat on the plates.

HOW TO POUND CUTLETS

1. Pour about 1 tablespoon water into a resealable plastic bag.

2. Add a boneless, skinless chicken breast half to the bag.

3. Remove excess air from the bag.

4. Seal the bag and pound the chicken using a meat pounder or rolling pin.

5. Continue pounding until the cutlet is very thin.

6. Remove the pounded cutlet from the bag and proceed with the recipe.

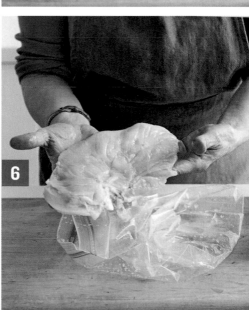

BAKED CHICKEN THIGHS
WITH PANCETTA, OLIVES, AND CHERRY TOMATOES

START TO FINISH: I HOUR 5 MINUTES / **HANDS-ON TIME:** 35 MINUTES / **SERVES:** 4 TO 6

"

I ought to have named this recipe the Henry Moulton Special in honor of my father. That's how much he loves it. Whenever I visit Dad these days, I have to whip up a special batch and freeze it in individual portions.

It's all about a few key Mediterranean ingredients—pancetta, olives, tomatoes—melding together to make a knockout Mediterranean sauce. Pancetta is Italian bacon. It's cured, but not smoked, which results in a rich pork flavor that doesn't overwhelm the other ingredients. Make sure to use oil-cured olives. I think of them as the raisins of the olive family because of their jammy texture and deep flavor.

Why chicken thighs instead of chicken breasts? Because if you're looking for foolproof juiciness and rich chicken flavor, you're always going to choose dark meat over white. Unlike white meat, the thighs won't dry out when baked.

"

BUY YOUR OLIVES WITH PITS

Pitted olives lose flavor and texture much faster than olives with their pits, so try to buy olives with pits and remove them yourself. It's very easy: Simply lay the olives on their side, smash them lightly with the dull side of your knife, and the pit will come charging out (or at least be loosened enough so you can pull it out easily).

8 small bone-in chicken thighs (3 to 3$\frac{1}{4}$ pounds)

Kosher salt and freshly ground black pepper

2 tablespoons extra-virgin olive oil

2 ounces chopped pancetta (about $\frac{1}{2}$ cup)

$\frac{1}{2}$ cup dry white wine

1 tablespoon minced garlic

1$\frac{1}{2}$ tablespoons fresh rosemary, chopped

1 to 2 teaspoons hot red pepper flakes

$\frac{3}{4}$ cup oil-cured black olives, pitted

1$\frac{1}{2}$ cups cherry tomatoes, halved (see page 181)

> Preheat the oven to 350°F. Season the chicken on all sides with salt and pepper. Heat the oil in a large ovenproof skillet over medium heat. Working in 2 batches, add the chicken thighs, skin side down, and cook them until the skin is golden brown, 6 to 8 minutes. Turn and cook another 4 minutes. Transfer the chicken to a shallow baking dish that just holds all the thighs in one layer.

> Pour off all but 2 tablespoons of fat from the skillet. Add the pancetta and cook over medium-low heat, stirring occasionally, until it is golden, 3 to 4 minutes. Transfer the pancetta and any fat from the skillet to the baking dish. Add the wine to the skillet and deglaze the pan over medium heat, scraping up the brown bits from the bottom of the pan. Pour the deglazing liquid over the chicken.

> In a small bowl combine the garlic, rosemary, and red pepper flakes and sprinkle the mixture along with the olives over the chicken, distributing them evenly around the chicken. Tuck the cherry tomatoes between the chicken pieces. Bake on the middle shelf of the oven until the chicken is just cooked through (160°F), about 20 minutes. Remove the baking dish from the oven carefully and let the chicken rest for 10 minutes before serving. Transfer the chicken to plates and spoon some of the tomato-olive mixture and juices from the skillet over each portion.

Cooking with *Hiroko Shimbo*

SPICY MISO CHICKEN WINGS

Adapted from *Hiroko's American Kitchen: Cooking with Japanese Flavors* (Andrews McMeel, 2012).

66

When it comes to Japanese cooking, there's no one I trust more than Hiroko Shimbo. She's written three award-winning books and teaches and lectures on the subject from coast to coast. *Hiroko's American Kitchen,* her most recent book, is a brilliant hands-across-the-water effort to help home cooks in America understand Japanese cuisine. She does so by applying Japanese techniques and sauces to American ingredients and seasonality.

I'm featuring Hiroko's Spicy Miso Chicken Wings here because I love chicken wings, especially fried ones, and because Hiroko's new twist on this all-American standard strikes me as fresh and delicious. The wings are fried twice—the first time at a lower temperature to cook the chicken; the second time at a higher temperature to crisp the skin.

A note from Hiroko: Your guests will need a large supply of paper napkins. A strongly flavored lager beer makes an excellent accompaniment for these wings.

99

START TO FINISH: 55 MINUTES / **HANDS-ON TIME:** 35 MINUTES / **SERVINGS:** 4

1¹/₂ pounds chicken wings

2 teaspoons onion powder

³/₄ teaspoon sea salt

1 medium egg, lightly beaten

1 tablespoon sake or water

6 tablespoons cornstarch

¹/₄ cup all-purpose flour

2 tablespoons ginger juice from freshly grated ginger (from 4- to 5-inch knob of ginger, see Notes), divided

¹/₄ cup Spicy Miso Sauce (page 131)

2 teaspoons rice vinegar

1 teaspoon soy sauce

2 to 3 teaspoons hot paprika

1 scallion, green part only

Vegetable oil, for frying

> Remove the wing tips (save them in the freezer for making stock), and separate the other two joints by cutting them in half where they join. Combine the onion powder, salt, egg, sake, cornstarch, flour, and 1 tablespoon of the ginger juice in a large bowl. Add the wings, coat with the mixture, and let stand for 20 minutes.

> In another large bowl, combine the Spicy Miso Sauce, vinegar, soy sauce, paprika, and the remaining 1 tablespoon ginger juice and set aside. Cut the scallion into very thin slices diagonally and set aside.

> Heat 3 inches of oil in a wok or deep skillet to 330°F. Stir the wings to make sure they are well coated with the cornstarch-flour mixture. Working in 2 batches, add the wings and cook them for 6 minutes, turning from time to time. Transfer the wings to a wire rack set over a baking sheet.

> Increase the temperature of oil to 350°F. Working in 3 batches, return the wings to the hot oil and cook them for 1 minute, or until the outside is crisp. Remove the wings from the oil and drain on the wire rack. While the wings are hot, toss all of the cooked wings in the Spicy Miso Sauce mixture until well coated. Transfer the chicken wings to a large platter, garnish with the sliced scallion, and serve.

Notes: To make the ginger juice, peel the ginger and grate it on a microplane or a Japanese grater. Place the grated ginger in a paper towel, a piece of cheesecloth, or a garlic press and squeeze to extract the juice.

Oroshigane are Japanese graters with raised surface bumps instead of perforated holes. Traditionally made of copper, modern ones are made of stainless steel and are dishwasher safe. These are very useful for making very fine pastes of ginger, garlic, or other roots and vegetables (see Sources, page 351).

SPICY MISO SAUCE

START TO FINISH: 18 MINUTES / **HANDS-ON TIME:** 18 MINUTES / **SERVINGS:** MAKES ABOUT 1½ CUPS

1 cup aged brown miso (see the definition at right)
½ cup plus 1 tablespoon sugar
¾ cup mirin
¼ cup plus 2 tablespoons sake
¼ cup fresh lemon juice
1 to 2 teaspoons red pepper flakes

Place the miso, sugar, mirin, and sake in a medium pot and whisk until smooth. Place the pot over medium heat and bring it to a simmer. Cook the mixture, stirring constantly, 4 to 5 minutes. Add the lemon juice and cook for 8 minutes, stirring occasionally. Turn off the heat, add the red pepper flakes, and stir. Any unused sauce will keep in the freezer for up to 3 months.

HIROKO'S MISO PRIMER

Miso is a paste made from fermented soybeans. Almost all the miso sold in the United States is *kome-miso,* made from a combination of rice and soybeans. Depending on the length of fermentation, miso will have different degrees of saltiness, color, and flavor.

▸ **White miso** is aged for 3 to 4 weeks and has a very sweet soybean flavor with mild saltiness.

▸ **Light brown miso** is aged longer than white and is stronger in flavor and saltier.

▸ **Brown miso** is aged the longest and the flavor is rich, complex, and robust. It is the saltiest of the three.

▸ **How to buy miso paste:** You'll find many types and brands of miso paste at Japanese or Asian markets. To choose, first check the ingredient list on the English nutrition label. It should have this simple, short list: soybeans, rice or barley, and salt. You may sometimes see alcohol as an added preservative. Next, check the price. Choose a miso whose price is in the middle or somewhat higher range. Good-quality miso has gone through a proper lengthy fermentation process and is not just salty brown paste.

▸ **How to store miso paste:** You may store miso in the freezer for up to 6 months. Freezing does not change its texture or nutritional value, and there's no need to bring it to room temperature before using.

BUFFALO CHICKEN NUGGETS

START TO FINISH: 2 HOURS 30 MINUTES / **HANDS-ON TIME:** 15 MINUTES / **SERVINGS:** 4 TO 6

One of my favorite local grocery stores regularly offers chicken tenders at a good price. A chicken tender is the flap of meat attached to the bottom of a chicken breast. It's too small to be good for much of anything, except in a stir-fry or this kind of recipe—a crowd-pleaser that's equally welcome at family meals and football Sundays.

White meat chicken is notoriously dry when overcooked, and overcooking is easy to do because we're all so concerned about salmonella. To make sure these tenders *remain* tender, I start by soaking the chicken in a buttermilk brine flavored with smoky hot sauce and garlic. Like all dairy, buttermilk is a tenderizer; adding salt to it simultaneously seasons the chicken and helps to keep it from drying out.

To make a low-fat version, follow the instructions and ingredients (substituting store-bought low-fat mayonnaise for the regular mayonnaise) up to the point after you coat the chicken with the crumbs. Arrange the breaded chicken in a single layer on the baking sheet. Spray the tops of all the chicken pieces lightly with olive oil spray and bake at 425°F on the middle shelf of the oven for 10 minutes. Turn them over and bake for an additional 5 minutes or until they are just cooked through.

2 garlic cloves, smashed and peeled

1 teaspoon kosher salt

$1/4$ cup plus 2 tablespoons hot sauce (my favorite for this recipe is Tabasco Chipotle), divided

2 cups plus 6 tablespoons low-fat buttermilk, divided

$1^1/4$ pounds chicken tenders or chicken breasts cut into 3-inch by 1-inch by $1/2$-inch-thick pieces

$1/4$ cup Homemade Mayonnaise (pages 52–53) or store-bought mayonnaise

$1/4$ cup crumbled blue cheese

$1/4$ cup finely chopped celery

$1/2$ teaspoon fresh lemon juice

$3/4$ cup Italian seasoned breadcrumbs

$1/4$ cup panko breadcrumbs

$1/2$ cup extra-virgin olive oil, divided

> In a medium bowl, combine the garlic, salt, 2 tablespoons of the hot sauce, and 2 cups of the buttermilk. Whisk until the salt is dissolved. Add the chicken tenders and stir to coat well with the marinade. Cover and chill at least 2 hours or up to 10 hours.

> Preheat oven to 300°F. Line a baking sheet with parchment paper.

> Meanwhile, in a small bowl, combine the remaining 6 tablespoons buttermilk, mayonnaise, blue cheese, celery, and lemon juice and stir well. Transfer to a ramekin for dipping. Pour the remaining $1/4$ cup hot sauce into a second ramekin. Set aside.

> In a shallow bowl, combine the seasoned breadcrumbs and panko breadcrumbs. Drain the chicken in a colander but do not pat it dry. Dip each chicken piece in the breadcrumb mixture, making sure it is coated well on both sides with the crumbs. Heat 2 tablespoons of the oil over medium-high heat in a large nonstick skillet and add half the chicken in one layer. Cook until golden brown, about 2 minutes, flip the chicken pieces, and add another 2 tablespoons oil to the skillet. Cook until golden brown on the second side, about 1 minute, and transfer to the baking sheet. Repeat the procedure with the remaining chicken, crumbs, and olive oil, transferring it when done to the baking sheet.

> Bake the chicken on the middle shelf of the oven for 10 minutes and serve right away with the blue cheese sauce and hot sauce.

DUCK BREASTS
WITH WARM LENTIL SALAD

START TO FINISH: 45 MINUTES / HANDS-ON TIME: 15 MINUTES / SERVINGS: 4

1 cup green lentils, preferably lentilles du Puy (see Note)

Kosher salt

4 Pekin duck breast halves (2 to 2½ pounds total; see Sources, page 350)

Freshly ground black pepper

1 tablespoon sherry, white wine, or red wine vinegar

1 teaspoon Dijon mustard

3 tablespoons extra-virgin olive oil

> Combine the lentils and 1 teaspoon salt with enough cold water to cover them by 2 inches in a small saucepan. Bring the water to a boil, reduce the heat, and simmer, partially covered, until the lentils are just tender, 20 to 25 minutes.

> While the lentils are cooking, using a very sharp knife, lightly score the skin on each duck breast half in a crisscross pattern, cutting all the way down through the skin but not into the meat.

> Pat the duck dry and season the skin with salt and pepper. Place the duck, skin side down, in a large, cold skillet. Turn the heat to medium and cook the duck breasts until the skin looks very crispy, about 12 minutes. There will be a lot of fat in the pan, but do not pour it off; the deep hot liquid fat in the pan helps to render out the fat under the skin.

> When the duck skin is crisp, transfer the breasts to a plate. Pour off all but 1 tablespoon of the fat from the pan, reserving the remaining fat in a bowl (see Notes). Season the meat side of the duck with salt and pepper and return it to the skillet, meat side down. Cook the breasts another 3 to 5 minutes for medium-rare. Transfer the duck to a clean plate, skin side up. Cover it loosely with foil and let it rest for 10 minutes before slicing.

> When the lentils are tender, drain them well and add to the skillet that the duck was cooked in, along with the vinegar, mustard, olive oil, and salt and pepper to taste. Add any juices that have collected on the plate the duck breasts are on, stir well, and heat the mixture over medium heat until hot.

> Spoon the warm lentil salad onto 4 plates, thinly slice the duck, and arrange it on top of the salad.

Notes: Lentilles du Puy are tiny green lentils that cook in no time and have a wonderful firm texture (see Sources, page 351).

Store any leftover duck fat in a lidded jar in the fridge or freezer, for use in Duck Confit (page 248), Duck Fat Popovers (page 311), or for sautéing potatoes and other vegetables.

66 ~~~~~~~~~~~~~

Duck is one of my favorite foods. It's just plain scrumptious no matter how you make it: roasted, braised, the legs confit-ed, the wings fried, the breasts grilled or sautéed. And then there's whole duck, slow roasted. That one's *really* a treat. But it's not exactly a dish to dash off, so I save it for special occasions.

Duck breasts are the quickest and easiest of all duck parts to cook. My family probably eats them for dinner once a week. Here's why: 1) They're so delicious all by themselves that they require almost no dressing up; 2) Eaten without the skin, they are as lean as white meat chicken; 3) They contain more iron per serving than most other poultry and some cuts of beef; and 4) They're as easy to cook as steak and can be prepared in 15 to 20 minutes. Indeed, it's so simple that my son, when he was a teenager, learned how to do it the first time I showed him. Follow the step-by-step photos on page 135, and you'll see how easy it is, too.

One whole duck breast—two halves—can feed two to three people. (Each breast weighs from 1 to 1¼ pounds.) I recommend cooking the breasts with the skin on, even if you don't plan on eating the skin; it prevents the breasts from drying out and guarantees better flavor.

~~~~~~~~~~~~~ 99

COOKING DUCK BREASTS

1. Using a very sharp knife, lightly score the skin on each duck breast half in a crisscross pattern, cutting all the way down through the skin but not into the meat.

2. Pat the duck dry with paper towels. Season the skin with salt and pepper.

3. Place the duck, skin side down, in a large, cold skillet.

4. Cook the duck breasts over medium heat, leaving the fat that renders out in the pan.

5. When the skin looks very crispy, transfer the breasts to a plate. Pour off all but 1 tablespoon of the fat from the pan and finish cooking the duck on the second side.

6. Let the duck rest for 10 minutes before thinly slicing. It's easiest to slice the duck with the skin side down.

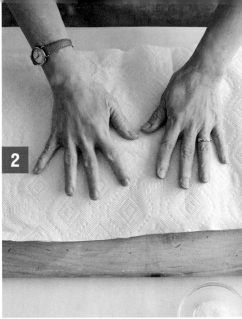

TURKEY-SPINACH BURGERS
WITH PEPPERONCINI SAUCE

START TO FINISH: 45 MINUTES / **HANDS-ON TIME:** 20 MINUTES / **SERVINGS:** 4

2 tablespoons extra-virgin olive oil, divided, plus olive oil cooking spray

1/2 cup finely chopped onion

5 ounces baby spinach

Kosher salt and freshly ground black pepper

1/4 cup plain nonfat Greek yogurt

1/4 cup low-fat mayonnaise

2 tablespoons minced seeded pepperoncini

1 tablespoon liquid from the pepperoncini jar

1 to 2 teaspoons fresh lemon juice or to taste

1 teaspoon minced garlic

3 ounces crumbled feta cheese

2 tablespoons chopped fresh oregano

1 pound ground turkey, a mix of white and dark meat (see page 138 if you would like to grind your own)

4 whole-wheat hamburger buns, toasted

Lettuce and sliced tomatoes for garnish

> Heat 1 tablespoon of the oil in a skillet over medium heat. Add the onion, and cook, stirring occasionally, until golden brown, about 8 minutes. Increase the heat to medium-high, add the remaining 1 tablespoon olive oil and the spinach, and cook, stirring, until the spinach is wilted. Season with salt and pepper and transfer the mixture to a bowl. Chill in the refrigerator until cooled to room temperature.

> Meanwhile, combine the yogurt, mayonnaise, pepperoncini, pepperoncini liquid, lemon juice, garlic, and salt and pepper to taste in a small bowl and set aside.

> Preheat the grill to medium. Once the spinach has cooled, remove it from the refrigerator and add the feta, oregano, ground turkey, 1/4 teaspoon salt, and 1/4 teaspoon pepper. Mix just until combined and shape into 4 patties, each about 1/2 inch thick.

> Spray the burgers lightly with olive oil cooking spray, then grill over medium heat until just cooked through, about 6 minutes per side. Spread some of the yogurt sauce on the bottom half of each bun, then top with lettuce and tomato slices and a burger. Spoon the remaining sauce over the burgers and top with the remaining bun halves. Serve immediately.

"
We love hamburgers because they're flavorful and juicy, but the (literally) heart-breaking source of all that flavor and juice is fat. As you decrease the fat content in a burger, its flavor tends to go bye-bye, too. This is a real problem if you want your burgers and you also want the blood to continue whistling through your veins. The solution? Turkey.

I know. I know. You tried turkey burgers and it was like chewing wet cardboard. Indeed, turkey cries out for additional flavor and moisture. Happily, any number of vegetables can answer this call by providing their own juices, including sautéed onions, bell peppers, or mushrooms, shredded raw napa cabbage, or carrots. I think of each and every one of these stalwarts as standard-issue Turkey Helper. These burgers get the Greek treatment with added spinach, garlic, and onions, all of it seasoned with crumbled feta and fresh oregano.

In search of a simpatico sauce, I built one out of yogurt, mayo, and pepperoncini—the little pickled green peppers that add heat to every Greek salad. Believe me, nobody in my house cries "Where's the beef?" when we pull these burgers off the grill.
"

CUBANO BURGERS

START TO FINISH: 45 MINUTES / **HANDS-ON TIME:** 45 MINUTES / **SERVINGS:** 4

Anyone convinced that there's no way to improve upon the grilled cheese sandwich has probably never tried a Cubano sandwich. Here's how they do it down in Florida: roast pork, ham, pickles, cheese, and mustard nestled together and grilled between two slices of Cuban bread. Oh. My. God. This recipe repurposes all of those elements, minus the bread (alas, it's tough to find real Cuban bread outside of Florida), and incorporates them into a burger.

The base is ground pork flavored with finely chopped ham and pickle. (If the only ground pork you can find happens to be lean, add several slices of finely chopped bacon to it.) Although I slather my bread with a mixture of mayo and Dijon mustard, yellow (aka. "ballpark") mustard is the Cubano standard. I'm not a fan, but by all means make the substitution if you prefer.

Why bother to grind meat at home? Because you can never know exactly what went into the ground beef or pork or turkey you buy at the supermarket; the mixture might contain any amount of random meat scraps. I prefer to be sure that my burger is made of 100 percent of the cut of meat that I've chosen (with no skin added).

Grinding meat at home also allows you to create your own custom burger blends or make your own sausage patties.

1 pound (not lean) ground pork (see below if you would like to grind your own)

4 ounces boiled ham, finely chopped

1/2 cup finely diced onion

1/4 cup very finely chopped dill pickle, plus 12 (1/4-inch-thick) lengthwise slices (2 to 3 whole pickles)

2 teaspoons chopped fresh oregano

2 teaspoons finely minced garlic

3/4 teaspoon ground cumin

1/2 teaspoon freshly grated orange zest

Freshly ground black pepper

2 tablespoons vegetable oil, preferably grapeseed

Kosher salt

4 slices Swiss cheese (about 3 ounces)

3 tablespoons Dijon mustard

3 tablespoons Homemade Mayonnaise (pages 52–53) or store-bought mayonnaise

8 slices rustic bread

› Combine the pork, ham, onion, chopped pickle, oregano, garlic, cumin, orange zest, and 1/2 teaspoon pepper in a large bowl and stir just until combined. Form the meat into 4 patties, each about 1/2 inch thick.

› Heat the oil in a large skillet over medium-high heat and reduce the heat to medium. Season the patties on both sides with salt and pepper and add them to the skillet; cook until they are almost cooked through but still pink inside, 1 to 2 minutes a side. Cover each burger with several slices of dill pickle (enough to cover the burger in one layer) and 1 slice of cheese, put a lid on the skillet, and cook the burger until the cheese melts, 1 minute more.

› While the burgers are cooking, combine the mustard and mayonnaise in a small bowl and toast the bread. Spread the mustard mayonnaise on the toast and transfer the cooked burgers to the toasts to make 4 burgers.

HOW TO GRIND YOUR OWN MEAT

If you happen to own a meat grinder or a stand mixer with a meat-grinding attachment (KitchenAid makes an excellent model), by all means read the instructions and use it.

If you're not the happy owner of one of these gadgets, here's what to do instead: Cut the meat into 1-inch cubes, and pop them into the freezer for about 30 minutes. Then, working in smallish batches, pulse the cubes in the food processor until they look properly ground. Be careful not to overdo it— you're making burgers, not mush.

GRILLED PORK TENDERLOIN
WITH WATERMELON-CUCUMBER SALSA
AND FETA DRESSING

START TO FINISH: 40 MINUTES / **HANDS-ON TIME:** 30 MINUTES / **SERVINGS:** 4

$^1\!/_2$ cup thinly sliced red onion

4 ounces feta cheese, crumbled, divided

$^1\!/_3$ cup low-fat buttermilk

$^1\!/_4$ cup Homemade Mayonnaise (pages 52–53) or store-bought mayonnaise (low-fat if you prefer)

1 tablespoon fresh lemon juice

1 tablespoon extra-virgin olive oil, plus extra for brushing the pork

Freshly ground black pepper

1 (1-pound) pork tenderloin, trimmed

Kosher salt

$1^1\!/_2$ cups $^1\!/_4$-inch cubed and seeded watermelon

$^3\!/_4$ cup $^1\!/_4$-inch cubed seedless cucumber

$^3\!/_4$ cup fresh mint leaves

$^3\!/_4$ cup fresh cilantro leaves

3 tablespoons fresh lime juice

Pita Crisps (page 305), optional

> Preheat the grill to medium. Set the sliced red onion to soak in ice water for 20 minutes (this will remove their "bite"). Drain and pat dry; set aside.

> Combine half of the feta, the buttermilk, mayonnaise, lemon juice, and olive oil in a blender and blend until smooth. Season with pepper and stir in the remaining feta. Set the dressing aside.

> Brush the pork lightly all over with some oil, season it lightly with salt and pepper, and grill it directly over the heat, giving it a quarter turn at a time, until a thermometer inserted at the thickest part registers 140°F for medium, about 2 minutes per side for a total of 8 minutes. Transfer the pork to a plate, cover it loosely with foil, and let it rest for 10 minutes.

> Toss together the onion, watermelon, cucumber, mint, cilantro, lime juice, and salt and pepper to taste.

> Place a mound of the salsa on each of 4 plates. Add the pork juices from the resting pork to the feta dressing, whisking to incorporate. Slice the pork crosswise into rounds $^1\!/_2$ inch thick and arrange a quarter of the slices on top of each serving. Spoon the dressing on top of the pork and divide the pita crisps among the plates, if using.

66

Here is the perfect summer meal on a plate, refreshing and filling at the same time. I thickened up the feta dressing with some buttermilk. It's my sly way of creating the creaminess we all want in a salad dressing without resorting to a ton of fat.

Homemade baked pita crisps top the dish. These are so easy to make that I never bother with packaged croutons, which are usually deep-fried and loaded with fat.

99

SAUTÉED PORK CHOPS
WITH CHORIZO-TOMATO SAUCE

START TO FINISH: I HOUR 45 MINUTES INCLUDING I HOUR PRESALTING
HANDS-ON TIME: 30 MINUTES / **SERVINGS:** 4

4 (1-inch-thick) boneless pork loin chops (6 to 7 ounces each)

Kosher salt

Wondra flour (see page 265) or all-purpose flour for dredging

3 tablespoons extra-virgin olive oil, divided

1 (4-ounce) piece Spanish chorizo (see Sources, page 350), quartered lengthwise and sliced thin crosswise

1½ cups thinly sliced onion

2 cups cherry tomatoes, halved (see page 181)

½ cup coarsely chopped fresh cilantro, optional

These days, much of the pork raised in the United States is bred to be so lean that pork chops are often dry and flavorless. Sure they're "healthier" than old-fashioned full-fat chops, but why bother to put a single forkful into your mouth if it has the taste and texture of leather?

This recipe demonstrates a couple of methods to ensure that your chops are juicy and the meat develops a nice crust when browned. It is best to salt the meat for an hour or so before cooking, but if you don't have the time, this recipe's flavorful sauce makes the dish plenty moist. (The Spanish pork sausage chorizo delivers the essence of porkiness.) A quick dip in flour before frying ensures a good crust. It's your choice to serve the chops whole or to slice them. Slicing them creates more surface area, and more surface area means that more of the meat is lavished with sauce.

You'll notice cilantro—one of those love-it-or-hate-it herbs—among the ingredients. If you're a hater, swap in some basil, which would also serve very nicely here.

> Season the pork chops on both sides with salt and let them stand, at room temperature, for 1 hour. If you don't have time, season the chops as far in advance as you can.

> Spread out the flour on a piece of parchment on the counter. Heat half the oil in a large skillet over high heat. Pat the chops dry, coat them lightly with the flour, lifting the parchment paper on both sides to help coat the pork, and shake off the excess. Reduce the heat to medium and add the chops to the pan. Sauté them for 2 to 3 minutes per side for medium and transfer them to a platter. Cover the chops with foil and let them rest while you make the sauce. (As they sit, the chops will continue to cook.)

> Remove the pan from the heat and let it cool slightly before adding the remaining oil and the chorizo. Cook over medium-low heat, stirring, until the chorizo releases its oil, 1 to 2 minutes. Transfer the chorizo with a slotted spoon to the other side of the platter with the pork. Measure the fat left in the skillet and pour off all but 2 tablespoons.

> Add the onion to the skillet and cook over medium heat, stirring, until the onion begins to brown, about 8 minutes. Add the tomatoes, ¼ cup water, and a pinch of salt, cover, and cook, stirring occasionally, until the tomatoes have softened and formed a chunky sauce, about 8 minutes. Add more water as necessary.

> Add the pork chops, the pork juices from the platter, and the chorizo to the skillet and cook, stirring, 1 minute. Transfer the chops to 4 plates (slicing them first, if you choose) and top each portion with some of the sauce and a sprinkling of cilantro, if using.

SAUTÉED HUNGARIAN PORK CHOPS

START TO FINISH: I HOUR 35 MINUTES INCLUDING I HOUR PRESALTING
HANDS-ON TIME: 30 MINUTES / **SERVINGS:** 4

4 (¹/₂-inch-thick) bone-in pork chops
  (2 to 2¹/₄ pounds)

Kosher salt

Wondra flour (see page 265) or all-
  purpose flour for dredging plus 1
  tablespoon for thickening the sauce

3 tablespoons vegetable oil, preferably
  grapeseed

2 tablespoons minced shallots

1¹/₂ tablespoons paprika, sweet, hot,
  or a mix

1 tablespoon caraway seeds

¹/₃ cup dry white wine

1 cup Homemade Chicken Stock
  (page 26) or store-bought chicken
  broth

¹/₃ cup sour cream

Freshly ground black pepper

Chopped fresh parsley or chives for
  garnish

› Pat the pork chops dry, season on all sides with ¹/₂ teaspoon salt, and let them stand, covered, at room temperature for 1 hour. If you don't have time, season the chops as far in advance as you can.

› Spread out the flour on a piece of parchment on the counter. Heat the oil in a large skillet over medium-high heat (use half the oil if working in batches). Working in 2 batches, if necessary, pat the chops dry, coat them lightly with the flour, lifting the parchment paper on both sides to help coat the pork, and shake off the excess. Reduce the heat to medium and add the chops to the pan. Cook 2 to 3 minutes per side for medium.

› Transfer the chops to a plate. Add the shallots, paprika, and caraway seeds to the pan, and cook, stirring, 1 minute. Add the wine and simmer, scraping up the brown bits from the bottom of the pan until the wine is reduced by half. Add the chicken stock to the pan and bring to a boil. Whisk together the 1 tablespoon flour with ¹/₄ cup water in a small bowl, add it to the sauce, whisking, and simmer for 2 minutes.

› Add the pork chops and any juices from the plate and simmer gently, turning the chops over several times, for 1 minute.

› Transfer the chops to 4 plates. Simmer the sauce until it reaches the desired consistency. Whisk in the sour cream and salt and pepper to taste and heat just until hot. Top each chop with some of the sauce and a sprinkling of parsley.

66

Another sautéed meat dish with a pan sauce, this recipe for pork follows the same rules as those for Sautéed Lemon Chicken with Fried Capers (see Cook's Notes, page 126).

Once upon a time, the specter of trichinosis in pork had us worrying about *under*cooking. Now that this problem has basically disappeared, the happy medium just to be safe (trichinosis is killed at an internal temp of 138°F) is to cook the chop to an internal temp of 140°F, which means it will still be pink inside even as any microscopic bugs are killed. A little extra flour stabilizes the sauce so that the sour cream can be heated without curdling.

The perfect accompaniments to this dish would be Sweet-and-Sour Shredded Beets (page 300) and the homemade German pasta called *spaetzle* (see page 66), but buttered egg noodles would be very nice, too.

99

COOK IT ON THE BONE

All animal protein—whether it's chicken, beef, pork, lamb, and even fish—tastes better when it's cooked on the bone. Bones also conduct heat within the meat, which allows it to cook more evenly and keeps it from drying out. It's more economical, too. You can always remove the bone afterward, if you prefer.

CLAIRE LEWIS'S QUICK TEXAS CHILI

START TO FINISH: 1 HOUR 15 MINUTES / **HANDS-ON TIME:** 30 MINUTES
SERVINGS: 4 TO 6 (MAKES 6 CUPS)

> For the most part, the recipes in this cookbook were tested by two stellar interns from New York's International Culinary Center. One of them is Claire Lewis, a native of Dallas. Although she's currently forsaken the Big D for the Big Apple, Claire remains as fond as ever of the cuisine of the Lone Star State. When I asked her to contribute a recipe of her own to the project, we agreed that it should be from Texas.
>
> Growing up, Claire ate this chili all the time. It was quick and easy and made everyone happy. Her mom used to whip up a batch before she went on trips, and then park it in the fridge for the family to help themselves. It's her dad's favorite dish.
>
> Simple as it is, this recipe comes with a couple of strict rules. Claire insists that there are NO BEANS in Texas chili, and she's equally adamant about what she calls "the accoutrements." Each is essential, especially the Fritos.

2 tablespoons vegetable oil, preferably grapeseed

2 pounds ground chuck (see page 138 if you would like to grind your own)

Kosher salt

2 cups finely chopped onion

1 cup finely chopped poblano

1 tablespoon minced garlic

3 tablespoons pure chile powder, preferably ancho

1½ tablespoons ground cumin

12 ounces Shiner bock beer (or any bock-style beer)

1 (28-ounce) can crushed tomatoes in tomato puree (see Note)

1 teaspoon liquid smoke

Cayenne

For topping the chili: Frito chips, lime wedges, sour cream, coarsely grated cheddar cheese, finely chopped raw onion, and Tabasco sauce

> Heat the oil in a large saucepan or Dutch oven over high heat. Add the ground chuck and 2 teaspoons salt, reduce the heat to medium-high, and cook, stirring and breaking up the meat, until lightly browned, about 6 minutes. Transfer the chuck with a slotted spoon to a bowl.

> Pour out and discard all but 2 tablespoons of the fat. Add the onion, poblano, and garlic to the pan and cook, stirring occasionally, until lightly golden, about 8 minutes. Add the chile powder, cumin, and ground chuck, and cook, stirring for 2 minutes.

> Add the beer, scraping up the brown bits from the bottom of the pot. Add the tomatoes and liquid smoke and bring to a boil. Reduce the heat and simmer, partly covered and stirring occasionally, 45 minutes.

> Season to taste with salt and cayenne. Spoon into bowls and serve with all the toppings.

Note: As an alternative to crushed tomatoes, you can combine 1 (15-ounce) can tomato puree and 1 (15-ounce) can whole tomatoes, crushed by hand.

SKILLET STEAK
WITH PICKLE SALSA VERDE

START TO FINISH: 35 MINUTES PLUS PRESALTING TIME / **HANDS-ON TIME:** 20 MINUTES / **SERVINGS:** 4

1¹/₂ pounds 1-inch-thick steaks, such as flat iron, tri-tip, or petite tender, (see page 153)

1¹/₂ teaspoons kosher salt

2 tablespoons finely chopped cornichons or other sour cucumber pickle

2 tablespoons finely chopped Quick Preserved Lemon Slices (page 47) or 2 teaspoons freshly grated lemon zest

1 tablespoon capers, rinsed, patted dry, and chopped

1 tablespoon minced shallots

1 tablespoon fresh lemon juice

1 teaspoon Dijon mustard

¹/₄ cup plus 2 tablespoons red pepper flakes, optional

¹/₄ cup plus 2 tablespoons olive oil, divided

1¹/₂ cups fresh parsley leaves, medium chopped

> Pat the steaks dry, season on all sides with the salt, cover, and chill for 4 hours. If you don't have time, season the steaks as far in advance as you can.

> Combine the cornichons, lemon, capers, shallots, lemon juice, mustard, and red pepper flakes, if using, with ¹/₄ cup of the oil and mix well. Add the parsley, toss well, and set the salsa aside.

> Pat the steaks dry. Heat the remaining 2 tablespoons oil in a large skillet over medium-high heat and reduce the heat to medium. Add the steaks and cook for 3 to 4 minutes per side for medium rare. Transfer to a plate, cover loosely with foil, and let rest for 8 minutes.

> Add the juices from the steak to the salsa. Slice the steak into ¹/₄-inch slices against the grain. Arrange one-fourth of the slices on each of 4 plates and top each portion with some of the salsa.

> "

M any cuisines feature their own version of green sauce, a sauce made of fresh chopped green herbs and flavorings. My salsa verde, loosely based on the Italian, features olive oil, parsley, and capers augmented with cornichons (or regular old sour pickles if you can't find cornichons) and chopped Quick Preserved Lemon Slices (page 47). The result, fresh and acidic, is the perfect counterpoint to a rich cut of meat. Pair this with Oven-Baked Creamy Polenta (page 310) and slices of fresh bread.

> "

HOW TO SEAR MEAT PROPERLY

If you want to get a beautiful brown crust on your steaks and chops, it is important to follow a few steps:

❿ Make sure the meat is patted dry on both sides. If it is wet it will steam, not sear.

❿ Make sure the skillet is well heated; it will cool down a bit when you add the meat and you need the heat to form the crust.

❿ Don't crowd the pan; the temperature will drop and the meat will steam.

❿ Don't try to turn the meat right away; let it sit undisturbed until it moves a little bit when you push it from the side. That's the indication that a crust has formed.

SEARED STEAK
WITH PEPPERCORN-COGNAC SAUCE

START TO FINISH: 35 MINUTES PLUS PRESALTING TIME / **HANDS-ON TIME:** 25 MINUTES / **SERVINGS:** 4

"
Steak *au poivre* is a French bistro classic, beloved for its rich and flavor-filled sauce. One of its key ingredients is beef or veal *demi-glace,* a rich brown sauce made by combining brown stock and *espagnole* sauce and reducing it by half. No self-respecting bistro is without it, but most of us are a little more lax about the need to keep a tub of the stuff in the fridge at home.

On the other hand, Homemade Brown Chicken Glace is a perfectly acceptable substitute. Infinitely less involved than traditional demi-glace, you can make it on a weekend and park it in the fridge or freezer for awhile.

Pair this steak with green beans and Hasselback Potatoes with Garlic Butter and Bacon (page 306).

Note: If you don't have Homemade Brown Chicken Glace in the fridge, you can use 1¹/₂ cups Homemade Brown Chicken Stock (page 27) or Homemade Chicken Stock (page 26), simmering the stock until it is reduced and thickened slightly before adding the mustard and cognac. You can also use 1 cup store-bought chicken broth, but you will need to thicken it after adding it to the skillet (it has no gelatin and will evaporate instead of reducing): Bring it to a boil in the skillet and whisk in 1 tablespoon cornstarch mixed with 2 tablespoons water.
"

1¹/₂ pounds 1-inch-thick steaks, such as flat iron, tri-tip, or petite tender (see page 153)

Kosher salt

2 tablespoons black peppercorns

2 tablespoons Clarified Butter (page 46) or vegetable oil, plus extra for brushing the steaks

2 tablespoons minced shallots

¹/₂ cup dry red wine

¹/₂ cup Homemade Brown Chicken Glace (page 27, or see headnote for alternatives)

2 teaspoons Dijon mustard

1 tablespoon cognac, optional

1 tablespoon unsalted butter

> Pat the steaks dry, season on all sides with 1¹/₂ teaspoons salt, cover, and chill for 4 hours. If you don't have time, season the steaks as far in advance as you can.

> Coarsely crush the peppercorns with a mortar and pestle or place them in a sturdy plastic bag and crush them using the bottom of a cast-iron skillet, meat pounder, or rolling pin. Spread the peppercorns evenly onto a plate. Pat the steaks dry, brush with some clarified butter or oil, and coat them on all sides with the peppercorns, pressing the peppercorns in.

> Heat the 2 tablespoons clarified butter in a large skillet over medium-high heat. Reduce the heat to medium, add the steaks, and cook for 3 to 4 minutes per side for medium rare. Transfer to a plate, cover loosely with foil, and let rest for 8 minutes. While the steaks are resting, make the pan sauce.

> Add the shallots to the skillet and cook over medium heat, stirring, 1 minute. Add the wine, bring to a boil, and simmer, scraping up the brown bits from the bottom of the pan, until almost all of the wine is reduced. Add the glace, ¹/₄ cup water, and any juices from the resting steak and bring to a simmer. Whisk in the mustard and cognac, if using. Add the butter and remove the sauce from the heat. Swirl the pan just until the butter is melted. Season with salt to taste.

> Slice the steak into ¹/₄-inch slices against the grain, arrange one-fourth of the slices on each of 4 plates, and top each portion with some of the sauce.

1. Some cuts of meat such as flank steak (shown here) can be eaten as a steak but must be sliced very thin and against the grain so that the meat is not too chewy.

2. Locate the grain (it's very obvious in these cuts) and cut across it and at an angle into very thin slices.

Cook's Notes: Discovering New Cuts of Beef

In the past few years, I've noticed new steaks at meat counters with names I've never heard before. I was intrigued not only by how this had come about (did someone discover a new part of the animal?) but also by the prices of these steaks, which were uniformly lower than the usual suspects.

At Brooklyn artisan butcher The Meat Hook, I got some clarification from one of their butchers, Sara Bigelow (above), and then followed up with a meat expert, Dr. Antonio Mata, to find out more about these new steaks. Antonio (Tony) Mata is a meat scientist, product development specialist, and self-proclaimed Meat Geek. In 1994, he started Mata & Associates, based in Texas, which consults with trade associations and restaurants.

Tony explained that for most of its history the U. S. beef industry has focused on the middle part of the carcass. However, Tony says, "Over the past several years, competitive pressures in the marketplace have forced the industry to explore areas of the beef carcass that had been previously ignored as potential sources of steaks, namely the chuck and the round." The chuck is the shoulder of the cow (above the brisket), while the round is the hind-quarter (behind the sirloin).

The five steaks on page 153 (with brief descriptions) are ones that Tony Mata recommends and thinks will become more and more available at the retail level. For more information about Tony and to learn about his latest steak discovery, the Vegas Strip Steak, visit meatgeek.com and VegasStripSteak.com.

NEW STEAKS ON THE BLOCK

1. Flat Iron
1 to 1¼ pounds
  • Great value
  • Very tender
  • Very juicy
  • Best when cooked to medium
  • Strong robust flavor

2. Denver Cut
3 to 8 ounces
  • Good value
  • Moderately tender
  • Sometimes labeled "Country Style Ribs" (Ask your Butcher. The term "Country Style Ribs" is loosely used in the industry.)

3. Chuck Eye (Delmonico)
6 to 8 ounces
  • Same muscles as in rib-eye steaks, every bit as tasty, and much more affordable

4. Petite Tender
8 to 12 ounces
  • Can be cut into medallions and cooked like steak
  • Moderately tender
  • Delicate flavor and texture

5. Tri-Tip (Bottom Sirloin)
4 to 10 ounces
  • Moderately tender
  • Triangular shape
  • Best grilled whole
  • Popular on the West Coast

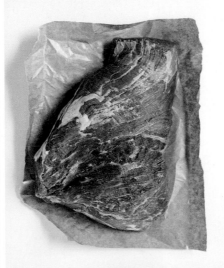

BEEF STROGANOFF BURGERS

START TO FINISH: 60 MINUTES / **HANDS-ON TIME:** 40 MINUTES / **SERVINGS:** 4

> It's not easy improving upon the all-American burger, but I've customized it here with porcini mushrooms, a stroke of inspiration suggested by Beef Stroganoff, a classic of Russian cuisine comprised of thin slices of pricey beef fillet topped with a sauce of sautéed mushrooms and sour cream. Call my burger a mutt if you must, but it's a delicious mutt and this healthy modern version delivers luxurious—even Stroganoffian—flavor using lean ground beef, soaked dried porcini, and low-fat sour cream.
>
> How'd I make moist burgers using lean ground beef? With the addition of caramelized onions and some of those mushrooms. In truth, though, the burgers are really just an excuse for the sauce. Made of caramelized onions, fresh cremini, and some porcini-soaking liquid, thickened with a tiny bit of flour, and finished with low-fat sour cream and Dijon mustard, this sauce—and the entire dish—is a mushroom lover's dream.

1 ounce dried porcini mushrooms (or shiitake, chanterelle, oyster, button, or a mix)

1½ cups Homemade Chicken Stock (page 26) or store-bought chicken broth

3 tablespoons vegetable oil, preferably grapeseed, divided

1 cup finely chopped onion

1 teaspoon minced garlic

4 ounces cremini mushrooms, sliced thin

1½ tablespoons all-purpose flour

¼ cup low-fat sour cream

2 teaspoons Dijon mustard

Kosher salt and freshly ground black pepper

1 pound ground round or ground sirloin (see page 138 if you would like to grind your own)

> Combine the porcini mushrooms with the stock in a small saucepan and bring the mixture to a boil. Cover and let stand, off the heat, until the mushrooms are soft, about 15 minutes. Strain the mixture through a strainer lined with a wet paper towel, reserving the liquid. Rinse the porcini mushrooms to rid them of any excess dirt and chop them.

> While the dried mushrooms are soaking, heat 1 tablespoon of the oil in a large nonstick skillet over medium heat. Reduce the heat to medium-low, add the onion, and cook, stirring occasionally, until the onion is golden brown, about 8 minutes. Add the garlic and cook, stirring, 1 minute. Using a slotted spoon, transfer half of the onion mixture to a medium bowl.

> Add 1 tablespoon of the oil and the cremini mushrooms to the skillet and cook, stirring, until the mushrooms give off all their liquid, about 4 minutes. Add the flour and cook, stirring, 1 minute. Add the reserved mushroom stock in a stream while whisking, bring it to a boil, reduce the heat, and simmer for 2 minutes. Whisk in the sour cream, mustard, and salt and pepper to taste. Transfer the sauce to a saucepan and keep warm. Wash the skillet and return it to the stove.

> Add the chopped porcinis to the onions in the bowl along with a hefty pinch of salt, black pepper to taste, and the ground beef. Mix well and form into 4 patties.

> In the cleaned skillet, heat the remaining 1 tablespoon oil over medium heat. Season the patties lightly with salt and pepper and cook to desired degree of doneness (3 minutes per side for rare and 5 for medium-well). Transfer the burgers to plates and pour some sauce over each one.

SPICED LAMB AND HUMMUS PITA PIZZAS
WITH HERB SALAD

START TO FINISH: 35 MINUTES / **HANDS-ON TIME:** 20 MINUTES / **SERVINGS:** 4

3 tablespoons extra-virgin olive oil, divided, plus extra for brushing the pitas

8 ounces ground lamb (see page 138 if you would like to grind your own)

Kosher salt

1/2 cup finely chopped onion

1 cup chopped plum tomatoes, with the juice and seeds

1 tablespoon minced garlic, plus 1 clove, cut in half

1 tablespoon fresh oregano, finely chopped

1 teaspoon ground cumin

1 teaspoon red pepper flakes

Freshly ground black pepper

4 (6-inch) pitas (whole, not split into rounds)

1 tablespoon fresh lemon juice

2 cups fresh parsley leaves

2 cups fresh cilantro leaves

1 cup plain hummus

> Preheat the oven to 350°F. Heat 1 tablespoon of the oil in a large skillet over high heat. Add the lamb and a pinch of salt, reduce the heat to medium, and cook, stirring and breaking up the meat, until lightly browned, about 3 minutes. Transfer the lamb with a slotted spoon to a bowl. Add 1 tablespoon of the oil, the onion, and a hefty pinch of salt to the pan, and cook, stirring occasionally, until golden, about 8 minutes. Add the tomatoes and cook, stirring occasionally for 3 minutes. Add the minced garlic, oregano, cumin, and red pepper flakes and cook, stirring, 1 minute. Return the lamb to the pan along with 2 tablespoons water and cook, covered, 2 to 3 minutes. Add salt and black pepper to taste.

> Meanwhile, arrange the pitas in a single layer on a baking sheet, brush them lightly with oil, and bake on the middle shelf of the oven until crisped, 8 to 10 minutes. Whisk the lemon juice with salt and pepper to taste in a medium bowl until the salt is dissolved. Whisk in the remaining 1 tablespoon oil, add the parsley and cilantro, and toss well.

> Transfer 1 pita to each of 4 plates. Rub the surface of each pita with the cut garlic clove and sprinkle it lightly with salt. Top each pita with one-fourth of the hummus, one-fourth of the lamb mixture, and one-fourth of the herb mixture.

This is my favorite kind of entrée because there are several layers of flavors and textures. You start with a crispy pita, spread it with a creamy hummus, top it with a spicy lamb mixture, and finish it with lemony fresh herbs. Everyone gets their own little pita pizza.

If you're not a fan of lamb, you can swap in ground beef or pork. If you have the time, you might make the spiced lamb mixture in advance, as much as a full day ahead. Then there's nothing to do but reheat it, which takes no time at all. And as an added benefit, the flavor will have become even deeper.

For hummus, just pick your favorite store-bought brand (there are lots of good ones available), but do not skimp on the fresh herbs. They brighten up the whole dish and should be added more frequently to any salad, especially now that they are so widely available. That said, if you were born with the anti-cilantro gene, you're welcome to substitute basil or mint. (Sounds weird, but it's a matter of fact. There really is a gene that makes people hate cilantro.)

SAUTÉED LAMB CHOPS
WITH WARM CAESAR SALAD SAUCE

START TO FINISH: 35 MINUTES / **HANDS-ON TIME:** I5 MINUTES / **SERVINGS:** 4

I'm a lifelong fan of lamb and lamb chops—all that sweet meat close to the bone, in particular. Unfortunately, rib and loin lamp chops are quite pricey. That's why, for this recipe, I've switched to blade and round bone chops from the shoulder. They're not quite as tender as the other chops, but they're tender enough, equally flavorful, and far more affordable.

This recipe is all about the dynamic combination of meat and acid—lemon juice, in this case, which, along with garlic and anchovy, flavors the salad of wilted bitter greens that are mounded on top of the chops. My green of first choice is escarole, if you can find it, which retains a nice crunch even after wilting. But I also love dandelion greens, not to mention that old stand-by, romaine.

This is a quick and easy recipe, requiring only 15 minutes of hands-on time, yet it tastes like restaurant fare. Serve it with Baked Tomatoes Puttanesca (page 289).

3 tablespoons extra-virgin olive oil, divided

4 (½-inch-thick) lamb shoulder or round bone chops

Kosher salt and freshly ground black pepper

4 anchovy fillets, chopped

2 tablespoons minced shallots

1 teaspoon minced garlic

¼ cup Homemade Chicken Stock (page 26) or store-bought chicken broth

2 tablespoons fresh lemon juice

4 cups chopped escarole, dandelion greens (tough stems removed), or romaine

1 ounce freshly grated Parmigiano-Reggiano

› Heat 1 tablespoon of the oil in a large skillet over medium-high heat, reduce the heat to medium, and add 2 of the lamb chops, sprinkled with salt and pepper. Sauté until lightly browned on both sides, 5 to 6 minutes total for medium-rare. Transfer to a plate and cover loosely with aluminum foil. Repeat with the remaining 2 chops in the oil remaining in the pan.

› Reduce the heat to medium-low, add 1 tablespoon of the oil, the anchovies, shallots, and garlic and cook, stirring, 1½ minutes. Add the chicken stock and lemon juice and cook, scraping up the brown bits on the bottom of the pan, 1 minute. Add the remaining 1 tablespoon oil, the escarole, and salt and pepper to taste and cook, stirring until the greens are slightly wilted, about 2 minutes. Add the juices from the resting lamb and remove from the heat.

› Transfer the chops to each of 4 plates and top each chop with one-fourth of the dressed wilted greens and the cheese.

5 *meal in* A PAN

There are many advantages to making a complete meal in a pan, whether that pan is a skillet, baking dish, or baking sheet. First of all, since you are making just one dish, there is no need to juggle disparate components to make a meal. One of the biggest issues home cooks have shared with me is timing: How to get everything on the table at the same time. A one-dish dinner eliminates that problem.

And there's a special kind of magic that happens when you combine several different components in a single pan. The result is a unique exchange of flavors, as in such dishes as Indian Cauliflower Stew with Crispy Chickpeas, Duck Confit with Braised Leeks and Sauerkraut, and Skillet Borscht with Meatballs (pictured opposite).

The perfect tutorial for building flavors in one pan is illustrated by Floyd Cardoz's Goan Shrimp Curry with Okra, which will introduce you to several key Indian ingredients and techniques on the way to the luscious finished product. Combining Chinese flavors is my buddy Grace Young's domain. She'll lay out all the steps for successful stir-frying with her Stir-Fried Beef with Broccoli and Red Peppers.

Another beauty of one-dish meals is that they can be built on items you have prepared ahead on the weekend or even leftovers, for example Barley with Clam Sauce; Sausage, White Bean, and Broccoli Rabe Stew; and Green Chile Rice and Chicken Skillet Dinner.

Finally, how nice it is, at the end of the meal, to have just one pan to wash.

INDIAN CAULIFLOWER STEW
WITH CRISPY CHICKPEAS

" Indian vegetarian cuisine is one of my all-time favorites. The layers of flavors and textures are so complex and exciting that even The Husband (a fairly unrepentant meathead) is a fan.

This dish is a seductive example. Although Indian food varies widely across the country's many regions, this cauliflower and potato stew is deeply flavored with spices and chiles typical of pan-Indian cuisine. The chickpeas are coated in their own spice mixture and provide a lovely contrasting crunch. In fact, they are good enough to stand on their own as a snack; put them out on the table in front of the TV during one of those endless football Sundays and watch them disappear like magic.

If you have found the time during the weekend to cook up a batch of grains (see page 34)—be it farro, wheat berries, or barley—you can swap them in for the basmati rice. "

START TO FINISH: 1 HOUR 10 MINUTES / **HANDS-ON TIME:** 40 MINUTES / **SERVINGS:** 4

For the stew:

¹/₄ cup Ghee (page 46) or vegetable oil, preferably grapeseed, divided

1 large russet potato (12 to 14 ounces), peeled and cut into ¹/₂-inch chunks

5 cups 1-inch cauliflower florets (about 1¹/₄ pounds)

Kosher salt

1 teaspoon mustard seeds

1 cup finely chopped onion

1¹/₂ tablespoons minced ginger

2 teaspoons minced garlic

1 finely chopped serrano chile with seeds

¹/₂ teaspoon turmeric

1¹/₂ cups Homemade Vegetable Stock (page 29) or store-bought vegetable broth

For the chickpeas:

2 tablespoons Ghee (page 46) or vegetable oil, preferably grapeseed

1¹/₂ cups cooked chickpeas (see page 36) or 1 (15-ounce) can chickpeas, rinsed, drained, and patted very dry

1 teaspoon smoked paprika

1 teaspoon cumin

¹/₂ teaspoon kosher salt

¹/₄ teaspoon cayenne

Basmati rice as an accompaniment

Coarsely chopped fresh cilantro and finely chopped scallions for garnish

> Preheat the oven to 450°F.

> **Make the stew:** Heat 2 tablespoons of the ghee in a large nonstick or stick-resistant skillet over medium-high heat. Add the potato to the skillet and cook, stirring occasionally, until the potato is golden brown on all sides, about 10 minutes. Transfer the potato with a slotted spoon to a bowl.

> Add 1 tablespoon of the ghee, the cauliflower, and a hefty pinch of salt to the skillet and cook, stirring, until the cauliflower is golden brown around the edges but not cooked through, about 14 minutes. Transfer the cauliflower with a slotted spoon to the bowl with the potato.

> Add the last tablespoon of the ghee and the mustard seeds to the skillet, and cook until fragrant (about 30 seconds—careful, they may pop, so have a lid handy to cover the skillet). Quickly add the onion and cook, stirring occasionally, until the onion is golden brown, about 8 minutes. Add the ginger, garlic, and serrano and cook, stirring, 2 minutes. Add the turmeric, 1/2 teaspoon salt, the cauliflower, potato, and the stock and bring the mixture to a boil. Reduce to a simmer, cover, and cook until both the cauliflower and potato are tender, about 10 minutes.

> **Meanwhile, make the chickpeas:** Pour the ghee into a rimmed baking sheet and place it on the middle shelf of the oven to heat for 3 minutes. Combine the chickpeas, paprika, cumin, salt, and cayenne in a bowl and toss well. Add the chickpeas to the baking sheet and stir to coat with the hot ghee. Bake until the chickpeas are crisp, about 20 minutes (be careful, they may pop when they come out of the oven). Transfer to paper towels with a slotted spoon and let cool.

> Spoon some rice onto each of 4 plates, top with the stew and chickpeas, and garnish with cilantro and scallions.

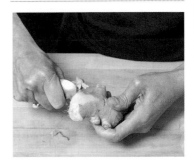

PEELING GINGER WITH A SPOON

With all its bumps and nobs, it can be difficult to remove the skin from fresh ginger using a peeler or a knife—but a spoon works perfectly. Simply slip the edge of the spoon under the skin and use it to push the skin away from the root. This method also keeps more of the ginger intact.

MUSHROOM AND LEEK SHEPHERD'S PIE

"

I grew up with my mom's very tasty version of shepherd's pie. She took advantage of leftover lamb stew and mashed potatoes and turned them into a second spectacular meal that was one of my favorites. And I have always loved the idea of re-purposing mashed potatoes, especially as a crust.

I think you'll be very pleasantly surprised by this meatless rendition of the Irish pub classic. It's an ode to mushrooms—with a potato topping—in which fresh mushrooms are married to dried porcinis and porcini stock. The finishing flavor touch is a spritz of truffle oil. If you're a mushroom lover, this one's for you.

"

START TO FINISH: 2 HOURS / **HANDS-ON TIME:** 1½ HOURS / **SERVINGS:** 6

1 ounce dried porcini mushrooms

2¼ cups Homemade Vegetable Stock (page 29), Homemade Chicken Stock (page 26), or store-bought vegetable or chicken broth

7 tablespoons unsalted butter, divided

4 medium leeks, trimmed of green part, halved lengthwise, cut into 1-inch lengths crosswise, washed, and dried

2 teaspoons minced garlic

Kosher salt

1 pound russet potatoes, peeled and cut into 1-inch chunks

Freshly ground black pepper

1 pound assorted fresh mushrooms, trimmed and quartered or sliced

2 teaspoons chopped fresh thyme

1 tablespoon tomato paste

3 tablespoons all-purpose flour

⅓ cup dry red wine

2 teaspoons truffle oil

An egg wash made by beating 1 egg with 1 tablespoon water

2 tablespoons freshly grated Parmigiano-Reggiano

> Preheat the oven to 375°F and arrange one of the racks in the upper third.

> Combine the porcini mushrooms with the stock in a small saucepan and bring the mixture to a boil. Cover and let stand, off the heat, until the mushrooms are soft, about 15 minutes. Strain the mixture through a strainer lined with a wet paper towel, reserving the stock. Clean the porcini mushrooms to rid them of any excess dirt and chop them. Set them aside.

> While the dried mushrooms are soaking, melt 2 tablespoons of the butter in a large skillet over medium heat. Reduce the heat to medium-low, add the leeks, garlic, and a hefty pinch of salt, and cover them with a round of parchment (see page 265) and a lid. Cook, stirring occasionally, until the leeks are very soft, 12 to 15 minutes.

> Meanwhile, combine the potatoes and 2 teaspoons salt in a large saucepan and cover with water by 1 inch. Bring to a boil, reduce the heat, and simmer until tender, 10 to 12 minutes. Drain well. Return to the pan, stir in 3 tablespoons of the butter and salt and pepper to taste, and mash coarsely.

> Transfer the leeks from the skillet to a bowl. Add the remaining 2 tablespoons butter, the fresh mushrooms, thyme, and a hefty pinch of salt to the skillet. Cook over medium heat, stirring occasionally, until most of the liquid released by the mushrooms is evaporated, about 8 minutes.

> Add the tomato paste and cook, stirring, 1 minute. Add the porcini, leeks, flour, and 1/2 teaspoon pepper and cook, stirring, 3 minutes. Whisk in the reserved stock and the wine and bring the mixture to a boil. Reduce the heat to a simmer and cook, covered, 10 minutes. Add the truffle oil and salt and pepper to taste and transfer to a 10-inch pie plate or round casserole dish.

> Spoon the potatoes over the entire surface of the filling, spreading them evenly. Brush the topping with the egg wash and sprinkle with the cheese. Transfer to the oven and bake until the pie is bubbling, about 15 minutes. Increase the oven temperature to broil, and cook on a shelf set 4 inches from the heat until the potatoes are golden brown, 3 to 4 minutes. Let stand for 15 minutes before serving.

A QUICKER WAY TO CLEAN MUSHROOMS

In cooking school, we learned that a fresh mushroom should never be washed but wiped with a damp paper towel, one at a time. The justification for this rule was that a washed mushroom became water-logged. I dutifully did as I was taught for several years, spending what felt like an eternity cleaning 5-pound baskets of white mushrooms.

Then I had the chance to do an apprenticeship in France, and if I learned nothing else, it was a speedy way to clean mushrooms. We did it by throwing the mushrooms, a handful at a time, into a large bowl of water, tossing them around briefly, then lifting them out and transferring them to a colander or kitchen towel. The brief bath cleaned the mushrooms without doing them any harm. (Portobellos are the exception. I still wipe them clean with a damp paper towel one at a time.)

STUFFED EGG ROULADE
WITH PROSCIUTTO, SPINACH, AND ROASTED RED PEPPER

START TO FINISH: 60 MINUTES / **HANDS-ON TIME:** 60 MINUTES / **SERVINGS:** 6 TO 8

5 tablespoons unsalted butter, plus extra for greasing the pan

6 tablespoons all-purpose flour, plus extra for dusting the pan

1¼ cups whole milk, heated

6 large egg whites and 4 large egg yolks, at room temperature

Kosher salt and freshly ground black pepper

Pinch of cream of tartar

2 tablespoons extra-virgin olive oil

10 ounces baby spinach

1 teaspoon minced garlic

8 ounces coarsely grated young Italian fontina or Gruyère cheese (about 2 cups)

3 ounces thinly sliced prosciutto

¾ cup medium chopped roasted red pepper

> Preheat the oven to 350°F. Line a buttered 15- x 10- x 1-inch rimmed baking sheet with parchment paper, letting it overhang by about 1 inch at each short edge. Butter the paper, dust with flour, and tap out the excess.

> Melt the 5 tablespoons butter in a small saucepan over medium heat. Add the flour and cook, stirring, 3 minutes. Add the milk in a stream, whisking, while you bring the mixture to a boil. Reduce to a simmer and cook for 5 minutes. Transfer the mixture to a large bowl and whisk in the egg yolks, one at a time. Stir in ½ teaspoon kosher salt and ¼ teaspoon black pepper.

> Beat the egg whites in a separate bowl with a pinch of cream of tartar and a pinch of salt, until they form soft peaks. Stir one-fourth of the whites into the yolk mixture, and then fold in the rest, gently but thoroughly (see page 344). Pour the batter into the prepared pan and smooth gently with a metal spatula. Bake on the middle shelf of the oven, turning the pan around half way through the cooking time, until golden and firm to the touch, about 15 minutes. Set the baking sheet on a rack to cool slightly.

> You can make the egg sponge up to this point, and then refrigerate it overnight or freeze it, well-wrapped first in plastic, then in foil, for up to 1 month. Defrost it in the refrigerator, and then heat it up slightly before proceeding with the filling. To do so, put the egg sponge back in the rimmed baking sheet, parchment side down, and then place the pan over two stovetop burners on low heat for just a couple minutes.

(recipe continues)

> 66
>
> Think of this roulade—a soufflé-like sheet of baked egg—as a one-stop omelet for eight. I learned how to make egg roulades when I worked in the test kitchen at *Gourmet* and now often make them for a crowd at home. An egg roulade will hold just about any filling you're in the mood for (although I always like to include cheese).
>
> Whichever fillings you use, be sure to cook any vegetables first to rid them of excess water. You don't want a wet filling. Here, I've chosen a savory filling of prosciutto, spinach, and cheese. You can bake the egg sponge ahead of time, and then store it overnight in the refrigerator or even freeze it.
>
> The only tricky part about making a roulade is getting the egg sponge to roll evenly around your chosen fillings. A damp towel is key here. Like the reed mat used to form sushi rolls, the towel helps to lift up the egg sponge completely and uniformly and to roll it tightly (see the photographs on page 169).
>
> 99

> Meanwhile, while the egg sponge is baking, heat the oil in a large skillet over medium-high heat. Add half of the spinach and cook, stirring until it starts to wilt, then add the remaining spinach and cook until all the spinach has wilted. Add the garlic and cook, stirring, 1 minute. Transfer the mixture to a colander, pressing lightly on the spinach to drain any excess liquid. Season with salt and pepper to taste.

> Increase the oven to 375°F. Cover the egg sponge with a buttered sheet of parchment paper, buttered side down. Cover with a damp kitchen towel and invert the sponge onto a work surface. Peel off the paper from the top.

> Sprinkle the cheese over the sponge, leaving a $^1/_2$-inch border on all sides. Lay the prosciutto in one layer on top, followed by the spinach. Arrange the roasted pepper in one line across the center (starting and ending at the short sides). Starting with one of the longer sides, use the towel to help roll up the sponge, enclosing the filling, jelly-roll fashion. Carefully pick up the roulade and place it seam side down on the baking sheet. Bake in the middle of the oven until the cheese has melted, 8 to 10 minutes. Use a serrated knife to cut the roulade crosswise into $^1/_2$-inch-thick slices.

HOW TO UNMOLD AND ROLL THE ROULADE

1. Cover the egg sponge with a buttered sheet of parchment paper, buttered side down. Then lay a damp kitchen towel on top.

2. Invert the sponge onto a work surface so the towel is on the bottom. Peel off the parchment paper that lined the pan.

3. Sprinkle the cheese over the sponge, leaving a ½-inch border on all sides. Lay the prosciutto in a single layer on top.

4. Follow with the spinach. Arrange the roasted pepper in one line across the center (starting and ending at the short sides).

5. Starting with one of the longer sides, use the towel to help roll up the sponge, enclosing the filling, jellyroll fashion.

6. Now the roulade is ready to be transported, seam side down, to a baking sheet.

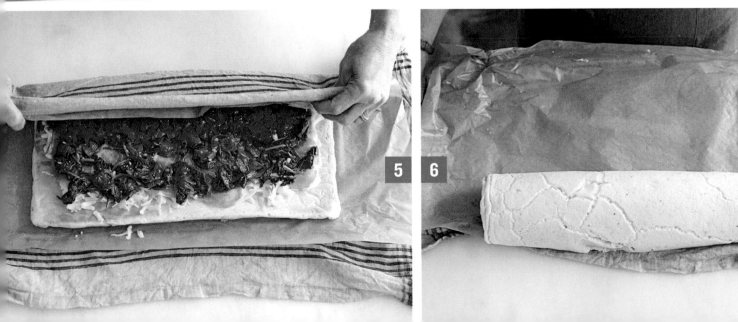

GREEK SHRIMP, FARRO, AND GREENS WITH FETA

START TO FINISH: 50 MINUTES / **HANDS-ON TIME:** 40 MINUTES / **SERVINGS:** 4

"

This whole meal is cooked in stages in one pan, and then finished in the oven. If you simply tossed all the ingredients into the pan at the same time, the shrimp would end up rubbery, the greens watery, and the flavor dull. You could use a separate pan for each ingredient, but why dirty extra pans when it's not necessary?

Saving and boiling down all the collected cooking juices from the various ingredients before adding them to the farro amps up the flavor in the final dish.

By the way, this dish sparkles in concert with whichever cooked grain you have in the house: brown rice, barley, wheat berries, and so on (see page 34), not to mention white rice left over from Chinese take-out.

"

¼ cup extra-virgin olive oil, divided

12 ounces peeled and deveined jumbo shrimp (16/20)

1 cup finely chopped onion

Kosher salt

1 tablespoon minced garlic

1 cup halved cherry tomatoes (see page 181)

2 teaspoons red pepper flakes

10 ounces baby spinach, torn kale, or torn mustard greens

Freshly ground black pepper

½ cup dry white wine

2 cups cooked farro

1 tablespoon chopped fresh oregano

4 ounces feta cheese, crumbled

1 cup Homemade Chicken Stock (page 26) or store-bought chicken broth

> Preheat the oven to 400°F. Heat 1½ tablespoons of the oil in a large skillet with an ovenproof handle over high heat. Add the shrimp and cook, undisturbed, until the shrimp turns golden, 1 minute. Turn them over and cook on the other side until barely golden, about 1 minute more (the shrimp should not be cooked through). Transfer the shrimp with tongs to a colander set over a bowl.

> Add another tablespoon of the oil to the skillet, reduce the heat to medium-low, and add the onion along with a hefty pinch of salt. Cook the onion, stirring occasionally, until it is golden, about 10 minutes. Add the garlic, tomatoes, and red pepper flakes and cook, stirring, 1 minute. Transfer the mixture to the colander with the shrimp.

> Increase the heat to high, add the remaining 1½ tablespoons oil and half the greens, and cook, stirring, until they start to wilt. Add the remaining greens, and continue cooking until all the greens are wilted. Add salt and black pepper to taste and transfer the greens to the colander that the shrimp are in and shake it to get as much cooking liquid from the colander into the bowl as possible.

> Add the wine and the cooking liquid from the bowl underneath the colander to the skillet and boil until the mixture is reduced to a few tablespoons. And the farro, oregano, half the feta, and the stock to the skillet and bring to a boil. Stir in all the ingredients from the colander and push the shrimp down slightly into the farro. Top the shrimp with the remaining crumbled feta and transfer the pan to the oven. Bake for 10 minutes or until the cheese is melted. Serve immediately.

Cooking with **Floyd Cardoz**

GOAN SHRIMP CURRY WITH OKRA

Adapted from *One Spice, Two Spice* (William Morrow, 2006).

START TO FINISH: 2 HOURS 40 MINUTES PLUS EXTRA TIME IF YOU ARE OPENING AND GRATING FRESH COCONUT / **HANDS-ON TIME:** 30 MINUTES / **SERVINGS:** 6

1½ cups roughly chopped white onion

1½ cups grated fresh coconut (see page 175) or frozen coconut

5 garlic cloves, peeled

1 tablespoon coriander seeds

1½ teaspoons cumin seeds

3 small dried red chiles (see Notes, page 174)

1 tablespoon sweet paprika

½ teaspoon ground turmeric

1 tablespoon vegetable oil, preferably grapeseed

4 cups Quick Shrimp Stock (see Notes, page 174) or water, divided

1 serrano chile, or more to taste, slit down one side

30 jumbo shrimp (16/20), peeled and deveined, heads left on if desired

Sea salt

2 tablespoons Tamarind Paste (page 174)

½ pound okra, trimmed (see page 174)

1 (13- to 14-ounce) can coconut milk (1¾ cups), stirred well

> Combine the onion, coconut, garlic, and ½ cup water in a blender and puree until smooth, starting at low speed and increasing to high. If necessary to keep the blades moving, add a little more water.

> Finely grind the coriander seeds, cumin seeds, and dried red chiles together in an electric coffee/spice grinder. Transfer to a small bowl or plate and combine with the paprika and turmeric.

> Heat the oil in a 4- to 6-quart pan over medium high heat until it shimmers and add the spice blend and coconut puree. Put 3 cups of the stock into the (uncleaned) blender and pulse to blend any residual puree. Add that mixture to the puree in the pan along with the serrano chile. Bring the sauce to a boil, stirring occasionally.

> Cook the sauce over medium high heat, stirring occasionally, until it is the consistency of thick paste, 15 to 20 minutes. (Do not let it scorch.) While the sauce is reducing, season the shrimp with salt and let them sit for about 20 minutes.

(recipe continues)

> Floyd Cardoz says this was his favorite curry as a child spending summers in the Indian state of Goa—and if it was good enough for Floyd, it's good enough for me. I always loved Tabla, the ground-breaking Indian-fusion New York restaurant where he served as chef until 2010. But when I booked Floyd onto my show, I was introduced to his skills as a teacher; he patiently attempted to teach yours truly, who is seriously rice-impaired, how to make basmati rice. A brave man.
>
> This recipe teaches so many techniques: how to make a quick shrimp stock, how to open a coconut, how to cook a fresh coconut puree, and the importance of seasoning shrimp before cooking it and using whole spices for better flavor. It's time-consuming, but so tasty—and you'll be so much wiser after making it.
>
> Floyd notes that this curry has a gentle heat that builds. If you want a spicier curry, add more dried red chile. Serve this with plain basmati rice or other cooked white rice.

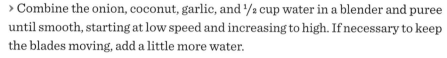

Use a sharp paring knife to trim the tops of the okra and cut off the brown tip of the tails.

> Stir the remaining 1 cup stock, the tamarind paste, and okra into the sauce and bring to a simmer. Simmer the mixture until the okra is barely tender, about 3 minutes. Stir in the coconut milk and bring the sauce to a boil. Add the shrimp and simmer until the shrimp are just cooked through, about 3 minutes. Season with salt before serving.

Notes: "Small dried red chile" refers to the cayenne type, about 2 inches long. Avoid the tiny Thai or bird chiles; they are too fiery. Floyd also likes dried pasilla de Oaxaca chiles for their mellow smokiness, or a mix of New Mexico and chipotle chiles. He also advises that if you ever see Kashmiri chiles, grab them; they are a true taste of India.

To make **Quick Shrimp Stock,** cover your shrimp shells with 4 cups cold water. Bring to a boil, and simmer, uncovered, 30 minutes. Strain the liquid through a sieve into a bowl, pressing hard on the shells with the back of a ladle, and use the liquid as stock.

TAMARIND PASTE

START TO FINISH: 1 HOUR 20 MINUTES / **HANDS-ON TIME:** 20 MINUTES / **MAKES:** ABOUT 2½ CUPS

¹⁄₂ pound tamarind (not concentrated) from 1 (1-pound) block (see Sources, page 351)

Tear off chunks of the tamarind pulp and put them in a 1-quart pan. Add 3 cups water and simmer, uncovered, for 30 to 35 minutes, mashing the pulp against the side of the pan with the back of a spatula or wooden spoon occasionally to help it soften.

Let the tamarind sit in the water off the heat for 30 minutes.

Strain the tamarind through a ricer or sieve into a bowl, pressing hard on the solids with the back of a wooden spoon.

Use your fingers to work the pulp free of seeds and fibers. Transfer the strained pulp back to the pan, taking care to include the pulp clinging to the underside of the ricer or sieve. If the paste is very thick, add 1 to 2 tablespoons more water, and bring the mixture to a vigorous boil.

Cool the paste completely and transfer to a glass jar or plastic tub. The tamarind paste keeps in the refrigerator for 1 month or in the freezer for 3 months and adds a nice touch of acid to any stew or soup.

HOW TO CRACK A FRESH COCONUT TO GET TO THE MEAT

1. Find the softest eye of the coconut and pierce it with a screwdriver.

2. You may need to use a hammer to help you. Then pierce a second eye, which will make the liquid pour out more easily.

3. Pour the coconut water into a bowl.

4. Bake the coconut in the middle of a preheated 400°F oven for about 15 minutes. If the coconut shell doesn't crack in the oven, break the shell with a hammer, rotating the coconut as you hit it.

5. The shell should fall off cleanly.

6. Remove the brown skin with a vegetable peeler.

BAKED ARCTIC CHAR
WITH ASPARAGUS, POTATOES, AND HERB BUTTER

START TO FINISH: 50 MINUTES / **HANDS-ON TIME:** 30 MINUTES / **SERVINGS:** 4

1½ bunches asparagus (about 1½ pounds), tough ends discarded and stems peeled if thicker than ⅓-inch

2 tablespoons olive oil, divided

Kosher salt and freshly ground black pepper

1¼ pounds Yukon gold or large boiling potatoes, sliced crosswise ¼ inch thick (leave the peel on)

1½ pounds arctic char (or other skinless fish fillets), cut into 4 portions

1 tablespoon fresh lemon juice

4 tablespoons Herb Butter (page 43), at room temperature

> Preheat the oven to 450°F. Toss the asparagus with 2 teaspoons of the oil and salt and pepper on a rimmed baking sheet and arrange them in a single layer. Bake them on the top rack of the oven until they are starting to brown and are crisp-tender, about 3 minutes for thin asparagus; 7 minutes for medium-thick asparagus. Transfer them to a plate and set aside.

> Toss the potatoes with 2 teaspoons of the oil and salt and pepper on the baking sheet and arrange them in a single layer. Bake the potatoes on the top rack of the oven, until they are barely golden, about 10 minutes.

> Remove the baking sheet from the oven and reduce the oven temperature to 400°F. Arrange the fish pieces in a single layer on top of the potatoes, sprinkle them with the lemon juice, drizzle them with the remaining 2 teaspoons oil, and season them with salt and pepper. Return the pan to the middle shelf of the oven and bake for 5 minutes. Add the asparagus to the pan and bake 2 to 3 minutes more or until the fish is just cooked through (see How Do You Know When Fish is Cooked?, page 239). Place one-fourth of the potatoes and asparagus on each of 4 plates. Transfer the fish to the plates and top each serving with a tablespoon of butter, and serve immediately.

" You can cook everything for this meal on a single rimmed baking sheet, but the trick here is to order each ingredient's turn on the pan so that, for example, the asparagus isn't incinerated while the potatoes are becoming tender.

Now let's talk asparagus. It's available in a range of thicknesses—pencil thin to wide-body—and I love them all. If you purchase some of the thin guys, which are less than ⅓-inch thick, don't bother peeling them. Just cut off an inch or two of the woody bottom. If they're thicker, peel each stalk from just under the head to the bottom. These preparations ensure that each stalk will cook evenly and be tender from head to toe.

This recipe's finishing touch is the herb butter. If you don't have the time to make it (or have none stashed away in the freezer), simply place a pat of regular old butter on top of the fish, along with an extra spritz of lemon and some chopped fresh herbs. "

BARLEY WITH CLAM SAUCE

START TO FINISH: 55 MINUTES / **HANDS-ON TIME:** 30 MINUTES / **SERVINGS:** 4

> "

*S*paghetti with Clams—*Spaghetti alle Vongole* to the Italians—is one of my favorite dishes: simple, flavorful, and satisfying. But really, it's hard to lose with clams, which spontaneously generate their own savory sauce as they're being cooked. All you have to do is steam them in a little liquid. When the shells open, the clam liqueur streams out, ready to glorify whatever it's added to.

In this case, I went in search of an alternative to white flour spaghetti, and settled on barley. Yes, barley takes longer to cook than spaghetti, but if you plan ahead and cook up a bunch of whole grains on the weekend, you'll have your barley ready to go.

If you can't find fresh fennel or just don't like it (not everyone's a fan of its slight scent of licorice), you can leave it out or replace it with some celery or leeks.

I've finished off this dish with one of my favorite little garnishes: sautéed breadcrumbs. They may sound ho-hum, but they're anything but. Once you make this recipe the first time, you might decide that there's hardly any dish that isn't improved when you sprinkle sautéed breadcrumbs on top.

"

⅓ cup panko breadcrumbs

3 tablespoons plus 2 teaspoons extra-virgin olive oil, divided

Kosher salt

1½ cups medium chopped fresh fennel bulb

1 cup finely chopped onion

1 tablespoon minced garlic

1 teaspoon red pepper flakes

½ cup dry white wine

2 cups cherry tomatoes, halved (see page 181)

3 dozen littleneck clams, scrubbed well

3 cups cooked pearl barley (see page 34)

⅓ cup chopped fresh flat-leaf parsley

> Combine the breadcrumbs, 2 teaspoons of the oil, and a pinch of salt in a small skillet. Cook over medium heat, stirring constantly, until golden brown, 2 to 3 minutes. Let cool.

> Heat the remaining 3 tablespoons oil over medium heat in a large saucepan or Dutch oven. Reduce the heat to medium-low, add the fennel and onion, and cook, stirring occasionally, until lightly browned, about 10 minutes. Add the garlic and red pepper flakes and cook, stirring, 1 minute. Add the wine, tomatoes, and clams and cover tightly. Steam over high heat, lifting the lid every so often to transfer opened clams to a bowl, 5 to 10 minutes. Discard any clams that don't open.

> Add the barley to the clam liquid in the saucepan and heat over medium heat, stirring, 3 minutes. Add the clams and cook, stirring, until the clams are heated through. Ladle the mixture into 4 pasta or soup bowls and top each portion with one-fourth of the sautéed crumbs and parsley.

SKILLET BORSCHT WITH MEATBALLS

Pictured on page 161

START TO FINISH: I HOUR I0 MINUTES / **HANDS-ON TIME:** 45 MINUTES / **SERVINGS:** 4 TO 6

> The Husband is a fiend for borscht, hot or cold. As a kid growing up in the 1960s, he used to drink this Eastern European beets-and/or-cabbage soup right out of the fridge (I believe the brand was "Mother's") like lemonade during the summer. On a winter's day in this century, he'll often stop at a deli around the corner and order a steaming bowl of it for lunch.

The Husband is a fiend for borscht, hot or cold. As a kid growing up in the 1960s, he used to drink this Eastern European beets-and/or-cabbage soup right out of the fridge (I believe the brand was "Mother's") like lemonade during the summer. On a winter's day in this century, he'll often stop at a deli around the corner and order a steaming bowl of it for lunch.

All the ingredients for this recipe are cooked in one skillet, as advertised. The vegetables—red cabbage and beets—go in first, with some balsamic vinegar and brown sugar added to give the soupy stew a sweet-and-sour appeal.

Then come the meatballs. You'll notice I didn't brown them to start. While testing this recipe, I tried adding them browned and without browning, and decided that it didn't make much difference. If anything, there's more of an exchange of flavors between the borscht and the meatballs when that step is skipped. The bread and milk mixture, also known as a *panade,* helps the meatballs hold their shape and retain moisture when cooked.

The garnish, sour cream and dill, is key, so don't omit it. A couple of slices of good toasted rye bread is all the side dish you need.

3 tablespoons vegetable oil, preferably grapeseed

3 cups finely chopped onion

Kosher salt

1 tablespoon minced garlic

3 cups finely shredded red cabbage, preferably using the slicing disk of your food processor

3 cups peeled and coarsely grated beets, preferably using the grating disk of your food processor (about 3 medium beets)

Freshly ground black pepper

¹/₂ cup balsamic vinegar

2 tablespoons firmly packed brown sugar

2 slices homemade-style white bread, crusts discarded

¹/₂ cup whole milk

1¹/₂ pounds ground chuck (see page 138 if you would like to grind your own)

1 large egg, beaten lightly

1 cup beef broth (I like Rachael Ray's Stock-in-a Box)

1 (14-ounce) can plum tomatoes, chopped (see page 30)

Sour cream and chopped fresh dill for garnish

> In a large skillet, heat the oil over medium-high heat, reduce the heat to medium, add the onion and a hefty pinch of salt, and cook until the onion is golden, about 8 minutes. Add the garlic and cook, stirring, 1 minute. Transfer ¹/₃ cup of the onion mixture to a medium bowl and set aside. Add the cabbage and beets and another hefty pinch of salt and pepper to the skillet and cook, covered, 5 minutes. Add the vinegar and brown sugar and cook, covered, stirring occasionally, until almost tender, 6 to 8 minutes.

> Soak the bread in the milk in a small bowl, until it is thoroughly saturated, about 5 minutes. Squeeze the bread dry and add it to the bowl with the reserved onions, along with the ground chuck, egg, 1 teaspoon salt, and ¹/₂ teaspoon pepper.

> Mix very well with your hands. Shape the ground meat mixture into walnut-sized meatballs (you should end up with about 24), dipping your hands in water from time to time to make it easier to roll the mixture.

> Add the broth, tomatoes, and meatballs to the skillet and bring the liquid to a boil. Turn down to a simmer, cover, and cook gently for 10 minutes. Uncover and simmer until the sauce is reduced to the desired consistency. Add salt and pepper to taste. To serve, spoon some of the mixture into soup plates and top each portion with a dollop of sour cream and a sprinkling of dill.

HOW TO QUICKLY HALVE A BUNCH OF CHERRY TOMATOES

You can quickly slice all the cherry tomatoes in half by lining them up between two plastic lids and then slicing through the middle of your plastic lid tomato sandwich with a serrated knife. Shazam! You're done. (Full disclosure: I learned this trick from Rachael Ray by way of Heather Moulton, my cousin's wife. And who did Rachael learn it from? An intern who worked on her Food Network Show, *30 Minute Meals.*)

1. Arrange several cherry tomatoes close together on a plastic lid.

2. Place another lid on top.

3. Press down just enough to hold them in place.

4. Using a serrated knife, slice though the tomatoes all at once.

5. When you take off the lid...

6. ...they will all be cut in half.

BAKED CHICKEN
WITH BRUSSELS SPROUTS, APPLES, AND BACON

START TO FINISH: I HOUR 5 MINUTES / **HANDS-ON TIME:** I5 MINUTES / **SERVINGS:** 4

> " Like the baked fish on page 177, this dish is cooked in stages. The bacon goes into the oven first; it provides a crispy garnish for the finished dish as well as the fat in which to cook the rest of the ingredients. Then the chicken makes its entrance, spending a little time on the top shelf to brown its skin. Finally, the sprouts and apples are added and the baking sheet is moved to the middle shelf.
>
> If you've bought a package of cut-up chicken parts, there's no guarantee that the pieces will be of uniform size, which means they'll finish cooking at different times. You can minimize this by trying to buy same-sized thighs or breasts, but the safest bet is to buy a whole chicken and cut it up yourself (see page 184). The pieces will certainly be of uniform size and—bonus!—you'll save money. "

6 slices bacon

1 (3½- to 4-pound) chicken, cut into 8 pieces (if the breasts are large, cut them in half crosswise)

Kosher salt and freshly ground black pepper

2 apples such as Golden Delicious, Gala, or Pink Lady, cored and cut into 8 wedges if the apples are small and 12 if they are large

1 pound Brussels sprouts, trimmed and halved, or quartered if large

1 cup Homemade Chicken Stock (page 26) or store-bought chicken broth

> Preheat the oven to 375°F. Arrange the bacon in a single layer on a rimmed baking sheet and bake on the middle shelf for 14 to 16 minutes or just until crisp. Remove the pan from the oven and, leaving the bacon fat in the pan, transfer the bacon to a paper towel–lined plate and set it aside. (Crumble when it has cooled.)

> Increase the oven temperature to 450°F. Add the chicken to the baking sheet and turn it to coat both sides with the bacon fat. Sprinkle it all over with salt and pepper and arrange the chicken, skin side up, in a single layer on the pan. Bake on the upper third shelf of the oven for 15 minutes.

> Carefully remove the baking sheet from the oven and add the apple wedges and Brussels sprouts to the pan, stirring to coat them with the fat in the pan. Season the Brussels sprouts with salt and pepper. Return the baking sheet to the middle shelf of the oven and bake, stirring the sprouts and apples once, until the vegetables are beginning to turn golden, about 10 minutes. Check the temperature of the chicken; if it registers 160°F, transfer the chicken to a plate, cover it loosely with aluminum foil, and continue to roast the apples and sprouts until golden brown, about another 10 minutes. If the chicken is not done, leave it in the oven with the sprouts and apples until it reaches the right temperature.

> When the Brussels sprouts, apples, and chicken are done, transfer them to 4 plates. Pour the stock into the baking sheet, place the pan on top of the stove across 2 burners set on medium, and deglaze the pan, scraping up the brown bits. Divide the juice over each serving and garnish with the bacon.

HOW TO CUT A WHOLE CHICKEN INTO PARTS

1. Lay the chicken on its side and lift it up by the wing. Cut it at the ball-and-socket joint. (If you are not sure where it is, wiggle the wing when it is attached to the body and feel where it is attached; that is where you want to go in with your knife.) Cut off the second wing.

2. Lay the chicken on its side and lift up the leg. Score the skin all around the leg.

3. Lay the chicken on its side and pull the leg and thigh joint up and over until it pops at the ball-and-socket joint.

4. Find the little nugget of meat (known as the "oyster") behind the leg on the back of the chicken and, using the tip of your knife, cut it away from the body of the chicken. Cut the leg and thigh joint off from the carcass. Repeat with the other leg and thigh piece.

5. Locate the fat line that runs between the leg and the thigh. Following that line, cut straight down through the joint to separate the leg from the thigh. Repeat with the second leg and thigh.

6. Lay the carcass on its side and locate the fat line under the breast. Using kitchen shears, cut through the fat line and down along one side of the backbone, and then repeat the procedure on the other side of the chicken until you have separated the whole breast from the backbone.

7. Stick the tip of a knife into the white spot at the top of the breast bone. Break open the two halves on either side of the breast bone. Isolate the breast bone and pull it out.

8. Turn the chicken breast skin side up and smooth the skin to make sure both halves are equally covered. Cut the chicken breast in half. If the breasts are large you can cut them in half again.

9. Here is what you should end up with, clockwise from the top right: 2 legs, the backbone (great for stock), 2 wings, 4 breast pieces, and 2 thighs.

1

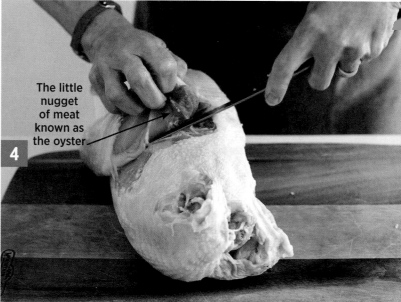

The little nugget of meat known as the oyster

4

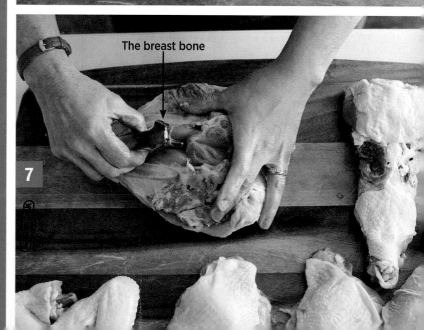

The breast bone

7

The ball and socket

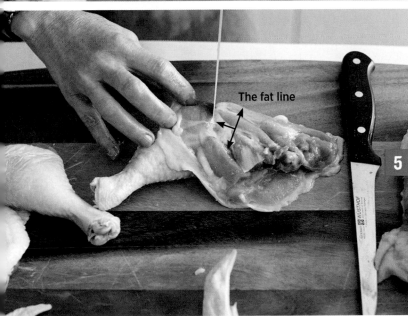
The fat line

The fat line

GREEN CHILE RICE AND CHICKEN SKILLET DINNER

START TO FINISH: 1 HOUR 10 MINUTES / **HANDS-ON TIME:** 30 MINUTES / **SERVINGS:** 6 TO 8

$^1/_2$ cup pine nuts

2 tablespoons butter or vegetable oil, preferably grapeseed

1 cup finely chopped onion

$^1/_2$ pound sweet potatoes, peeled and coarsely shredded, preferably using the grating disk on a food processor

1 teaspoon chili powder

$^1/_2$ teaspoon ground cumin

Kosher salt

1 cup sour cream

2 cups fresh cilantro, leaves and stems, plus leaves for garnish

3 cups cooked white or brown rice

2 cups shredded cooked chicken (rotisserie or leftover cooked chicken from Blasted Chicken, page 242)

$1^1/_2$ cups cooked black beans (see page 36) or 1 (15-ounce) can black beans, drained and rinsed

1 (4-ounce) can chopped green chiles (about $^1/_2$ cup), undrained

2 teaspoons hot sauce or to taste

4 ounces coarsely grated Monterey Jack cheese (about 1 cup)

> Preheat the oven to 350°F. Spread the pine nuts on a rimmed baking sheet and toast in the oven until golden, 5 to 6 minutes. Set aside.

> Heat the butter or oil in a large, ovenproof skillet over medium-high heat. Reduce the heat to medium, add the onion, and cook, stirring occasionally, until softened, about 5 minutes. Add the sweet potatoes, chili powder, cumin, and $^1/_2$ teaspoon salt and cook, stirring, until the sweet potatoes are almost tender, about 5 minutes.

> While the sweet potatoes are cooking, combine the pine nuts, sour cream, and cilantro in a blender and puree until smooth.

> Add the puree, rice, chicken, black beans, chiles, hot sauce, and salt to taste to the sweet potatoes in the skillet and stir well. Sprinkle the cheese evenly on top. Bake for 30 minutes or until bubbling around the edges. Garnish with the cilantro leaves.

"

Green chile rice is a favorite side dish on the church potluck circuit. The typical version consists of cooked rice, canned green chiles, sour cream, and either cheddar cheese or Monterey Jack, all of it baked in a casserole until the cheese is melted and bubbly around the edges. How far wrong can you go with those ingredients?

The plan here was to expand that side dish into a full meal. I started with a couple of stalwarts from the American Southwest, namely black beans and sweet potatoes. Then I added one of my favorite short-cut ingredients, rotisserie chicken, although you're welcome to replace it with any other cooked protein you have kicking around in the fridge.

This recipe is the perfect candidate for leftover (Chinese take-out) rice, but other cooked grains would work just as well (see page 34). One more suggestion: If you have the time and interest, replace the canned chiles with a fresh poblano, roasted, peeled, and chopped. (Incidentally, while creating this recipe I discovered that not all canned chiles have the same punch. I recommend avoiding any can that is labeled "mild.")

"

DUCK CONFIT
WITH BRAISED LEEKS AND SAUERKRAUT

START TO FINISH: 55 MINUTES / **HANDS-ON TIME:** 15 MINUTES / **SERVINGS:** 4

"This is a tasty, easy one-pot meal. It works on the assumption that you have duck confit (duck that has been seasoned and slow cooked in duck fat) at hand, either because you made it yourself (see pages 248–249) or you bought it. You didn't know there was such a thing as already-made duck confit? Well, there is. There are several online sources (see page 350), and you might even be able to find it at your local grocery store.

Well-loved for the moistness of its meat and the crispiness of its skin, the confit is teamed up here with sauerkraut as a counterbalance to the duck's richness. If you can't find leeks, use onions. If you'd prefer a different mushroom, use it. This is a fairly complete meal in itself, but if you have the time and the inclination, you might round it out with Duck Fat Popovers (page 311, as shown) and a simple green salad."

3 tablespoons duck fat or olive oil

4 duck confit legs (pages 248–249) or store-bought (see Sources, page 350)

2 medium leeks, trimmed of green part, halved lengthwise, cut into 1-inch lengths crosswise, washed, and dried

8 ounces cremini mushrooms, sliced

1 cup sauerkraut (do not rinse it)

1 cup Homemade Chicken Stock (page 26) or store-bought chicken broth

Kosher salt and freshly ground black pepper

› Preheat the oven to 350°F. Heat the duck fat in a large nonstick or stick-resistant skillet with an ovenproof handle over medium heat. Add the duck legs, skin side down, and cook until the skin side is crisp, about 10 minutes. Turn the duck legs over and bake them on the middle shelf of the oven for 20 minutes. Transfer to a platter and cover loosely with foil. Pour off all but 2 tablespoons of the duck fat in the skillet.

› Add the leeks to the skillet and cook over medium-low heat, stirring, until the leeks are slightly golden, about 12 minutes. Add the mushrooms and cook over medium heat, stirring occasionally, until the liquid released by the mushrooms has evaporated and the mushrooms are golden, about 6 minutes. Add the sauerkraut and chicken stock, bring the liquid to a boil, and simmer until almost all the liquid is reduced. Taste and add salt and pepper to taste. Return the duck legs to the skillet, skin side up, and cook over medium heat, until the duck is just heated through, 2 to 4 minutes.

› To serve, spoon a mound of the sauerkraut mixture onto each of 4 plates and top each portion with one of the duck legs.

CRISPY PORK FRIED RICE
WITH PICKLED RADISHES

START TO FINISH: 40 MINUTES / **HANDS-ON TIME:** 40 MINUTES / **SERVINGS:** 4

1/4 cup vegetable oil, preferably grapeseed, divided

2 large eggs

Kosher salt and freshly ground black pepper

1/2 pound Canadian bacon, cut into medium dice

1 cup finely chopped onion

2 teaspoons minced garlic

2 teaspoons grated ginger

1 cup sugar snap peas, strings removed and cut crosswise into 1/2-inch pieces

3 cups cooked rice or grains (see page 34)

2 cups coarsely shredded radishes (about 10 large radishes)

2 tablespoons seasoned rice vinegar

1 tablespoon low-sodium soy sauce

2 tablespoons sake or dry sherry

2 teaspoons sesame oil

1 cup blanched fresh or thawed frozen peas

> Heat 1/2 tablespoon of the vegetable oil in a large nonstick or stick-resistant skillet over medium-high heat. Lightly beat the eggs with a tablespoon of water, a pinch of salt, and some pepper in a small bowl. Add the eggs to the pan and tilt the pan to spread the eggs all around to make a flat pancake. Cook until almost set, 30 to 45 seconds. Turn over the egg and cook for another 10 seconds. Transfer the egg to a cutting board.

> Add 1 tablespoon of the vegetable oil and the bacon to the pan and cook until the bacon is browned at the edges, about 7 minutes. Transfer the bacon to a bowl with a slotted spoon. Reduce the heat to medium-low, add 1/2 tablespoon of the oil and the onion to the pan, and cook until the onion is golden, about 8 minutes. Add the garlic, ginger, and sugar snaps and cook, stirring, 1 minute. Transfer the mixture to the bowl with the bacon.

> Add the remaining 2 tablespoons vegetable oil to the skillet, then add the rice, pressing it flat with the back of a spatula. Cook until the rice is slightly crispy, turning it over with the spatula, 12 to 15 minutes.

> Combine the radishes, vinegar, and salt to taste in a small bowl. In another small bowl, combine the soy sauce, sake, and sesame oil. Chop the egg and add it along with the peas to the bowl with the bacon.

> When the rice is nicely crisped, add the contents of the bacon bowl, the peas, and the soy sauce mixture to the skillet and cook, stirring, until the mixture is heated through. Transfer the fried rice to 4 bowls and top each portion with some of the radishes.

> "Starchy, crunchy, and flavorful, fried rice is a deeply satisfying dish no matter what you add to it—and that includes just about any vegetable or protein you care to name, fresh or cooked. If a carton of leftover take-out restaurant rice suddenly appears on a shelf next to the milk, I'm good to go.

This recipe jazzes up a familiar and well-loved duo—rice and peas—with some raw radishes. You simply shred the radishes, toss them with a little seasoned rice vinegar, and sprinkle them on top of the finished dish for a pickle-like effect.

Protein-wise, this recipe calls for pork, but you're welcome to use the protein of your choice, or toss in mushrooms instead and call it a vegetarian's delight. Whatever you choose, I can pretty much guarantee that if you try this recipe even once, you'll be inspired to make variations of it again and again.

By the way, cooking the rice in the skillet until it is crispy is not traditional, but my son, Sam, prefers it crispy and has converted the whole family to his way of thinking."

SAUSAGE, WHITE BEAN, AND BROCCOLI RABE STEW

START TO FINISH: 60 MINUTES / **HANDS-ON TIME:** 40 MINUTES / **SERVINGS:** 6

"This recipe contains some of my favorite ingredients—Italian sausage, white beans, and broccoli rabe—simmered together and topped with toasted breadcrumbs. Both the sausage and the broccoli rabe are so flavorful that you don't have to add much else.

I mash a small amount of the beans to thicken the stew; it's one of my favorite little tricks. The broccoli rabe is blanched to take the edge off its bitterness, and then chopped so that its flavor makes it into every bite.

This dish is plenty satisfying all by itself, but you're welcome to round it out with a salad and/or my Grill Pan Garlic Bread (page 305)."

1 bunch broccoli rabe (about 1 pound), trimmed

¼ cup extra-virgin olive oil, divided

1½ cups fresh breadcrumbs

2 pounds Italian sausage links (sweet or hot), cut into 1½-inch lengths

1 large onion, sliced

1 tablespoon minced garlic

2 cups cooked white beans, pinto beans, or chickpeas (see page 36) or 2 cups rinsed and drained canned beans, ½ cup mashed and the rest left whole

1 tablespoon red wine vinegar

2 cups Homemade Chicken Stock (page 26) or store-bought chicken broth

Kosher salt and freshly ground black pepper

> Bring a large pot of salted water to a boil. Working in several batches, add the broccoli rabe to the water, boil for 2 minutes, and transfer to a bowl of ice and water. Drain the broccoli rabe well, pressing it down to get rid of excess liquid, and slice it crosswise ½ inch thick.

> Heat 2 tablespoons of the oil in a large skillet over medium heat, add the breadcrumbs and cook, stirring constantly, until they are golden and crisp, 8 to 10 minutes. Transfer the crumbs to a bowl and set aside.

> Add the remaining 2 tablespoons oil to the skillet and add the sausages. Cook them, turning occasionally, until browned, about 5 minutes. Transfer the sausages to a bowl and add the onion to the skillet. Cook, stirring occasionally, until it is golden, about 8 minutes. Add the garlic and cook, stirring, 1 minute. Add the whole and mashed beans, vinegar, stock, and sausages, bring to a boil, and simmer gently for 5 minutes.

> Add the broccoli rabe and salt and pepper to taste, stir well, and simmer until the broccoli rabe is just heated through, about 3 minutes.

> Spoon the stew into 6 soup plates and top each portion with some of the breadcrumbs.

STIR-FRIED BEEF
WITH BROCCOLI AND RED PEPPERS

START TO FINISH: 40 MINUTES / **HANDS-ON TIME:** 40 MINUTES / **SERVINGS:** 4

12 ounces lean flank steak

1 tablespoon minced ginger

1 tablespoon plus 2 teaspoons Shaoxing rice wine or dry sherry

2 teaspoons soy sauce

1½ teaspoons cornstarch

½ teaspoon salt

⅛ teaspoon freshly ground black pepper

1 teaspoon Asian sesame oil

2 tablespoons Homemade Chicken Stock (page 26) or store-bought chicken broth

2 tablespoons oyster sauce

2 teaspoons dark soy sauce

2 tablespoons peanut or vegetable oil, divided

1 tablespoon minced garlic

1 tablespoon fermented black beans, rinsed and mashed

¾ cup thinly sliced onion

1 large red bell pepper, cut into ¼-inch-wide strips

3 cups broccoli florets and stems, cut into ¼-inch-thick slices, blanched for 1 minute, then drained

Rice as an accompaniment

> Cut the beef with the grain into 2-inch-wide strips. Cut each strip across the grain into ¼-inch-thick slices. In a medium bowl, combine the beef, ginger, the 2 teaspoons rice wine, soy sauce, cornstarch, salt, and pepper. Stir to combine. Stir in the sesame oil. In a small bowl, combine the stock, oyster sauce, dark soy sauce, and the remaining 1 tablespoon rice wine.

> Heat a 14-inch flat-bottomed wok or 12-inch skillet over high heat until a bead of water vaporizes within 1 to 2 seconds of contact. Swirl in 1 tablespoon of the peanut oil, add the garlic and black beans, then, using a metal spatula, stir-fry 10 seconds or until the aromatics are fragrant. Push the garlic mixture to the sides of the wok, carefully add the beef and spread evenly in a single layer in the wok. Cook, undisturbed, 1 minute, letting the beef begin to sear. Then, stir-fry 1 minute, or until the beef is lightly browned but not cooked through. Transfer the beef to a plate.

> Swirl the remaining 1 tablespoon peanut oil into the wok, add the onion, and cook about 30 seconds or until just translucent. Add the bell pepper and stir-fry 30 seconds. Add the broccoli and stir-fry 15 seconds or until just combined. Return the beef with any juices that have accumulated to the wok. Swirl the oyster sauce mixture into the wok and stir-fry for about 30 seconds, or until the beef is just cooked through. Serve with rice.

I've known and admired Grace Young for years. We booked her time and again on a variety of my old Food Network shows and, more recently, on *Sara's Weeknight Meals.* The depth of Grace's love for and knowledge of Chinese cooking is inspiring. Her ability to teach others about it is without equal. She is also the author of three award-winning Chinese cookbooks, including her most recent, *Stir-Frying to the Sky's Edge* (Simon & Schuster, 2010) from which this recipe is adapted.

I've chosen this recipe by Grace because it illustrates just about everything you need to know about the proper way to stir-fry. I suggest looking at the tips and photos on pages 196–197 before starting to cook.

Although broccoli is available all year, Grace likes to make this dish in the autumn when broccoli appears in local farmers' markets. Young broccoli has slender stalks with florets that are almost bluish green in color. Halve or quarter large florets so that all of the pieces match in size to ensure that they cook in the same amount of time.

Cook's Notes: Grace's Tips for Successful Stir-Frying

▶ It's important to have all your ingredients prepped and ready to go, because once the wok is hot, the stir-fry comes together very quickly.

▶ Use a salad spinner or kitchen towels to pat vegetables dry. Adding wet vegetables will cool down your wok and turn your stir-fry into a steamy braise.

▶ Use a 14-inch flat-bottomed carbon-steel (not a nonstick) wok with a long wood handle and season it properly.

▶ Preheat the wok over high heat before stir-frying. Test the temperature with a drop of water—it should vaporize within a second or two of contact.

▶ Use an oil with a high smoking point, such as peanut, grapeseed, canola, or avocado—never extra-virgin olive oil or sesame oil.

▶ If the oil smokes wildly when you add the oil, you've overheated the wok. When you add the aromatics there must be a sizzle. If there's no sizzle, you've underheated the wok. If you overheat or underheat you need to begin again.

▶ When you add the protein, spread it in a single layer so that every piece is touching the hot well of the wok. Do not touch it for 1 minute, or until you can see that it's beginning to sear on the bottom side, before stir-frying.

▶ Use a flexible pancake or metal fish spatula. A wood spatula is too thick to get under ingredients and will cause sticking.

▶ You should hear a consistent sizzle throughout the stir-fry process. If you don't, the wok was either insufficiently preheated or you've crowded your wok with too many ingredients or ingredients that are too wet.

STEP-BY-STEP STIR-FRY

1. Add the marinade ingredients to the meat one at time, mixing until the cornstarch is no longer visible. Add the sesame oil last to lightly coat the meat and prevent sticking in the wok.

2. With all of the prepared ingredients within reach, swirl the oil along the side of the hot wok. Then tilt and turn the pan on all sides to coat the bottom.

3. With the garlic–black bean mixture pushed to the side, add the meat in one even layer and let it cook for 1 minute without touching until you can see that it's seared. Stir-fry for 1 minute. Remove when lightly browned but not cooked through.

4. Add the onions, red peppers, and broccoli, stir-frying briefly between each addition.

5. Return the meat and any accumulated juices to the wok and add the oyster sauce mixture, pouring it around the side of the wok so as not to cool down the pan. Stir-fry briefly, scooping and tossing, to combine.

6. Any of these spatulas are fine to use for stir-frying. A good Chinese spatula (top) can be difficult to find, but a flexible slotted fish spatula (center) or slotted spatula (bottom) will also work nicely.

6 | *vegetarian* & VEGAN

Whether or not you are a practicing vegetarian, a meatless meal is an appealing way to mix up the weekly dinner lineup. And it's more appetizing today than ever before. There are so many varieties of vegetables available, whether you shop at the supermarket, farmers' market, or have joined a CSA. (See the box on page 11 for details.) When I first started cooking, it was a challenge to find leeks, shallots, or any mushroom besides the white button kind. Now the produce aisles overflow with almost any vegetable in season, sometimes in an exotic array of varieties. (Purple carrots anyone?) There are so many new toys to play with.

In this chapter, the recipes highlight the versatility of vegetables, demonstrating how they take on a range of flavors and textures depending on the cooking method. They are easy to turn into main-course dishes and will take you all over the world, as so many cultures are less meat-centric than ours. In this chapter, you'll find flavors from Italy, India, and the Middle East.

My notable guest chefs in this chapter are Amanda Cohen, chef/owner of New York City's highly esteemed vegetarian restaurant Dirt Candy, and Adam Sobel, creator of the pioneering vegan food truck Cinnamon Snail, formerly in New York and now in Red Bank, New Jersey. Amanda's Broccoli Carpaccio with Broccoli Stalk Salad will wow your dinner guests on a weekend. Adam's Korean BBQ Tofu Tacos with Vegan Kimchi (pictured opposite) work equally well at a fun family meal or a backyard barbecue.

This chapter offers four strictly vegan recipes, although many others could satisfy vegans with a few minor adjustments—eliminating the cheese, for example, or replacing eggs with tofu.

198

INSIDE-OUT EGGPLANT-PARMESAN ROLLS

START TO FINISH: I HOUR IO MINUTES / **HANDS-ON TIME:** 50 MINUTES / **SERVINGS:** 6

2 large slices homemade-style white or whole-wheat bread, crusts discarded and bread cut into $1/4$-inch cubes (about $1^3/4$ cups)

1 tablespoon extra-virgin olive oil

Kosher salt

2 pounds large eggplants

Olive oil cooking spray

$1/2$ cup finely chopped roasted red pepper

4 ounces mozzarella, cut into $1/4$-inch cubes

1 ounce freshly grated Parmigiano-Reggiano

1 teaspoon minced garlic

$2^1/2$ cups Speedy Marinara Sauce (page 30) or store-bought marinara sauce

Shredded fresh basil for garnish

> Preheat the oven to 400°F and adjust the oven racks so there is one in the top third and one in the bottom third of the oven.

> Toss the bread cubes with the oil and a pinch of salt in a medium bowl. Spread the cubes in a single layer on a large rimless baking sheet and bake them in the bottom third of the oven until they are golden brown, 5 to 8 minutes. Transfer them back to the bowl.

> Leaving the skin on, slice the eggplant lengthwise into $1/4$-inch-thick slices, discarding the ends. Spray the baking sheet you used for the bread and a second large rimless baking sheet with the olive oil spray. Sprinkle the slices very lightly with salt on both sides, arrange them in a single layer on the pans, and spray lightly with more olive oil spray. Bake just until barely golden, 16 to 20 minutes, turning the slices over and swapping the pans in the oven halfway through. (Don't overcook the slices or they won't be pliable.)

> Add the red pepper, mozzarella, Parmigiano-Reggiano, and garlic to the bread cubes and toss well. Pour half the marinara sauce in a shallow baking dish. Arrange the eggplant slices on a clean kitchen surface, overlapping a few if they are small (to make a wide rectangle). You will need 12 portions total. Divide the filling among the eggplant slices, mounding it in the center. Roll up the slices to enclose the filling and transfer the rolls, seam sides down, to the baking dish. Spoon the remaining marinara sauce over the rolls and bake on the bottom third of the oven, 20 minutes, until the sauce is bubbling.

> Transfer 2 rolls to each of 6 plates, making sure that each portion has ample sauce, and top with shredded basil.

"

A vegetarian's delight, Eggplant Parmesan can nonetheless be very heavy. My mission here was to concoct a lighter recipe that managed to retain all the ingredients that make the traditional version so delicious.

Eggplant tends to soak up oil like a sponge, even more so if it's breaded. So the first thing I did was take a cue from my mom, who made an easy but inventive eggplant side dish by cutting it into half-inch slices, brushing them with her homemade vinaigrette, and then baking them all until tender and golden. Here, I simply spray each slice with a modest amount of cooking spray before baking.

Still, I didn't want to lose the bread. So I literally turned the recipe inside out, placing the bread—in the form of croutons—inside the rolled-up slices of eggplant. The croutons will soften up a bit when the dish is baked, but they'll also absorb and marry the other flavors in the filling.

I recommend the big eggplants for this recipe. Look for smooth skin and flesh that's firm to the touch. If you can't find large eggplants, use the smaller ones and just overlap the slices slightly to make substantial roll-ups.

PORTOBELLO CHEESESTEAKS

START TO FINISH: 60 MINUTES / **HANDS-ON TIME:** 60 MINUTES / **SERVINGS:** 4

The cheesesteak is one of those attractions that—like the Liberty Bell—makes Philadelphia a world-class tourist destination. This is my vegetarian version of the classic. It's meatless, but not a punk; not with that most steak-like of mushrooms, the portobello, in the starring role.

Portobellos have to be cleaned before they can be savored. Start by removing the dark gills on the underside, scraping them out with a teaspoon. (A grapefruit spoon works nicely, if you have one.) If you leave the gills in, they will stain the rest of the ingredients dark brown; also I am not a fan of their texture. Then simply rinse the cap on both sides—briefly—under cold running water to remove any dirt. Be sure to pat the caps dry afterward so that they'll be able to absorb the marinade.

Topping-wise, I've gone the Mediterranean route, but you're welcome to substitute a topping of your choice. Likewise, you can swap in thin slices of mozzarella, cheddar, or Italian fontina for the provolone. Finally, if don't like mayo on your sandwiches, use Dijon mustard instead.

However you customize it, I urge you to add this super-satisfying vegetarian ringer to the menu the next time you're grilling up hot dogs and hambies in the backyard—I know you'll win some converts.

2 tablespoons sherry vinegar

2 tablespoons extra-virgin olive oil, plus extra for brushing

1 tablespoon Dijon mustard

1 teaspoon minced garlic

Kosher salt and freshly ground black pepper

4 large portobello mushrooms, stems and gills removed

1/2 cup Homemade Mayonnaise (pages 52–53) or store-bought mayonnaise (low-fat if you prefer)

2 teaspoons finely minced fresh rosemary

1/2 cup medium chopped jarred roasted red peppers

1/2 cup kalamata or other Mediterranean olives, pitted and medium chopped

6 large scallions, trimmed but kept whole

8 slices rustic bread

4 thin slices provolone (about 3 ounces total)

> Preheat the grill to medium. In a small bowl, whisk together the vinegar, oil, mustard, garlic, and salt and pepper to taste. Brush the marinade on both sides of the mushrooms, transfer them to a resealable plastic bag along with any remaining marinade, and let them marinate at room temperature for 20 minutes.

> Meanwhile, in another small bowl, combine the mayonnaise and rosemary and add salt and pepper to taste. Combine the peppers, olives, and black pepper to taste in a medium bowl and set aside.

> Brush the scallions with some olive oil and grill them over medium heat, turning often, until they are charred on the edges and tender, 3 to 4 minutes. Transfer them to a cutting board and let cool slightly. Medium chop the scallions and add them to the bowl with the peppers and olives.

> Brush the bread on both sides with olive oil and grill it until lightly toasted on both sides, about 2 minutes a side.

> Grill the mushrooms over medium heat, 6 to 8 minutes a side, until tender when pierced with a knife. Transfer them to a cutting board and trim the edges so that they are roughly the same size as the bread. Chop the trimmed parts and add them to the olive mixture. Return the trimmed mushrooms to the grill, gill sides up, and spoon one-fourth of the olive mixture on top of each mushroom. Top with a slice of cheese, cover, and cook, until the cheese is melted, 1 to 2 minutes.

> Spread each slice of bread on one side with the mayonnaise mixture. Transfer the mushroom steaks to the mayonnaise side of 4 bread slices and top with another slice, mayonnaise side down. Cut in half and serve immediately.

BEANS AND GREENS GRATIN

START TO FINISH: I HOUR I5 MINUTES / **HANDS-ON TIME:** 40 MINUTES / **SERVINGS:** 6

1¼ cups fresh breadcrumbs (made by pulsing 2 to 3 slices homemade-style white bread in a food processor)

3 tablespoons extra-virgin olive oil, divided

½ teaspoon red pepper flakes

Kosher salt

1 cup finely chopped onion

1 tablespoon finely minced garlic

2 tablespoons fresh rosemary, finely chopped

4 cups packed coarsely chopped chard, kale, mustard greens, collard leaves, or a mix (tough stems removed)

2 cups cooked pinto, white, kidney, or black beans; chickpeas (see page 36); or rinsed and drained canned beans (a 19-ounce can)

1½ cups Homemade Vegetable Stock (page 29) or store-bought vegetable broth

1½ ounces freshly grated Parmigiano-Reggiano

1 cup chopped whole canned tomatoes (see page 30)

Freshly ground black pepper

› Preheat the oven to 375°F. Toss together the breadcrumbs, 1 tablespoon of the olive oil, the pepper flakes, and salt to taste in a small bowl.

› Heat the remaining 2 tablespoons oil in a large ovenproof skillet over medium heat. Add the onion and cook, stirring occasionally, until golden, about 8 minutes. Add the garlic and rosemary and cook, stirring, 1 minute. Add the greens in batches and cook until they are wilted. Mash ½ cup of the beans with a potato masher or fork and add the mashed beans along with the whole beans, stock, cheese, tomatoes, and salt and pepper to taste. Sprinkle the crumbs evenly on top of the mixture. Bake on an upper middle shelf of the oven until the crumbs are lightly browned and the beans are bubbling, 25 to 35 minutes.

> When you see the word *gratin* in the title of a recipe, it means that the dish is topped with a light brown crust usually consisting of baked breadcrumbs or grated cheese. The best known of these recipes is potato gratin (see my Foolproof Scalloped Potatoes, page 308), but why should potatoes get all the love?
>
> Here, I've combined two hearty ingredients: beans (of your choice, see page 36) and greens (again, of your choice, see page 34). Some of the beans are mashed, which is one of my favorite tricks for thickening a bean-centric dish. Classified as a vegetarian entrée, this dish would also shine as a side dish to a meat-based main.

INDIAN EGGS
WITH SPICY TOMATO-PEPPER SAUCE

START TO FINISH: 40 MINUTES / **HANDS-ON TIME:** 20 MINUTES / **SERVINGS:** 4

This is an adaptation of a recipe sent to me years ago by Aparna Subramanian, a fan of *Cooking Live,* one of the shows I used to host on Food Network. At first, the idea of putting hard-boiled eggs in a sauce struck me as odd, but as soon as I tried it, it made all the sense in the world. Eggs become downright meaty when they are hard-boiled and do a splendid job of absorbing all the flavors.

The sauce in this case is a tomato-vegetable stew spiked with cumin and mustard seeds, turmeric, cayenne, ginger, and chiles. The neutral eggs team up beautifully with this somewhat spicy sauce. By the way, do check out a new method of "boiling" eggs (see page 54). You'll be amazed by how tender a hard-boiled egg can be.

One last note: If you want a substitute for the eggs, try Paneer (page 50) or firm tofu, cubed and briefly sautéed before being added to the sauce. Serve with Shallow-Fried Beer-Battered Okra (page 292) with Smoked Paprika Dipping Sauce (page 293, as shown).

"

3 tablespoons vegetable oil, preferably grapeseed, divided

2 teaspoons mustard seeds

1½ teaspoons cumin seeds

1 cup finely chopped onion

Kosher salt

1 red and 1 green bell pepper, cut into thin strips about 1½ to 2 inches long

1 tablespoon finely grated ginger

2 teaspoons minced garlic

1 serrano or jalapeño chile, or to taste, sliced thin crosswise, with seeds and ribs

½ teaspoon ground turmeric

¼ teaspoon cayenne or to taste

2 cups chopped ripe tomatoes

6 large Hard-"Boiled" Eggs (page 54), peeled and cut in half lengthwise

Brown or white rice, or the grain of your choice (see page 34) as an accompaniment

¼ cup chopped fresh cilantro

› Heat half of the oil in a large skillet over medium heat. Add the mustard and cumin seeds and cook, stirring, until fragrant, about 30 seconds (careful, they may pop, so have a lid handy for the skillet). Add the onion and a hefty pinch of salt and cook, stirring, until the onion is softened, about 5 minutes. Add the remaining oil and the bell pepper strips and cook, stirring, until the peppers are just tender, about 5 minutes.

› Add the ginger, garlic, and chile to the skillet and cook, stirring, 1 minute. Add the turmeric and cayenne and cook, stirring, 1 minute. Add the tomatoes and cook until soft, about 5 minutes. Season with salt to taste.

› Arrange the eggs, cut sides up, in the sauce and heat until the sauce bubbles and the eggs are hot. Spoon rice evenly onto each of 4 plates. Spoon some of the sauce and 3 egg halves on top of the rice. Sprinkle with cilantro.

SAAG PANEER
WITH CAULIFLOWER

START TO FINISH: I HOUR 20 MINUTES / **HANDS-ON TIME:** 50 MINUTES / **SERVINGS:** 4

4 cups chopped cauliflower, cut into
½-inch pieces

¼ cup plus 1 tablespoon Ghee (page
46) or vegetable oil, preferably
grapeseed, divided

Kosher salt and freshly ground black
pepper

1 recipe Homemade Semisoft Cheese
(Paneer; page 50), cut into 1-inch by
¾-inch cubes

1 cup thinly sliced onion

1½ cups finely chopped plum tomatoes
(about 12 ounces)

1 tablespoon minced garlic

1 small serrano, sliced thin crosswise,
with seeds and ribs, optional

1 teaspoon finely grated ginger

¼ teaspoon garam masala

¼ teaspoon cayenne

¼ teaspoon turmeric

1 to 1¼ pounds spinach, finely chopped
(about 12 cups)

¼ cup heavy cream, optional (leave it
out if you want a lighter dish)

> Preheat the oven to 425°F. Toss the cauliflower with 2 tablespoons of the ghee and salt and pepper to taste, arrange in a single layer on a rimmed baking sheet, and bake in the upper third of the oven until golden brown, 15 to 20 minutes. Set aside.

> Meanwhile, heat 1½ tablespoons ghee in a large nonstick or stick-resistant skillet over medium heat. Add the paneer cubes and sauté, turning once, until browned on both sides, about 5 minutes. Transfer to a bowl and set aside.

> Add the remaining 1½ tablespoons ghee and the onion to the skillet and cook over medium heat, stirring occasionally, until the onion is golden, about 8 minutes. Add the tomatoes and cook, stirring, until tender, about 5 minutes. Add the garlic, chile, if using, and ginger and cook, stirring, 2 minutes. Add the garam masala, cayenne, and turmeric and cook, stirring, 1 minute. Add the spinach, cover, and cook, stirring occasionally, until the spinach is very tender, 25 to 30 minutes. Add the paneer, roasted cauliflower, salt and pepper to taste, and cream, if using. Cook just until heated through and serve hot.

“

Saag paneer is a South Asian dish consisting of cubes of fresh farmer cheese (that's the paneer) combined with greens (or saag) in a creamy sauce. It's flavored with ginger, garlic, chiles, and garam masala—a blend of ground spices that differs from region to region in India, but usually contains a mix of coriander, cumin, cardamom, cloves, cinnamon, black pepper, and nutmeg. You can find garam masala at most grocery stores these days, but it's also available online (see Sources, page 350).

If you choose not to make your own paneer, tofu would be a fine stand-in (see Stir-Fried Tofu on page 223); just be sure to freeze it or press out the excess water (as described in the first step on page 223) before proceeding with the recipe.

One night I was in a rush while making this recipe and didn't feel like chopping the spinach, so I took a short cut. Right after adding the garam masala, cayenne, and turmeric, I increased the heat under the skillet to high, added only 10 ounces of whole, unchopped baby spinach, and cooked it, stirring, until just wilted. Then I immediately added the paneer, cauliflower, and cream. This quicker version, although not traditional, is very tasty, too.

”

JILL LEVY'S RISOTTO
WITH CARROT AND ZUCCHINI SAUCE

START TO FINISH: 40 MINUTES / **HANDS-ON TIME:** 40 MINUTES / **SERVINGS:** 4

Jill Levy was the first of the two A-plus interns recruited by the International Culinary Center (formerly the French Culinary Institute) to work with me on this book. Jill grew up in a food-loving family: Both her mom and her beloved Aunt "Muffin" are great cooks. But it wasn't until she spent a semester studying in Florence, Italy, that Jill first began thinking about cooking as a profession.

This dish, which marries traditional risotto to ingredients that typically fill ravioli, is a product of Jill's Italian adventure. The risotto is prepared in a high-sided sauté pan. It's a labor-intensive process—you have to add the stock in several increments—but it's definitely worth it in the end. The risotto's ready when the rice is *al dente* and has released its natural starches, which comprise a creamy sauce. For maximum impact, Jill suggests serving this dish as soon as it's done cooking. It is, she reports, 'a favorite among my family.'

2 tablespoons extra-virgin olive oil

1 1/2 cups carrots, peeled and cut into small dice

1 1/2 cups zucchini, cut into small dice

1 1/2 large leeks, white and light green parts, sliced thin, washed, and dried

3 garlic cloves, crushed and peeled

Kosher salt and freshly ground black pepper

5 1/2 to 6 1/2 cups Homemade Vegetable Stock (page 29) or store-bought vegetable broth

3 tablespoons unsalted butter, divided

2 cups Arborio rice

1/2 cup dry white wine

1 ounce freshly grated Parmigiano-Reggiano

1/2 cup torn fresh basil

› Heat a large, high-sided skillet over high heat. Turn the heat down to medium and add the olive oil. Add the carrots and sauté, stirring occasionally, 5 minutes. Add the zucchini, leeks, and garlic and sauté, stirring occasionally, until the vegetables are soft and lightly browned, 10 to 15 minutes. Season the mixture with salt and pepper. Transfer all of the garlic with half of the vegetables to a blender. Transfer the remaining vegetable mixture to a bowl and set it aside.

› Add 1/2 cup of the stock to the mixture in the blender and puree until smooth. Add salt and pepper to taste. Bring the remaining stock to a simmer in a medium saucepan.

› In the same skillet used to cook the vegetables, heat 2 tablespoons of the butter over medium heat. Add the Arborio rice and cook, stirring, 2 minutes. Add the wine and cook, stirring, until the wine is absorbed, about 1 minute. Add the simmering stock 1/2 to 3/4 cup at a time, letting the rice absorb the liquid before the next addition, stirring constantly, until all the stock is absorbed and the rice is al dente. This process takes 20 to 25 minutes.

› Add the reserved cooked vegetables, the vegetable puree, the cheese, and the remaining 1 tablespoon butter to the risotto and gently stir to combine. Season to taste with salt and pepper and serve immediately, topped with the fresh basil.

ROASTED PUMPKIN FARROTTO
WITH FRIED SAGE LEAVES

" Farrotto is risotto made with farro, an ancient variety of wheat, instead of the usual medium-grain white rice. Farrotto isn't as creamy as risotto, but farro is more robustly flavorful than white rice and boasts significantly more nutrients. It's a trade-off I can live with.

I cooked this farrotto using a method recommended for risotto by Chef Andrew Carmellini. Rather than adding liquid in small amounts and stirring constantly (as in Jill Levy's Risotto with Carrot and Zucchini Sauce, page 210), Andrew adds the liquid in just two stages, stirring only occasionally. Although the result is not quite as creamy, as someone who prefers not to be glued to the stove, I found his method quite liberating.

The pumpkins I recommend for this recipe are the tiny guys with cutesy names like Jack Be Little. Thought of mostly as decorative objects, they happen to be the best-tasting pumpkins you'll ever eat. If you can't find them, use roasted butternut squash instead.

Note: I suggest you scoop out the seeds *after* roasting the pumpkins (because it is easier), but if you want to toast the seeds for a snack, scoop them out *beforehand* and follow the recipe on page 213. "

START TO FINISH: I HOUR 45 MINUTES / **HANDS-ON TIME:** 25 MINUTES / **SERVINGS:** 4 TO 6

2 pounds small (½ to 3 inches across, see headnote at left) pumpkins, cut in half vertically (see Note, left)

Vegetable oil, preferably grapeseed, with a high smoke point (see Cook's Notes on page 225) for the baking sheet and for frying the sage leaves

36 sage leaves (from 1 small bunch)

Kosher salt

2 tablespoons unsalted butter

½ cup finely chopped onion

6 cups Homemade Vegetable Stock (page 29) or store-bought vegetable broth

2 cups pearled farro (the quicker-cooking variety)

1 cup dry white wine

1 ounce finely grated Parmigiano-Reggiano, plus extra for sprinkling

Freshly ground black pepper

> Preheat the oven to 350°F. Arrange the pumpkins, cut sides down, in a single layer on a rimmed baking sheet brushed lightly with oil. Bake on the middle shelf of the oven for 45 to 60 minutes, or until a knife goes through the flesh with no resistance. Using tongs, turn the pumpkin halves cut sides up and let them cool until they can be handled. Scoop out and discard the seeds (or reserve them to make Toasted Squash Seeds). Then scoop out the pulp and mash it with a potato masher (you should have about 2 cups). Set it aside.

> Heat 1 inch of vegetable oil in a 4-quart saucepan to 360°F (tip the pan to take the temperature). Add about 6 sage leaves and fry them for 10 to 15 seconds. Transfer with a slotted spoon to paper towels to drain and sprinkle them with salt. Repeat with the remaining leaves in small batches and set aside.

> Pour off the oil from the saucepan, add the butter, and melt over medium heat. Reduce the heat to medium-low, add the onion, and cook, stirring occasionally, until the onion is softened, about 5 minutes. Meanwhile, in a small saucepan, bring the vegetable stock to a bare simmer.

> Add the farro to the softened onions in the larger saucepan and cook, stirring, until all the grains are nicely coated with butter. Add the wine, bring it to a simmer and simmer until most of the wine is absorbed. Add half the stock, bring to a simmer, and cook, stirring occasionally, until most of the stock has been absorbed, 10 to 15 minutes.

> Add the remaining stock and cook, stirring occasionally, until most of the stock has been absorbed, 10 to 15 minutes. Stir in the cheese, mashed pumpkin, and salt and pepper to taste and cook just until heated through. Spoon onto plates and top each portion with additional cheese and the fried sage leaves.

Note: Cutting pumpkins in half from top to bottom is much less dangerous than cutting them horizontally, but be careful nonetheless. It is easy to slip and cut yourself.

TOASTED SQUASH SEEDS

START TO FINISH: 2 HOURS 40 MINUTES / **HANDS-ON TIME:** 40 MINUTES
SERVINGS: VARIES DEPENDING ON THE SIZE OF THE PUMPKIN

Squash seeds from butternut, acorn, pumpkin, or any winter squash
Kosher salt
Vegetable oil, preferably grapeseed

Scoop the seeds from the winter squash, removing as much fiber as you can; rinse and drain the seeds. Make a solution of ½ teaspoon salt per 1 cup water (enough for the seeds to float in), add the seeds, and soak for 2 hours.

Preheat the oven to 300°F. Drain the seeds, pat them very dry, and toss them with the oil and salt to taste on a rimmed baking sheet. Spread in a single layer and bake on the middle shelf of the oven until toasted and crispy, about 18 minutes. They will crisp up further as they cool.

BUTTERNUT SQUASH, CHESTNUT, AND GRUYÈRE CROSTATA

START TO FINISH: 2 HOURS / **HANDS-ON TIME:** 45 MINUTES / **SERVINGS:** 6

4 cups sliced (about ⅛ inch thick) butternut squash, cut in 2-inch by 1-inch pieces (about 2 pounds)

3 tablespoons extra-virgin olive oil, divided

Kosher salt

2 leeks, white and light green parts, thinly sliced crosswise ½ inch thick

1 large red bell pepper, sliced thin and then slices halved crosswise

1 tablespoon minced fresh sage or 1 teaspoon dried

Freshly ground black pepper

1 cup coarsely chopped roasted, peeled chestnuts, jarred, or see box at right

1 recipe Pie Dough (page 40) or 1 store-bought pie dough (about 12 ounces)

Flour for dusting

1 cup coarsely grated Gruyère

An egg wash made by beating 1 egg with 1 tablespoon water

A crostata is an Italian pie that can be sweet or savory. It's made free form on a baking sheet with the edges folded in willy-nilly—no fancy crimping or shaping required. The finished product is supposed to look rustic and homemade, and it does. It's the perfect pie for the baking-impaired.

> Preheat the oven to 450°F and line a rimmed baking sheet with parchment.

> Toss the squash with 1 tablespoon of the oil and ½ teaspoon salt and spread it in a single layer on the prepared baking sheet. Bake the squash in the middle of the oven, stirring once, until it is tender and golden, about 25 minutes. Reduce the oven to 400°F.

> Meanwhile, heat the remaining 2 tablespoons oil in a large skillet over medium heat; reduce the heat to medium-low and add the leeks, bell pepper, and a hefty pinch of salt. Cook the mixture, stirring, until the leeks are golden brown, about 20 minutes. Add the sage and salt and pepper to taste and cook for 1 minute.

> When the squash is done, add it to the skillet along with the chestnuts, stir the mixture well, and let it cool to room temperature. Reserve the baking sheet and line it with a fresh sheet of parchment.

> Roll out the dough into a 13-inch round on a lightly floured surface with a lightly floured rolling pin (see Tips for Rolling Out Pie Dough, page 331). Transfer the dough to the prepared baking sheet; sprinkle half the cheese in the center, leaving a 2- to 3-inch border, and spread the filling on top of the cheese. Sprinkle the remaining cheese over the top. Fold the dough in on itself to cover the outer rim of the filling, pleating the dough. Brush the edges of the crostata with the egg wash. Bake in the lower third of the oven until the crust is cooked through and the edges are golden, 35 to 45 minutes. Let cool on a rack for 10 minutes before serving.

ROASTING AND PEELING FRESH CHESTNUTS

Fresh chestnuts are in season in the fall, and I learned a great way to prepare them from food blogger Tori Avey (toriavey.com). If you've never roasted them, try it—your house will smell heavenly.

Slice through the flat side of a chestnut shell using a serrated knife, making an incision about 1 inch long, ⅛ inch deep down to the flesh. (Be very careful not to slip.) Put the scored chestnuts in a small saucepan, cover with water, and bring them just to a simmer. Using a slotted spoon, transfer the chestnuts to a baking sheet and bake in a preheated 425°F oven until the shells peel back, about 15 minutes. Transfer them to a bowl, cover with a towel, and let stand for 15 minutes. Now both the shell and the dark peel should be very easy to remove.

ROOT VEGETABLES BOURGUIGNON

START TO FINISH: 1 HOUR 45 MINUTES / **HANDS-ON TIME:** 45 MINUTES / **SERVINGS:** 4 TO 6

The word *bourguignon* in the name of a recipe indicates that the recipe is "in the style of Burgundy," one of the most celebrated food and wine regions of France. Those of us of a certain age remember Julia Child energetically popularizing boeuf bourguignon on TV a generation ago.

What does this vegetarian stew have in common with the beef-based classic? Well, red wine for starts, as well as garlic, onions, thyme, mushrooms, and tomato paste. Those last two items, plus the addition of soy sauce, add umami, the kind of meatiness even a vegetarian can love. But the stars of this show remain the root vegetables.

This wonderful stew tastes even better a few days after you make it. Accordingly, you might want to cook up a double batch on a weekend and freeze half of it. You'll be delighted to rediscover it a month down the road, when you come home on a cold night after a long day at work and don't feel like cooking. Serve with Oven-Baked Creamy Polenta (page 310), cooked grains (see page 34), or Grill Pan Garlic Bread (page 305).

1/3 cup dried porcini mushrooms

4 cups Homemade Vegetable Stock (page 29) or store-bought vegetable broth

1/4 cup plus 1 tablespoon extra-virgin olive oil, divided

12 pearl onions, blanched and peeled, or 1 cup 1-inch chunks onion

2 large carrots (about 1 pound), cut into 1-inch pieces

Kosher salt

1/2 pound small turnips, cut into 1-inch pieces

1/2 pound parsnips, cut into 1-inch pieces

1/2 pound cremini mushrooms, cut into quarters or eighths if the mushrooms are large

1 tablespoon minced garlic

1 tablespoon fresh thyme leaves

1 tablespoon tomato paste

1/2 cup dry red wine

3 tablespoons all-purpose flour

1 teaspoon sweet smoked paprika

1 tablespoon soy sauce (preferably mushroom soy sauce)

2 tablespoons fresh lemon juice

Freshly ground black pepper

> Combine the porcini and stock in a medium saucepan and bring the mixture to a boil. Cover, remove from heat, and let stand.

> Heat 2 tablespoons of the oil in a Dutch oven over medium-high heat. Reduce the heat to medium and add the onions, carrots, and a hefty pinch of salt. Cook until golden brown, 18 to 20 minutes. Transfer with a slotted spoon to a bowl. Add 2 tablespoons of the oil, the turnips, parsnips, and a hefty pinch of salt and cook until golden brown, 18 to 20 minutes. Transfer them to the bowl with the onions and carrots.

> While the vegetables are browning, drain the porcini mushrooms through a strainer lined with a wet paper towel, reserving the soaking liquid. Clean the porcini mushrooms to rid them of any excess dirt and chop them.

> Add the remaining tablespoon oil and the cremini mushrooms to the Dutch oven and cook, stirring occasionally, until the liquid the mushrooms give off has evaporated. Add the garlic, thyme, and tomato paste and cook, stirring, 1 minute. Add the porcini soaking liquid and the wine and bring the mixture to a boil, whisking. Combine the flour and 1/3 cup water in a small bowl and whisk well. Add the flour mixture to the Dutch oven in a stream, whisking; bring back to a boil and simmer for 2 minutes.

> Return all the vegetables and the cleaned porcini to the Dutch oven along with the paprika and soy sauce and simmer, uncovered, until the vegetables are barely tender, 20 to 30 minutes. Increase the heat to high and boil until the broth has thickened to the desired consistency. Stir in the lemon juice and add salt and pepper to taste.

SPICY GREENS RAVIOLI

START TO FINISH: 40 MINUTES / **HANDS-ON TIME:** 30 MINUTES / **SERVINGS:** 4

All-purpose flour for dusting
   parchment paper

3 tablespoons extra-virgin olive oil

9 cups packed spicy or bitter greens,
   such as arugula, escarole, watercress,
   or mustard greens, finely chopped
   (about ³/₄ pound)

¹/₄ cup plus 2 tablespoons Homemade
   Ricotta-Style Cheese (page 48) or
   store-bought ricotta

3 tablespoons freshly grated pecorino
   cheese, plus extra for sprinkling

Pinch of freshly grated nutmeg

Kosher salt and freshly ground black
   pepper

32 square wonton wrappers

1 large egg white, lightly beaten with
   1 teaspoon water

2 tablespoons unsalted butter

¹/₂ cup chopped toasted walnuts

> Bring 6 quarts of water to a boil in a large saucepan or stockpot. Line a baking sheet with parchment and dust the parchment with flour.

> Heat the oil in a large skillet over medium-high heat, add the greens, and cook, stirring until they are wilted, about 3 minutes. Transfer them to a strainer set over a bowl and let them drain until they are cool enough to handle. Working with a small handful at a time, squeeze out the greens over the colander, reserving the liquid. Transfer the greens to a bowl. Set the skillet aside.

> Add the ricotta and the 3 tablespoons pecorino to the greens, combine well, and add the nutmeg and salt and pepper to taste. Working with a few wonton wrappers at a time (keeping the others covered tightly with plastic wrap), arrange 3 wrappers on the counter and spoon a rounded tablespoon of the filling on top of each. Moisten the edges of the wrappers with the egg white mixture, place a second wrapper on top of the filling, and press down with your fingers, first to remove the air and then to seal the edges tightly. Transfer the filled ravioli to the prepared baking sheet.

> When the pot of water is boiling, add 2 tablespoons salt and the ravioli. Simmer gently, stirring occasionally, until al dente, 5 to 6 minutes.

> Meanwhile, heat the reserved cooking liquid from the greens in the reserved skillet over medium-high heat. When the ravioli are done, reserve 1 cup of the pasta cooking liquid and drain the ravioli. Add them to the skillet along with the butter and enough of the pasta cooking liquid to make a sauce. Transfer the ravioli to 4 shallow bowls and spoon some of the sauce on top along with a sprinkling of walnuts and more pecorino cheese.

66

I love the combination of sautéed bitter greens and cheese—and this is one of my favorite ways to prepare them: tucked into ravioli and topped with a sauce based on the greens' juices.

You will be able to pull this recipe together on a weeknight by using wonton wrappers, which are one of my favorite shortcut ingredients. Fresh squares of pasta dough, wonton wrappers are a mainstay in the refrigerated section of supermarkets everywhere, right alongside the tofu and miso. Just be sure that the two wonton wrappers sandwiching the filling are properly sealed, so the filling doesn't spill out when you simmer the ravioli.

I topped my ravioli with toasted walnuts, but pine nuts or pistachios would be lovely, too. And if you can't find pecorino, reach for the Parmigiano-Reggiano; it's slightly less salty than its southern Italian cousin.

99

KOREAN VEGETABLE PANCAKES

START TO FINISH: I HOUR 5 MINUTES / **HANDS-ON TIME:** 25 MINUTES / **SERVINGS:** 4

> Thin pancakes studded with vegetables and/or meat or fish, Korean pancakes are usually served as a side dish or an appetizer with a dipping sauce. Paired up with a buddy dish or two—Sesame Kale Salad (as shown at right, recipe page 286), for example, or Baked Eggplant with Miso-Ginger Glaze (page 294)—they're a strong component in a full vegetarian meal.
>
> You're welcome to vary the vegetables added to the pancake batter. Just keep in mind that they won't spend a lot of time in the pan, so they'll need to be cut very small—or grated or blanched—before adding to the batter so that they cook through.
>
> This recipe happens to live in the vegetarian chapter, but I think it would be a delightful accompaniment to any fish or meat entrée, too.

For the pancakes:

120 grams (about 1 cup) all-purpose flour

1 teaspoon baking powder

1/2 teaspoon fine sea salt or table salt

1 large egg

1 tablespoon soy sauce

5 1/2 tablespoons vegetable oil, preferably grapeseed, divided

2 cups thinly sliced shiitakes (about 4 ounces)

Kosher salt

1/2 bunch thin scallions, white and green parts

1 cup coarsely grated carrot

1 small serrano chile, minced (remove seeds and ribs first, if desired)

For the dipping sauce:

1/4 cup soy sauce

1 1/2 tablespoons unseasoned rice vinegar

2 teaspoons finely grated fresh ginger

1 teaspoon sugar

> **Make the pancakes:** Whisk together the flour, baking powder, salt, 1 cup cold water, egg, and soy sauce just until smooth. Let stand for 30 minutes. Preheat the oven to 250°F.

> Meanwhile, heat 1 tablespoon of the oil in a large nonstick or stick-resistant skillet over medium-high heat. Add the shiitakes and a hefty pinch of Kosher salt, reduce the heat to medium, and sauté until the mushrooms are tender and golden at the edges, 4 to 5 minutes. Transfer to a bowl and let cool slightly.

> While the mushrooms are cooking, trim off and discard about 1/2 inch of the scallion greens. Cut the remaining scallions in half lengthwise and then into 1-inch lengths. Add them to the batter, along with the cooled shiitakes, carrot, and chile.

> Add 1 1/2 tablespoons of the remaining oil to the skillet and heat over high heat until a flick of water evaporates quickly. Add one-third of the batter to the skillet and spread out to completely coat the bottom of the pan. Turn the heat down to medium and cook until lightly golden on the bottom, 1 1/2 to 2 minutes. Turn over carefully using two spatulas and cook until golden on the second side, 1 1/2 to 2 minutes. Transfer to paper towels to drain, and then to a rimmed baking sheet. Move the pan to the oven to keep the pancake warm while you repeat the procedure two times with the remaining oil and batter.

> **Make the dipping sauce:** Combine the soy sauce, rice vinegar, ginger, sugar, and 1 tablespoon water in a small bowl. Cut the warm pancakes into wedges and serve with the dipping sauce on the side.

STIR-FRIED TOFU
IN CHILE-ORANGE SAUCE

START TO FINISH: 1 HOUR 15 MINUTES / **HANDS-ON TIME:** 40 MINUTES / **SERVINGS:** 4

1 (14-ounce) package extra-firm
 water-packed tofu

For the sauce:

1 tablespoon cornstarch

1/4 cup fresh orange juice

2 tablespoons hoisin

1 tablespoon soy sauce

2 tablespoons chili garlic sauce

1/2 teaspoon sesame oil

For the vegetables:

1/4 cup vegetable oil, preferably
 grapeseed, divided

Kosher salt

1 red bell pepper, cut into thin strips

6 cups medium broccoli florets,
 blanched until crisp tender and
 drained

2 teaspoons finely grated ginger

2 teaspoons minced garlic

Brown or white rice, or the grain of
 your choice (see page 34) as an
 accompaniment

Toasted cashews for garnish

> Cut the tofu in half horizontally, layer with paper towels, and press down with a heavy plate topped with a weight (such as a can of tomatoes), until it is very firm, 20 to 30 minutes. Cut the planks into 1/2- to 3/4-inch cubes.

> **Make the sauce:** Whisk together the cornstarch, orange juice, 1/4 cup water, hoisin, soy sauce, chili garlic sauce, and sesame oil in a bowl. Set aside.

> **Stir-fry the tofu and vegetables:** In a large nonstick or stick-resistant skillet, heat 1 1/2 tablespoons of the vegetable oil over medium-high heat. Add half the tofu, sprinkle with salt, and cook, stirring occasionally until golden brown on all sides, 8 to 10 minutes. Transfer with a slotted spoon to a bowl. Repeat the procedure with another 1 1/2 tablespoons of the oil and the remaining tofu.

> Add the remaining 1 tablespoon oil to the skillet and heat over medium-high heat. Add the bell pepper and cook, stirring, until it is almost tender, about 3 minutes. Add the broccoli and cook for 2 minutes more. Add the ginger and garlic and cook, stirring, 1 minute. Whisk the sauce in the bowl to dissolve the cornstarch, add the sauce to the skillet and bring it to a boil while whisking. Add the tofu and cook just until heated through.

> Arrange a mound of rice on each of 4 plates, spoon the tofu mixture over the rice, and top with cashews.

66

I'm a nut for sauces, and often prefer a milder-tasting protein to serve as a base for whatever I'm ladling on top. I realized recently that tofu is an excellent vehicle for a tasty sauce. When properly prepared, it is firm, not flabby—a natural sponge for flavor.

Losing the excess water in tofu will not only improve the texture but also keep it from watering down the dish. Press the tofu as described in the first step. It becomes less mushy and more firm the longer you press it, and when cooked will have a springy texture and crispy exterior. You can achieve the same effect by freezing the tofu. Just pat it dry and proceed with the recipe.

Frozen tofu also absorbs sauce more readily, which makes it a wonderful foil for this recipe's intense chile-orange sauce. Served on white or brown rice, it's a light but filling one-dish meal. My husband, a die-hard carnivore, had no idea this was a healthy vegetarian dish. He just scarfed it down and said thank you.

99

VEGETABLE FRITTERS
WITH GREEN CHILE–COCONUT CHUTNEY

❝

A popular street snack throughout India and Pakistan, *pakoras* are fritters of vegetables dipped in a spiced batter, deep-fried, and served with a flavorful chutney. The typical batter calls for seasoned chickpea flour combined with water and often a leavener such as baking powder. In search of an extra-light texture for this fritter, I took a cue from Japanese tempura, substituting seltzer for water, and then folding in some beaten egg whites at the last moment.

Delicious here, the green chile–coconut chutney also partners beautifully with any savory pancake (like the Korean Vegetable Pancakes on page 220), as well as with grilled fish or chicken. A simple side dish like Sautéed Shredded Carrots with Pine Nuts (page 301, shown here), Sesame Kale Salad (page 286), or Tomato-Avocado Salad with Gingered Tomato Vinaigrette (page 284) makes these fritters a meal.

❞

START TO FINISH: 45 MINUTES / **HANDS-ON TIME:** 45 MINUTES / **SERVINGS:** 6

170 grams (about 2 cups) chickpea flour (see Sources, page 350)

1 tablespoon ground cumin

1 tablespoon ground coriander

1½ teaspoons kosher salt

1 teaspoon cayenne

½ teaspoon baking powder

1¾ cups plain seltzer

2 large egg whites

Vegetable oil, preferably grapeseed, for deep-frying

10 (2-by 1-inch) cauliflower or broccoli florets

10 (½- by 1- to 2-inch, ½-inch thick) carrot or butternut squash slices

10 (½-inch-thick) onion rings

Green Chile–Coconut Chutney (page 225)

› In a medium bowl, whisk together the chickpea flour, cumin, coriander, salt, cayenne, and baking powder. Add the seltzer in a stream, whisking until the mixture is smooth. Right before frying, whisk the egg whites in a bowl with electric beaters until they reach soft peaks and fold them into the batter (see page 344).

> Heat 2 inches of oil in a large deep saucepan to 365°F. Working in batches of 5 or so pieces at a time, dip the vegetables in the batter, add carefully to the oil, and fry, turning often, until golden, about 5 minutes for the harder vegetables and 2 minutes for the onion rings.

> Transfer to paper towels to drain. Serve hot with the chutney on the side.

GREEN CHILE–COCONUT CHUTNEY

START TO FINISH: 15 MINUTES / **HANDS-ON TIME:** 15 MINUTES / **SERVINGS:** MAKES ABOUT 1½ CUPS

2 cups packed fresh cilantro, leaves and stems

½ cup chopped scallions, white and light green parts

¼ cup sweetened flaked coconut

2 serrano chiles, chopped with seeds (about 2 heaping tablespoons)

3 tablespoons vegetable oil, preferably grapeseed

1½ tablespoons finely grated ginger

2 tablespoons fresh lime juice

2 tablespoons water

1 to 2 teaspoons packed brown sugar, or to taste

Kosher salt and freshly ground black pepper

Puree all the ingredients in a blender, adding salt and pepper to taste.

Cook's Notes: Proper Deep-Frying

▶ **Pick your oil carefully.** Read the label to be sure that it's appropriate for frying. The bottle should say "for high heat," meaning that it has a high smoke point. The smoke point is the temperature at which an oil starts to break down. Above that temp, it can catch fire. When you're frying food, the oil you use should have a smoke point of 400°F or higher.

▶ Oil and water don't mix. **Make sure the food you add to the oil is dry** or well-coated in batter; water makes the oil spatter.

▶ Fry safely. For safety's sake, heat the oil in a deep pan and **use a deep-fat thermometer** to monitor its temperature. Most frying recipes stipulate a temperature in the low to high 300°Fs. If your oil reaches 400°F, pull the pan off the burner and let the oil cool down, or add a tiny bit more oil.

▶ **Maintain your temperature.** The correct temperature is key to frying properly. Too low and the food will absorb more oil and taste oily; too high and the food will get too brown on the outside before it is cooked on the inside.

▶ **Fry the food in batches** so that the oil stays at a constant temperature; when you crowd the pan, the temp drops. Turn the food with a spider (see pages 18–19) or a slotted spoon and, when it's done, transfer it to a baking sheet lined with paper towels to absorb any excess oil.

CHICKPEA FLOUR: A GREAT ALTERNATIVE

Chickpea flour is much more readily available than it used to be, perhaps because it's gluten-free. (Supermarkets these days often stock the kind made by Bob's Red Mill. You'll find online sources on page 350). I love the nuttiness chickpea flour brings to the batter for these fritters, but it has many other uses:

▶ For thin pancakes, whisk together equal parts water and chickpea flour and let the batter stand for 30 minutes before using.

▶ Add chickpea flour to sautéed vegetables to coat and flavor them and to amp up the nutrition.

▶ Add chickpea flour to yogurt to stabilize it and keep the yogurt from breaking down as quickly in a cooked sauce.

ZUCCHINI PATTIES
WITH GARLICKY YOGURT SAUCE

START TO FINISH: 60 MINUTES / **HANDS-ON TIME:** 45 MINUTES
SERVINGS: 4 (MAKES ABOUT 16 PATTIES)

1 cup plain Greek yogurt (full-fat or low-fat)

3¹/₂ teaspoons minced garlic, divided

¹/₂ teaspoon freshly grated lemon zest

Kosher salt and freshly ground black pepper

1 pound zucchini (about 3 medium)

1 cup cooked chickpeas (see page 36) or drained, rinsed, canned chickpeas

¹/₄ cup plus 1 tablespoon extra-virgin olive oil, divided

¹/₂ cup minced onion

³/₄ teaspoon ground cumin

¹/₂ teaspoon ground coriander

¹/₂ cup dry breadcrumbs

¹/₄ cup toasted pine nuts, chopped

¹/₂ cup packed fresh parsley leaves, finely chopped

¹/₃ cup packed fresh mint leaves, finely chopped

4 6-inch pitas with pockets, halved

Shredded lettuce

Grated Carrot Salad

> Preheat the oven to 200°F. Combine the yogurt, 1¹/₂ teaspoons of the garlic, the lemon zest, and salt and pepper to taste in a small bowl and set aside.

> Coarsely grate the zucchini in a food processor fitted with the medium shredding disk. Toss with 1 teaspoon salt in a colander and let stand 15 minutes to drain. Wipe out the food processor, fit it with the cutting blade, and add the chickpeas and 1 tablespoon water. Process until fairly smooth.

> Heat 1 tablespoon of the oil in a large nonstick or stick-resistant skillet over medium heat, add the onion, and cook until golden, about 8 minutes. Add the remaining 2 teaspoons garlic, the cumin, and coriander and cook, stirring for 1 minute. Transfer to a medium bowl and set the skillet aside.

> Working with a small handful at a time, squeeze out the zucchini to remove excess moisture; add it to the bowl with the onion. Add the chickpeas, breadcrumbs, pine nuts, parsley, mint, and salt and pepper to taste; combine well, using your hands if necessary. Roll 2-tablespoon portions into balls (you should get about 16) and flatten them into patties ¹/₂ inch thick and 2 inches wide.

> Heat 2 tablespoons of the remaining oil in the skillet over medium heat, add half the patties, and cook, turning once, until golden on both sides, about 6 minutes. Transfer them to a rimmed baking sheet and keep warm in the oven. Repeat procedure with remaining oil and patties. To serve, arrange several patties in each pita half, top with the yogurt sauce, lettuce, and Grated Carrot Salad.

Grated Carrot Salad: Whisk together 2 tablespoons white vinegar, ¹/₂ teaspoon sugar, and ¹/₄ teaspoon kosher salt in a medium bowl. Add 2 cups coarsely grated carrots and toss well.

"

This is a meal in a sandwich—a zucchini burger that's blended with mashed chickpeas and breadcrumbs and nicely seasoned with spices and fresh herbs. It's equally appropriate on a summer's day in the backyard as on a wintry night in front of the fire. The pine nuts add crunch and, well, nuttiness. The garlicky yogurt sauce is crucial; it provides a tangy, creamy contrast.

As ever, the zucchini needs to be salted, drained, and squeezed before it's added to the mix. This will not only rid it of excess water (you'll be amazed at how much it shrinks down), but also help to concentrate the flavor.

As you shape the mix into patties, don't flatten them too much. They're somewhat delicate. Serve these stuffed pita halves with a quick salad of grated carrots.

"

LEMONY CARROT "FETTUCCINE"
WITH TOASTED PISTACHIOS

START TO FINISH: 35 MINUTES / **HANDS-ON TIME:** 30 MINUTES / **SERVINGS:** 4

1/2 cup chopped pistachios

2 pounds large carrots, peeled and stem ends discarded

1 cup Homemade Vegetable Stock (page 29) or store-bought vegetable broth, divided

1 tablespoon freshly grated lemon zest

Kosher salt and freshly ground black pepper

6 to 8 ounces Neufchâtel (1/3-less-fat cream cheese)

1 teaspoon fresh lemon juice

2 tablespoons chopped fresh chives

> Preheat the oven to 350°F. Spread the pistachios in a single layer in a shallow baking dish and bake them on the middle shelf of the oven until fragrant, about 5 minutes. Remove and set aside.

> Meanwhile, using a swivel blade or a Y-shape vegetable peeler, peel the carrots into long, fettuccine-like strands, discarding the core (or save it for a snack or a stock).

> Combine the vegetable stock, lemon zest, a hefty pinch of salt, and several grinds of pepper in a large skillet; whisk the mixture until the zest is well distributed.

> Break up the cream cheese into small pieces and add it to the skillet along with the carrot strands. Cover the skillet tightly and bring the stock to a boil. Reduce the heat and simmer the carrots, covered, 3 minutes. Remove the lid, and stir the carrots gently with tongs to make sure that the cheese is well distributed. Cover and simmer just until the carrots are tender, 1 to 2 minutes more.

> Stir in the lemon juice and salt and pepper to taste. Mound the carrot "fettuccine" on each of 4 plates and top each portion with one-fourth of the toasted pistachios and the chives.

"This dish—featuring ribbons of carrot masquerading as pasta in a creamy sauce reminiscent of Fettucine Alfredo—is a great way to get your kids eating more vegetables.

Start with big, long, fat carrots. Just peel off and discard the outermost layer, and then continue peeling on all sides until you've reached the woody core. I find it easiest to start at the middle of the carrot and peel down the bottom half, then flip it over and peel the top half.

The sauce for this "fettuccine" is quite simple. It's based on Neufchâtel, the variation on cream cheese that is miraculously creamy and has one-third less fat than most other types of cream cheese. Add the full 8 ounces if you want an extra-creamy sauce.

I counter-balance the carrot's natural sweetness with lemon (both zest and juice) although lime would work just as well. The pistachios add crunch, nutty taste, and some nutrition, but any nut will do.

The carrots cook quickly—so prep them ahead of time, and measure out all the rest of the ingredients as well. Once cooked, you'll want to serve before the strands go soft. Happily, cooking this dish is simple enough to do at the last minute. And it's both delicious and filling. Pair with Tomato-Avocado Salad with Gingered Tomato Vinaigrette (page 284, as pictured here) for a complete meal."

Cooking with *Amanda Cohen*

BROCCOLI CARPACCIO
WITH BROCCOLI STALK SALAD

Adapted from *Dirt Candy* (Clarkson Potter, 2012).

START TO FINISH: 45 MINUTES / **HANDS-ON TIME:** 45 MINUTES / **SERVINGS:** 4 TO 6

3 large broccoli stalks, about 1¹/₂ inches in diameter and about 9 inches long

For the broccoli planks:

3 tablespoons minced fresh Thai basil, cilantro, or mint

1 teaspoon minced peeled ginger

1 teaspoon minced garlic

¹/₄ teaspoon chopped red bird's-eye chile or other hot chile

Kosher salt

3 tablespoons fresh lime juice

2 very firm but ripe avocadoes

1¹/₂ to 2 tablespoons extra-virgin olive oil

For the broccoli stalk salad:

Vegetable oil for deep-frying

¹/₄ cup cornstarch

2 cups mesclun mix

¹/₄ cup thinly sliced red onion

1 tablespoon extra-virgin olive oil

1 tablespoon fresh lime juice

Pinch of freshly ground black pepper

> Following the photos on page 233, trim the tough outsides of the broccoli stalks, shaping each stalk into a long rectangular block. Using a mandoline, slice 2 of the blocks thinly (¹/₈ inch or thinner). You should get 8 slices from each stalk; set what's left aside for the next step.

> Using a vegetable peeler, shave the stalks from the previous step into thin ribbons and set them aside. Julienne the remaining third broccoli stem (you should have about ¹/₃ cup) and put the julienned strips in a large bowl.

> In a small bowl, mix the basil, ginger, garlic, chile, and ¹/₂ teaspoon salt into a rough paste and set aside. Use a mortar and pestle if you like, but be sure that all the ingredients are finely minced beforehand.

> Put the broccoli slices in a bowl and add the lime juice and ¹/₂ teaspoon salt. Toss to coat. With a vegetable peeler, peel the avocado and then peel about 16 thin (about ¹/₈ inch or thinner) slices from the fruit. Arrange 4 slices each of the avocado and broccoli slices alternating on a board and trim them neatly around the edges. Carefully transfer the slices onto the plate and drizzle with the olive oil. Repeat for the remaining servings.

> In a large pot, heat 2 inches of vegetable oil to 325°F.

(recipe continues)

"

The vegetarian restaurateuse Amanda Cohen, one of the most creative chefs I know, is not exactly a well-kept secret. The original Dirt Candy, her highly regarded shoe box–sized spot on New York's Lower East Side, was so popular that it was darn near impossible to get a reservation. Indeed, the food was so good that even The Husband, a devout carnivore, was impressed. (I was afraid he'd suggest going out for 'a real meal' immediately afterwards, but nope, he was content.) Happily, Amanda has relocated Dirt Candy to a larger space and has garnered even greater critical acclaim.

As Amanda explains, the latest trend of nose-to-tail cooking, in which every part of the animal is served, has expanded into all types of cuisine, including vegetarian. This recipe makes use of broccoli stalks, which are normally thrown in the trash. Amanda thinks the broccoli stalks have a sweeter taste than the florets. Look for firm, hard stalks to achieve the best result. This elegant dish, which boasts a variety of textures and flavors, is perfect for entertaining.

"

› Coat the broccoli ribbons in cornstarch and deep-fry until they hold their shape and turn a very light brown color, about 30 seconds. Watch the vegetable ribbons carefully and be ready to pull them from the oil—they will crisp up very quickly. Remove to a paper towel and sprinkle with salt.

› Mix the julienned broccoli with the mesclun, onion, olive oil, lime juice, 1 teaspoon salt, and pinch of pepper and toss to coat.

› To serve, sprinkle the basil paste across the top of the broccoli and avocado slices. Pile the dressed salad on the side and garnish it with the fried broccoli ribbons right before serving (so they don't get soggy).

Cook's Notes: Amanda on Vegetables

▸ We throw away so many parts of vegetables that we could be eating, like broccoli stalks. Taste everything. Don't be scared. It won't hurt you. Taste carrot greens, radish greens, and see if you like the flavor. If you do, use them as you would any other more common greens.

▸ We're so used to cutting and cooking vegetables in the same ways over and over (potatoes are mashed, cucumbers are raw, root vegetables are roasted) that we get bored of them, even though they are so versatile. So experiment—if you're not thrilled with the results, it won't be a waste of your time. We even make sauerkraut from the vegetable peelings.

MAKING BROCCOLI SALAD WITH AMANDA

1. Cut off the broccoli florets and save them for another use. Trim the tough outsides of the broccoli stalks, shaping each stalk into a long rectangular block.

2. Using a mandoline, slice 2 of the blocks thinly (⅛ inch or thinner). You should get 8 slices from each stalk; set what's left aside for the next step. (Please use the guard that comes with the mandoline!)

3. Using a vegetable peeler, shave the stalks from the previous step into thin ribbons and set them aside.

4. Julienne the remaining core of the third broccoli stem (again, if you are going to do it on the mandoline, please use the guard).

5. Peel the avocado with a vegetable peeler, peeling thin (about ⅛ inch or thinner) slices from the fruit.

6. Arrange 4 alternating slices each of the avocado and broccoli on a board and trim them neatly around the edges. Transfer them to a plate and drizzle with oil. Sprinkle with the herb mixture. Arrange the salad on the plate and top with the fried broccoli ribbons.

KOREAN BBQ TOFU TACOS
WITH VEGAN KIMCHI

Adapted from *Street Vegan* (Clarkson Potter, 2015).

Pictured on page 199

START TO FINISH: 45 MINUTES / **HANDS-ON TIME:** 25 MINUTES / **SERVINGS:** 4

> Veganism is touted as the cuisine most healthful to humans and least damaging to the environment. But the idea that it tastes good? Not that I'd heard. Then I visited Adam Sobel's food truck, Cinnamon Snail. I expected to see a clientele of young folks, "hipsters," and other would-be rebels. In fact, the customers in line for lunch on a weekday were mostly businessmen and businesswomen, as well as ladies who lunch and grannies.
>
> The second surprise was the food itself. It wasn't merely edible, it was really delicious—and I didn't even get the chance to try one of Adam's donuts, the most popular item on his menu.
>
> This recipe is for the dish that Adam and I prepared when he made a guest appearance on *Sara's Weeknight Meals*. Only the kimchi takes some planning, but it's well worth it, and you'll be able to use the extra in soups and sandwiches for several weeks after making it.

For the gochujang roasted tofu filling:

2 tablespoons gochujang (Korean chili paste; see Sources, page 350)

3 tablespoons sesame oil

2 tablespoons maple syrup

1 pound extra-firm tofu

For the Sriracha cream:

1 minced scallion, white and light green parts

1/2 cup Vegenaise or other vegan mayonnaise alternative

2 tablespoons Sriracha sauce

2 tablespoons maple syrup

For the tacos:

8 (5- to 6-inch) Homemade Corn Tortillas (page 270) or store-bought tortillas

2 cups baby arugula

2/3 cup Vegan Kimchi (page 235)

1/4 cup gochujang, optional for garnish

3 tablespoons toasted sesame seeds, optional for garnish

1/4 cup thinly sliced scallions, white and light green parts, optional for garnish

> Preheat the oven to 400°F. Line a baking sheet with parchment paper and lightly oil the paper.

> **Make the gochujang roasted tofu filling:** In a small bowl, whisk together the gochujang, sesame oil, and maple syrup. Cut the tofu into thin strips, about 1/4 inch thick, 1/2 inch wide, and 2 to 3 inches long. Gently toss the tofu in the marinade so that all the sides are coated. Arrange the tofu strips and all the marinade on the prepared baking sheet, leaving a little space between the strips. Bake until golden brown and a little crispy, 15 to 18 minutes.

> **Make the Sriracha cream:** Meanwhile, combine the scallion, Vegenaise, Sriracha, and maple syrup in a small bowl, whisking for about 30 seconds, until an even orange color develops. Set aside.

> Warm the tortillas on both sides by placing them over a gas burner for about 10 seconds on each side. Flip the tortillas with tongs. Alternatively, wrap the tortillas in foil and warm for 10 minutes in a 350°F oven.

> **Make the tacos:** Lay out the tortillas. On each, spread about 1 tablespoon of the Sriracha cream, a small pile of arugula, 2 to 3 tablespoons of kimchi, and 4 strips of tofu. Garnish each taco with additional gochujang, sesame seeds, and scallions if you like.

VEGAN KIMCHI

START TO FINISH: 1 WEEK / **HANDS-ON TIME:** 45 MINUTES / **SERVINGS:** MAKES ABOUT 1 QUART

½ head napa cabbage (about 1½ pounds), any wilted outer leaves discarded

½ daikon radish, peeled, halved lengthwise, and cut crosswise into thin ½-inch moons

4 red radishes, scrubbed and sliced thin

¼ cup plus ½ teaspoon sea salt

2 tablespoons minced onion

1½ teaspoons minced ginger

1½ teaspoons minced garlic

1 teaspoon evaporated sugarcane juice (see Notes) or granulated sugar

⅙ cup Korean ground chile pepper (gochugaru, see Notes)

Roughly chop the cabbage, discarding the center core. In a large bowl, toss together the cabbage, daikon, and red radishes.

Combine ¼ cup salt and 2 cups water in a ½-gallon jar (or other large nonreactive container). Pack the cabbage and radishes into the jar and let them sit at room temperature in the brine for 5 hours. Drain and rinse the brined vegetables in a colander with cool water.

Combine the onion, ginger, garlic, sugarcane juice or sugar, Korean ground chile, ½ teaspoon salt, and 1½ tablespoons of water in a bowl and stir to form a smooth bright red paste. In a bowl, massage the chile paste into the drained vegetables to coat all sides. Press the chile-coated vegetables into a 1-quart glass jar, and really tamp them down to remove extra air.

Cover the jar and let the vegetables ferment at room temperature (between 60° and 78°F) for 3 days. Open the jar and press the kimchi down again to remove any air bubbles. Move the jar to the refrigerator and let the kimchi ripen for at least 4 more days before using. The kimchi will keep for a few weeks in the fridge.

Notes: Sugarcane juice is the juice extracted from sugarcane. Look for it in the soft-drink aisles of Latin, Asian, or Middle Eastern markets; in health food stores; or at big-box retailers.

Gochugaru, Korean ground chile pepper, can be found in Korean or other Asian markets (see Sources, page 350).

NOT ALL KIMCHI IS VEGAN

If you are topping your tacos with store-bought kimchi, and you want to make sure that every part is vegan, check the ingredient list to be sure it doesn't contain fish sauce or brined shrimp paste, which are traditionally part of the recipe.

7 | *cooking when you have* MORE TIME

Cooking on a weekend, or whenever you have a little more time, is a splendid idea for so many reasons. For starters, you can take the time to make a special meal. That's such a gift to your family and friends, whether for a holiday or simply for Sunday night dinner when everyone could use a little lift before contemplating the long work or school week ahead.

On a weekend you can tackle a slightly more complicated dish and learn something new in the process, such as how to prepare preserved duck (pictured opposite) or butterfly, stuff, and tie a pork loin roast. I bet you've never considered making homemade tortillas. Rick Bayless explains the process so well that you might never reach for the store-bought variety again. He also offers some tasty fillings that will satisfy both the carnivores and vegetarians in the family.

Another benefit of cooking ahead is that many dishes, especially braised or stewed items, taste much better a day or two later. Also, how about stockpiling leftovers? Some of the recipes in this chapter generate leftovers that can be repositioned later, including Blasted Chicken and Red Wine–Braised Short Ribs of Beef. Elizabeth Karmel's Smoked Brisket, cooked slow and low on an outside grill, is going to be a crowd-pleaser in the middle of summer or as the star of a hot sandwich later on in the fall.

Finally, there's a paint-by-number kit for Roast Turkey and its sidemen, including a Basic Stuffing formula with variations and Make-Ahead Turkey Gravy. It embodies all the tips I picked up during the years I covered Thanksgiving for *Good Morning America*.

BAKED ARCTIC CHAR
WITH CHERMOULA

START TO FINISH: 60 MINUTES / **HANDS-ON TIME:** 40 MINUTES / **SERVINGS:** 4 TO 6

1 teaspoon minced garlic

¹/₂ teaspoon sweet paprika

¹/₂ teaspoon ground cumin

¹/₄ teaspoon kosher salt

¹/₄ teaspoon cayenne

1 tablespoon fresh lemon juice

¹/₄ cup extra-virgin olive oil

¹/₂ cup finely chopped fresh cilantro

¹/₂ cup finely chopped fresh parsley

¹/₂ cup chopped olives of your choice

2 tablespoons chopped Quick Preserved Lemon Slices (page 47) or 2 teaspoons freshly grated lemon zest

1¹/₂ pounds arctic char fillet (see page 112 for instructions on removing the skin, if needed)

Freshly ground black pepper

> Preheat the oven to 400°F. Combine the garlic, paprika, cumin, ¹/₄ teaspoon salt, cayenne, lemon juice, oil, cilantro, parsley, olives, and preserved lemon in a medium bowl and stir well.

> Spread half of the mixture on the bottom of a shallow baking dish just large enough to hold the fish in a single layer. Season the fish on both sides with salt and pepper and place it on top of the chermoula. Top the fish with the remaining chermoula, spreading it to cover the surface. Cover with foil and bake for 15 to 20 minutes or until the fish is just cooked through.

> *Chermoula*, the Arabic word for marinade, is a North African blend of olive oil, lemon juice, garlic, cilantro, and spices. It can be used on meats or vegetables, but it's a particularly wonderful match for fish because it brings a salty, acidic pungency to a fairly neutral protein.
>
> Almost any fish would work in this recipe, keeping in mind that if you use fillets thinner or thicker than arctic char, you'll need to adjust the cooking time. This is one of my favorite ways to cook fish because the fish and the sauce meld as they bake together in the oven, and the fish becomes deeply flavored.

HOW DO YOU KNOW WHEN FISH IS COOKED?

Fish cooks from the outside in. The best way to find out if it is cooked through is to stick a paring knife straight down through the fish. If the knife goes through with a little resistance in the middle, then the fish is still uncooked in the center.

If you like your fish medium-rare (many people prefer their salmon cooked this way), then take the fish out when there is still a little bit of resistance in the middle. If you like your fish cooked through, take it out when the knife slides through with no resistance.

TOASTED PASTA
WITH SHRIMP AND CHORIZO

" This is a pasta version of *paella,* in which all the ingredients are cooked together in one pan. Its star is *fideo,* a very short thin Spanish noodle that is like Italian vermicelli or spaghetti.

Making this dish requires a little vigilance to make sure that the pasta gets cooked properly. The pasta is toasted in a skillet until golden, removed from the pan while the sauce is coming together, and then added back and simmered until almost tender. Finally, the whole dish is finished under the broiler, turning the tips of the pasta quite crunchy and brown.

Preseasoning the shrimp is key: It concentrates its flavor in advance of cooking. Also, don't skimp on the garlic mayo: The dish tastes so much more interesting with a drizzle of it on top. "

START TO FINISH: I HOUR 20 MINUTES / **HANDS-ON TIME:** 60 MINUTES / **SERVINGS:** 4 TO 6

1 pound peeled and deveined large (26/30) shrimp (see page 81)

3 tablespoons plus 2 teaspoons extra-virgin olive oil, divided

1 tablespoon minced garlic, divided

Kosher salt

8 ounces fideo (see Sources, page 350), spaghettini, or thin spaghetti, broken into 1- to 2-inch lengths

6 ounces Spanish chorizo (see Sources, page 350), peeled, quartered lengthwise, and sliced ¼ inch thick crosswise

1 cup finely chopped onion

1³⁄₄ cups Speedy Marinara Sauce (page 30) or your favorite store-bought tomato sauce

1 teaspoon smoked paprika

1 teaspoon sweet or hot paprika

12 ounces broccoli rabe or broccoli, trimmed, coarsely chopped, and briefly blanched (about 2 cups, see Note)

¹⁄₂ cup dry white wine

3 cups Homemade Chicken Stock (page 26) or store-bought chicken broth

Garlic Mayonnaise (page 241)

> Toss the shrimp with 1 tablespoon of the oil, 1 teaspoon of the garlic, and $1/4$ teaspoon salt in a bowl, cover, and set aside.

> Toss the fideos with 2 teaspoons of the oil in a large, broiler-safe skillet and toast over medium-high heat, stirring frequently, until the pasta is golden brown, 6 to 8 minutes. (Be careful, this process can happen very quickly and the pasta can burn.) Transfer the fideos to a bowl.

> Add the remaining 2 tablespoons oil to the skillet and heat over medium-low heat. Add the chorizo and cook, stirring, 2 minutes. Transfer with a slotted spoon to the bowl with the pasta and pour off and discard all but 3 tablespoons of the remaining fat in the skillet. Add the onion to the skillet, increase the heat to medium, and cook, stirring occasionally until golden, about 10 minutes. Add the remaining 2 teaspoons garlic and cook, stirring, 1 minute more.

> Add the marinara sauce, bring to a simmer, and cook, stirring occasionally, until the mixture is thick, about 4 minutes. Add the two paprikas and cook, stirring, 1 minute. Add the pasta, chorizo, and the broccoli rabe to the pan and stir to combine. Pour in the wine and chicken stock and bring the mixture to a boil. Preheat the broiler.

> Simmer the pasta mixture, stirring occasionally, until the liquid is slightly thickened and the fideos are just al dente, 8 to 10 minutes. Scatter the shrimp over the pasta and press them into the pasta to partially submerge. Transfer the skillet to the top shelf of the oven set about 4 inches from the heat and broil until the shrimp are opaque and the top of the pasta is dry and crisped in spots, 3 to 4 minutes.

> Serve each portion topped with a spoonful of the Garlic Mayonnaise.

Note: For a variation, substitute 2 cups defrosted frozen peas for the broccoli rabe, adding the peas to the skillet for the last 4 minutes of cooking before the pan is set under the broiler.

GARLIC MAYONNAISE

START TO FINISH: 5 MINUTES / **HANDS-ON TIME:** 5 MINUTES / **SERVINGS:** MAKES ABOUT ¾ CUP

$3/4$ cup Homemade Mayonnaise (pages 52–53) or store-bought mayonnaise

1 to $1^{1}/_{2}$ teaspoons minced garlic

2 teaspoons fresh lemon juice

Kosher salt and freshly ground black pepper

Combine the mayonnaise, garlic, and lemon juice in a bowl and add salt and pepper to taste.

BLASTED CHICKEN

START TO FINISH: I HOUR 5 MINUTES / **HANDS-ON TIME:** 5 MINUTES / **SERVINGS:** 4

1 (3½-pound) chicken, trimmed of excess fat and patted dry
Extra-virgin olive oil for brushing

Kosher salt and freshly ground black pepper

> Preheat the oven to 450°F. Brush the chicken all over with the oil and season it well with salt and pepper to taste. Place the chicken, breast side up, on a rack in a roasting pan. Roast on the middle shelf of the oven until a thermometer inserted into the thickest part of the thigh, not touching the bone, registers 160°F, about 45 minutes. Transfer the chicken to a cutting board, cover loosely with foil, and let stand for 15 minutes before carving.

Cook's Notes: Tips for Successful Roast Chicken

▶ **The timing is based on a "broiler," or 3½-pound chicken,** so try to stick to that weight. (It feeds four people nicely.)

▶ **Your oven must be very clean** or it will start smoking.

▶ **You must let the chicken rest** for a full 15 minutes after you pull it from the oven and before you start carving, or it will lose all its juices and become dry.

▶ **You might want to get into the habit of roasting two of these birds at once,** so that the second can provide leftovers for meals later in the week. Think of it as your own homemade rotisserie chicken.

> "This is my favorite way to roast chicken and I hope it'll become yours. I learned how to make it during my last restaurant job, where it was frequently the centerpiece of our family meal. Family meal is the one shared by the staff at the end of the afternoon before the doors open to the public. Given all the time and energy required to prepare for service, we spent very little time or energy on niceties for ourselves. This chicken was oiled, seasoned with salt and pepper, and tossed without further ado (no trussing required) into an oven blasting away at 500°F. That's the temperature at which everything was cooked and why I call this recipe "Blasted Chicken." (I've reduced the temperature to 450°F for home-roasting purposes). You might imagine that such a simply prepared bird would be a bust, but it turns out to be the most delicious roast chicken on the planet: The skin is wonderfully crispy; the meat is perfectly moist."

BLASTED CHICKEN, PERUVIAN STYLE

> Peruvian chicken, a whole chicken marinated in spices and spit-roasted or grilled, has become quite popular in my neck of the woods. The reason: a great little franchise of Peruvian restaurants called Pio Pio. When I don't feel like cooking dinner, we call Pio Pio. They deliver.
>
> But good as the chicken is, the real attraction—the *addictive* attraction—is their green sauce. Hot—but not too hot—and uniquely flavorful, it's tantalized me for years. How do they do it? What are the recipe's secret ingredients? Over and over again I've tried to bust it and failed—and the Pio Pio folks are definitely keeping the solution to this puzzle to themselves.
>
> Happily, I'm pretty sure I've finally discovered the missing ingredient. It's *aji amarillo,* a bright-orange, thick-fleshed chile with a medium-to-hot heat level, native to South America and ubiquitous in Peruvian cuisine. You can find aji amarillo paste at Latin markets and online (see Sources, page 350).
>
> I don't think my green sauce is going to put Pio Pio out of business, but I'm very pleased just to have come within shouting distance of the original. Add it to soups, stews, vegetable dishes—it dazzles anywhere you'd drizzle hot sauce. Serve this dish with Crispy Jerusalem Artichokes on page 291.

START TO FINISH: I HOUR I5 MINUTES PLUS 6 TO 24 HOURS MARINATING TIME
HANDS-ON TIME: I5 MINUTES / **SERVINGS:** 4

¹/₄ cup soy sauce

2 tablespoons extra-virgin olive oil

2 tablespoons roughly chopped garlic

2 teaspoons ground cumin

2 teaspoons smoked paprika

2 teaspoons dried oregano

1 tablespoon aji amarillo paste (see Sources, page 350)

¹/₄ cup fresh lime juice

1 (3¹/₂-pound) chicken (see Note), trimmed of excess fat and patted dry

Green Sauce (page 245) as an accompaniment

❯ Process the soy sauce, oil, garlic, cumin, paprika, oregano, aji amarillo paste, and lime juice in a blender until a smooth. Using a grapefruit spoon, curved side up, your fingers, or the handle of a wooden spoon, carefully loosen the skin over the thighs and breast. Put the chicken in a resealable plastic bag and pour half the marinade beneath the skin of the chicken. Pour the remaining marinade over the outside surface of the chicken. Seal and chill at least 6 hours up to 24 hours, turning the bag several times.

> Preheat the oven to 450°F. Remove the chicken from the bag and arrange on a rack in a roasting pan. Cover loosely with foil and roast for 20 minutes. Uncover and roast until a thermometer inserted in the thickest part of the thigh, not touching the bone, registers 160°F, about 25 minutes more. Remove from the oven and let it rest for 15 minutes before carving.

> Serve with green sauce.

Note: The timing of this recipe is based on a "broiler," or 3½-pound chicken, so try to stick to that weight.

GREEN SAUCE

START TO FINISH: 20 MINUTES / **HANDS-ON TIME:** 20 MINUTES / **SERVINGS:** MAKES ABOUT I CUP

½ cup roughly chopped scallions, white and light green parts

⅓ cup packed fresh cilantro, leaves and stems

¼ cup roughly chopped jalapeño or serrano, with seeds and ribs

½ cup Homemade Mayonnaise (pages 52–53) or store-bought mayonnaise

1 tablespoon aji amarillo paste (see Sources, page 350)

½ ounce crumbled fresh goat cheese (about 2 tablespoons)

½ teaspoon minced garlic

1 tablespoon vegetable oil, preferably grapeseed

1 teaspoon white vinegar

½ teaspoon fresh lime juice

½ teaspoon kosher salt

Combine all the ingredients in a blender and puree until smooth. Cover and chill. The green sauce will keep in the fridge for 10 days.

WHAT TO DO WITH THE LEFTOVERS

Use the extra chicken from these roasted chickens wherever you would have reached for rotisserie or cooked chicken, including Green Chile Rice and Chicken Skillet Dinner (page 187), Thai-Style Chicken Salad (page 94), and Speedy Korean Chicken Noodle Soup (page 71).

CHICKEN IN A POT
WITH MOROCCAN SPICES

"

A French country dish known as *poule au pot* that dates back to the seventeenth century, chicken in a pot typically consists of a whole stuffed chicken poached with vegetables. All the ingredients contribute to a rich broth, which is then served with the chicken and vegetables. This version, minus the stuffing, is a lean dish that still delivers big flavor. It's a wonderful meal to serve to a crowd.

Given that all animal protein becomes tough when boiled, the key to success here is to cook the chicken gently, ensuring that it stays moist and tender. All of this care pays off in the finished texture of the star of the show. Rubber chicken is a dish only a comedian could love.

Spice-wise, I have taken this French dish to Morocco, adding ginger and harissa, a hot chile paste popular in northern Africa. I like to serve it with flatbread or Grill Pan Garlic Bread (page 305), although you're welcome to ladle the chicken and vegetables onto couscous to complete the Moroccan theme.

"

START TO FINISH: 2 HOURS / **HANDS-ON TIME:** 50 MINUTES / **SERVINGS:** 8

3 tablespoons vegetable oil, preferably grapeseed

2 large leeks, trimmed of green part, halved lengthwise, cut into 1-inch lengths crosswise, washed, and dried

1/2 pound cremini mushrooms, quartered

1 1/2 tablespoons minced garlic

1 1/2 tablespoons finely grated ginger

1 (3 1/2-pound) chicken

3 quarts Homemade Chicken Stock (page 26) or store-bought chicken broth

1 pound carrots, peeled and cut into 1-inch pieces

1/2 pound parsnips, peeled and cut into 1-inch pieces

1/2 pound turnips, peeled and cut into 1-inch pieces

1/2 pound boiling potatoes, cut into 1-inch pieces

Kosher salt and freshly ground black pepper

Harissa (page 247)

Chopped fresh cilantro or parsley for garnish

> Heat the oil over medium heat in a 7- to 8-quart pot. Add the leeks and cook, stirring occasionally, until softened, about 3 minutes. Add the mushrooms and cook, stirring occasionally, 5 minutes. Add the garlic and ginger and cook,

stirring, 1 minute. Add the chicken, breast side down, pour the stock over the chicken, and bring the stock just to a boil. Reduce the heat and simmer, skimming the scum that comes to the surface, for 10 minutes. Cover and simmer gently for another 15 minutes. Turn off the heat, cover, and let the chicken sit in the hot stock for 30 minutes. Carefully remove the chicken from the pot and let it cool until it can be handled.

› Add the carrots, parsnips, turnips, and potatoes to the stock and bring the stock to a boil. Reduce the heat and simmer, covered, until the vegetables are just tender, 12 to 15 minutes.

› Meanwhile, pull off and discard the skin from the chicken and remove the meat from the bones in large chunks. When the vegetables are tender, return the chicken meat to the pot and simmer gently, just until heated through. Season with salt and pepper to taste. Ladle the soup into each of 8 soup bowls and top each portion with a spoonful of the harissa and some cilantro.

HARISSA

START TO FINISH: 10 MINUTES / **HANDS-ON TIME:** 10 MINUTES / **SERVINGS:** MAKES ABOUT 1 CUP

1 (12-ounce) jar roasted red peppers, drained

1 tablespoon extra-virgin olive oil

2 teaspoons minced garlic

2 teaspoons fresh lemon juice

1 teaspoon cumin seeds

1 teaspoon red pepper flakes

1/2 teaspoon coriander seeds

1/2 teaspoon caraway seeds

1/2 teaspoon kosher salt

Combine all the ingredients in a blender and process until smooth. The harissa will keep in the fridge for about 1 week.

DUCK CONFIT
COOKED IN A SLOW COOKER

Pictured on page 237

START TO FINISH: 4 HOURS 35 MINUTES PLUS 12 TO 36 HOURS MARINATING TIME
HANDS-ON TIME: 15 MINUTES / **SERVINGS:** 6

1 Turkish bay leaf, crumbled, plus
  2 whole bay leaves, divided

3 tablespoons chopped fresh thyme
  leaves plus 5 small sprigs of thyme,
  divided

3 tablespoons kosher salt

3 tablespoons minced shallots

2 tablespoons minced garlic

2 teaspoons black peppercorns, lightly
  crushed

1 teaspoon ground allspice

6 pair duck legs with thighs attached

8 cups duck fat (see Sources, page 350)

1 head of garlic, cut in half through the
  middle

> Combine the crumbled bay leaf, the chopped thyme, the salt, shallots, minced garlic, peppercorns, and allspice in a small bowl. Sprinkle half the mixture in the bottom of a shallow baking dish. Add the duck legs, meat sides down, and sprinkle the remaining spice mixture over the top. Cover and chill for at least 12 hours or up to 36 hours.

> Remove the duck legs from the dish, rinse them well with cold water, and pat dry.

> Place the duck fat, the whole bay leaves, the thyme sprigs, and the head of garlic in the insert of a large (5½- to 7-quart) slow cooker. Cover and turn the heat to high (see Note). When the fat has melted, carefully add the duck and turn the slow cooker to low. Cover and cook until the duck is very tender, about 4 hours.

> If you are going to eat it right away, remove the duck carefully from the slow cooker with tongs and cook it in a nonstick skillet, skin sides down, over medium heat, until the skin is crisp, about 10 minutes.

> If you are not going to eat the duck right away, transfer it to a bowl, cover with the fat and juices from the cooker, and chill until you are ready to serve. To reheat the duck, arrange the legs in a single layer in a baking pan, cover, and cook in a preheated 350°F oven for 15 minutes. Transfer to a nonstick or stick-resistant pan and cook, skin sides down, until the skin is crisp.

> Reserve all the duck fat from the recipe for future uses such as roasting potatoes or sautéing vegetables. It will keep for 6 months in the freezer.

Note: To speed this part of the process, combine the fat with the bay leaves, thyme sprigs, and garlic in a large saucepan, heat until it is melted and hot to the touch, and then carefully pour it into the slow cooker and proceed with the recipe.

"Southwest France is ground zero for the so-called "French Paradox," which seeks to explain why the local folks—devoted to a diet of duck and duck fat, goose and goose fat, and foie gras, all of it washed down with vats of red wine—are nonetheless long-lived. Since this paradox was first identified, various studies have pointed out the health benefits of red wine. More recently, it's come out that duck fat has its values, too. Because it's composed of poly- and monounsaturated fats (in addition to saturated fat) duck fat has some of the same healthy benefits as olive oil.

I share this to soften the blow about how duck confit is prepared: Duck legs are marinated for several days in garlic, salt, and spices, and then immersed in duck fat and cooked low and slow until tender. But duck confit is *so good*—one of my favorite foods on the planet; my family loves it, too.

Serve either of these duck confits with Foolproof Scalloped Potatoes on page 308."

DUCK CONFIT
COOKED IN AN OVEN BAG

START TO FINISH: 3 HOURS 20 MINUTES PLUS 12 TO 36 HOURS MARINATING TIME
HANDS-ON TIME: 20 MINUTES / **SERVINGS:** 4

3 tablespoons chopped fresh thyme leaves

2 tablespoons kosher salt

2 tablespoons minced shallots

1 Turkish bay leaf, crumbled

1½ tablespoons minced garlic

2 teaspoons black peppercorns, lightly crushed

¾ teaspoon ground allspice

4 pair duck legs with thighs attached

Vegetable cooking spray

1 tablespoon all-purpose flour

> Combine the thyme, salt, shallots, bay leaf, garlic, peppercorns, and allspice in a small bowl. Sprinkle half of the mixture in the bottom of a shallow baking dish. Add the duck legs, meat sides down, and sprinkle the remaining spice mixture over the top of the duck. Cover and chill the duck legs for at least 12 hours or up to 36 hours.

> Rinse the duck legs well with cold water and pat them dry.

> Preheat the oven to 250°F. Spray the inside of an oven cooking bag with vegetable cooking spray. Add the flour to the bag, shaking the bag to spread the flour, and place the duck legs in the bag in a single layer. Follow the bag manufacturer's instructions for providing proper ventilation during cooking. Place the bag in a large baking dish and bake until the duck is tender when pierced with the tip of a knife, about 3 hours. (You will need to remove the baking dish from the oven and carefully open the bag, avoiding any steam, to check the doneness of the duck.)

> If you are going to eat it right away, remove the duck from the bag with tongs and cook it in a nonstick skillet, skin sides down, over medium heat until the skin is crisp.

> If you are not going to eat the duck right away, transfer to a bowl, cover with the fat and juices from the bag, and chill until you're ready to serve. To reheat the duck, arrange the legs in a single layer in a baking pan, cover, and cook in a preheated 350°F oven for 15 minutes. Transfer to a nonstick or stick-resistant pan and cook, skin sides down, until the skin is crisp.

> Reserve all the duck fat from the recipe for future uses such as roasting potatoes or sautéing vegetables. It will keep for 6 months in the freezer.

> "I am sharing two methods for making duck confit. If you have duck fat stockpiled in the freezer (perhaps because you have been thrifty and saved it every time you cooked duck breasts, see page 134) then cooking duck confit in a slow cooker is the way to go.
>
> However, cooking the legs in an oven bag is convenient if you don't have a lot of duck fat kicking around. I learned it from a viewer who called in during my *Cooking Live* days. "

WHAT TO DO WITH THE LEFTOVERS

Leftover confited duck can be used in the same way as chicken (see page 245) or beef (see page 264). Here are some other suggestions:

▶ As a substitute for the kielbasa in Warm Red Cabbage, Potato, and Kielbasa Salad (page 98 but omit the deglazing of the pan), or the shrimp in the Warm Shrimp Salad with Carrot-Ginger Dressing (page 80), or the chicken in Grilled Chicken with Peach Salad and Blue Cheese Dressing (page 93)

▶ Duck confit nachos

▶ Duck fried rice

▶ Duck and wild mushroom risotto

ROAST TURKEY AND ITS POSSE
THANKSGIVING BASICS

How Much Food Should You Make?

For many of us, Thanksgiving is the biggest meal we'll cook all year—we not only want enough food to feed our guests, but to allow for the all-important leftovers. Here are some guidelines:

▶ **How much turkey?** Allow for 1 to 1½ pounds turkey per person (depending on whether you want leftovers). Keep in mind that smaller birds have less meat, so you might want to go with that higher ratio.

▶ **How much stuffing?** About ¾ cup per person or per pound of turkey. Not all of that stuffing will fit in the cavity if you are planning on stuffing the bird. You will have to cook some of it in a casserole dish separately from the bird.

▶ **How much gravy?** About ½ cup per person, which allows for leftovers.

What's the best way to defrost a frozen turkey?

It's best to thaw your turkey in a refrigerator that's 40°F or cooler. A good rule of thumb is to allow 24 hours of thawing time for every 4 to 5 pounds of turkey.

If you've run out of time, you can defrost the turkey in a sink filled with cold water. Thaw the turkey, breast side down, in its unopened wrapper, in enough cold water to cover it completely. Change the water frequently to keep the turkey chilled. Estimate a minimum thawing time of 30 minutes per pound for a whole turkey.

How long should I cook the turkey?

To ensure a moist bird, do not let its temperature exceed 160°F. Insert the thermometer on the inside of the leg/thigh joint—making sure not to touch the bone—and start checking a full 45 minutes *before* the earliest recommended time the turkey's supposed to be done (see the chart, page 254). (Yes, the USDA suggests a temp of 165°F. That's not a problem—with carry-over cooking time, it will rise to at least 165°F as it rests.)

Should I let the turkey rest before carving?

Yes! Whatever else you do, let the bird rest for at least 20 minutes—and preferably 30 minutes (and don't worry; it will stay hot for up to an hour)—before carving it. Folks tend to carve the turkey too soon—and who can blame them? The sight of that big golden bird is mouth-watering. Even so, I counsel restraint. Carving the turkey too soon will cause all the juices to come streaming out of it, leaving the meat dry. The juices need time to redistribute.

66 ~~~~~~~

I've confessed before that I never make turkey on Thanksgiving Day. (At our house we roll with Red Wine–Braised Short Ribs of Beef, page 263.) I know it's traditional, and a roast turkey is a great way to feed a crowd, but it's a tough dish to get right, especially when company's coming and you're also making a feast's worth of other dishes.

No matter. For most of us, it's not Thanksgiving unless there's a roast turkey in the center of the table. I happen to have learned a lot about the big bird and its fixin's during the years I served as *Good Morning America*'s go-to person for Thanksgiving Day. The segment was called "Turkey 911"—and for good reason. Then and now, I like to make the job easier for the home cook.

We'll start with some tips for the overall meal, and then you'll find recipes for Roast Turkey (page 252), Basic Turkey Stuffing or Dressing (page 253), and Make-Ahead Turkey Gravy (page 255). For the Smoothest Mashed Potatoes, see page 307.

~~~~~~~ 99

ROAST TURKEY

START TO FINISH: 3¾ TO 5 HOURS PLUS 24 TO 36 HOURS BRINING TIME
HANDS-ON TIME: 15 MINUTES / **SERVINGS:** 8 TO 10 WITH LEFTOVERS

1 (12- to 15-pound) fresh or defrosted turkey, giblets, neck, and wing tips reserved for Homemade Turkey Stock (page 28)

3 tablespoons plus 2 teaspoons kosher salt

1 stick butter

Freshly ground black pepper

2 cups Homemade Chicken Stock (page 26) or store-bought chicken broth

> Using a grapefruit spoon, curved side up, your fingers, or the handle of a wooden spoon, loosen the skin over the thighs and breast, taking care not to break the skin. Rub 1 tablespoon salt evenly inside the cavity, 1½ teaspoons under the skin of each breast, and 1½ teaspoons under the skin of each leg/thigh. Wrap the turkey in plastic wrap or tightly in a plastic bag and chill for 24 to 36 hours.

> Rinse the turkey well to remove excess salt and pat the turkey very dry (see Note).

> Preheat the oven to 325°F. Arrange an oven shelf in the lower third of the oven.

> If you are stuffing the turkey (see box, page 254), do so right before roasting and return the legs to tucked position. (Many turkeys come with the legs tucked into a flap of the skin; if that is not the case with your turkey, simply tie the legs together with kitchen string.)

> Arrange the turkey, breast side up, in a rack (preferably a V-rack) set in a heavy large roasting pan. Melt the butter and use one-third of it to brush the turkey all over. Season the turkey with the pepper and cover the whole turkey loosely with foil. Pour the chicken stock into the bottom of the roasting pan and roast the turkey in the lower third of the oven for 1 hour.

> Uncover and baste with another third of the butter. Re-cover the turkey and roast until approximately halfway through the total cooking time (see chart, page 254). Uncover the turkey, baste with the remaining butter, and roast, uncovered, until a thermometer inserted in the inside thickest part of the thigh joint, and not touching the bone, reaches 160°F.

> Transfer the turkey to a platter, leaving the drippings in the pan for the gravy (see page 255), and cover the turkey loosely with foil. Let the turkey rest for at least 20, preferably 30 minutes, or up to 1 hour before carving.

Note: The USDA does not recommend rinsing the turkey, as you'll spread turkey juices, which might contain bacteria, all over your sink. But if you have salted the turkey ahead of time, you must rinse the turkey and clean the sink well afterward, either with Comet, Ajax, or water mixed with a little bleach.

"I've cooked turkey in every way known to man or woman. There are a lot of good methods, but not all of them are practical for every home kitchen. My favorite way to cook a turkey is to deep-fry it, which reliably delivers the crisp skin and moist meat we all work so hard to achieve. Unfortunately, not all of us are blessed with a concrete backyard and a handy fire extinguisher.

My *second* favorite method is to brine the big bird before roasting it. Featured in *Cook's Illustrated,* this technique was actually Introduced in Jean Anderson's award-winning *The Food of Portugal* (William Morrow, 1986). (See Jean's recipe for Pimiento Mac and Cheese, page 309.) Soaking the turkey in a mixture of water and salt not only deepens its flavor but it's the perfect method for keeping the bird—and especially the white meat—juicy and succulent.

I simply don't have enough space in my fridge to park a turkey in a vat of water for several days. Instead, I presalt the turkey and skip the water, as described here. Even if you don't want to presalt your turkey, follow the advice on cooking and resting times and you'll still have a juicy bird."

BASIC TURKEY STUFFING OR DRESSING

START TO FINISH: I HOUR 45 MINUTES / **HANDS-ON TIME:** 25 MINUTES
SERVINGS: 8 TO IO (MORE WITH ADD-INS)

1 pound firm white, homemade-style sandwich bread

1 stick unsalted butter

2 cups finely chopped onion

1 cup finely diced celery

2 teaspoons finely chopped fresh sage

2 teaspoons finely chopped fresh thyme

3 cups Homemade Turkey Stock (page 28), Homemade Chicken Stock (page 26), or store-bought chicken broth

Kosher salt and freshly ground black pepper

> Preheat the oven to 250°F. Cut the bread into ½-inch cubes and arrange the cubes in a single layer on 3 baking sheets. (If you don't have 3 baking sheets, bake the cubes in batches.) Bake until the edges are dried but the center is moist, rotating the trays in the oven a few times so all the cubes cook evenly, about 45 minutes to 1 hour. Let cool to room temperature.

> Meanwhile, melt the butter in a large skillet over medium heat. Add the onion and celery and cook, stirring occasionally, until softened, about 5 minutes. Transfer the vegetables and butter to a large bowl and stir in the bread, herbs, and enough of the stock to moisten the cubes but not saturate them. Add salt and pepper to taste.

> If you're not using the mixture as a stuffing in the turkey, transfer it to a baking dish and stir in additional chicken stock to make it fairly moist. Cover and bake in a 350°F oven for 15 minutes. Uncover and bake until slightly browned and crisp on top, 20 to 25 minutes more (see Note).

Note: You can pop the dressing in the oven while the turkey is resting. You can also make the dressing a day ahead—just take it out of the fridge an hour ahead of putting it in the oven.

> Making stuffing well requires as much attention as the rest of the feast. To start, please avoid ready-made stuffing mixes. They're filled with bad ingredients. Second, dry your bread cubes in the oven. Leaving them out overnight only makes them stale. They'll absorb too much liquid, resulting in soggy stuffing.

WHAT ABOUT ADD-INS?

Your stuffing will be safer to eat and will taste better if you cook your add-ins before tossing them into the mix. Raw sausage should not be slowly heating up in the bird for hours and raw vegetables will give off excess liquid, taste watery, and make the stuffing watery, too. Here are some suggestions for add-ins in amounts appropriate for this recipe:

▶ 2 sautéed sliced apples

▶ ½ pound sausages, cooked and sliced ½ inch thick

▶ 1 cup chopped toasted walnuts, almonds, or pistachios

▶ 1 cup dried cranberries, cherries, or chopped apricots

▶ 1 cup coarsely chopped roasted chestnuts (see page 215)

▶ ½ pound sautéed sliced mushrooms

TURKEY COOK TIMES
(ROASTED AT A CONTINUOUS 325°F)

Turkey Weight (Pounds)	Cook Times
8 to 12 pounds	$2^3/_4$ to 3 hours unstuffed 3 to $3^1/_2$ hours stuffed
12 to 14 pounds	3 to $3^3/_4$ hours unstuffed $3^1/_2$ to 4 hours stuffed
14 to 18 pounds	$3^3/_4$ to $4^1/_4$ hours unstuffed 4 to $4^1/_4$ hours stuffed
18 to 20 pounds	$4^1/_4$ to $4^1/_2$ hours unstuffed $4^1/_4$ to $4^3/_4$ hours stuffed
20 to 24 pounds	$4^1/_2$ to 5 hours unstuffed $4^3/_4$ hours to $5^1/_4$ hours stuffed

Note: These are the times recommended by the USDA. I suggest checking the turkey 45 minutes before the lowest cooking time listed here.

Cook's Notes: Gravy 101

‣ When making any type of gravy, I like to use **Wondra flour** (see page 265). If you can't find Wondra, all-purpose flour will do.

‣ **The formula for thickening the stock** into gravy is 2 tablespoons each of fat and flour for every 1 cup of liquid.

‣ **Flour tastes raw unless you cook it** both before and after you add the liquid. So start by melting the butter in a saucepan, adding the flour, and cooking it for several minutes.

‣ Before adding it to the roux, **heat the liquid to roughly the same temperature,** and whisk constantly while combining the two. In my experience, this step gets me that much closer to lump-free perfection. **Use a flat whisk** (see page 18) to get into the corners of the saucepan where the roux tends to stick.

‣ To maximize the flour's thickening ability, it must be heated to no less than 200°F. **Bring the gravy up to a boil,** turn it down to a simmer, and then let it simmer for at least as many minutes as you have tablespoons of flour. Season it, and place a sheet of parchment paper or plastic wrap on the gravy's surface to prevent a skin from forming while it cools (see page 255), then chill it.

MAKE-AHEAD TURKEY GRAVY

START TO FINISH: 30 MINUTES (SPREAD OUT OVER TWO DAYS)
HANDS-ON TIME: 10 MINUTES / **SERVINGS:** 8

1/2 cup butter or turkey fat (from Homemade Turkey Stock, page 28)

1/2 cup Wondra flour (see page 265) or all-purpose flour

4 cups Homemade Turkey Stock (page 28), Homemade Chicken Stock (page 26), or store-bought chicken broth, heated

Kosher salt and freshly ground black pepper

1 cup dry white wine or water

> Heat the butter in a medium saucepan over medium-low heat until melted. Add the flour and whisk until the roux (the butter-flour mixture) looks like wet sand, 2 to 3 minutes. Add the stock in a stream, whisking (preferably with a flat whisk, see page 18), and bring it to a boil. Reduce the heat and simmer the gravy, whisking occasionally, 8 minutes. (Don't worry if the gravy seems thick, you will be adding more liquid when you finish it on Thanksgiving Day.) Add salt and pepper to taste. Let cool slightly, transfer to a bowl, and cover the surface of the gravy with parchment to avoid a skin forming. Cover the bowl with plastic wrap and chill until ready to use.

> On Thanksgiving Day, when the turkey is cooked and resting on a platter, it is time to finish the gravy. Pour off the liquid at the bottom of the roasting pan and put it into a fat separator (see page 21). Pour off the fat (which you can freeze and use in the roux the next time you make gravy) and reserve any of the clear turkey juices. (If you don't have a fat separator, pour the liquid into a heatproof measuring cup and skim off the fat that rises to the top using a spoon.)

> Place the roasting pan across two burners and heat the pan over medium heat. Add the wine to the pan and simmer, scraping up the brown bits at the bottom of the pan with a metal spatula until the liquid is reduced by half. Add the gravy, whisking, and some of the reserved turkey juices and simmer the gravy in the pan until it is reduced to the desired consistency. Add salt and pepper to taste.

> The crux of the problem for the Thanksgiving cook is not only the extravagant length of the menu, but the need to serve every dish piping hot at exactly the same moment—a problem made all the more acute by the fact that the oven is probably going to be hogged by the big bird for most of the day. What's a home cook to do?

I'll offer two pieces of advice: First, keep in mind that the turkey will stay rip-roaring hot for up to an hour after you pull it out of the oven. This allows ample time to bake the dressing, side dishes, and pies. Second, many dishes can be made a day ahead. The obvious candidates are casseroles and the dressing itself. But there's one you may not have considered—the gravy. (I want to give a shout-out to Rick Rodgers, who first came up with this idea in his very excellent book, *Thanksgiving 101,* Harper Collins, 2007.)

Start by making the turkey stock the day before Thanksgiving and thicken the cooked stock with a roux. Then, on the great day itself, after you've transferred the turkey to a platter to rest, deglaze the bottom of the pan with white wine, "marry" the made-ahead gravy to the pan drippings, and heat it up.

This strategy not only saves you the stress of having to conjure up a boatload of gravy at the eleventh hour, I think the gravy tastes even better when made this way.

PORK POSOLE

START TO FINISH: 3 HOURS 45 MINUTES / **HANDS-ON TIME:** 45 MINUTES
SERVINGS: 8 WITH LEFTOVERS

1 pound fresh tomatillos, husked, rinsed, and quartered

1 cup coarsely chopped scallions, white and light green parts

1 cup chopped fresh cilantro, leaves and stems

3 serranos, coarsely chopped, with seeds and ribs

4 large garlic cloves, smashed and peeled

¼ cup fresh lime juice

4 tablespoons vegetable oil, preferably grapeseed, divided

Kosher salt

2 cups sliced onion

3 cups Homemade Chicken Stock (page 26) or store-bought chicken broth

4 pounds pork shoulder, cut into 2-inch cubes

2 (15-ounce) cans hominy, rinsed and drained

Freshly ground black pepper

Lime wedges, fresh cilantro leaves, grated Monterey Jack cheese, and sliced serranos for garnish

Tortilla Strips (page 59) or 2 cups store-bought tortilla chips

> Preheat the oven to 325°F. Combine the tomatillos, scallions, cilantro, chopped serranos, garlic, lime juice, 2 tablespoons of the vegetable oil, and 2 teaspoons salt in a food processor and pulse until the ingredients are almost smooth with a few small chunks.

> Heat the remaining 2 tablespoons oil in a Dutch oven over medium heat, add the onion and cook, stirring occasionally, until softened, about 5 minutes. Add the vegetable puree, bring to a simmer, and cook for 5 minutes.

> Add the chicken stock and pork, bring the mixture to a boil, and reduce the heat to a bare simmer. Cover with a round of parchment (see page 265) and then a lid. Bake on a shelf in the lower third of the oven until very tender, 2½ to 3 hours. Remove from the oven, add the hominy, and cook over medium-low heat on the stove just until the hominy is heated through. Add salt and pepper to taste. Ladle the stew into 8 bowls and let each person garnish their own dish.

SLOW-COOKER VERSION

> Make the vegetable puree as directed. Heat the remaining 2 tablespoons oil in a large skillet over medium heat, reduce to medium-low, add the onion, and cook, stirring occasionally, until softened, about 5 minutes. Add the puree, bring to a simmer, and cook for 5 minutes. Transfer the puree to the insert of a large (5½- to 7-quart) slow cooker. Add the chicken stock and pork, cover, and cook until the pork is very tender, on high for 4 hours or on low for 8 hours. Add the hominy, cover, and cook for another 15 minutes. Add salt and pepper to taste.

> "Posole, a hearty, soupy stew from the state of Guerrero in southern Mexico, is traditionally made with pork and hominy. The right cut for this stew is pork shoulder. It boasts a generous percentage of flavorful fat, guaranteeing that the meat itself will become very tender after long, slow cooking. Buy it on the bone without the skin, and cut it into chunks yourself—it'll still be cheaper than buying it with the bone removed. If you can't find pork shoulder in the market, but see something labeled as "pork stew meat," ask the butcher if in fact that meat comes from the shoulder.

> There are red and green versions of posole. The green version (the kind we're making) is flavored with a puree of tomatillos, chiles, garlic, lime, and cilantro. If you can't find all the ingredients, substitute good-quality store-bought green salsa.

> Hominy is a kind of dried corn from which the hulls and germs have been removed. (Ground-up hominy is called grits.) I've specified using canned hominy here because, unlike dried hominy, it's widely available.

> Although it takes 2½ hours for this stew to become tender, preparing it requires very little work. And the finished product is so richly flavored that everyone will assume you must have worked really hard to make it taste so good. The garnishes add a lot to the stew; don't stint on them. "

SALAMI AND PROVOLONE–STUFFED PORK LOIN

START TO FINISH: I HOUR 55 MINUTES PLUS 24 HOURS MARINATING TIME
HANDS-ON TIME: 35 MINUTES / **SERVINGS:** 8 TO IO

To "butterfly" a piece of meat is to transform a thick and blocky slab into a thinner and more expansive cut. The usual procedure is to lay the meat on a cutting board and cut through it horizontally, starting on one side and stopping just before you reach the other side. Then you open up the two halves of meat like the leaves of a book—or the wings of the aforementioned butterfly.

For years I thought this was the only method. Then I learned about a roll-cut method while I was working at *Gourmet*. For larger roasts, this is a far better technique than the traditional method because the final thickness of the meat is much more uniform. I developed this pork loin recipe to demonstrate this technique (see page 260 for a step-by-step), but it works just as well with beef tenderloin.

Try to plan ahead so you can leave the meat in the marinade overnight. Doing so deeply seasons it. As for the stuffing, you can opt for the salami and provolone here or make up your own. Either way, this roast is a show-stopper. Once you've mastered it, you'll make it over and over again. Serve with the Sautéed Artichoke Hearts with Pancetta on page 295.

1 (3¼ to 3½-pound) center-cut boneless pork loin roast (4 to 5 inches in diameter), trimmed, leaving a ¼-inch layer of fat if possible

For the marinade:

1 tablespoon minced garlic

2 teaspoons kosher salt

2 teaspoons freshly ground black pepper

2 tablespoons finely chopped fresh rosemary

2 tablespoons fresh lemon juice

¼ cup extra-virgin olive oil

6 ounces thinly sliced salami or prosciutto

6 ounces thinly sliced provolone or about 2 ounces freshly grated Parmigiano-Reggiano (2 cups)

> Butterfly the pork loin in a roll cut following the step-by-step photos (see page 260). Sprinkle water on top of the butterflied pork, cover it with a sheet of plastic wrap, and pound to ½ inch thick with a smooth meat pounder or rolling pin. Remove the plastic wrap.

> **Make the marinade:** Combine the garlic, salt, pepper, rosemary, lemon juice, and olive oil in a small bowl and rub it all over the pork. Put the pork either in a covered bowl or a resealable plastic bag and chill it overnight.

> Preheat the oven to 450°F. Put the pork, fat side down, on a cutting board with a short end facing you. Arrange the salami or prosciutto evenly over the meat, leaving a 1-inch border at the short end that is furthest from you. Either arrange the provolone or sprinkle the Parmigiano-Reggiano evenly on top of the meat. Beginning with the short end closest to you, roll up the loin tightly and turn it, seam side down, on the cutting board. Tie the roast with kitchen string at 1-inch intervals (see page 260).

> Put the pork on an oiled rack in a foil-lined (to catch any cheese that comes out) roasting pan. Roast in the middle of the oven for 15 minutes. Reduce the oven temperature to 325°F and roast the pork until it reaches an internal temperature of 140°F, 25 to 30 minutes more. Remove from the oven and let rest on a platter, covered loosely with foil, for 25 minutes before carving.

HOW TO BUTTERFLY AND TIE A PORK LOIN ROAST

1. Lay the pork loin, fat side down. Beginning at one of the long sides, about ½ inch from the edge, start to cut down at a 45° angle.

2. When the knife is about ½ inch from the bottom of the meat, angle it parallel to the cutting board and continue to cut the meat.

3. Pull the meat back as you cut. You'll end up with a flat piece of meat, roughly ½-inch thick. Make cuts about ½-inch deep along any thick ridges of meat. Then pound the meat between dampened pieces of plastic wrap until it is flat.

4. After the meat has marinated, place it fat side down on a cutting board and layer in the filling ingredients, leaving a 1-inch border near the short end of the roast. Starting from the short end (opposite where you have left your border), roll up the pork tightly to enclose the filling. Turn the roast, seam side down, fat side up. Tie a piece of kitchen twine tightly around the roast at one end.

5. Pull the other end of the twine out to form a loop; turn the loop over so one half of the string is under the other where the strings cross.

6. Pull the loop to the end of the roast, then under the roast.

7. Then pull the string at the top of the loop back and forth until it is tight around the roast. Continue making loops and tying the roast at 1-inch intervals until you have reached the end of the roast.

8. Flip the roast over, and weave the string through the ties along the bottom of length of the roast.

9. Flip the roast back over and tie the end of the string to the end of the string from the first tie you made.

RED WINE–BRAISED SHORT RIBS OF BEEF

START TO FINISH: 6½ TO 7½ HOURS / **HANDS-ON TIME:** ABOUT I HOUR 45 MINUTES
SERVINGS: 6 WITH LEFTOVERS

3 tablespoons extra-virgin olive oil

7 pounds beef short ribs (flanken or English cut) with the bone

Kosher salt and freshly ground black pepper

3 cups thinly sliced onions

2 medium carrots, medium chopped

2 tablespoons minced garlic

2 tablespoons tomato paste

2 fresh thyme sprigs or 2 teaspoons dried

1 Turkish bay leaf or ½ California bay leaf

One 750-ml bottle dry red wine

4 cups Homemade Chicken Stock (page 26), Homemade Brown Chicken Stock (page 27), or store-bought chicken broth

¼ cup plus 1 tablespoon Wondra flour (see page 265) or all-purpose flour

2 tablespoons Dijon-style mustard

1 tablespoon fresh lemon juice

> Preheat the oven to 325°F. Divide the oil between two large skillets and heat over medium-high heat until hot. Pat the ribs dry and season them on all sides with salt and pepper. Reduce the heat to medium, add half the ribs to each skillet, and brown them on all sides, about 10 minutes. Transfer them with tongs to a large Dutch oven or deep baking dish.

> Pour off all but 2 tablespoons of fat from each skillet, reduce the heat to medium-low, and add half the onion and carrots to each of the skillets. Cook, stirring occasionally, until golden brown, 25 to 30 minutes.

> Add the garlic to the onion-carrot mixture in either pan and cook 1 minute. Add the tomato paste, thyme, and bay leaf to the same pan and sauté for 2 minutes. Transfer the vegetable mixture to the Dutch oven. Off the heat, add half the wine to each of the two skillets. Bring the skillets back to the heat, bring the wine to a boil, scraping up the brown bits, then let simmer until it is reduced by about three-fourths.

> When the wine is reduced in each of the skillets (you should have a total of 1 cup from both), divide the chicken stock and 1 cup water among the skillets and bring the liquid to a boil. Pour the liquid over the contents of the Dutch oven and cover the surface with a piece of parchment paper (see page 265). Put the lid on the pot and braise the ribs in the lower third of the oven until the meat is very tender (the bones may fall off before the meat is completely tender), 4 to 5 hours.

(recipe continues)

Every year for a dozen years I'd appear on *Good Morning America* on Thanksgiving Day to conduct a little seminar called "Turkey 911." But when the segment was over and I returned to home and family, what did I prepare for our big feast? Braised short ribs of beef. My family just isn't wild about turkey (although stuffing and gravy are always welcome.) But those short ribs? Man, oh, man. They can make any day a holiday.

Short ribs are delicious thanks to the high proportion of fat to muscle. They also freeze beautifully, which means you can cook them well ahead of time and they'll taste even better. And that's a good thing, because tenderizing them takes a lot of time in a slow oven.

To maximize the depth of flavor, start with meat on the bone, and brown both the meat and the vegetables well. Finally, don't skimp on the wine. One bottle may seem like a lot, but three-quarters of it will evaporate during cooking and the ribs will boast a wonderful acidity.

To cut down on time, I brown the meat and vegetables in two large skillets. If you'd prefer not to dirty two pans, brown everything in batches in the Dutch oven. I place a piece of parchment directly on the surface of the short ribs (I learned this quick way to cut out the proper-sized circle, page 265, from Jacques Pépin), and then put on the lid of the Dutch oven, to makes sure that none of the precious liquid escapes while they're cooking.

”

❯ Transfer the ribs to a platter with tongs and let stand until they are cool enough to be handled. Meanwhile, strain the sauce into a bowl. Discard the solids and return the liquid to the Dutch oven. Skim off any fat that floats to the surface (or use a fat separator, or chill overnight; see Cook's Notes, page 265). Whisk together the flour and ⅓ cup water. Bring the cooking liquid to a boil and add half the flour mixture in a steady stream, whisking. Bring the sauce to a boil, check the consistency, and, if you would like it thicker, whisk in more of the flour-water mixture. Simmer for 8 minutes. Whisk in the mustard, lemon juice, and salt and pepper to taste.

❯ Meanwhile, discard the bones and trim any excess fat and gristle from the rib meat. Transfer 2 cups of the smaller pieces of meat to a storage container and top them with ⅓ cup of the sauce; chill or freeze for future recipes (see What to Do with the Leftovers, at left). Add the big rib chunks to the pot along with any juices from the platter they were on, and cook gently just until heated through. To serve, arrange some rib meat on each plate and generously spoon some of the sauce over each portion.

SLOW-COOKER VERSION

❯ Brown the ribs and vegetables as instructed above and transfer them to the insert of a large (5½- to 7-quart) slow cooker. Reduce the wine in the skillets, add the chicken stock (omit the water), and bring the stock to a boil. Add to the slow cooker, cover, and cook on low until the meat is very tender, 8 to 10 hours. Proceed with the recipe as written.

Cook's Notes: The Easiest Way to Skim Off the Fat

This recipe tastes even better a few days after you make it. And, if you make it ahead, it's easier to remove the fat. Here is what you do:

▶ After the ribs are tender, transfer them to a bowl and strain the cooking liquid over them, discarding the vegetables. Let the mixture cool, cover, and chill overnight. The fat will solidify on top and be easy to lift off. (You can freeze the fat and use it to sauté vegetables for stews or soups.)

▶ Gently reheat the ribs and the liquid in a large saucepan until the ribs are warm. Strain the liquid and set it aside. Discard the bones and trim the excess fat and gristle from the ribs.

▶ Thicken the liquid following the instructions in the recipe, reserve 2 cups of the smaller pieces of meat mixed with ⅓ cup sauce for future recipes (see What to Do with the Leftovers, page 264) and add the big ribs chunks to the thickened liquid; heat and serve.

WHAT IS WONDRA FLOUR?

Wondra flour (aka instantized flour), the stuff that comes in that unique round blue container, is the flour that my grandmother used to thicken gravies. You can still find it in most supermarkets in the baking section. It has been moistened and dried into granules that blend instantly in hot and cold liquids. So no lumps in your gravy, hooray!

Wondra is one of my favorite coatings for foods that I am going to fry or sauté. I learned this from David Waltuk, the chef/owner of the now-closed, three-star restaurant in New York City called Chanterelle, when I visited his restaurant to do a story on "family meal," the meal that restaurants serve to their staff right before service. He dipped his fish fillets in Wondra before he sautéed them. It gave the fish a wonderful light crisp coating. You will never get that crunch with regular old all-purpose flour.

CUTTING PARCHMENT TO FIT YOUR PAN

1. To make a round that fits snugly on top of the short ribs, fold one of the short sides of a piece of parchment to meet the other short side. Bring the bottom half of the folded parchment up to line up with the top half. Now form a triangle by bringing one of the folded (not open) sides up to meet the other folded side. Repeat several more times until you have a long thin triangle. Measure the radius of the pot and cut off the part that hangs over the edge.

2. Unfold the paper, crumple it, which will help it lie flat, and lay it over the short ribs. Tuck the parchment paper in around the sides.

SMOKED BRISKET

START TO FINISH: 6 HOURS / **HANDS-ON TIME:** 30 MINUTES / **SERVINGS:** 8 TO 10

Post-oak or white oak wood chips, soaked in water for 30 minutes

1 whole beef brisket, untrimmed (9 to 12 pounds)

Lockhart Dry Rub (page 267)

12 ounces bottled beer (such as Lone Star or Corona)

Tangy Red Chile Hot Sauce (page 267), optional

Accoutrements: Pickled okra, avocado slices, jalapeños, white onion, longhorn cheddar cheese, and saltine crackers or sliced white bread

66

I first met Elizabeth Karmel, a native of North Carolina's barbecue belt, years ago when she was working for Weber Grill. It was always clear to me that she knew way more than anyone else about the nuances of the grills and how to cook on them. She was also more expert than any of the celebrity grill chefs who emerged later, all of whom happened to be men and several of whom learned everything they knew from her. That's why I applauded Elizabeth when she started her own company, Girls at the Grill, an online source for grilling instructions and recipes that features her gadgets and products. Her latest venture, CarolinaCueToGo.com, is an online barbecue shack that ships North Carolina whole-hog barbecue with all the fixin's directly to your home.

Elizabeth is the founding executive chef of Hill Country Barbecue Market, a great Texas-styled barbecue restaurant that opened in New York in 2007. This brisket, direct from the Hill Country menu, is the best I've ever eaten. I had to have it in this book, and Elizabeth kindly agreed to share it.

99

> Build a charcoal fire or preheat a gas grill. If using a gas grill, place the soaked wood chips in a smoker box directly on top of the flavorizer bars or ceramic rock during the preheating stage. Once the charcoal reaches white-gray ash stage, or the grill is heated to 500°F, reconfigure for indirect medium-low heat. (For indirect heat, make sure there is no heat directly under the food.)

> Pat the brisket dry with paper towels. Do not trim any excess fat off the meat. This fat will naturally baste the meat and keep it moist during the long cooking time.

> Using your hands or a shaker-top jar, sprinkle the meat liberally with the rub—saving any extra rub to season meat for future grillings. Let it sit for about 5 minutes. Pat the spices into the meat but do not rub. This mixture will form a dark savory crust on the meat often referred to as the sought-after "burnt ends." Set aside on a clean tray until ready to cook.

> If using a charcoal grill, place the drip pan between the 2 piles of white-gray ashed briquettes (on the charcoal grate). Pour the beer into the drip pan. Before placing the meat on the grill, place the soaked wood chips directly on the coals. You will need to add charcoal every hour to maintain the heat.

> If using a gas grill, place a drip pan with the beer in the upper left corner of the gas grill directly on top of the flavorizer bars or ceramic rock, next to the smoker box.

> Place the brisket in the center of the cooking grate, fat side up, over indirect medium-low heat. Cover and cook for 5 to 6 hours at 300° to 325°F, or until an instant-read thermometer inserted in the middle of the brisket registers 190° to 200°F. *Do not* turn the meat during the entire cooking time. When done, the meat should be very tender and falling apart. It will feel like the consistency of soft butter when inserted with the probe of the thermometer. Let the meat rest for 20 minutes or until cool enough to handle.

> The brisket can be made in advance up to this point and once it is cool, wrapped in 3 layers of heavy-duty aluminum foil. To reheat the brisket, leave it in foil and heat for 1 to 2 hours in a 250°F oven. For a crispier crust, remove the foil at the end and put it back into the oven for another 15 to 20 minutes.

> Slice against the grain of the meat (see box, page 152) and serve with Tangy Red Chile Hot Sauce, if using, and the assorted accoutrements.

LOCKHART DRY RUB

START TO FINISH: 5 MINUTES / **HANDS-ON TIME:** 5 MINUTES / **SERVINGS:** MAKES ABOUT ¾ CUP

½ cup kosher salt

3 tablespoons coarsely ground black pepper

2 teaspoons cayenne pepper

In a medium bowl, combine the salt and peppers and mix well. Store the rub in an airtight container or shaker-top jar.

TANGY RED CHILE HOT SAUCE

START TO FINISH: 5 MINUTES / **HANDS-ON TIME:** 5 MINUTES / **SERVINGS:** MAKES 1½ CUPS

1 cup white vinegar

½ cup apple cider vinegar

2 tablespoons cayenne pepper or more to taste

1 tablespoon red chile flakes or more to taste

Whisk together the white vinegar, apple cider vinegar, cayenne, and chile flakes in a medium nonreactive bowl. Pour the sauce into a glass bottle with a top. It will keep indefinitely, covered, in or out of the refrigerator.

Note: The longer the sauce sits, the hotter it gets.

ELIZABETH'S TIPS FOR MAKING TEXAS-STYLE BRISKET

▶ Make sure to purchase a whole untrimmed brisket with both the point (or the deckle), which is the "moist" meat, and the flat, which is the "lean" meat. It is essential to cook the brisket as a whole muscle. You can separate the point and the flat after cooking.

▶ Pat the spices into the meat but do not rub. Rubbing can damage the meat fibers.

▶ DO NOT turn the meat during the entire cooking time. When you cook using indirect heat, you do not need to turn the meat because the heat rotates in a circle around it. Also, when cooking meat with a fat cap, you want to cook it fat-side up so that as the fat melts it renders through the muscle and flavors it.

▶ Slice against the grain of the meat (see box, page 152). You may have to turn the meat several times to keep cutting against the grain. If the slice of meat has a honeycomb pattern, you are cutting it against the grain and have a correct slice; if it looks "long and stringy," you are cutting with the grain and the slice of meat will be tough and fall apart.

Cooking with *Rick Bayless*

TACO NIGHT WITH TWO FILLINGS

Adapted from *Rick Bayless Mexico One Plate at a Time* (Scribner, 2000).

How weird is it that one of today's great Mexican chefs—Rick Bayless—is a non-Mexican based in Chicago? Exactly as weird (or not) as the fact that one of yesteryear's great teachers of French cuisine—Julia Child—was a non-Frenchwoman based in Cambridge, Massachusetts. Me, I accept the world's cosmopolitanism and keep it moving.

Although not very time-consuming, homemade corn tortillas with a variety of fillings are a great meal for a summer weekend—particularly if you have guests. Why make corn tortillas from scratch? As Rick says: 'Mexican food without corn tortillas is like Chinese food without rice ... [but] many of us north of the border don't choose corn tortillas with our Mexican food. The reason: We may never have eaten a good fresh one—a just-made one. Corn tortillas, you see, are at their peak for only a few hours after they're made.'

In addition to the crucial tortilla info on pages 270–271, Rick provides us with recipes for these fillings: skirt steak, grilled portobellos, and charred poblanos and onions.

START TO FINISH: 60 MINUTES PLUS MARINATING TIME (1 HOUR TO OVERNIGHT)
HANDS-ON TIME: 20 MINUTES / **SERVINGS:** 4 AS A LIGHT MEAL (MAKES 12 TACOS)

3 medium white onions, sliced into ½-inch rounds (keep the rounds intact for easy grilling)

6 garlic cloves, peeled and roughly chopped

¼ cup plus 3 tablespoons fresh lime juice

½ teaspoon cumin, preferably freshly ground

Kosher salt

1 pound beef skirt steak, trimmed of surface fat as well as the "silverskin" (see pages 278–279)

6 (4- to 5-inch) portobello mushrooms (about 1¾ pounds), stems removed and caps wiped clean and gills removed, if desired

6 medium fresh poblano chiles (about 18 ounces)

Vegetable or olive oil for brushing

12 warm, fresh Homemade Corn Tortillas (page 270)

A small bowlful of lime wedges

Chopped fresh cilantro

Guacamole (your own homemade or your favorite store-bought brand)

Salsa (see Sources, page 351)

> In a food processor or blender, combine two-thirds of the onion, the garlic, 6 tablespoons lime juice, cumin, and 1 teaspoon salt. Process to a smooth puree. Place the skirt steak in a nonreactive baking dish. Using a spoon, smear half of the marinade over both sides of the skirt steak. Cover and chill for at least 1 hour or up to 8 hours. Chill the remaining marinade. One hour before you're ready to grill, use a spoon to smear the remaining marinade over both sides of each mushroom cap. Cover and let stand at room temp for 1 hour.

> Turn the oven to its lowest setting. Preheat a gas grill to medium-high heat or let a charcoal fire burn until the coals are covered with gray ash and very hot. Turn the burners in the center of the gas grill to medium-low, or bank the coals to the sides of the charcoal grill for indirect cooking. Set the cooking grate in place, cover the grill, and let the grate heat up, 5 minutes or so.

> Lay the chiles on the hottest part of the grill and cook, turning occasionally, until the skin is blistered and uniformly blackened all over, about 5 minutes. Be careful not to char the flesh, only the skin. Remove the chiles from the grill and cover with a kitchen towel.

> While the chiles are roasting, brush or spray the remaining onion slices with oil and lay the whole rounds of onions on the grill in a cooler spot than you chose for the chiles. When they're starting to soften and are browned on the first side, about 10 minutes, use a spatula to flip them and brown the other side. Transfer to an overproof serving dish and separate the rings (if they haven't started separating during grilling).

> Rub the blackened skin off the chiles then pull out the stems and seed pods. Rinse briefly to remove any stray seeds and bits of skin. Slice into $1/4$-inch strips and stir into the onions. Taste the mixture and season with salt, usually about $1/4$ teaspoon, and the remaining 1 tablespoon lime juice. Keep warm in the oven.

> Remove the steak and the mushrooms from the marinade, spray or brush with oil, and lay over the hot part of the grill (place the mushrooms gill sides up). Grill the steak, turning once, until richly browned and done to your liking, about $1^1/2$ to 2 minutes per side for medium-rare (the way Rick likes skirt steak). Cook the mushrooms until browned in spots, about 5 minutes, then flip and move to the center of the grill—the cooler part—and continue grilling until they feel a little limp but still have some body, about 10 minutes more.

> Cut the long piece of skirt steak into 3- to 4-inch lengths, and then cut each section against the grain (see box, page 152) into thin strips and season with a little salt. Place the meat in a serving dish. Cut the mushrooms into $1/4$-inch strips and scoop into a serving dish. Mix the chiles and onions and place in a serving bowl, season with a little salt, and set on the table along with the warm tortillas, lime wedges, and suggested accompaniments for your guests to make into soft tacos.

FILLING TIPS

Thin steaks like skirt taste best with a relatively short tour in the marinade—1 to 8 hours. Leave them longer, and the marinade overpowers the flavor and saps the rosy color of the meat. The poblano and onion strips can be made several hours ahead and left at room temperature; rewarm before serving. The steak, of course, must be grilled just before you're ready to eat.

HOMEMADE CORN TORTILLAS

START TO FINISH: 20 MINUTES / **HANDS-ON TIME:** 20 MINUTES / **SERVINGS:** MAKES 15 TORTILLAS

1 pound fresh-ground corn masa
for tortillas or 1³/₄ cups powdered
masa harina for tortillas (such as
Maseca brand) mixed with 1 cup plus

2 tablespoons hot tap water, or more
as needed (up to 1³/₄ cups)

> Prepare the tortilla dough as described at right (Step 1). Heat a heavy rectangular griddle (or two skillets) to two different temperatures: one side (or one skillet) over medium to medium-low, the other over medium-high. Cut two pieces of plastic to just cover the plates of a tortilla press (to be on the safe side, cut them from a food-storage bag; the thicker plastic is easier for beginners to work with) and shape and press the tortilla dough (Steps 2 and 3 at right).

> Lay the tortillas onto the cooler side of the griddle (or into the cooler skillet). Don't flip them off your hand—this always results in rumpled tortillas. Instead, as you slowly sweep the tortilla away from you, let the dangling part catch on the hot surface, then roll your hand out from under the tortilla (the movement looks a little as if you are sweeping something off the griddle with the back of your hand). Cook for 15 to 30 seconds, and then transfer to the hotter side and cook for 30 to 45 seconds (Steps 5 and 6 at right).

> Transfer the cooked tortillas to a cloth-lined basket and continue making tortillas, stacking them one on top of another and keeping them covered. As the cloth traps the steam, the tortillas will complete their final little bit of "cooking."

Cook's Notes: Tips for Buying a Tortilla Press

▶ Cast-iron presses are heavier than aluminum ones and stay put better during pressing. Ones that have at least an 8-inch diameter offer more flexibility than smaller ones. Though some traditional cooks prefer wooden presses, they can be bulky and cumbersome for occasional use.

▶ Rick uses tortilla presses purchased from Mexico or in Mexican markets, but you can also find them in many Mexican groceries, hardware stores in Mexican communities, well-stocked cookware stores, and online. Rick has developed his own cast-iron press, made by Gorham (see Sources, page 351).

▶ Note that a tortilla press should only to be used to press corn tortillas between two sheets of plastic; it cannot be used for flour tortillas, as they won't be thin enough.

MAKING CORN TORTILLAS

1. Knead the masa with just enough hot water to make it soft but not sticky. The softer the dough, the more tender the tortillas—but don't make it so soft that it sticks to your hands.

2. Open the press; lay one piece of plastic on the bottom. Scoop out a walnut-sized piece of dough, roll into a ball, and place in the center of the plastic. Cover with a second sheet of plastic.

3. Close the press and pull the handle over it to flatten the ball into a 5- to 6-inch disk. Open the press, turn the plastic-covered disk 180° and press gently to even the thickness. Open the press; peel off the top piece of plastic.

4. Flip the uncovered side of the tortilla onto your palm, lining up the top of the tortilla with the top of your index finger. Starting at the top, peel off the remaining sheet of plastic. Part of the tortilla will be dangling off the side of your hand.

5. Quickly lay the tortilla onto the cooler side of the griddle as directed in the recipe, and cook for 15 to 30 seconds—just until the tortilla releases itself from the griddle.

6. Flip onto the hotter side of the griddle and bake until splotchy brown underneath, 30 to 45 seconds. Turn once again, leaving it on the hot side, and bake for another 30 to 45 seconds.

Cooking with *Marc Vetri*

SAL'S OLD-SCHOOL MEATBALLS

Adapted from *Rustic Italian Food* (Ten Speed Press, 2011).

Marc Vetri, the chef and owner of eight well-loved restaurants in Philadelphia, was a guest on season three of *Sara's Weeknight Meals*. We had a ton of fun cooking together—and just as much fun shopping together beforehand in Philly's historic Italian Market.

We started at Esposito's Meats on Ninth Avenue where we bought exactly the right mix of meats for this recipe. Then we moved on to Di Bruno Bros., the most amazing cheese store, for Parmigiano-Reggiano and the right can of tomatoes, San Marzano from Italy.

Sal is Marc's father. Turns out that great meatballs were only part of the legacy he's passed on to his son. 'My father instilled three things in me,' Marc said on our show. 'One, always work for yourself—no matter what, be the boss. Two, always have integrity—you're only as good as your word. And three, always use veal, pork, and beef in meatballs. Life really is that simple!'

These meatballs are seriously good.

START TO FINISH: 2 HOURS 20 MINUTES / **HANDS-ON TIME:** I HOUR I5 MINUTES
SERVINGS: 8 TO I0 (SEE NOTES)

1 pound ground veal

1 pound ground pork

1 pound ground beef

4 slices white sandwich bread, torn

1¹/₂ cups milk

3 large eggs

2 cups packed (about 4 ounces) freshly grated Parmigiano-Reggiano, plus more for garnish

1 cup packed (about 2 ounces) freshly grated pecorino cheese

6 tablespoons chopped fresh flat-leaf parsley, plus more for garnish

2 tablespoons kosher salt

¹/₂ teaspoon freshly ground black pepper

1 garlic clove, minced

2 tablespoons extra-virgin olive oil

1 medium onion, chopped

1 garlic clove, minced

2 pounds Yukon gold potatoes, peeled and cut into small cubes

4 cups San Marzano tomatoes (1¹/₄ [28-ounce] cans)

1¹/₂ cups 00 flour (see Notes) or all-purpose flour

¹/₄ cup vegetable oil, preferably grapeseed

> **Make the meatballs:** Combine the veal, pork, beef, bread, milk, eggs, 2 cups of Parmigiano-Reggiano, 1 cup of pecorino, 6 tablespoons parsley, salt, pepper, and garlic in a stand mixer fitted with the flat blade. Mix on medium-low speed for 1 minute.

> Scoop out 2-tablespoon pieces of the meat mixture and gently roll them between your hands into balls about the size of a golf ball (you should have about 60 [1-ounce] meatballs). The meat will be soft, so don't compress it too much. Place the meatballs in the refrigerator for about 30 minutes to chill them slightly.

> **While the meatballs are chilling, make the sauce:** Heat the olive oil in a large skillet over medium-low heat. Add the onion and garlic and cook until softened. Add the potatoes and tomatoes and simmer until the potatoes are tender, about 30 minutes. Mash with a whisk and add salt and pepper to taste.

> **Finish the meatballs:** Put the flour in a bowl and toss the chilled meatballs in the flour before cooking. Heat the vegetable oil over medium heat in a large skillet and, working in batches, add the floured balls, cooking them until golden brown all over, 8 to 10 minutes. The internal temperature should be about 155°F.

> Divide the meatballs among plates, top with the sauce, and sprinkle with Parmigiano-Reggiano and parsley.

Notes: This recipe will also make 30 (2-ounce) meatballs or 20 (3-ounce) meatballs.

Italian flour, or 00 flour, is excellent for making soft, pliable doughs. The "00" refers to the grind of the flour, and it is available in low- to high-protein versions. Look for 00 flour in Italian or baking specialty stores. King Arthur Flour makes their own version, available from their website as "Italian-Style Flour" (see Sources, page 350).

MARC'S TIPS FOR BETTER MEATBALLS

◗ Make sure to mix the mixture for the meatballs well so the three different meats are blended evenly.

◗ Once you have rolled the meatballs, place them in the refrigerator for about a half hour to chill. Frying them when they are cold will yield a better result, as it keeps them from falling apart.

◗ Before frying the meatballs, test the seasoning by frying a small piece of the mixture. Taste the cooked meat to make sure the seasoning is to your liking.

SLOW-ROASTED RIB ROAST
WITH BÉARNAISE SAUCE

START TO FINISH: 4½ TO 5¾ HOURS / **HANDS-ON TIME:** 40 MINUTES / **SERVINGS:** 8 TO 10

8 to 10 pounds first-cut beef rib roast (3 to 4 ribs), the top 2 inches of the bones frenched (see page 278), if desired

Kosher salt and freshly ground black pepper

1 tablespoon vegetable oil, preferably grapeseed

½ cup dry white wine

½ cup white wine vinegar

2 tablespoons minced shallots

1 tablespoon dried tarragon

½ teaspoon kosher salt

¼ teaspoon freshly ground black pepper

4 large egg yolks

2½ sticks butter, cut into ½-inch pieces and chilled

2 to 3 tablespoons chopped fresh tarragon, or to taste

> Heat the oven to 200°F. Trim the surface layer of fat on the top side of the roast to ¼ inch thick. Score the fat in a crisscross pattern, cutting down to, but not into, the meat. Season the roast all over with salt and pepper.

> Heat the oil in a large skillet over high heat until hot. Reduce the heat to medium-high, add the roast, and brown on all sides except the bone side. Transfer the roast, fat side up, to a rack set in a roasting pan. Roast on the middle shelf of the oven until an instant-read thermometer reads 115° to 120°F for rare, or 120° to 125°F for medium-rare, 4 to 5 hours. Begin checking at 4 hours. Transfer the roast to a platter and cover loosely with foil. Let stand for 20 minutes before carving.

> While the meat is roasting, combine the white wine, vinegar, shallots, dried tarragon, ½ teaspoon kosher salt, and ¼ teaspoon pepper in a small saucepan. Bring the mixture to a simmer and simmer gently until reduced to about 4 tablespoons. Pour the mixture through a fine strainer into a medium metal bowl, pressing hard on the solids (you should have about 3 tablespoons liquid). Discard the solids and set the liquid aside until the meat is cooked and resting.

> While the roast rests, combine the yolks with the reserved liquid in a medium metal bowl and whisk until combined well. Set the bowl over a saucepan of simmering water (the water should not touch the bottom of the bowl) and whisk constantly, until the mixture feels quite warm to the touch (do not let it get too hot or the eggs will scramble).

> Immediately start adding the butter, several pieces at a time, whisking until the pieces are almost melted before adding the next. When all the butter is added, remove the bowl from the saucepan; whisk in the fresh tarragon and some of the meat juices that have accumulated on the platter, if desired. Slice the meat and serve each portion topped with béarnaise.

" Have you ever noticed that beef roasts, when cooked the traditional way (at 350°F or higher), have a brown exterior and only a bull's-eye of pink meat in the center? What if your whole family, like mine, prefers rare (or medium-rare)? This low-heat roasting method solves that problem. The finished product is always more succulent and more evenly cooked than if you roast it at high heat. There will be rare meat for everyone and there'll be more of that meat. And, low-heat roasts shrink less as they cook than high-heat roasts.

A standing rib roast, aka prime rib, is considered by many to be the most choice cut of meat on the animal because it combines a deep, beefy flavor with a tender, juicy texture. I like to finish it with a classic accompaniment, béarnaise sauce, which is rich like the roast but also provides a tangy contrast.

One note about the hunting and gathering before the cooking: Ask your butcher for a first-cut rib roast, which has less fat and more meat than the shoulder side of the roast. Then have him or her remove the chine bone, so that you can cut between the ribs when the roast is done. Serve with Smoothest Mashed Potatoes (page 307). "

RACK OF LAMB FOR TWO
WITH ROSEMARY CRUMB CRUST

START TO FINISH: 55 MINUTES / HANDS-ON TIME: 30 MINUTES / SERVINGS: 2

> "
> **M**ost of us never get to enjoy this elegant dish except at a fine restaurant, but it's surprisingly easy to make at home and the perfect candidate for a romantic meal for two.
>
> A single rack of lamb is comprised of eight chops, or half of the rib cage. At the supermarket these days you'll usually find a choice of New Zealand or American racks (the former are smaller than the latter and taste slightly more lamb-y). Either kind will work here, but in both cases make sure to have the butcher remove the chine bone so you can cut the rack into chops.
>
> Normally I would leave a layer of fat on the meat to keep it from drying out, but this recipe's crumb coating will keep the meat moist. You have to remove the rack's layer of fat along with the silverskin. You can ask your butcher to do this or follow the steps and photos on pages 278–279 to do it yourself.
>
> After you sear the meat, you top it with the mustard-mayonnaise mixture ("the glue") and the crumbs. You can prep the roast to this stage earlier in the day, and then park it for an hour. When dinner's about 30 minutes away, just pop it in the oven. (By the way, this recipe is adapted from a wonderful version by Kemp Minifie, an old buddy of mine from *Gourmet* magazine.)
> "

1 rack of lamb, 7 to 8 ribs (about 1¼ pounds)

2½ tablespoons extra-virgin olive oil, divided

¼ teaspoon red pepper flakes, optional

1 teaspoon minced garlic

3 medium scallions, white and 1 inch of the green parts, thinly sliced (about ¼ cup)

1 teaspoon dried rosemary

¾ cup fresh breadcrumbs (made by pulsing 1 large slice homemade-style white bread in a food processor or blender)

Kosher salt and freshly ground black pepper

2 tablespoons Homemade Mayonnaise (pages 52–53) or store-bought mayonnaise

1 teaspoon Dijon mustard

> Using a very sharp paring or boning knife, trim the meat and french the bones following the photos starting on page 278.

> Heat 1½ tablespoons of the oil over medium-high heat in a medium ovenproof skillet. Add the pepper flakes, if using, and garlic and cook, stirring, 30 seconds. Stir in the scallions and rosemary and cook, stirring, until the scallions are slightly softened, about 30 seconds. Stir in the breadcrumbs and remove from the heat. Add salt and pepper to taste and transfer to a bowl. Wipe out the skillet.

> Preheat the oven to 400°F. Heat the remaining 1 tablespoon oil in the skillet over medium-high heat. Season the lamb with salt and pepper and add to the skillet, meat side down. Sear until well browned on the meat side and the ends, about 5 minutes. Remove the skillet with the lamb from the heat and pour off the fat.

> Combine the mayonnaise and the mustard in a small bowl. Spread the mixture evenly over the meat side of the lamb and press the rosemary crumbs on top. Transfer the skillet to the middle shelf of the oven and roast until a meat thermometer reads 120°F for medium-rare, 10 to 12 minutes. Let the meat rest on a cutting board for 10 minutes before slicing into chops. Arrange decoratively on two plates, overlapping the rib bones and serve. (If some of the crumbs fall off, just sprinkle them over the plated chops.)

HOW TO TRIM AND FRENCH A RACK OF LAMB

1. If your rack of lamb comes with a thick piece of meat and fat on top of it, cut off that piece. Find the seam along the length of the meat side (not the bone side) of the lamb where the fatty piece is attached to the top of the rack and, using a sharp boning knife, start to slice it off...

2. ...pulling the piece of meat back as you go.

3. Continue until the whole piece is off and you can see the meat and bones underneath. (This might be what your rack of lamb looks like when you buy it, as that piece of meat and fat might already have been removed.)

4. To remove the tough silverskin, insert the tip of a sharp boning or paring knife just under the skin, on top of the meat, and, holding the knife at a 20° angle, slice in one direction.

5. When you reach the end of that strip of silverskin, lift up the skin and slice in the opposite direction.

6. Continue slicing off strips of silverskin until you have removed it all.

7. To french the bones, cut out the meat between the bones...

8. ...and scrape the bones clean of all sinew and tendons...

9. ...until your rack of lamb looks like this.

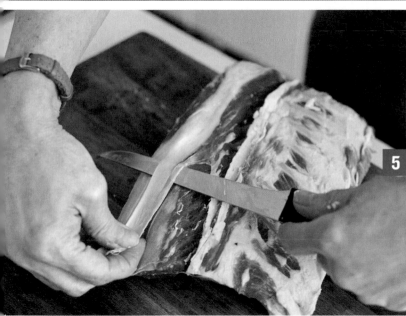

PERSONAL PIZZAS

START TO FINISH: 30 MINUTES TO PREHEAT THE OVEN AND 12 MINUTES ASSEMBLY
HANDS-ON TIME: 12 MINUTES ASSEMBLY / **SERVINGS:** MAKES 6 PERSONAL PIZZAS

1 recipe 10-Minute Pizza Dough (page 38) or 1½ pounds room temperature store-bought pizza dough

1½ cups Speedy Marinara Sauce (page 30) or your favorite store-bought variety

3 cups coarsely grated mozzarella, cheddar, Monterey Jack, or good melting cheese of your choice

4½ cups assorted toppings (see choices below right)

> Thirty minutes before you roll out the dough, preheat the oven to 500°F. Arrange a rack on the lowest shelf of the oven.

> Divide the dough into 6 equal pieces. On a lightly oiled surface, roll out one piece of the dough to a 9-inch circle (see page 39). Transfer the dough carefully to a baking sheet and smooth it out. Repeat with the remaining dough.

> Top the dough first with marinara, spreading it to within ½ inch of the edges. Then sprinkle the cheese evenly on top of the marinara, followed by the toppings. For each personal pizza you will need ¼ cup marinara, ½ cup cheese, and ¾ cup (combined) toppings (see box, below right).

> Bake the pizzas on the rack in the lowest part of the oven until the bottom is golden and the cheese is melted, about 7 minutes.

Note: For a crispier crust, roll out the dough into a 10-inch circle, transfer to a baking sheet, and smooth out. Bake for 3 minutes. Remove the crust from the oven, spread it with the marinara, cheese, and toppings, and bake until the cheese is melted, about 5 minutes.

GRILLED PIZZA VARIATION

> Preheat the grill to high with the lid down for 10 minutes. Reduce the heat to medium. Roll out the pizza dough on a lightly oiled counter (see page 39) that you can carry to the grill and brush the top of the dough with olive oil. Lift up the edge closest to you, and working very quickly, invert the dough, oiled side down, onto the grill. Close the lid and grill the dough for 1 to 3 minutes or until you can peek underneath and see that it is nicely marked on the bottom. Brush the top side of the dough with olive oil. Pick up the dough with tongs and place it, grilled side up and oiled side down, on the cutting board.

> Turn off a few of the burners on the grill to set up an area with indirect heat. Top the dough as instructed above and slide it back onto the grill with the help of tongs. Cover the grill and cook the pizza until the bottom crust is golden, 7 to 10 minutes.

> "Make pizza from scratch on a weeknight? Why bother when you can snap your fingers and have it delivered to your door?

Here's why: Homemade pizza tastes way better than commercial pizza and it takes much less time and effort than you might've guessed. Additionally, this recipe is for individual personal pizzas, which allows everyone to customize their toppings. Making the dough takes 10 minutes flat. Then, during the next hour, while the yeast is working its magic, there's plenty of time to prepare whatever toppings you like.

Starting with rolled-out prebaked crusts speeds up the whole dinner process. You can prebake the crusts (see Note) and freeze them. Let them cool completely, and then wrap them well in plastic wrap and foil and pop them in the freezer. When you are ready to use them, let them defrost on the counter for 30 minutes, and then top and bake them."

SUGGESTED PIZZA TOPPINGS:

▶ Sliced mushrooms sautéed in oil

▶ Thin sliced salami or prosciutto, cut into strips

▶ Chopped roasted red peppers

▶ Thin strips of fresh green bell peppers

▶ Thinly sliced onion

▶ Cooked crumbled Italian sausage

▶ Chopped fresh tomatoes

8 *on the* SIDE

Side dishes, like supporting actors, don't always get the love they deserve, even though they're often perfectly capable of outshining the so-called star of the meal. This chapter is my attempt to rectify that injustice.

Here are recipes for the summer, including Tomato-Avocado Salad with Gingered Tomato Vinaigrette, and the winter, such as Jean Anderson's stellar Pimiento Mac and Cheese. You'll meet veggies that may be new to you in recipes like Smashed Crispy Jerusalem Artichokes and Grilled Okra and learn new ways to prepare old pals like Roasted Radishes and Sautéed Lemony Radish Tops.

Techniques-wise, there's a new way to pare down artichokes to their hearts much more quickly than you may have been taught. I'm proud of my recipes for Smoothest Mashed Potatoes and Foolproof Scalloped Potatoes. Likewise, I guarantee that my Cream Biscuits are the most tender you'll ever taste.

Rawia Bishara, the owner of Tanoreen, a great Middle Eastern restaurant in New York, has shared two of the recipes on her menu, including her extraordinary Brussels Sprouts with Panko dressed with tahini. Come to think of it, if you made several of these side dishes for one meal, you could tell the main dish to take the night off. Dinner wouldn't be typical, but it certainly wouldn't be boring either.

TOMATO-AVOCADO SALAD
WITH GINGERED TOMATO VINAIGRETTE

Pictured on page 229

START TO FINISH: 45 MINUTES / **HANDS-ON TIME:** 25 MINUTES / **SERVINGS:** 4

At the peak of its ripeness, a tomato in season is one of the things that makes life worth living. This recipe is my ode to the tomato in summer.

The best place to shop for tomatoes is at a farm stand or farmers' market. How do you know if the tomato in question is ripe ripe ripe? Smell the stem end; its perfume should fairly shout, "Tomato!" And once you get them home, do *not* put your tomatoes in the fridge. It will kill their flavor and texture. You can heighten that flavor by presalting your tomatoes and letting them drain for 15 to 20 minutes, as I have done here.

I've teamed up the tomatoes with one of their best friends, an avocado. But come to think of it, tomatoes have many best friends. Certainly, there isn't a fresh green herb that doesn't play nicely with tomatoes. That includes the prescribed mint, as well as basil, cilantro, chives, oregano, dill, parsley, and tarragon.

Topping the salad are some thinly sliced serrano chiles, which provide a jolt of heat to counterbalance the tomato's sweetness.

For the dressing:
1 small ripe tomato (4 to 6 ounces), coarsely chopped
$1/2$ small garlic clove, smashed and peeled
2-inch piece ginger, coarsely chopped
2 tablespoons seasoned rice vinegar
2 tablespoons vegetable oil, preferably grapeseed
2 teaspoons low-sodium soy sauce
Kosher salt and freshly ground black pepper

For the salad:
2 large beefsteak tomatoes, sliced $1/3$ inch thick, plus 1 cup chopped assorted small tomatoes
1 firm ripe avocado, quartered, pitted, sliced, and sprinkled lightly with salt
$1/2$ to 1 serrano chile, sliced thin crosswise, optional
$1/4$ cup shredded fresh mint
$1/4$ cup chopped toasted peanuts

› **Make the dressing:** Combine the tomato, garlic, ginger, rice vinegar, oil, and soy sauce in blender and puree until smooth. Add salt and pepper to taste.

› **Make the salad:** Lightly salt the sliced tomatoes and let them drain on a rack for 20 minutes. Toss the chopped tomatoes with salt and drain in a colander for 20 minutes.

› Arrange alternating slices of the large tomatoes, patted dry, and the avocados on a platter and season them lightly with pepper. Drizzle the tomatoes and avocados with most of the dressing and top them evenly with the chopped tomatoes. Season the chopped tomatoes lightly with pepper and scatter the serrano slices, if using, mint, and peanuts evenly on top. Serve the remaining dressing on the side.

HOW TO PIT AN AVOCADO SAFELY

I can't blame home cooks for attempting to pit an avocado the way celebrity chefs do it on television. There's something so dashing about it—holding the fruit in the air, slicing it in half with a big knife, separating the two halves with a quick twist, forcefully burying the heel of the knife in the pit, and finally pulling out the pit like a giant tooth. *Ta-da!*

Dramatic it may be, but this technique has occasioned many a trip to the emergency room. Here's a much safer way to pit an avocado, by cutting it in quarters.

1. Lay the avocado on its side and cut down to the pit.

2. Move the knife around the outside rim of the avocado, rotating it as you cut.

3. Leaving the avocado in the same position and working from the top side, cut down to the pit from the top to the bottom of the avocado.

4. Then flip it over to do the same on the second side.

5. Pull the 4 quarters off the pit (they will come off very easily).

6. Now each avocado quarter is ready to be scored in a crisscross pattern using a paring knife, and then scooped out with a spoon (to form cubes), or scooped out uncut with a spoon and sliced or cubed afterward.

SESAME KALE SALAD

Pictured on page 221

START TO FINISH: 25 MINUTES / **HANDS-ON TIME:** 25 MINUTES / **SERVINGS:** 4

1 small garlic clove, minced

2¹/₂ teaspoons sesame oil

2 tablespoons vegetable oil, preferably grapeseed

3 tablespoons rice vinegar

2 tablespoons low-sodium soy sauce

10 cups packed chopped kale leaves (about 1 large bunch, see Note)

2 tablespoons sesame seeds (toasted in a small skillet over low heat until golden), optional

Kosher salt and freshly ground black pepper

› In a large bowl, whisk together the garlic, sesame oil, vegetable oil, vinegar, and soy sauce. Add the kale and massage it with your hands for 4 to 5 minutes, or until it has become shiny and a little translucent and reduced in volume by one-third to one-half. Sprinkle with the sesame seeds, if using, and salt and pepper to taste, and toss well.

Note: Kale is available in curly, ornamental, and dinosaur varieties. Generally, smaller leaves are milder in flavor.

Kale is wonderful, but I wanted a new way to prepare it. Garlicky kale sautéed in olive oil? Been there. Baked kale chips? Done that. I decided to go the salad route and give it the Asian treatment, dressing the kale with soy, sesame oil, and rice vinegar.

Kale's one problem, especially with the larger-leaved varieties, is that it's tough. You can tenderize it by cutting it into thin shreds or, oddly enough, you can massage it. I was always taught to be gentle with greens because they bruise easily, but kale is the punching bag of the greens world.

WHITE BEAN AND FENNEL SALAD

START TO FINISH: 35 MINUTES / **HANDS-ON TIME:** 35 MINUTES / **SERVINGS:** 6

2 cups cooked white beans (see page 36) or 1 (19-ounce) can, rinsed and drained, divided

¹/₂ teaspoon freshly grated lemon zest

1¹/₂ tablespoons fresh lemon juice

8 anchovy fillets, finely chopped

¹/₂ teaspoon freshly ground black pepper

¹/₄ cup plus 1 tablespoon extra-virgin olive oil

¹/₂ cup thinly sliced red onion, soaked in ice water for 20 minutes, drained and patted dry

1¹/₂ cups thinly shaved (about ¹/₈ inch thick) fresh fennel (see Note) plus ¹/₂ cup coarsely chopped fennel fronds

1 cup halved cherry tomatoes (see technique, page 181)

¹/₂ cup medium chopped fresh flat-leaf parsley

Kosher salt

› Mash ¹/₂ cup of the beans in a small bowl. Combine the lemon zest, lemon juice, anchovies, and black pepper in a salad bowl and mix well. Add the oil in a stream, whisking. Stir in the mashed beans. Add the whole beans, onion, fennel, tomatoes, parsley, and salt to taste and toss well.

Note: Fennel, like celery, is stringy. When you're prepping the bulb, slice it *against* the grain.

Cooked beans tossed with olive oil and lemon are always a treat. Complement the beans' creaminess with some crunchy fennel, red onions, and cherry tomatoes, and you're looking at one very tasty salad.

The anchovies' role in this salad is not to make it fishy, but to add saltiness and depth of flavor. You're welcome to leave them out, if you prefer. Likewise, if you're no fan of fennel, replace it with celery. (Some folks don't like fennel's licorice taste.)

Why soak the onions in ice water? To tamp down their sharp edge and take a big bite out of onion breath.

SWEET POTATO AND GRILLED CORN SALAD
WITH SPICY CILANTRO DRESSING

START TO FINISH: 40 MINUTES / **HANDS-ON TIME:** 25 MINUTES / **SERVINGS:** 6

1 garlic clove, smashed and peeled

1/2 chipotle chile in adobo sauce

1 small shallot, coarsely chopped

1 cup chopped fresh cilantro, leaves and stems

1 cup seasoned rice vinegar

Kosher salt

4 ears corn, husked

Vegetable cooking spray

1 1/2 pounds sweet potatoes, peeled and cut into 1/2-inch cubes

2 cups cooked black beans (see page 36) or 1 (19-ounce) can, rinsed and drained

4 scallions, white and light green parts, sliced thin

> Preheat the grill to high.

> Combine the garlic, chipotle, shallot, cilantro, and rice vinegar in a blender and puree until smooth. Add salt to taste and set aside.

> Spray the corn with vegetable cooking spray. Reduce the heat to medium-high and grill the corn, turning it often, until it is lightly browned in spots on all sides, about 10 minutes. Remove the corn from the grill and let it cool until it can be handled. Cut off the corn from the cob. (You should have at least 2 cups.)

> Place the potatoes in a steamer rack set over boiling water, cover, and steam until they are just tender, about 8 minutes.

> Drain the potatoes and toss them while still hot with a hefty pinch of salt and half the dressing. Let them cool, then stir in the corn, black beans, scallions, and as much additional dressing as desired.

> Everyone knows potato salad is good—there's a reason it's a summertime perennial—but that doesn't mean it's good *for you*. This crafty version swaps in sweet potatoes for white potatoes and loses the standard recipe's abundant mayonnaise in favor of a dressing high in flavor and low in fat.

Sweet potatoes have great nutritional value. For the best texture, steam them just until they become tender, then stop. Overdo it, and they'll turn to mush.

Here, I've grilled the corn, which amps up the flavor and decreases the need for fat. In fact, with the exception of the spray used to coat the corn before grilling, there's no oil in this recipe. How'd I manage that little trick? By composing a dressing so flavorful—the keys are chipotle, cilantro, and garlic—that no one will notice the lack o' fat.

One final note: Toss the sweet potatoes with the dressing while they're still warm. It helps them absorb the dressing and become deeply flavored.

SPICY CREAMED CORN
THE SUMMER VERSION

START TO FINISH: 30 MINUTES / **HANDS-ON TIME:** 30 MINUTES / **SERVINGS:** 4

3 cups fresh corn kernels (from 4 to 6 ears of corn), divided

¾ cup Homemade Chicken Stock (page 26), Homemade Vegetable Stock (page 29), store-bought chicken or vegetable broth, or water, divided

2 tablespoons vegetable oil, preferably grapeseed, or olive oil

Kosher salt

½ cup finely chopped scallions, white and light green parts

1 serrano chile, seeds and ribs discarded if desired, and minced (about 1 tablespoon)

1 to 2 tablespoons fresh lime or lemon juice or to taste

2 tablespoons shredded fresh basil or chopped fresh cilantro, leaves and stems

Freshly ground black pepper

› Add 1 cup of the corn kernels and ½ cup of the stock to a blender and puree.

› Heat the oil over medium heat in a large skillet until hot, add the remaining 2 cups corn and a pinch of salt, and sauté for 2 minutes. Add the scallions and serrano and sauté for 2 minutes. Add the pureed corn, bring the puree to a simmer, and cook for 2 minutes.

› Stir in the remaining ¼ cup chicken stock, the lime juice, basil, and salt and pepper to taste and simmer 1 minute more.

THE WINTER VERSION

› Preheat the broiler. Rub 1 medium poblano chile all over with vegetable oil (preferably grapeseed), and broil it 4 inches from the heat source, turning it often, until it is charred on all sides, about 10 minutes. Transfer to a bowl, cover with plastic wrap, and let steam for about 10 minutes. Remove and discard the peel and the seeds and chop the poblano finely. Heat 1 tablespoon vegetable oil (preferably grapeseed) in a large skillet over medium heat. Add 1 cup thinly sliced onion and a pinch of kosher salt and cook, stirring occasionally, until the onion is golden brown, 8 minutes. Add 1 (16-ounce) bag of frozen corn, 2 ounces Neufchâtel (⅓-less-fat cream cheese), the chopped poblano, and ½ to ¾ cup chicken or vegetable stock and cook, stirring occasionally, until the corn is hot. Stir in 1 tablespoon fresh lime or lemon juice, ¼ cup shredded fresh basil or chopped fresh cilantro, and salt to taste.

BAKED TOMATOES PUTTANESCA

Pictured on page 159

START TO FINISH: 55 MINUTES / **HANDS-ON TIME:** 25 MINUTES
SERVINGS: 8 TOMATO HALVES

4 ripe medium tomatoes
(about 5 ounces each)

Kosher salt

2 tablespoons extra-virgin olive oil

1/4 cup finely chopped onion

2 teaspoons minced garlic

4 anchovy fillets, chopped

1/4 cup medium chopped pitted
Mediterranean olives

1 1/4 cups fresh breadcrumbs (made
by pulsing 2 slices homemade-style
white bread in a food processor)

Freshly ground black pepper

Shredded fresh basil for garnish

> Cut the tomatoes in half horizontally, sprinkle the cut sides generously with salt, and turn them upside down on a rack to drain for 30 minutes.

> Preheat the oven to 375°F. Heat the oil in a medium skillet over medium heat, add the onion, and cook, stirring occasionally, until softened, about 5 minutes. Add the garlic and anchovies and cook, stirring, 3 minutes. Add the olives and breadcrumbs and combine well. Remove from the heat and season with salt and pepper to taste.

> Turn the tomatoes right side up, pat them dry, and transfer to a shallow baking dish. Mound the breadcrumbs evenly on top of the tomatoes. Bake on the middle shelf of the oven until golden and just tender, about 20 minutes.

> Top each tomato half with some basil and serve immediately.

"
Spaghetti *a la puttanesca* is one of southern Italy's best-loved recipes. A classic pasta dish consisting of spaghetti topped with a tomato sauce flavored with garlic, onions, anchovies, and olives, it gets its name from *puttana,* the Italian word for prostitute. The story goes that the sauce was favored by these ladies of the evening because they could cook it quickly between visits by clients.

Here, I've retired the spaghetti in favor of some breadcrumbs, and repurposed the sauce ingredients on top of halved, baked tomatoes. Be sure to salt and drain the tomatoes before you bake them. It rids them of their excess water and amps up their tomato flavor.

You can set up the tomatoes with their topping an hour ahead of time, and then pop them into the oven 20 minutes before dinner. However, you don't need to serve them piping hot. They're very tasty at room temperature, too.
"

ROASTED RADISHES AND SAUTÉED LEMONY RADISH TOPS

Pictured on page 120

START TO FINISH: 50 MINUTES / **HANDS-ON TIME:** 20 MINUTES / **SERVINGS:** 4

2 bunches radishes (about 1¼ pounds) with fresh-looking tops

2 tablespoons extra-virgin olive oil, divided

Kosher salt and freshly ground black pepper

1 tablespoon fresh lemon juice

2 teaspoons Dijon mustard

> Preheat the oven to 425°F.

> Cut off the radish tops, discarding the tough ends, wash them well, and coarsely chop them. Clean the radishes and quarter them lengthwise.

> Toss the radishes with 1 tablespoon of the oil and season them with salt and pepper. Arrange them in a single layer on a rimmed baking sheet and roast on the middle shelf of the oven until they are golden brown, 25 to 30 minutes. When they are done, mash them lightly on the baking sheet with a potato masher.

> Heat the remaining 1 tablespoon oil in a large skillet over medium-high heat. Add the radish tops and sauté them for 1 to 2 minutes. Add the roasted radishes to the tops along with the lemon juice, mustard, and salt and pepper to taste, and cook until heated.

Mostly, when we eat radishes, we eat them raw. Their spiciness and crisp texture make them a terrific ingredient in all sorts of salads and raw dishes. But a *cooked* radish is a totally different, if equally delightful, animal: sweet, tender, and pink.

Like beets, turnips, and carrots, radishes—when considered whole—are a two-fer. Those leafy tops that we often thoughtlessly cut off and toss away are not only edible, they can be delicious. In fact, there's a world of flavor and nutrition in such supposedly worthless vegetable by-products as leaves, stems, and peels, as we see with Amanda Cohen's Broccoli Carpaccio with Broccoli Stalk Salad (page 231). You also can enter that world through the door of a book I highly recommend: Tara Duggan's *Root-to-Stalk Cooking: The Art of Using the Whole Vegetable* (Ten Speed Press, 2013).

Accordingly, when purchasing a bunch of radishes for this recipe, be sure to pick ones with fresh-looking greens attached. Those greens are very quickly sautéed in oil, then combined with the roasted mashed radishes. The first time you serve this dish, your diners may not be able to put their finger on just what it is they're eating. But they will know that they love it.

SMASHED CRISPY JERUSALEM ARTICHOKES

Pictured on page 244

START TO FINISH: 40 MINUTES / **HANDS-ON TIME:** 25 MINUTES / **SERVINGS:** 4

1 pound Jerusalem artichokes, scrubbed (but not peeled)

¼ cup extra-virgin olive oil

3 tablespoons freshly grated Parmigiano-Reggiano

Kosher salt and freshly ground black pepper

> If the Jerusalem artichokes are more than 2 inches long, cut them in half crosswise. Put them in a small saucepan, add cold salted water to cover by 2 inches, and bring the water to a boil. Reduce the heat and simmer until almost tender, 12 to 15 minutes. Drain, transfer to a cutting board, and lightly crush them with a potato masher or a fork until they are about ¾ inch thick, keeping the Jerusalem artichokes intact as much as possible.

> Heat the oil in a large skillet over medium-high heat. Transfer the Jerusalem artichokes with a spatula to the skillet, and cook, turning them, until golden brown, about 12 minutes total. (Watch the heat, and turn them over more often if they are getting too brown.) Transfer them with a slotted spoon to paper towels to drain.

> Sprinkle with the cheese, season generously with salt and pepper, and serve immediately.

66

Jerusalem artichokes, or sunchokes, aren't actually artichokes and have nothing to do with Jerusalem. They're the tuberous roots of a native North American plant in the sunflower family. (How they got their name is a long story we'll save for another time.) Raw, they have a crunchy texture reminiscent of water chestnuts. Cooked, they become creamy, with a taste that faintly resembles, yep, artichokes. Either way, they're delicious.

99

HOW TO PREP JERUSALEM ARTICHOKES

Jerusalem artichokes are easy to prep: Just scrub them and you're done. (Peeling is optional because their skins are so thin.) If you want to eat them raw, be sure to toss them with a little lemon juice after slicing, or put them in a bowl of water combined with the juice of half a lemon. Otherwise, like potatoes or apples, they'll quickly turn brown.

Okra, Two Ways

SHALLOW-FRIED BEER-BATTERED OKRA

Pictured on page 207

START TO FINISH: 60 MINUTES / **HANDS-ON TIME:** 30 MINUTES / **SERVINGS:** 6

Okra doesn't always get a lot of love, particularly because when it's been sliced and allowed to cook for awhile, it gives off a uniquely gelatinous slime. In Louisiana that's considered a good thing: It's this liquid that thickens the local gumbo. Other folks, less charmed by this dense goo, will have nothing to do with it. The trick to avoiding the goo is to cook the okra whole and to cook it briefly, as I do in these preparations. Both of the following recipes feature whole okra. The first is beer-battered and fried, the second is grilled. The grilled okra is partially split open, but cooks so quickly that the goo doesn't make an appearance.

The Smoked Paprika Dipping Sauce is a great partner for either version and it works beautifully with other grilled or fried vegetables, and with grilled fish or chicken, too.

1 cup unbleached all-purpose flour, plus extra for dredging the okra

Kosher salt

1 (12-ounce) bottle beer of your choice (if you want pronounced beer flavor, use a full-bodied beer)

1 teaspoon Dijon mustard

Freshly ground black pepper

Vegetable oil, for shallow-frying (see page 225)

½ pound okra (about 20 pods), trimmed (see box, page 174)

Smoked Paprika Dipping Sauce (page 293)

> Preheat the oven to 300°F. Whisk together 1 cup of the flour and ½ teaspoon kosher salt in a medium bowl. Add 1 cup of the beer and the mustard and whisk until almost smooth with a few lumps still remaining. Strain the batter through a medium-mesh strainer into another bowl, cover, and let stand for 30 minutes. Reserve the extra beer for another use.

> Spread out additional flour on a piece of parchment on the counter and season it with salt and pepper. Check the batter; it should have the consistency of a thick pancake batter. If it seems too thick, whisk in up to ¼ cup more beer.

> Heat ½ inch oil in a large skillet over medium-high heat until it reaches about 360°F. (Tipping the pan slightly will make it easier to take the temperature.) Working with half of the okra at a time, toss them in the flour, lifting the parchment on both sides to move them around and coat them with the flour. Transfer the okra to a medium-mesh strainer and shake them to get rid of excess flour. Dip the okra in the batter, letting the excess drip off, and add them to the skillet. Cook the okra, turning once, until they are golden, 1 to 2 minutes per side. Transfer the okra to a rimmed baking sheet, sprinkle lightly with salt, and keep warm in the oven while you cook the rest.

> Repeat the procedure with the remaining okra and serve them with the Smoked Paprika Sauce on the side.

GRILLED OKRA

START TO FINISH: 20 MINUTES / **HANDS-ON TIME:** 20 MINUTES / **SERVINGS:** 8 TO 10

1 pound okra (about 40 pods)

1¹/₂ tablespoons vegetable oil, preferably grapeseed

1 teaspoon kosher salt

¹/₄ teaspoon freshly ground black pepper

Smoked Paprika Dipping Sauce

> Preheat the grill to high. Cut each okra pod lengthwise, leaving about ¹/₂ inch uncut at the stem end. Toss the okra with the oil, salt, and pepper in a bowl. Grill the okra, turning it once, until the pods are slightly charred and have started to split wide open, about 5 minutes. Transfer to a platter and serve with the Smoked Paprika Dipping Sauce.

SMOKED PAPRIKA DIPPING SAUCE

Pictured on page 207

START TO FINISH: 10 MINUTES / **HANDS-ON TIME:** 10 MINUTES / **SERVINGS:** MAKES ABOUT ½ CUP

¹/₂ cup Homemade Mayonnaise (pages 52–53) or store-bought mayonnaise

2 teaspoons fresh lemon juice

1 teaspoon minced garlic

1 teaspoon hot smoked paprika or 1 teaspoon smoked paprika plus ¹/₄ teaspoon cayenne

Kosher salt

Combine the mayonnaise, lemon juice, garlic, paprika, and salt to taste and mix well.

BAKED EGGPLANT
WITH MISO-GINGER GLAZE

START TO FINISH: 35 MINUTES / **HANDS-ON TIME:** 20 MINUTES / **SERVINGS:** 4

"Miso, the fermented soybean paste that's key to Japanese cuisine, has been one of the happier culinary discoveries of my recent years. It makes whatever it's added to just taste better: soup, noodles, fish, meat, or vegetables. It's sweet and salty and has a thick texture, which provides a wonderful glaze. There are several varieties of miso and each one reflects how long it's been aged, becoming darker, saltier, and more robust as time passes (see box, page 131). Miso keeps in the fridge for months. I recommend buying a little tub and experimenting with it.

Given that eggplant is a sponge for oil, I'd rather bake it than fry it—and this glaze offers a lot of flavor in the process. It's also quite versatile and would be right at home on top of any number of vegetables, including carrots, turnips, onions, and broccoli."

1³/₄ pounds eggplant, peeled and sliced ¹/₂ inch thick

¹/₄ cup plus 2 teaspoons vegetable oil, preferably grapeseed, divided

Kosher salt and freshly ground black pepper

2 teaspoons finely grated ginger

2 teaspoons minced garlic

¹/₄ cup sake or mirin

2 tablespoons white miso

1 tablespoon unseasoned rice vinegar

2 teaspoons packed brown sugar

1 teaspoon hot sauce or to taste, optional

2 teaspoons sesame oil

Chopped scallions, white and light green parts, for garnish

> Preheat the oven to 400°F. Brush both sides of the eggplant slices with ¹/₄ cup of the oil and season with salt and pepper. Arrange in a single layer on 2 parchment-lined, rimmed baking sheets and bake on the upper and lower third shelves of the oven, switching the pans halfway through, until tender, 12 to 15 minutes.

> In a small skillet, heat the remaining 2 teaspoons oil over medium heat, add the ginger and garlic, and cook, stirring, 1 minute. Add the sake, miso, vinegar, brown sugar, and hot sauce, if using, whisking, and cook about 1 minute. Stir in the sesame oil.

> Spoon the sauce on the top of the eggplant slices and bake for 5 minutes more. Sprinkle with the scallions and serve.

SAUTÉED ARTICHOKE HEARTS
WITH PANCETTA

Pictured on page 259

START TO FINISH: 40 MINUTES / **HANDS-ON TIME:** 25 MINUTES / **SERVINGS:** 4 TO 6

1 lemon, plus 1 tablespoon fresh lemon juice, divided

6 globe artichokes

3 tablespoons extra-virgin olive oil

2 ounces ¼-inch-thick slices pancetta, finely chopped

1 teaspoon minced garlic

Kosher salt and freshly ground black pepper

> Juice the whole lemon into a large bowl and throw in the halves along with 1 quart cold water. Working with 1 artichoke at a time, follow the steps on page 296 to trim down to the heart. Cut into fourths, remove the chokes, and drop the hearts into the acidulated water. Proceed with the remaining artichokes.

> Drain the artichokes hearts and pat dry. Heat the oil in a large skillet over medium-high heat. Reduce the heat to medium, add the artichoke hearts, and sauté, stirring often, until golden brown on all sides, 8 to 10 minutes. Transfer to a bowl with tongs.

> Add the pancetta to the skillet, reduce the heat to medium-low, and cook, stirring frequently, until golden, about 2 minutes. Return the artichokes to the pan along with the garlic and sauté for 1 minute. Add the remaining 1 tablespoon lemon juice and salt and pepper to taste, and serve.

> Artichokes are the armadillos of the vegetable kingdom. There is a tender and succulent heart at the center of each specimen, but getting past its armor of prickly leaves is daunting at best.

By contrast, steaming—and eating—a whole artichoke is relatively easy: Cut off the stem and the top, trim the tips of the leaves, place in a steamer, and cook for about 45 minutes. You eat one leaf at a time, ignoring the spiky tip in favor of the plump tasty nugget at the base. It's a very pleasant way to clear away the brush until the happy moment when you arrive at the undefended heart.

But if the goal is to trim the artichoke down to the heart and nothing but the heart, I always thought it a pretty tough slog. Then I went to an artichoke seminar in Castroville, California, where one of the chefs showed us a much less labor-intensive way to lose the leaves, which is demonstrated in the photos on pages 296–297. Amazed and grateful, I've done it that way ever since.

HOW TO TRIM AN ARTICHOKE TO GET TO THE HEART

1. Lay the artichoke on its side and start to cut down one side about ½ inch from the edge.

2. Cut down and circle around, following the curve of the artichoke with your knife, until you have removed all the tough green outer leaves and gotten down to the light green inner part of the artichoke.

3. Cut off the remaining leaves where they meet the light green part of the artichoke.

4. Using the tip of a sharp paring knife, make a cut, straight down, about ⅛ inch deep, around the base of the stem.

5. Then cut off the tough dark green part around the stem.

6. Notice the lighter green core in the center of the stem; it is tender and delicious like the artichoke heart.

7. Peel the stem using a vegetable peeler or paring knife until you get down to the light green center of the stem.

8. Cut the trimmed artichoke heart in half, and then in quarters.

9. Then cut out the tough, hairy choke in the center of each quarter with a paring knife.

REFRIED BEANS

Pictured on page 123

START TO FINISH: 35 MINUTES / **HANDS-ON TIME:** 20 MINUTES / **SERVINGS:** 4

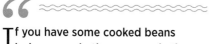

If you have some cooked beans in-house—whether you made them yourself (see page 36) or because there's a can in the cupboard—you'll find this to be a very quick weeknight side dish. And if your freezer contains any leftover pork, beef, or duck fat, you'll be able to whip up an extra-tasty Mexican/Tex-Mex version of it. I encourage you to stockpile those fats as a matter of course. Every time you make a meat-based sauce or cook some duck and have to skim off the fat, think of it as liquid gold. Don't toss it, save it and use it (see Notes, page 134).

3 tablespoons pork fat, beef fat, duck fat, or vegetable oil, preferably grapeseed

1 cup minced onion

2 teaspoons minced garlic

2 teaspoons ground cumin

1 teaspoon chili powder

3 cups cooked pinto beans (see page 36), plus 1 cup bean cooking liquid, or rinsed, drained canned pinto beans plus 1 cup Homemade Chicken Stock (page 26), Homemade Vegetable Stock (page 29), or store-bought chicken or vegetable broth

Kosher salt and freshly ground black pepper

Optional garnishes: Mexican crema, chopped raw onion, grated Monterey Jack or sharp cheddar cheese, chopped fresh cilantro

› Heat the fat in a large skillet over medium heat, add the onion, and cook, stirring occasionally, until golden, about 8 minutes. Add the garlic, cumin, and chili powder to the skillet and cook, stirring, 1 minute. Add the beans and the bean liquid and bring the liquid to a boil. Reduce to a simmer, cover, and cook until most of the liquid has evaporated, about 12 minutes. Remove from the heat and mash the beans with a potato masher or fork until they are smooth, with some lumps. Add salt and pepper to taste. Serve as is or with some of the garnishes.

ROASTED CABBAGE
WITH WARM BACON-AND-BLUE CHEESE DRESSING

START TO FINISH: 40 MINUTES / **HANDS-ON TIME:** 20 MINUTES / **SERVINGS:** 4

$^1/_2$ medium green cabbage
(1 to 1$^1/_2$ pounds)

1 tablespoon extra-virgin olive oil

Kosher salt and freshly ground black
pepper

3 slices bacon

2 tablespoons minced shallots

3 tablespoons sherry wine vinegar

1 teaspoon Dijon mustard

$^1/_2$ cup crumbled blue cheese

> Preheat the oven to 450°F. Cut the cabbage half into 4 wedges and cut out and discard the thick core. Sprinkle the cut sides of the cabbage with the oil, season them with salt and pepper, and transfer the wedges to an oiled baking sheet. Roast on a shelf in the upper third of the oven for 12 minutes. Carefully turn the wedges over and roast until browned on the second side, 6 to 8 more minutes.

> Meanwhile, cook the bacon in a medium skillet over medium heat until crisp, about 5 minutes. Transfer the bacon to paper towels to drain, then crumble it. Discard all but 1 tablespoon of the bacon fat from the pan, add the shallots, and cook over medium heat, scraping up the brown bits, until the shallots have softened, 3 to 4 minutes. Remove from the heat and whisk in the vinegar, mustard, blue cheese, crumbled bacon, and salt and pepper to taste.

> Transfer the cabbage wedges to each of 4 plates, pour some of the sauce over each portion, and serve immediately.

"
Roasting any vegetable brings out the natural sugars and intensifies its flavor. Here, I've cut the cabbage into wedges before roasting to increase the surface area and help it cook more quickly. While the cabbage is in the oven, you can cook the bacon and make the sauce in the drippings.

This is a simple but elegant side dish and the combination of cabbage, smoky bacon, sharp sherry vinegar, and blue cheese is magical. It would be equally welcome at a weeknight dinner or a weekend dinner party.
"

SWEET-AND-SOUR SHREDDED BEETS

Pictured on page 144

START TO FINISH: 35 MINUTES / **HANDS-ON TIME:** 25 MINUTES / **SERVINGS:** 4

1³/₄ to 2 pounds beets
3 tablespoons extra-virgin olive oil
Kosher salt

3 tablespoons balsamic vinegar
Freshly ground black pepper

› Peel the beets, cut them into pieces that fit through the feed tube of a food processor, and coarsely grate them, using the grating disk of the food processor.

› Heat the oil in a large skillet over high heat. Reduce the heat to medium, add the beets and a hefty pinch of salt, cover, and cook for 5 minutes. Add the balsamic vinegar, stir well, and cook, covered and stirring occasionally, until tender, 6 to 8 minutes. Add salt and pepper to taste.

" This side dish, like my Skillet Borscht with Meatballs (page 180), is inspired by The Husband. He loves beets. I hated them for years. (To me, they tasted like dirt.) Even cooking beets for the family was a drag: They took forever to become tender and stained my hands when I peeled them. In recent years, I somehow came to appreciate their taste, but my other beefs with beets remained.

Then one day when I was staring at a dusty box of never-used food processing disks, a light bulb went off. If it were possible to use the shredding disk to shred beets, this whole psychodrama would disappear. Sure enough, as soon as I started using the proper tool, it took no more than 15 minutes to shred and cook some beets. And the bonus? Peeling raw beets before shredding them stains the hands much less than peeling cooked beets after boiling them. (Of course, I'd have come to this solution much much sooner if only I'd read the manual when I first bought the food processor. Duh!) Suddenly, I started shredding and sautéeing every vegetable I could lay my hands on.

By the way, you might want to move your food processor from that high cupboard above the fridge to a more accessible place—you'll be more likely to use it if it's in plain sight. "

SAUTÉED SHREDDED ZUCCHINI
WITH LEMON AND THYME

Pictured on page 125

START TO FINISH: 30 MINUTES / **HANDS-ON TIME:** 30 MINUTES / **SERVINGS:** 4 TO 6

2 pounds zucchini

1 1/2 teaspoons kosher salt, plus more to taste

3 tablespoons extra-virgin olive oil

1 cup thinly sliced onion

1/2 teaspoon freshly grated lemon zest

2 teaspoons fresh lemon juice

2 teaspoons chopped fresh thyme

Freshly ground black pepper

> Trim off and discard the ends of the zucchini. Coarsely grate the zucchini, preferably using the grating disk of a food processor. Transfer the zucchini to a colander and toss with the salt; let drain for 15 minutes. Using your hands and working with small handfuls, gently but firmly squeeze out as much moisture as possible.

> While the zucchini is draining, heat the oil in a large skillet over medium heat, add the onion, and cook, stirring occasionally, until browned, about 10 minutes. Add the zucchini and cook, stirring, 2 minutes. Add the lemon zest, lemon juice, and thyme and cook for 1 minute. Season with salt and pepper to taste.

> "As any home gardener can tell you, the zucchini embodies one of nature's great paradoxes: How can one vegetable be so bland and so prolific at the same time? On a summer's day years ago, faced with yet another truckload of these aggravating squashes, I set myself the task of figuring out what to do with them. It turns out that if you shred and salt zucchini, and then squeeze out its excess water (they're very watery), you'll discover a sweet and very flavorful vegetable. Try this recipe, and see for yourself."

SAUTÉED SHREDDED CARROTS
WITH PINE NUTS

Pictured on page 224

START TO FINISH: 20 MINUTES / **HANDS-ON TIME:** 10 MINUTES / **SERVINGS:** 4 TO 6

1/4 cup pine nuts

2 tablespoons extra-virgin olive oil

2 tablespoons unsalted butter

1 1/2 pounds large carrots, peeled and coarsely grated, preferably using the grating disk of a food processor

1/2 teaspoon kosher salt, plus more to taste

1/4 teaspoon red pepper flakes, optional

A squeeze of fresh lemon juice

> Preheat the oven to 375°F. Put the pine nuts in a shallow baking dish and bake until golden, 3 to 4 minutes. Remove from the oven; set aside.

> Combine the oil and butter in a large skillet and heat over medium-high heat. Add the carrots and salt and cook, stirring, until tender, about 4 minutes. Stir in the pine nuts, pepper flakes, if using, and a squeeze of lemon. Season with salt to taste.

> "Carrots shredded and quickly sautéed are not only much tastier than steamed or boiled carrots, they're also *much* quicker to cook. If you start with the big fellas known as horse carrots, you reduce your prep time, too, with fewer carrots to peel and grate.

> I have called for pine nuts, but any nut adds its own little mojo to the mix. (Pistachios would be lovely, too.) Hot pepper flakes nicely counterbalance the natural sweetness of the carrots, but are optional. Don't forget the squeeze of lemon as a last step."

Cooking with **Rawia Bishara**

BRUSSELS SPROUTS WITH PANKO

Adapted from *Olives, Lemons & Za'atar* (Kyle Books, 2014).

START TO FINISH: 40 MINUTES / **HANDS-ON TIME:** 40 MINUTES / **SERVINGS:** 3 TO 4

Corn oil for shallow-frying

2 pounds Brussels sprouts, outer leaves
    removed, cut in half

Thick Tahini Sauce (page 304)

1/2 cup low-fat plain yogurt

1 tablespoon pomegranate molasses
    (see Sources, page 351)

1 tablespoon extra-virgin olive oil

1/4 teaspoon minced garlic

1/2 cup panko breadcrumbs

Pinch of sea salt

> Pour 1/4 to 1/2 inch of corn oil in a large skillet and place over high heat until hot. To test the temperature, slip half a Brussels sprout into the pan; if it makes a popping sound, the oil is hot enough. Working in batches, fry the Brussels sprouts, turning occasionally, until they are browned all over, 2 to 3 minutes per batch. Using a slotted spoon, transfer the sprouts to a paper towel–lined plate to drain.

> Meanwhile, whisk together the Thick Tahini Sauce, yogurt, and pomegranate molasses in a medium bowl. Set aside.

> In a small skillet, heat the olive oil over medium-high until hot. Add the garlic and sauté until fragrant, about 1 minute. Add the panko and stir constantly until the crumbs are golden brown, about 2 minutes. Season with salt and remove the breadcrumbs from the heat. Transfer to a paper towel–lined plate to cool.

> Place the Brussels sprouts in a serving dish, drizzle with the sauce, and top with the panko crumbs. Serve immediately.

" In the introduction to her cookbook, Rawia Bishara writes: 'I was born into a food-loving Palestinian Arab family in Nazareth, a beautiful town in southern Galilee. Though the words *organic, locavore,* and *sustainable* were unknown then, my parents' approach to food and cooking qualified on all counts. They were 'foodies' before the word was coined.'

Her parents' values and cuisine live on not only in Rawia's book, but in Tanoreen, the restaurant she opened in Bay Ridge, Brooklyn, in 1998. It is Middle Eastern home cooking to the core, but customized to reflect Rawia's personal journey.

For example, this Brussels sprouts recipe. Growing up, Rawia never encountered Brussels sprouts, but she embraced them after marrying and moving to America. Her treatment of the sprouts—shallow-fried and topped with a thick tahini yogurt and pomegranate sauce and garlic panko crumbs—is all her own, and it's so tasty. "

THICK TAHINI SAUCE

START TO FINISH: 10 MINUTES / **HANDS-ON TIME:** 10 MINUTES / **SERVINGS:** MAKES ABOUT ½ CUP

As Rawia tells us: 'Tahini sauce, a smooth blend of toasted sesame paste, lemon juice, garlic, and olive oil, is ubiquitous in Middle Eastern kitchens. It is *the* condiment. There is hardly a dish that isn't enhanced by it. At Tanoreen, I mix it into salad dressings and drizzle it into cauliflower casseroles. My daughter? She dips French fries into it! Learn to make this and you will have a simple, delicious, versatile sauce to add to your repertoire. Try it on a sandwich instead of mustard.'

Note: Tahini, like any other seed or nut paste needs to be stored in the fridge after you open it, or it will become rancid.

³/₄ cup well stirred tahini (sesame paste, see Note at left)

1 to 2 garlic cloves, crushed and peeled

Juice of 2 to 3 lemons or to taste (about ¹/₂ cup)

¹/₂ teaspoon sea salt

Chopped fresh parsley for garnish

In the bowl of a food processor, combine the tahini, garlic, lemon juice, and salt and process on low speed for 2 minutes or until thoroughly incorporated. Turn the speed to high and blend until the tahini mixture begins to whiten. Gradually add up to ¹/₄ cup water until the mixture reaches the desired consistency.

Transfer the sauce to a serving bowl and garnish with the parsley. Leftover tahini sauce can be stored, tightly covered, in the refrigerator for up to 2 weeks.

Spicy Tahini Sauce: Add 2 tablespoons pomegranate molasses and 1 tablespoon chile paste to the bowl of the food processor and pulse until thoroughly incorporated.

Fetti Sauce: Combine ¹/₂ cup of the tahini sauce with ¹/₂ cup plain yogurt in the bowl of a food processor and pulse until smooth to make a wonderful, simple sauce.

RICE AND VERMICELLI PILAF

Pictured on page 302

Adapted from *Olives, Lemons & Za'atar* (Kyle Books, 2014).

START TO FINISH: 35 MINUTES / **HANDS-ON TIME:** 10 MINUTES / **SERVINGS:** 4 TO 5

Rawia's pilaf is an all-purpose side dish, half rice and half pasta. She toasts the pasta in oil and ghee until it turns golden brown, then adds the rice, cooking it until it's opaque. Finally, she adds the water. It's that preliminary toasting that makes this dish much more flavorful than steamed rice or boiled pasta.

Rawia prefers using Egyptian rice here. It's unique—the kernels are small, round, and broken—but it's not easy to find. The next best choices are Chinese or Carolina rice.

¹/₃ cup extra-virgin olive oil

2 tablespoons Ghee (page 46) or butter

¹/₂ pound vermicelli

2 cups Egyptian rice (see Sources, page 351), or Chinese rice or Carolina rice

¹/₂ tablespoon sea salt or to taste

› Combine the oil and ghee in a large saucepan and heat on high until hot. Add the vermicelli and stir until golden brown, 7 to 10 minutes. Add the rice and stir until opaque, 3 to 5 minutes. Pour in 4¹/₂ cups boiling water and salt, reduce the heat to low, cover, and simmer until the rice is fluffy, about 12 minutes, stirring once halfway through. Remove the pan from the heat, stir once more, cover, and let stand 5 minutes. Serve warm.

Note: Rawia says to ensure fluffy rice, be sure that your water is already boiling when you add it to the rice.

GRILL PAN GARLIC BREAD

Pictured on page 74

4 to 6 (¹/₂-inch-thick) slices country bread

Extra-virgin olive oil for brushing the bread

1 garlic clove, halved

Kosher salt

> Preheat a grill pan over high heat. Brush both sides of the bread slices with extra-virgin olive oil. Add the bread to the preheated grill pan, reduce the heat to medium, and cook until it's nicely marked and crispy on both sides (about 2 minutes per side).

> Remove the bread from the pan and, while it's still hot, rub one side of each slice with a cut clove of garlic, then sprinkle it very lightly with kosher salt. Or just do it on your backyard grill. (If you're lucky enough to have a backyard. And a grill).

FAUX GRILL PAN GARLIC BREAD

> Sometimes I don't feel like hauling out the grill pan and disconnecting the smoke detector, so here's an alternative way to grill bread in the kitchen: Pop the bread in the toaster (naked, no oil yet) and toast until golden. Remove the bread from the toaster, brush it with extra-virgin olive oil, rub it with a cut clove of garlic, and sprinkle it with kosher salt. I have a toaster with just two slots, so I can only toast two pieces at a time, but that's not a problem. I toast them when there are lulls in the soup-making; by the time the soup is done, I have a basket full of "grilled" bread.

I love all kinds of soups, but what I really love is using a piece of grilled bread as a spoon to eat that soup. My family agrees. If I serve any soup at home without that "garnish," everyone complains.

Just as long as I disconnect my smoke detector (don't try this at home), I can grill bread in my kitchen on a grill pan.

PITA CRISPS

Pictured on page 140

START TO FINISH: 20 MINUTES / **HANDS-ON TIME:** 12 MINUTES / **SERVINGS:** MAKES 32 CRISPS

2 (6-inch) whole-wheat pitas with pockets

Olive oil for brushing the pitas

Kosher salt

> Heat the oven to 400°F. Split each pita horizontally into 2 rounds. Brush the rough sides of each round lightly with some olive oil, and then sprinkle lightly with salt. Cut each round into 8 triangles (you should get 32). On a rimmed baking sheet, arrange the triangles in a single layer. Bake on the middle shelf of the oven until golden and crisp, about 8 minutes. Set aside to cool.

These pita crisps are pretty addictive and very easy to make. They can be used as the perfect scooper for any dip, the crunchy garnish for any soup, or the crouton for any salad, such as Grilled Pork Tenderloin with Watermelon-Cucumber Salsa and Feta Dressing (page 141).

HASSELBACK POTATOES
WITH GARLIC BUTTER AND BACON

Pictured on page 151

START TO FINISH: 1 HOUR 30 MINUTES / **HANDS-ON TIME:** 25 MINUTES / **SERVINGS:** 4

4 tablespoons unsalted butter

1/2 teaspoon fine sea salt or table salt, plus additional salt for sprinkling

2 garlic cloves, smashed and peeled

1 tablespoon finely chopped fresh thyme

4 russet (baking) potatoes, 6 to 8 ounces each

Freshly ground black pepper

2 slices bacon

First served in Sweden in the 1700s, Hasselback potatoes are enjoying a huge comeback—and with good reason. Great-looking baked potatoes sliced to fan out like an accordion (they're known as accordion potatoes in some quarters), Hasselbacks are always a hit at a dinner party. More importantly, they're delicious, boasting that magical combo of crispy on the outside and tender on the inside.

The slices create much more surface area, which means that more of the potato becomes browned and crusty. And because we're working with high-starch russets (as opposed to waxy boiling potatoes), the insides end up fluffy and soft.

> Preheat the oven to 400°F. Combine the butter, salt, garlic, and thyme in a small saucepan. Turn the heat to medium-low and melt the butter, stirring until the salt is dissolved. Remove from the heat and set it aside while you prepare the potatoes.

> Peel the potatoes, dropping them into a bowl of cold water after you peel each one. Working with 1 potato at a time cut a thin slice off the bottom (from the long side) so that the potato lays flat. Place 2 chopsticks along each long side of the potato and, using a chef's knife, slice down to the chopsticks at 1/8-inch intervals, leaving the potato attached at the bottom. Return the cut potato to the water, while you prepare the remaining potatoes.

> Remove all the potatoes from the water, pat them dry, and arrange them flat side down on a parchment-lined, rimmed baking sheet. Brush 1 tablespoon of the seasoned butter over the potatoes and sprinkle lightly with pepper. Bake the potatoes on the middle shelf of the oven for 30 minutes.

> Remove the potatoes from the oven and spread open the potato slices carefully with a butter knife. Brush the potatoes with more seasoned butter, making sure to get some of it down between the slices. Return the potatoes to the oven and bake until golden brown around the edges and tender, another 30 to 40 minutes.

> Meanwhile, cook the bacon in a small skillet over medium heat until crisp, about 5 minutes. Transfer to paper towels to drain, then crumble it.

> When the potatoes are done, transfer to 4 plates, drizzle with remaining seasoned butter and sprinkle with a little salt and the bacon.

SMOOTHEST MASHED POTATOES

Pictured on page 274

START TO FINISH: 50 MINUTES / **HANDS-ON TIME:** 15 MINUTES / **SERVINGS:** 8

3 pounds russet or Yukon gold potatoes
½ cup whole milk
½ cup heavy cream
1 teaspoon kosher salt

6 tablespoons unsalted butter, cut into pieces and softened
Freshly ground black pepper

> Peel the potatoes and cut them into 1-inch chunks. As you peel and cut them, add the potatoes to a large bowl of cold water and swish them around to get rid of excess starch. Transfer the potato chunks to a large steamer insert and set the steamer over a pot of boiling water. Reduce the heat to medium and steam the potatoes, covered tightly, 10 minutes. Lift out the steamer insert, return the potatoes to the bowl filled with fresh cold water, and continue running cold water on top of the potatoes for a few minutes. Add several ice cubes and let the potatoes cool completely in the ice water. Drain the potatoes, return them back to the steamer insert, and steam, covered, until tender when pierced with the tip of a paring knife, 12 to 15 minutes.

> Meanwhile, heat the milk and cream with the salt in a medium saucepan over medium heat until hot.

> When the potatoes are tender, lift them out in the insert, and pour off the water from the bottom of the steamer. Transfer the potatoes to a ricer in batches and rice them, while still hot, back into the pot. Add the butter and stir until it is incorporated. (Putting the butter in first is key; it coats the potatoes with fat and prevents them from becoming gummy when you mix in the liquid.) Add the milk mixture and stir until incorporated. Add salt and pepper to taste and serve immediately.

MAKE-AHEAD MASHED POTATOES

> Follow the procedure given for cooking the potatoes up to the point of ricing the potatoes. Rice the potatoes directly into a large, microwave-safe bowl. Cover the bowl and chill until you are ready to finish the potatoes. When you are ready, heat the milk and cream with the salt, and soften the butter. Microwave the riced potatoes, covering the bowl partially with plastic wrap, in 2-minute increments, stirring the potatoes each time, until they are very hot, and then add the butter and milk mixture as instructed in the recipe.

"I've made mountains of mashed potatoes in my little life by faithfully adhering to the method I learned in cooking school. And I've always been reasonably happy with the taste, but not the slightly lumpy texture. So I set out to find a foolproof method for making smooth mashed potatoes.

First, I had to select the best potato. I had equally good results with russets and Yukon golds. The russets (aka baking potatoes) are better at absorbing cream and butter. The Yukons (a cross between a baking and a boiling potato) are sweeter and more assertively potato-y.

In my research on cooking the spuds for maximum smoothness, one recommendation kept popping up: Boil them only halfway, then chill them completely before finishing the cooking process. Why? Because mashing a fully cooked potato unleashes a ton of gummy starch. But if it's cooked only halfway, and then cooled, that starch becomes locked in and the finished product is much less gummy.

The best way to mash potatoes is to rice them with a ricer. It gets the job done, but more gently than a food mill or a hand masher. This gentleness helps to keep the starchiness to a minimum.

Whatever you do, do not reach for a food processor. It's the tool I used to mash some potatoes exactly one time, before I knew any better. The potatoes were inedible, but on the plus side, they were so gluey I could've used them to put up wallpaper."

FOOLPROOF SCALLOPED POTATOES

Pictured on page 237

START TO FINISH: I HOUR 30 MINUTES / **HANDS-ON TIME:** 35 MINUTES / **SERVINGS:** 8

> "Scalloped potatoes are always a big hit in our house, but it takes some care to ensure that the potatoes are properly seasoned, properly tender, and creamy as a dream.
>
> I've made scalloped potatoes using russets (aka baking potatoes) and Yukon golds (a cross between a baking potato and a boiling potato), and both versions have their merits. The russets picked up more of the flavor of the cream, while the Yukons were firmer, with more potato flavor. I ruled in favor of richness: The russets got the nod.
>
> Whichever you pick, the potatoes must be sliced to the same thickness or they'll cook unevenly. For a home cook working by hand, this task can be a bit of a challenge. Fortunately, there are a couple of tools to streamline the process: A food processor fitted with the slicing blade (in which case the potatoes will need to be trimmed to fit through the feed tube) or a mandoline.
>
> When I first learned how to make scalloped potatoes, the routine was to season each layer before adding the next, and then to pour the cream on top. But somehow the final dish never seemed properly seasoned. A better method is to add an exact amount of salt, garlic, and thyme to the milk and cream mixture, and then pour it—deeply seasoned and hot—onto the potatoes. The potatoes soak in all the flavor and the finished product is anything but bland."

1½ cups whole milk
1½ cups heavy cream
1 teaspoon chopped fresh thyme
1 Turkish bay leaf
2 garlic cloves, smashed and peeled
1½ teaspoons kosher salt
½ teaspoon freshly ground black pepper
3 pounds russet potatoes
3 ounces freshly grated Parmigiano-Reggiano

> Preheat the oven to 375°F and adjust the oven rack to the middle position.

> Combine the milk, cream, thyme, bay leaf, garlic, salt, and pepper in a medium saucepan and bring the mixture to a boil. Remove from the heat, cover, and let steep while you prepare the potatoes.

> Peel the potatoes and using a mandoline (see Note) or the slicing disk of a food processor, slice them crosswise ⅛ inch thick. Remove and discard the bay leaf and garlic cloves from the milk mixture and pour one-fourth of the mixture into a 9- x 13-inch baking dish. Add the potatoes and the remaining milk mixture to the baking dish. Stir the potatoes to make sure they are separated, and then press them down to distribute them evenly. Bake the potatoes on the middle shelf of the oven until the liquid has thickened and the top is golden, about 40 minutes. Sprinkle the cheese evenly over the top of the potatoes, return the pan to the oven, and bake until the top is browned, about 10 minutes.

> Cool for 5 minutes before serving.

Note: When using a mandoline, be sure to use the guard and proceed carefully when slicing.

PIMIENTO MAC AND CHEESE

Adapted from *From a Southern Oven* (Houghton Mifflin Harcourt, 2012).

START TO FINISH: 55 TO 60 MINUTES / **HANDS-ON TIME:** 30 MINUTES / **SERVINGS:** 6

Vegetable cooking spray

1 tablespoon unsalted butter

1/2 cup finely chopped yellow onion

57 grams (1/4 cup) unsifted all-purpose flour

1/2 teaspoon salt, or to taste

1/4 teaspoon freshly ground black pepper, or to taste

1 1/2 cups milk

2 cups coarsely grated sharp cheddar cheese, divided

2 cups elbow macaroni, cooked according to package directions and well drained

2 (2-ounce) jars diced pimientos, well drained

1/3 cup firmly packed mayonnaise or, if you prefer, mayonnaise-relish sandwich spread (Hellmann's or Duke's)

For the topping:

1 1/2 cups moderately fine, soft white breadcrumbs

1 1/2 tablespoons melted unsalted butter

› Preheat the oven to 350°F. Spritz a 2-quart casserole or baking dish about 2 1/2 inches deep with vegetable cooking spray and set aside.

› Melt the butter in a large heavy saucepan over medium heat. Add the onion and cook, stirring now and then, until wilted and golden, about 5 minutes.

› Whisk the flour, salt, and pepper into the milk and when smooth, gradually whisk into the onion and cook, stirring constantly, until thickened, 3 to 5 minutes. Whisk in 1 1/2 cups of the grated cheese and when melted, fold in the macaroni, pimientos, and mayonnaise. Taste for salt and pepper and adjust as needed.

› **Make the topping:** Toss the breadcrumbs and the melted butter together until the crumbs are well coated with the butter.

› Scoop the macaroni mixture into the prepared casserole or baking dish, spreading it to the edges. Scatter the remaining 1/2 cup cheese evenly across the top, and then cover with the buttered breadcrumbs.

› Bake, uncovered, on the middle oven rack until bubbling and brown, 25 to 30 minutes.

"

I met the esteemed cookbook author and photographer Jean Anderson while I was the chef at Cybele's Restaurant in Boston. Thinking of relocating to New York, I'd gone home for the weekend. Jean had recently moved into the same New York City apartment building where my parents lived, so as soon as my mom discovered how Jean earned her daily bread, she invited her up for drinks so that the two of us could meet.

Jean and I hit if off instantly and she's mentored me ever since. In the early 1980s, before I had kids, I was Jean's assistant on magazine assignments to Holland, Portugal, and Brazil. When I was hosting *Cooking Live* and viewers called in with questions that stumped me, Jean was my red phone. She always had the answer.

If you're not from the South, you may never have heard of pimiento cheese. It's a sandwich spread made of sharp cheddar cheese, mayonnaise, and bottled chopped pimientos. The late North Carolina novelist Reynolds Price describes the stuff as 'the peanut butter of my childhood.' Here, Jean has combined its key ingredients with macaroni to come up with a lip-smacking new twist on mac and cheese. Serve as the main course of a simple lunch or supper. A tossed salad of crisp greens, tartly dressed, is all you need to accompany.

"

OVEN-BAKED CREAMY POLENTA

Pictured on page 148

START TO FINISH: 50 MINUTES / **HANDS-ON TIME:** 5 MINUTES / **SERVINGS:** 4 TO 6

1 quart water or 2 cups water combined with 2 cups Homemade Vegetable Stock (page 29), Homemade Chicken Stock (page 26), or store-bought vegetable or chicken broth, if you want to add some vegetable or chicken flavor

1 tablespoon unsalted butter

1 cup cornmeal

1 teaspoon kosher salt

Freshly ground black pepper

> Preheat the oven to 350°F. Stir together the water, butter, cornmeal, salt, and pepper to taste in a 1-quart casserole dish. (If using vegetable or chicken stock, omit the salt). Bake, uncovered, in the middle of the oven for 45 minutes. Remove from the oven, stir, and serve immediately.

CRISPY POLENTA SQUARES

> Follow the recipe above, but bake the polenta an additional 30 minutes or until the polenta reaches a very thick consistency. Pour out onto a lightly oiled baking sheet and spread into a 1/2-inch thick rectangle. Chill until very firm, about 2 hours. Cut the polenta into squares and dip them in panko breadcrumbs if you want, for extra crunch. Sauté them in olive oil or butter in a large nonstick or stick-resistant skillet, until lightly browned and crispy, about 5 minutes a side. Top the polenta squares with sautéed mushrooms, or serve them in place of rice with vegetarian dishes.

I've always loved polenta. A staple of northern Italian cuisine made of cornmeal and liquid, there's something elemental and deeply satisfying about it. But I almost never made polenta at home. I just didn't have the patience to stir and stir for 40 minutes—staying on guard the whole time against the Vesuvian bubbling of this hot mush—until it was finally done, creamy and perfect.

Then, years ago on a flight, I met a flight attendant (and home cook) named Dobbs who watched my show and told me how to bake polenta in the oven. I tried it as soon as I got home and—eureka!—it worked. Making polenta has been a snap ever since.

Now polenta is part of my regular lineup of side dishes. It's the perfect backdrop for stews, and, topped off with nothing more complicated than a ladleful of marinara sauce, it proudly stands on its own. Sometimes, about 10 minutes before the polenta's finished cooking, I'll stir in some cheese, which makes it even creamier and more luxurious.

DUCK FAT POPOVERS

Pictured on page 189

START TO FINISH: 40 MINUTES PLUS I DAY AND I HOUR RESTING TIME
HANDS-ON TIME: IO MINUTES / **SERVINGS:** MAKES IO TO II POPOVERS

4 large eggs

2 cups whole milk

³/₄ cup plus 1 teaspoon melted duck fat
(see pages 134 and 248 or Sources,
page 350), divided

240 grams (2 cups) unbleached
all-purpose flour

¹/₂ teaspoon table salt

> Whisk the eggs in a large bowl, add the milk and ¹/₄ cup of the duck fat, and combine well. Add the flour and salt and stir just until combined. Cover and chill overnight. The next day, remove the batter from the fridge and let it stand at room temperature for 1 hour. Whisk the batter briefly to re-mix it.

> Preheat the oven to 450°F.

> Pour 2 teaspoons of the remaining duck fat into each of 11 nonstick popover cups (or, if you don't have a nonstick tin, grease each of 11 regular popover cups with 2 teaspoons duck fat). Place the pan on the lower third of the oven and preheat for 5 minutes.

> Remove the pan from the oven, fill the tins three-fourths full with batter, and bake the popovers in the lower third of the oven with plenty of room above them for 14 minutes. Without opening the oven, reduce the heat to 350°F and bake for an additional 15 minutes.

> Let the popovers stand in the tins for 5 minutes before serving.

66 ～～～～

Growing up I spent my summers at our family's farmhouse in New England, which allowed me to hang out a lot with my grandmother, Ruth Moulton. Granny was a walking encyclopedia of Olde New England cuisine. As a young girl—and guiltless little chubbette—I was especially enamored of two of Granny's more caloric standards: Yorkshire pudding and popovers. Made from the same batter, these dishes are variations on a theme. Yorkshire pudding is more like a sturdy soufflé. Popovers are individual muffins.

One of the side benefits of my grown-up love of Duck Confit (page 250) is that there is often a plentiful supply of luscious duck fat in my refrigerator. One day (thank you, Granny!) it struck me: Given how well beef fat works in Yorkshire pudding, maybe duck fat would be a tasty base for popovers.

This recipe is an adaption of the popovers served at the Jordan Pond House Restaurant, a justly famous restaurant in Maine's Acadia National Park. The batter needs to rest overnight, but otherwise it's very simple—whipping up the batter takes 5 minutes. And the results are spectacular.

You can bake the popovers in muffin tins, but they'll come out higher if you use popover tins; they're deeper. An individual popover tin has either 6 or 12 cups. If you use a 6-cupper, you'll have to bake the extra batter in a separate batch.

～～～～ 99

CREAM BISCUITS

START TO FINISH: 35 MINUTES / **HANDS-ON TIME:** 20 MINUTES / **SERVINGS:** 12 BISCUITS

Working in *Gourmet*'s test kitchens in the mid-1980s, I was put on the quest for the Best Biscuit. I tested dozens of versions, but cream biscuits won hands down. An all-American favorite popularized by James Beard, cream biscuits were the tastiest and most tender—and the quickest and easiest to make as well. Cream biscuits have fewer ingredients than any other kind, because a single ingredient (the cream) provides both the fat and the liquid required to make the biscuit heavenly.

It's best to weigh the flour if you have a scale. And if you don't have a scale, measure your flour by loosely dropping it into your measuring cup, and then leveling it off (see Cook's Notes, page 40). Also, after you add the cream to the dry ingredients, work the dough as little as possible. The less you manipulate the protein (the gluten) in the flour, the tenderer the biscuits.

240 grams (2 cups) unbleached all-purpose flour, plus more for dusting

1 tablespoon baking powder

1/4 teaspoon table salt

1 to 1 1/2 cups heavy cream, plus more for brushing the tops of the biscuits

> Preheat the oven to 425°F and line a baking sheet with parchment paper.

> Stir together the flour, baking powder, and salt in a large bowl. Pour in enough of the cream to just form a dough.

> On a lightly floured surface, knead the dough briefly, two or three times, just until it comes together, and form it into a disk. Roll it out into a round, until it is 3/4 inch thick. Cut the round into 12 triangles and brush each triangle lightly with some cream. Transfer the triangles to the baking sheet and bake, on the middle shelf of the oven, until pale golden, 12 to 15 minutes. Transfer to a rack and let cool slightly before serving.

NO-KNEAD WALNUT-ROSEMARY BREAD

Pictured on page 106

START TO FINISH: 14 HOURS 20 MINUTES TO 21 HOURS 20 MINUTES
HANDS-ON TIME: 20 MINUTES / **SERVINGS:** 1 (10-INCH) LOAF

1/2 cup coarsely chopped walnuts (50 grams), toasted and cooled

2 cups bread flour (266 grams)

1 cup whole-wheat flour (133 grams)

1 1/4 teaspoons table salt (8 grams)

3/4 teaspoon instant yeast

2 tablespoons chopped rosemary (6 grams)

1 1/3 cups cool water (about 55° to 65°F, 350 grams)

Additional flour, wheat bran, or cornmeal for dusting

> In a medium bowl, stir together the walnuts, bread flour, whole-wheat flour, salt, yeast, and rosemary. Add the cool water and stir briefly with a wooden spoon or your hands, just until the dough is barely mixed, about 30 seconds. The dough should be quite wet and tacky; if it is not, add 1 to 2 tablespoons more water. Cover the bowl and let the dough rise at room temperature for 12 to 18 hours.

> Generously sprinkle a work surface with flour and gently, with the help of a plastic bench scraper, scoop out the dough onto the counter. Working very quickly, with floured hands, fold in all the sides of the dough to the center to form a seam and turn the dough over to form a nice round with the seam on the bottom. Generously sprinkle a (lint-free) tea towel with flour and transfer the dough round, seam side down, to the towel. Sprinkle the top lightly with flour and loosely fold the ends of towel over the dough.

> Let the dough rise in a warm place for 1 to 2 hours or until it is almost doubled in bulk. You will know it is ready when you poke the dough and it holds your imprint (like an "innie" belly button). If the dough bounces back, it's not ready.

> About 30 minutes before you think the dough is ready preheat the oven to 475°F, put a rack in the lower third of the oven, and place a 4 1/2- to 5 1/2-quart casserole dish with a lid (like a Dutch oven) on the shelf to preheat.

> When the dough has risen, remove the casserole dish from the oven and take off the lid. With the aid of the tea towel, flip the dough gently, seam side up, into the casserole dish. Replace the lid and return it to oven. Bake for 30 minutes. Carefully remove the lid and bake the dough until it is dark brown but not burnt, another 15 to 20 minutes.

> Remove the casserole dish from the oven and, with a spatula or dish towel, carefully transfer the bread to a rack to cool completely.

" Generally speaking, in the culinary world there are bakers and there are cooks. Me, I'm a cook.

But I do love to bake bread. In fact, I've been on a bread-baking kick for several years. Recently, however, I learned a method so wonderful that it will likely become my standard.

I took a class with the legendary Jim Lahey, founder of Sullivan Street Bakery, at the International Culinary Center in New York City. I first saw Jim's method years ago, when *The New York Times* ran his sensational recipe for no-knead, slow-rise bread. I was skeptical—no way baking bread could be so easy.

But it can. I followed his instructions, then put my own twist on the recipe, adding extra whole-wheat flour, toasted walnuts, and rosemary, and, wow! I baked up a darned good-looking, excellent-tasting loaf of bread.

One of the ways to ensure your success here is by weighing, not measuring, the flour. And don't be thrown off by the wetness of the dough, the temperature of the water added (it's cool), or the temperature at which the dough first rises (it's room temp).

You do need to plan ahead to accommodate the long rise, and the bread has to cool down completely before you can eat it. But you may find yourself enjoying really heavenly fresh bread several times a week. "

9 | *something* SWEET

Some of the desserts in this chapter are ridiculously easy, like Baked Summer Fruit with French Toast Crust, and some are seriously intricate, like Joanne Chang's Hazelnut-Almond Dacquoise (pictured opposite). No matter. If you follow the instructions carefully, you'll be successful.

Although there are only 10 desserts here, they allow us to dig into several key techniques. You'll learn how to work with gelatin in the Chai Tea Panna Cotta, get over your fear of crepe-making with Bananas Foster Crepes, acquire a secret trick for slicing apples on the way to making a perfect apple tart, discover how to temper chocolate in the microwave thanks to the King of Chocolate, Monsieur Jacques Torres, and become an expert soufflé maker.

Bottom line: I am more cook than baker. If I can master these techniques, so can you.

THAI-FLAVORED PUMPKIN CUSTARD

START TO FINISH: 50 MINUTES PLUS AT LEAST 6 HOURS CHILLING TIME
HANDS-ON TIME: 20 MINUTES / **SERVINGS:** 6

3 large eggs

1/2 cup packed brown sugar, preferably dark

1/2 cup well-stirred coconut milk

1 (5-ounce) can evaporated milk

2 teaspoons finely minced makrut lime leaf (aka kaffir lime leaf, see Sources, page 351), or 1 1/2 teaspoons freshly grated lime zest

1 1/2 tablespoons fresh lime juice

2 tablespoons dark rum, optional

Seeds from 1 vanilla bean or 1 1/2 teaspoons pure vanilla extract

1/4 teaspoon table salt

1 cup solid pack canned pumpkin puree

1/4 cup finely chopped crystallized ginger or toasted coconut for garnish

> Preheat the oven to 350°F. Beat the eggs in a large bowl with electric beaters. Add the brown sugar and beat just until any lumps have dissolved. Add the coconut milk, evaporated milk, lime leaves, lime juice, rum, if using, vanilla seeds or extract, salt, and pumpkin puree and beat just until smooth.

> Pour the mixture into 6 (1-cup) ramekins. Set the ramekins into a rectangular baking pan (like a lasagna pan). Working quickly, set the pan on the middle shelf of the oven and pour enough hot water into the pan to come halfway up the sides of the ramekins.

> Bake the custards until a knife inserted in the center comes out clean, about 30 minutes. Using tongs, remove the ramekins from the water bath and cool on a wire rack. Cover with plastic wrap and refrigerate until very well chilled, about 6 hours. Serve each portion topped with some of the crystallized ginger or coconut.

> "Pumpkins are always paired up with the same partners—cinnamon, nutmeg, allspice, cloves, and ginger—and I think sometimes the pumpkin flavor gets buried under all those spices. So I decided to take pumpkin puree on an Asian detour and team it up with coconut milk, vanilla, and lime to produce a cleaner, more pumpkin-y taste in these Thai-flavored custards.
>
> This recipe calls for canned pumpkin, an ingredient at which I used to turn up my nose. Happily, I figured out that pumpkins, like tomatoes, don't suffer from canning. They're harvested at the peak of their ripeness, then cooked and canned immediately, which insures that both the flavor and the health benefits of the giant berry are retained. But be sure to read the label: You want "solid pack" canned pumpkin, with no added sugar, salt, or other ingredients."

CHAI TEA PANNA COTTA

START TO FINISH: 40 MINUTES PLUS AT LEAST 6 HOURS CHILLING TIME
HANDS-ON TIME: 25 MINUTES / **SERVINGS:** 6

1 tablespoon unflavored gelatin

2 cups heavy cream, divided

1 cup half-and-half

1 tablespoon loose black tea or 3 black tea bags

³/₄ teaspoon ground cinnamon

³/₄ teaspoon ground cardamom

³/₈ teaspoon ground ginger

¹/₄ teaspoon freshly ground black pepper

¹/₄ teaspoon ground cloves

¹/₄ teaspoon table salt

¹/₃ cup honey

1¹/₂ teaspoons vanilla extract

> In a very small saucepan, sprinkle the gelatin over ¹/₄ cup of the cream, stir with a fork, and set aside for 5 minutes. Cook over low heat, stirring occasionally and scraping the sides, until the gelatin is completely dissolved.

> Meanwhile, in a medium saucepan, combine the remaining **1³/₄** cups cream with the half-and-half, tea, cinnamon, cardamom, ginger, pepper, cloves, salt, and honey and bring to a boil over medium-high heat, stirring. Remove the pan from the heat, stir in the gelatin mixture, and let stand for 10 minutes. Strain the mixture through a fine strainer into a medium metal bowl, discarding the solids. Stir in the vanilla.

> Set the metal bowl over another bowl of ice and water and cool, stirring often, until quite cool to the touch.

> Divide the mixture among 6 lightly oiled ¹/₂-cup ramekins and chill for at least 6 hours before serving.

> "I know this is going to sound all *Downton Abbey,* but every day at 4 o'clock I break for tea time. I have no opinion about whether or not this routine is "civilized," but I do appreciate it as a kind of stepping stone between lunch and dinner. And the tea itself is exactly as restorative as advertised.
>
> My cuppa is usually chai tea with milk. (An Indian slant on tea, *chai*—which means tea in Hindi—is black tea spiced with cinnamon, cloves, ginger, cardamom, and black pepper.) I love the three-way mix of tea, spices, and dairy. This recipe teams up that combo with panna cotta to make a smooth and refreshing dessert.
>
> *Panna cotta* (the Italian term for cooked cream) is like cream Jell-O; it gets its texture from unflavored gelatin.
>
> If you'd like your panna cotta spicier, by all means add more of the spices."

WORKING WITH GELATIN

Gelatin has to soak briefly in a liquid until all the granules are completely dissolved or it won't do its job. But it'll turn out rubbery if you overdo it and add too much; the perfect ratio is 1 teaspoon of gelatin for every 1 cup of liquid.

In this recipe, if you haven't a) completely dissolved the gelatin before adding it to the other ingredients, and b) cooled the mixture before placing the ramekins in the fridge, the panna cotta might separate into layers.

CREAMSICLE PUDDING CAKE

START TO FINISH: 60 MINUTES / **HANDS-ON TIME:** 35 MINUTES / **SERVINGS:** 6

> "This recipe is a mash-up of two of my all-time favorite desserts: the Creamsicle (that unbeatable combo of vanilla ice cream and orange sherbet on a stick) and the pudding cake (the utterly seductive, if unlikely, concoction that is, as advertised, a pudding on the bottom and a cake on top).
>
> I wanted a cake in which both the orange and vanilla flavors were booming. For the orange, both the juice and zest are added. For the vanilla, I used a whole vanilla bean and scraped out its seeds. Yes, vanilla beans are expensive, but nothing else delivers such intense vanilla flavor. Besides you can re-use them. Just pop the scraped-out vanilla pod into your sugar canister and discover how quickly the sugar takes on the scent of vanilla."

1 cup fresh orange juice

2 tablespoons freshly grated orange zest

1/2 cup heavy cream

4 tablespoons unsalted butter, melted, plus more for greasing the baking dish

1 tablespoon fresh lemon juice

Seeds from 1 1/2 vanilla beans or 1 1/2 tablespoons vanilla bean paste (see Sources, page 351)

120 grams (about 1 cup) unbleached all-purpose flour

1/2 cup sugar

2 teaspoons baking powder

1/4 teaspoon table salt

Vanilla ice cream as an accompaniment

> Preheat the oven to 350°F. Lightly grease an 8-inch-square baking dish with butter.

> Bring the orange juice and 1/4 cup water to a boil while you prepare the batter. In a small bowl, whisk together the zest, cream, melted butter, lemon juice, and vanilla bean seeds or paste.

> Whisk together the flour, sugar, baking powder, and salt in a medium bowl. Add the cream mixture and stir just until combined. Transfer the batter (it will be quite stiff) to the prepared dish, smoothing the top with a rubber spatula. Set the baking dish on the middle shelf of the oven and carefully pour the boiling orange juice over the surface of the batter. (This may sound odd, but it's this mercurial.) Bake for 27 to 35 minutes, until the cake on top has a crisp golden surface and the pudding sauce on the bottom bubbles.

> Spoon the pudding cake onto each of 6 plates and top each portion with a small scoop of ice cream. Serve immediately.

BANANAS FOSTER CREPES

START TO FINISH: I HOUR IO MINUTES / **HANDS-ON:** 40 MINUTES / **SERVINGS:** 4

For the crepes:
5 tablespoons unsalted butter
1 cup whole milk
180 grams (about ³/₄ cup) unbleached
    all-purpose flour
2 large eggs
¹/₄ teaspoon table salt
For the filling:
2 under-ripe (slightly green around the
    edges) bananas

3 tablespoons unsalted butter
¹/₃ cup packed dark brown sugar
¹/₄ teaspoon ground cinnamon
1 tablespoon fresh lemon juice
¹/₄ cup dark rum
Coffee or vanilla ice cream and chopped
    toasted walnuts as accompaniments

> **Make the crepes:** Melt the butter in a 10-inch nonstick or stick-resistant skillet over low heat. Transfer 2 tablespoons of the butter to a ramekin and 3 tablespoons of butter to the blender. Set aside the skillet (do not wipe it out) and add the milk, flour, eggs, and salt to the butter in the blender. Blend until smooth, scraping down the sides. Strain through a sieve into a bowl, cover, and set aside at room temperature for 30 minutes to allow the gluten (protein) in the flour to rest and ensure that your crepes are tender.

> Heat the skillet over medium-high heat until hot but not smoking. Reduce the heat to medium. Make the crepes following the procedure on page 324, brushing the skillet as necessary with some of the remaining melted butter. You should end up with 8 to 10 crepes. Once they are cool, set aside 4 crepes for this recipe and wrap and freeze the remaining crepes for another use.

> **Make the filling:** Peel the bananas, cut them in half lengthwise, and then in quarters crosswise. Combine the butter, sugar, cinnamon, and lemon juice in a large skillet and cook over medium heat, stirring, until melted. Add the bananas and cook, gently turning them over 1 or 2 times, until they are just golden at the edges, about 5 minutes.

> Remove the skillet from the heat and add the rum. Return the pan to the heat, bring to a simmer, stirring, and simmer until the sauce is the consistency of honey, turning the bananas often to coat them with the sauce.

> Arrange 1 crepe on each of 4 plates, spoon one-fourth of the banana mixture down the middle of each and roll up the crepe to enclose the filling. Turn the crepe so the seam is on the bottom. Top each filled crepe with a scoop of ice cream, a drizzle of the sauce, and a sprinkling of walnuts.

"

Bananas Foster is the deluxe dessert invented at Brennan's restaurant in New Orleans back in 1951. I gathered up its trademark components—bananas sautéed with butter and brown sugar and spiked with rum—then wrapped them in a crepe topped with ice cream and toasted walnuts. But my true agenda here is to teach you how to make crepes.

It takes a little bit of practice, but follow the step-by-step instructions and photos (see pages 324–325), and you'll be a complete pro after knocking out two or three of them. With crepes in the fridge or the freezer, and just a few other ingredients on hand (leftovers definitely included), dinner or dessert is always just minutes away.

"

Cook's Notes: For Successful Crepes

▶ **The one key tool required is the right pan.** I use a stick-resistant ceramic or enamel pan. (My favorite ones are made by Chantal.) A nonstick pan will also do the trick; just don't overheat it.

▶ Transporting the batter from the bowl to the pan can be messy. **I keep the mess to a minimum by setting the measuring cup on a plate placed right next to the stove,** then pouring out the batter ¼ cup at a time. All the drips from the measuring cup will go on the plate, not the counter.

▶ After the crepes have cooled, if you are not going to use them all right away (or if you have made a double batch, you smart person), **wrap them in the amounts you will use them later on—stacks of 4, 6, or 8.**

▶ Wrap the stacks first in plastic, then in foil. Contrary to what I was taught in cooking school, **crepes can be stacked on top of each other.** You don't have to put a piece of parchment between each one.

▶ **Label the crepes and pop them in the freezer** for future entrées or desserts. Let the stacks defrost in the fridge. If the crepes stick together (because the butter in the crepes is cold), when you are ready to use them, remove the plastic wrap, wrap them in the foil and pop them in a 350°F oven for 5 minutes and they will come apart easily.

FILLINGS FOR CREPES

▶ Line the crepes with thinly sliced Gruyère cheese, top with smoked salmon and softly scrambled eggs mixed with a little freshly grated lemon rind, roll the crepes up, and bake them until the cheese is melted.

▶ Stuff them with creamed spinach, sautéed mushrooms, and prosciutto and warm them in the oven.

▶ Spread them with Nutella and top them with coffee or chocolate ice cream.

▶ Stuff them with sautéed apples and top them with caramel ice cream.

▶ Slice fresh strawberries, toss with sugar and freshly grated orange rind, let stand 1 hour, and then roll them in crepes and top with whipped cream.

HOW TO MAKE CREPES

1. Brush the pan very lightly with butter and heat it until a tiny bead of water, when added, skips across its surface.

2. Pour ¼ cup of batter into the pan. Immediately lift the pan and tilt it all around until you have covered the whole bottom of the pan with the batter.

3. After 30 to 45 seconds, peek to see if the bottom of the crepe is golden brown.

4. When it is nicely browned, slide your spatula underneath. And—with no hesitation—quickly flip the whole crepe over.

5. Transfer the cooked crepes to a rack, where they'll cool off slightly. A crepe's pretty side is the first one you cooked (pictured on the right in the photo). When you roll up a crepe, keep the pretty side on the outside.

6. When the crepes have cooled you can stack them. (No, they won't stick to each other; that is a myth.)

BAKED SUMMER FRUIT
WITH FRENCH TOAST CRUST

START TO FINISH: I HOUR 25 MINUTES / **HANDS-ON TIME:** 20 MINUTES / **SERVINGS:** 6

" This is my favorite kind of dessert because it's so simple, so versatile, and so doggone delicious. Best of all, you don't have to be an accomplished dessert cook to pull it off. Just be sure to use the ripest summer fruits: Apricots, peaches, and cherries are excellent substitutes for the plums and nectarines.

I like Grade B maple syrup because it is the most intensely maple-y of all the maple syrups. Darker in color and stronger in flavor than the other grades, Grade B is made from the sap harvested in the spring at the end of the season.

It is my favorite pancake syrup, too. Happily, Grade B's more widely available now than it used to be as more cooks discover its robust taste. If I were doing the grading, I'd give it an 'A.' "

4 plums, quartered and sliced ¼ inch thick

2 nectarines, quartered and sliced ¼ inch thick

⅓ cup Grade B maple syrup

1 tablespoon fresh lemon juice

¼ teaspoon table salt

2 large eggs

⅓ cup whole milk

2 teaspoons vanilla extract

7 slices homemade-style white or whole-wheat bread, crusts discarded, cut in half

1 tablespoon sugar

Vanilla ice cream for serving, optional

> Heat the oven to 400°F. Toss the fruit with the maple syrup, lemon juice, and salt in a 9-inch square baking dish. Cover with foil and bake on the middle shelf of the oven for 35 minutes.

> Meanwhile, whisk together the eggs, milk, and vanilla extract in a medium bowl.

> When the fruit is tender, remove the foil. Dip the bread halves in the egg mixture and arrange them in a single layer over the fruit, cutting the bread as necessary to cover all of the fruit. If there is any egg mixture left, pour it over the bread. Sprinkle with the sugar, and then bake until the bread is golden, 15 to 20 minutes.

> Serve right away, topped with a small scoop of vanilla ice cream, if using.

Dessert Calzones, Two Ways

STRAWBERRY CANNOLI CALZONES

"As a grade-schooler, my father's first crush was on a girl named Pauline Moffat, aptly known as Babes. A great beauty and something of a wild child, Babes ended up marrying a Frenchman. A generation later, when I was in high school, my mom and dad took us on vacation to France, where, among other attractions, we met Babes and her family. Babes was all right, but she paled in comparison to the mid-afternoon snack she served us one day. It was six inches of baguette, sliced lengthwise and stuffed with chunks of dark chocolate.

I was a little wary of this odd thing until I took a bite. Wow! What a brilliant combination! The unsweetened bread was the perfect counterpoint to the bittersweet chocolate. It made me think of a well-made pie—the unsweetened crust cradling the sweet filling.

Here, I've taken this French snack on a detour to Italy by stuffing pizza dough (very similar to baguette dough) with sweet filings. Calzones are nothing more than stuffed, folded pizzas, but I have never seen a sweet one. Here are two."

START TO FINISH: I HOUR IO MINUTES / **HANDS-ON TIME:** 55 MINUTES
SERVINGS: 12 CALZONES

$^1/_4$ cup plus 1 tablespoon finely chopped strawberries

1 teaspoon sugar

3 ounces Neufchâtel ($^1/_3$-less-fat cream cheese)

1 teaspoon freshly grated orange zest

$1^1/_2$ ounces dark chocolate, finely chopped

12 ($1^1/_2$-ounce) balls 10-Minute Pizza Dough made with vegetable oil (page 38) or store-bought pizza dough

Vegetable oil, preferably grapeseed, for rolling out the dough

An egg wash made by beating 1 egg with 1 tablespoon water

> Preheat the oven to 375°F. Toss together the strawberries and sugar in a small bowl and let stand for 15 minutes.

> Combine the Neufchâtel, orange zest, and chocolate well in a medium bowl. Add the strawberries and the strawberry juices from the bowl and stir just until combined.

> Working with 1 ball at a time, roll out the dough to a 4-inch round on a lightly oiled surface (see page 39). Mound 1 tablespoon of the filling on the lower half of the round. Moisten the edges of the round with water and fold the top half of the round over the filling. Pinch the edges together very tightly, crimping them to seal. Place the calzones on a parchment-lined baking sheet. Brush the tops with the egg wash and make 3 slits in the top of each with the tip of a paring knife.

> Bake the calzones on the middle shelf of the oven until golden, 12 to 15 minutes.

> **SEPARATE YOUR CUTTING BOARDS**
>
> To keep your strawberries from tasting like garlic, reserve one of your cutting boards for use with desserts only.

CHOCOLATE-HAZELNUT CALZONES

START TO FINISH: 50 MINUTES / **HANDS-ON TIME:** 35 MINUTES / **SERVINGS:** 12 CALZONES

12 (1½-ounce) balls 10-Minute Pizza Dough made with vegetable oil (page 38) or store-bought pizza dough

Vegetable oil, preferably grapeseed, for rolling out the dough

¼ cup plus 2 tablespoons Nutella

3 ounces bittersweet chocolate, finely chopped

An egg wash made by beating 1 egg with 1 tablespoon water

Kosher salt for sprinkling, optional

> Preheat the oven to 375°F. Working with 1 ball at a time, roll out the dough to a 4-inch round on a lightly oiled surface (see page 39). Mound ½ tablespoon of the Nutella and ½ tablespoon of the chocolate on the lower half of the round. Moisten the edges of the round with water and fold the top half of the round over the filling. Pinch the edges together very tightly, crimping them to seal. Place the calzones on a parchment-lined baking sheet. Brush the tops with the egg wash and make 3 slits in the top of each with the tip of a paring knife. Sprinkle lightly with the salt, if using.

> Bake the calzones on the middle shelf of the oven until golden, 12 to 15 minutes.

FRENCH APPLE TART

START TO FINISH: 2 HOURS 40 MINUTES / **HANDS-ON TIME:** 50 MINUTES
SERVINGS: 1 (10-INCH) TART, ABOUT 8 SERVINGS

1 recipe Pie Dough (page 40), or
   1 (12-ounce) store-bought pie
   dough (see Note)

All-purpose flour for rolling out the
   dough

6 Golden Delicious apples

3 tablespoons sugar

4 tablespoons cold butter, sliced thin

$^1/_2$ cup apricot jam combined with
   2 tablespoons water, heated, and
   strained

Vanilla ice cream or sweetened
   whipped cream as an accompaniment

> Preheat the oven to 375°F. On a lightly floured surface, roll out the dough to a 13-inch round and fit it into a 10-inch tart tin with a removable fluted rim, trimming the excess. Prick the dough all over with the tines of a fork. Cover and chill for 1 hour.

> While the tart shell is chilling, following the directions on page 332, peel , halve, and core the apples. Arrange the apples, cut side down, on a cutting board and use a very sharp knife to slice them crosswise, but not all the way through, .

> Arrange 8 apple halves like the spokes of a wheel on the pastry and the remaining slices in diminishing concentric circles in the middle of the spokes. Sprinkle the sugar evenly on top of the apples and top with butter slices. Bake in the middle of the oven for 45 to 50 minutes or until the crust is cooked through and the apples are golden brown. Brush with the heated apricot jam while the tart is still hot. Serve each portion with a small scoop of ice cream or a small spoonful of whipped cream.

Note: If you are using store-bought pie dough (which usually comes all rolled out, fitted into an aluminum pie tin, and fluted at the edges), let it warm up a little bit on the counter so that it is malleable, then lift it out of the tin and lay it on a lightly floured surface. Roll it out slightly and transfer it to the tart tin.

Ever walked past a French bakery with an apple tart in the window, boasting apple slices fanned out in the shape of a flower? Incredible, right? But if you then daydreamed about making such a thing yourself, you might've figured that it required skills well beyond those of a home cook. Happily, that's not so.

Okay, when I learned how to do it, I was in fact working as a professional chef. But what's required is the ability to slice an apple paper-thin, and it turns out that there's a simple trick (see Step 2, page 332) that allows anyone to do it, even someone without great knife skills.

The ingredients of the tart itself are purely elemental: apples, pie dough, sugar, butter, and apricot jam. The apples are Golden Delicious, which aren't my favorite to eat raw, but which turn into a different animal—intense and honeyed—when baked. They hold their shape beautifully, too.

TIPS FOR ROLLING OUT PIE DOUGH

Make sure there is a light dusting of flour on the counter before you start rolling out the dough. Lightly dust the top of the dough and the rolling pin with flour, too. The dough should be able to move on the counter at all times; if it starts to stick, sprinkle a little more flour on the counter. If it sticks, you will end up overworking it.

To roll the dough into a circle, roll over the disk going just to but not over the edge, and then turn it an eighth of a turn. Roll it again and turn it an eighth of a turn. Repeat until you have a circle of dough about $^1/_8$-inch thick. If you turn it a quarter of a turn each time, you will end up with a square or rectangle.

WHICH APPLE?

Golden Delicious is my apple preference for the star of this tart, but if you want to try a different kind, be my guest. However, stay away from McIntosh, Macoun, Cortland, and Empire. They won't hold their shape when baked, and you'll end up with an applesauce tart. If you want to try a different apple, just research its properties first on the Internet.

SLICING AND ARRANGING THE APPLES

1. Peel and halve all the apples, then arrange them cut side down on a cutting board. Using a melon baller, remove and discard the cores.

2. With a very sharp knife, slice the apples crosswise, but don't cut all the way down with the back side of the knife; stop just before it reaches the cutting board so that the apples stay attached at the bottom.

3. Here is what happens if you slice all the way down to the cutting board: The apples will become detached, fly all over the counter, and be very difficult to arrange in a pattern. You want them to stay lined up like the Rockettes.

4. When you have sliced all the apples, turn each on its side to expose the bottom. Cut off about ¼ inch of the bottom to remove the part of the apple that has not been sliced through.

5. Arrange 8 apple halves like the spokes of a wheel on the pastry, leaving a gap in the center of the spokes, and press down on the apple halves to spread the slices slightly.

6. Arrange the remaining apple slices in concentric circles in the center of the tart starting from the outside and working your way in...

7. ...further and further...

8. ...until there's a small space left in the center.

9. Shape the center apple slice into a cone to resemble the shape of the center of a rose.

Cut off the bottom of the apple half to detach the slices; now they can be fanned out.

Don't cut all the way down at the back end.

2

3

If you cut all the way down on both sides, the apple will fly all over.

5

6

8

9

Cooking with *Jacques Torres*

RASPBERRY BONBONS

Adapted from *A Year in Chocolate* (Stewart, Tabori & Chang, 2008).

START TO FINISH: 50 MINUTES / **HANDS-ON TIME:** 20 MINUTES
SERVINGS: MAKES ABOUT 30 BONBONS

1 pound chocolate, preferably
   bittersweet

1 recipe Raspberry Ganache

2 trays polycarbonate or plastic bonbon
   molds (see Sources, page 351)

> Line a rimmed baking sheet with parchment paper. Place 1 or 2 wire racks large enough to hold the candy molds on the baking sheet. Set aside.

> Temper the chocolate following the steps and photos on pages 336–337.

> Place the tempered chocolate in a room temperature glass bowl and follow the procedure for making the bonbons on pages 336–337.

RASPBERRY GANACHE

START TO FINISH: 40 MINUTES / **HANDS-ON TIME:** 40 MINUTES
SERVINGS: MAKES ABOUT 4 CUPS

1$^1/_3$ cups Fresh Raspberry Puree
   (see text at right)

$^1/_3$ cup light corn syrup

$^1/_4$ cup heavy cream

13 ounces milk chocolate, finely
   chopped

3 ounces bittersweet chocolate, finely
   chopped

4 tablespoons unsalted butter,
   cut into small pieces, at room
   temperature

3 tablespoons raspberry eau de vie
   (a clear, fruit brandy available at
   many liquor stores)

In a heavy saucepan, combine the raspberry puree, corn syrup, and cream. Bring to a boil, remove from the heat, and whisk to lower the temperature slightly.

Combine the two chocolates in a medium glass bowl. Pour the raspberry mixture over the chocolate and stir until the chocolate has melted and the mixture is cooled to just barely under 130°F on an instant-read thermometer.

Add the butter and eau de vie and, using an immersion blender or a whisk, mix until the ganache registers 110°F. If necessary, place over a pan of hot water to keep slightly warm until ready to use. Just be sure that the bottom of the bowl (or pan) holding the ganache does not touch the hot water or it will cause the ganache to be too warm and soft.

> "Jacques Torres possesses a child's wide-eyed love of all things chocolate and the pastry-and-candy-making skills of a roomful of master chocolatiers. So, who better to teach us how to temper chocolate and make bonbons? Tempering is the crucial process of heating and cooling chocolate to prepare it for dipping and coating. Tempered chocolate has a smooth texture, a glossy shine, and a pleasing "snap" when bitten or broken. Untempered chocolate is a mess.
>
> Here, Jacques shows how to temper chocolate in the microwave and how to mold chocolate with no fancy equipment required. I recommend you read those instructions and study the step-by-step photos on pages 336–337 first before making Jacques's bonbons.
>
> Ganache is typically a mixture of chocolate and heavy cream, heated, stirred, and then whipped into a silky rich confection. For a lush fruit component, Jacques adds a pure raspberry puree and raspberry eau de vie to his ganache filling. **Fresh Raspberry Puree:** Blend 2 cups fresh raspberries until smooth. Strain through a sieve to remove the seeds."

Cook's Notes: How to Temper Chocolate in the Microwave

Rather than stand at the stove, stirring chocolate over a double boiler, here is Jacques's method to easily temper chocolate in the microwave.

1. Chop the chocolate using a serrated knife and place it in a large, glass, microwave-safe bowl.

2. Melt chocolate in the microwave on high for 20 seconds, then remove from the oven and stir.

3. Continue to microwave the chocolate for 20-second intervals, stirring completely in between to let the residual heat melt the unmelted pieces. Do not rush the process—you don't want to overheat the chocolate and you don't want all of it to melt.

4. When the chocolate is about two-thirds melted, with one-third of the chocolate still solid, transfer the chocolate to another bowl (which is at room temperature), and mix the chocolate to a smooth consistency, preferably using an immersion blender.

5. While mixing, begin taking the temperature of the chocolate, which should ideally be 90°F or close to it. Jacques uses a laser thermometer (see Sources, page 351), but any good instant-read thermometer will do.

6. Point a hair dryer, turned to the hot setting, over the bowl when necessary to maintain the 90°F temperature of your tempered chocolate while you work with it.

HOW TO MOLD AND FILL BONBONS

1. Carefully ladle the tempered chocolate into the molds.

2. Turn the molds upside down over the bowl of tempered chocolate, allowing the excess chocolate to drip out, leaving just a thin coating (about 1/16 inch) inside each cup. Use a paring knife, pastry scraper, or metal spatula to scrape the excess chocolate off the top of the molds, returning the excess chocolate to the bowl of tempered chocolate.

3. Invert the molds and bang them gently, open side up, to release any air bubbles that might remain in the chocolate. Place the chocolate-coated mold, open side down, on a wire rack. Let stand for about 5 minutes.

4. Meanwhile, fill a pastry bag with raspberry ganache. Carefully fill the chocolate cups. Place the filled molds on a wire rack set over a baking sheet. Place the pan in the refrigerator for about 5 minutes to allow the chocolate to set completely.

5. When the ganache is set, melt the remaining tempered chocolate again and carefully ladle the chocolate over the filled molds, covering the filling with a layer and scraping off the excess chocolate with a paring knife or pastry scraper.

6. Set aside to firm for about 30 minutes and unmold.

1

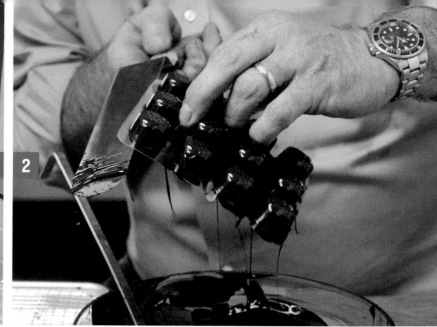

2

3

4

5

6

HAZELNUT-ALMOND DACQUOISE

Adapted from *Flour: Spectacular Recipes from Boston's Flour Bakery + Cafe* (Chronicle Books, 2010).

We booked Joanne Chang onto *Sara's Secrets* shortly after she opened Flour, her first bakery, in Boston's South End, which was an instant hit. A whirlwind of energy, Joanne today is the chef/owner of four bakeries and a Chinese restaurant in the Boston area and the author of three well-regarded cookbooks, including her most recent, *Baking with Less Sugar* (Chronicle Books, 2015).

She also turns out to be an excellent teacher. Here is Joanne's recipe for Hazelnut-Almond Dacquoise. *Dacquoise* is a term that refers to both the baked meringue layers of the cake and the composed cake itself. It's just about as challenging—and as delicious—as it sounds, requiring the intrepid baker to navigate the intricacies of meringue, buttercream, and ganache. Still, I promise you: Follow Joanne's instructions exactly, and you'll end up with a cake that looks just like the one in this photo. If I can do it, you can, too.

START TO FINISH: 11 HOURS 45 MINUTES / **HANDS-ON TIME:** 2 HOURS
SERVINGS: MAKES 1 (10-INCH-LONG) RECTANGULAR CAKE, SERVING 10 TO 12

For the meringue:

Vegetable cooking spray

$^1/_2$ cup blanched whole hazelnuts, plus $^1/_4$ cup blanched whole hazelnuts, toasted

$^1/_2$ cup blanched whole almonds, plus $^3/_4$ cup sliced almonds, toasted

$1^1/_3$ cups confectioners' sugar

$^1/_8$ teaspoon kosher salt

6 large egg whites

$^1/_3$ cup granulated sugar

For the chocolate ganache:

1 pound semisweet or bittersweet chocolate, chopped

2 cups heavy cream

For the espresso buttercream:

$^3/_4$ cup granulated sugar

$^1/_4$ cup water

2 large eggs

1 large egg yolk

$1^1/_2$ cups (3 sticks) unsalted butter, at room temperature, cut into 2-inch chunks

1 tablespoon instant espresso powder, 2 tablespoons instant coffee powder, or $^1/_4$ cup cooled brewed espresso

$^1/_4$ teaspoon kosher salt

> **Make the meringue:** Position a rack in the center of the oven, and heat the oven to 225°F. Line an 18- x 13-inch baking sheet (if you don't have a sheet that large, line 2 smaller sheets) with parchment paper. Draw 3 (10- x 3-inch) rectangles at least 3 inches apart on one side of the parchment paper (the meringues will expand in the oven), then turn the parchment over and liberally coat the other side of the paper with vegetable cooking spray or butter.

> In a food processor, pulse the ½ cup whole hazelnuts until ground to a fine powder. (Stop grinding once they are powdery; if you continue, they will become a paste.) Transfer to a medium bowl. Repeat with the ½ cup whole almonds; add the ground almonds to the ground hazelnuts. Sift the confectioners' sugar into the bowl holding the ground nuts. Add the salt and stir with a rubber spatula until all of the ingredients are well mixed. Set aside.

> Using a stand mixer fitted with the whip attachment (or a handheld mixer), beat the egg whites on medium speed for 3 to 4 minutes, or until they hold soft peaks. (This will take 6 to 7 minutes with a handheld mixer.) The whites will start to froth and turn into bubbles, and eventually the yellowy viscous part will disappear. Keep whipping until you can see the tines of your whip leaving a slight trail in the whites. To test for the soft-peak stage, stop the mixer and lift the whip out of the whites; the whites should peak and then droop.

> On medium speed, add the granulated sugar in three equal additions, mixing for 30 seconds after each addition. When all of the granulated sugar has been incorporated, increase the speed to high and beat for about 15 seconds longer. The meringue should be slightly glossy and white and somewhat stiff. Scrape the meringue into a large bowl.

> Sprinkle the nut-sugar mixture on top of the meringue. Working quickly and gently, use a rubber spatula to fold the nuts into the meringue, scraping the sides of the bowl to catch any loose nuts. The final consistency will be soupy, gloopy, and pudding-like.

> Fit a pastry bag with a ½-inch round plain tip and fill the bag with the meringue. Following the guidelines you drew on the underside of the parchment paper, pipe 3 rectangles of meringue; "fill in" the rectangles to form your individual layers.

> Bake for about 3 hours, or until the dacquoise rectangles are firm to the touch. Turn off the oven and leave the rectangles in the closed oven for at least 6 hours or for up to 12 hours.

(recipe continues)

JOANNE'S TIPS FOR MAKING THE HAZELNUT-ALMOND DACQUOISE

▶ The cake is not difficult to make, but all of its components make it important. Read the recipe from start to finish so you can organize your prep schedule.

▶ Each component can be made in advance, which makes the final assembly of the cake easier.

▶ Be sure you spray the parchment paper for the dacquoise meringues very well or they will be a bear to remove from the pans!

▶ Don't overwhip the egg whites. You want them just at firm peaks so that there's a little room for the meringues to grow when they bake in the oven.

> **Make the chocolate ganache:** Place the chocolate in a medium heatproof bowl. In a small saucepan over medium-high heat, scald the cream (bubbles start to form around the edge of the pan, but the cream is not boiling). Pour the hot cream over the chocolate and let sit for about 1 minute, then slowly whisk the chocolate and cream together until the chocolate is completely melted and the mixture is smooth. You should have about 4 cups.

> Let cool, cover, and store at room temperature for up to overnight. (The ganache can be made up to 1 week in advance and stored in an airtight container in the refrigerator. Remove it from the refrigerator 1 day before using.)

> **Make the buttercream:** In a small saucepan, stir together the granulated sugar and water. Place the pan over high heat, bring to a boil, and cook, without stirring, 3 to 4 minutes, or until the syrup registers 238°F on a candy thermometer (the soft-ball stage).

> Meanwhile, fit the stand mixer with the whip attachment (or use a handheld mixer) and beat together the eggs and egg yolk on medium speed for 3 to 4 minutes, or until pale and light. When the syrup is ready, remove from the heat. On low speed, slowly add the syrup into the eggs, drizzling it down the side of the bowl to keep it from hitting the whip and spattering. Turn the speed up to medium and whip for 6 to 8 minutes, or until the mixture turns light and fluffy, pale, and cool to the touch. Turn the speed down to low and add the butter, a few chunks as a time. Increase the speed to medium and continue to whip for 4 to 5 minutes. The mixture will break and look curdled at first, but don't worry. It will soon become smooth and silky. Add the espresso powder and salt and whip until completely combined. You should have about 3 cups.

> Use within 30 minutes, or cover and leave at room temperature for up to 8 hours, and then beat vigorously with a wood spoon until smooth before using. (Or, transfer to an airtight container and store in the refrigerator for up to 5 days, then bring to room temperature and beat with the stand mixer fitted with the paddle attachment for a few minutes until smooth before using.)

> **Assemble the cake:** When the dacquoise rectangles are ready, carefully peel off the parchment paper. Using a small paring knife or a small, serrated knife, trim the edges so they are even and the rectangles are all about the same size. The rectangles are fairly delicate at this point, and if you are not careful, they could shatter. The best way to avoid this is to shave off a little piece at a time until the rectangles are roughly uniform. If a rectangle shatters as you are trimming it, don't fret. That rectangle can be the middle layer. If 2 or all 3 rectangles shatter, again don't fret. You can piece them together as you assemble the cake. The cake will not be quite as neat, but the final product will taste the same.

> Cut a piece of cardboard the size of the dacquoise rectangles and place one rectangle on the cardboard. Fit a pastry bag with the ¹/₂-inch round plain tip and fill with about half of the ganache. Pipe a layer of ganache about ¹/₂ inch thick on top of the dacquoise. Gently press a second dacquoise rectangle directly on top of the ganache layer and press lightly to adhere the dacquoise to the ganache.

> Fill the pastry bag with about two-thirds of the espresso buttercream and pipe a layer of buttercream about ¹/₂ inch thick on top of the second dacquoise layer. Top the buttercream with the last dacquoise rectangle, placing it upside down so the flat side is on top. Press lightly to adhere this last rectangle to the buttercream. Use a small offset spatula to spread the remaining buttercream into the gaps between the layers and to spread a very thin layer all over the dacquoise. Do your best to make the exterior of the cake as smooth as you can—you will need to use a fair amount of buttercream to fill in all the gaps.

> Place the cake in the refrigerator for at least 1 hour to chill all of the layers. (At this point, the cake can be well wrapped in plastic wrap and stored in the refrigerator for up to 2 days or in the freezer for up to 2 weeks. If frozen, thaw overnight in the refrigerator before serving.)

> When ready to serve, spoon the remaining ganache into a small heatproof bowl, place over (not touching) simmering water in a saucepan, and heat just until melted. (Or, place in a microwave-safe bowl and microwave on low power for 30 to 45 seconds, or just until melted and warmed enough to pour freely—no warmer than that).

> Place a wire rack on a baking sheet (to catch the drips), and place the cake on the rack. Pour the melted ganache evenly over the entire dacquoise, so it covers the top and drips down the sides. Use a small offset spatula to level off the ganache on the top of the cake. Then, with the spatula, spread the ganache that drips down the sides so that it covers the sides evenly. Some of the ganache may mix into the buttercream, which is okay, because the sides will be covered with sliced almonds.

> Now, press the sliced almonds into the sides of the cake, covering them completely. (It helps to tilt the cake with one hand and press the almonds with your other hand.) Place the cake on a cake plate and press the whole hazelnuts along the top edge for decoration. The cake can be stored in an airtight container in the refrigerator for up to 2 days.

WHAT'S THE BEST WAY TO STORE NUTS?

Nuts and seeds (sesame, poppy, flax, sunflower) become rancid very quickly, so don't store them in your pantry. If you're planning to use them in a week or two, store them in the fridge. If you are not sure how soon you will use them, wrap them well and store them in the freezer.

LA TULIPE'S APRICOT SOUFFLÉS

Adapted from *Gourmet* magazine (March 1996).

START TO FINISH: I HOUR 10 MINUTES / **HANDS-ON TIME:** 35 MINUTES / **SERVINGS:** 6

6 ounces dried California apricots (see Note)

³/₄ cup granulated sugar, divided, plus additional for coating the ramekins

1 tablespoon fresh lemon juice

1 tablespoon cognac or dark rum, optional

¹/₂ teaspoon pure vanilla extract

Fine sea salt or table salt

Melted butter for the ramekins

5 large egg whites, at room temperature

¹/₄ teaspoon cream of tartar

Confectioners' sugar, lightly sweetened whipped cream, and small mint sprigs for garnish

> Combine the apricots, 1¹/₂ cups water, and ¹/₂ cup of the granulated sugar in a small saucepan. Bring the water to a boil, reduce the heat, and simmer the mixture, covered, 20 minutes. Transfer the mixture to a blender and puree until very smooth. Transfer the puree to a large bowl and stir in the lemon juice, cognac, if using, vanilla, and a pinch of salt. Cool the puree completely. (The puree may be made 2 days ahead, kept in a small bowl, the surface covered directly with plastic wrap, and chilled. Or it may be frozen for up to 1 month, but bring it back to room temperature and transfer it to a large bowl before proceeding with the recipe.)

> Preheat the oven to 350°F. Generously butter 6 (7-ounce: 3¹/₂- x 1³/₄-inch) ramekins and coat them with the additional granulated sugar, dumping out the excess. Chill the ramekins while you beat the egg whites.

> In a large bowl (preferably copper) with an electric stand mixer, beat the egg whites with a pinch of salt until foamy. Add the cream of tartar and beat until the whites just hold soft peaks. Continue beating, while adding the remaining ¹/₄ cup sugar a little bit at a time; beat the whites until they just hold stiff peaks. Add one-fourth of the whites to the apricot puree and whisk until combined well. Fold in the remaining whites, gently but thoroughly. Ladle or spoon the batter into the prepared ramekins and shape the soufflés (see page 344), if desired. Set the ramekins on a rimmed baking sheet. Bake the soufflés on the middle shelf of the oven, until they are puffed, golden brown, and just set in the center, 20 to 25 minutes.

> Remove the soufflés from the oven, sift a little of the confectioners' sugar on top and transfer to plates. Using a soup spoon, lift off a mound of the soufflé, place a spoonful of whipped cream in the indentation, and top the whipped cream with the mound. Garnish with the mint sprigs and serve immediately.

Note: Do not use Turkish apricots; they will not give you the bright, sunny flavor required.

In the early eighties I worked at La Tulipe, a little gem of a French restaurant In Greenwich Village as the *chef tournant,* covering a different station every day, which allowed all the other chefs a second day off every week. It was a terrific gig because I had to learn *everything,* including those things I might not have focused on otherwise, like desserts.

La Tulipe's chef/owner was Sally Darr. Sally had no formal restaurant training, but she had a world-class palate and she was a perfectionist who expected perfection from everyone in her kitchen. I probably learned more from Sally than from anyone else in my career.

This recipe is a wonderful example of her talent. Traditional soufflés are notoriously delicate. They can fail to come together properly at any number of steps along the way. But Sally's apricot soufflé is basically bullet-proof. The base consists of nothing but sweetened pureed dried apricots. The soufflé batter is sturdy enough to be shaped and to hold that shape when baked. And the soufflés in their ramekins are so rugged that you can park them in the fridge for an hour or two ahead of time before popping them into the oven to bake them off—without worrying for a second that they'll collapse or fail to rise.

We ran an adaption of this recipe in *Gourmet* years ago, but I decided it also needed to live on in this book, especially because I wanted to share the technique about how to shape the soufflés for dramatic effect (see page 344).

MAKING AND SHAPING THE SOUFFLÉS

HOW TO FOLD EGG WHITES

1. Beat your eggs only until they reach soft peaks, before adding the sugar. (If you beat your whites in a copper bowl, your meringue will be more stable and your soufflé will stay up longer. If you do a lot of baking involving egg whites you might want to invest in a copper bowl.)

2. Add one-fourth of the whites to the apricot puree and whisk until combined well.

3. Add the remaining whites to the bowl. Position a large spatula at the bottom of the bowl and lift the mixture with the spatula so that it falls on itself. Turn the bowl a quarter turn and fold in the same manner. Continue folding by lifting the mixture and letting it fall on itself until the mixture is just combined (if there are any little lumps of egg white at this point, just work them into the mixture where they are, using your finger). Do not press down on the mixture or stir vigorously.

HOW TO SHAPE THE APRICOT SOUFFLÉS

4. Spoon the batter into the prepared ramekins, making sure to get none of the batter on the sides of the ramekin (if the outside of the ramekin gets sticky you will not be able to execute the next step properly). Smooth the outside of the mixture with a small spatula to form a pointed mountain shape.

5. Turning the ramekin with one hand, dig a circular trench with the index finger of your other hand about 1 inch in from the edge of the ramekin. Move the ramekin, not your finger.

6. Drop the batter from your finger on top of the soufflé to form a little top knot.

7. Scoop off and level the batter around the center mound using an offset spatula.

8. Clean the rim with a towel.

9. Bake the shaped soufflés until nicely browned.

Be careful not to get any of the soufflé mixture on the sides of the ramekin.

2

3

Lift the mixture with the spatula so it falls on itself. Don't press down.

5

Move the ramekin, *not* your finger.

6

8

9

GUEST CHEFS

Jean Anderson is the author of more than 20 cookbooks including the best-selling *Doubleday Cookbook* (with Elaine Hanna; Doubleday, 1975), *The Food of Portugal* (William Morrow Cookbooks, 1994), and *A Love Affair with Southern Cooking* (William Morrow Cookbooks, 2007). A six-time best cookbook award winner (James Beard, IACP, and Tastemaker), Jean was named Editor of the Year by the James Beard Foundation in 1992, inducted into the James Beard Who's Who in Food & Beverage in America in 1994, and into the James Beard Cookbook Hall of Fame in 1999. A founding member of both Les Dames d'Escoffier and the New York Women's Culinary Alliance, Jean now makes her home in Chapel Hill, North Carolina. Her most recent book is *Crisps, Cobblers, Custards & Creams* (Houghton Mifflin Harcourt, 2016). Follow Jean at jeanandersoncooks.com.

Rick Bayless has done more to bring authentic Mexican cooking to America than any other cookbook author and chef. He is a five-time James Beard Award winner, the host of *Mexico: One Plate at a Time* on PBS, and the chef-owner of Frontera Grill, Topolobampo, and Xoco. Among his eight cookbooks are *Mexican Kitchen* (Scribner, 1996; IACP Cookbook of the Year), *Mexican Everyday* (W. W. Norton & Co., 2005), and *More Mexican Everyday* (Norton, 2015). Rick's Frontera Farmer Foundation provides grants for capital improvements to small Midwestern farms, while the Frontera Scholarship sends a Mexican-American Chicago Public School student to Kendall College to study culinary arts. His award-winning Frontera line of salsas, cooking sauces and organic chips can be found coast-to-coast and online at rickbayless.com and fronterafiesta.com.

Rawia Bishara, a Palestinian Arab chef from Nazareth, Israel, opened her restaurant Tanoreen, featuring Middle Eastern home cooking, in Brooklyn in 1998. The small, take-out/eat-in restaurant with seven tables soon had lines around the block. The current, larger restaurant has been lauded by everyone from *The New York Times* and *Gourmet* to Food Network's *The Best Thing I Ever Ate*. Tanoreen has been named to Michelin's Bib Gourmand guide four years running and has received "Best In" category scores in Zagat as well as being named in their top 50 New York City restaurants. For more information, visit tanoreen.com. Rawia's first cookbook is *Olives, Lemons & Za'atar* (Kyle Books, 2014).

Floyd Cardoz began his career in his native Bombay and furthered his culinary training in Switzerland before moving to New York, where he rose to Executive Sous Chef at the famed Lespinasse. As executive chef and partner in the beloved restaurant Tabla, he introduced New York to his groundbreaking New Indian cuisine; his newest restaurant, The Bombay Canteen, opened in Mumbai in 2015. He is the author of *One Spice, Two Spice: American Food, Indian Flavors* (William Morrow Cookbooks, 2006) and *Floyd Cardoz: Flavorwalla* (Artisan, 2016). In 2012 he won Season Three of Bravo TV's *Top Chef Masters*. His grand prize of $100,000 was donated to the Young Scientist Cancer Research Fund at New York's Mt. Sinai School of Medicine, which supports young researchers trying to make a difference in cancer research. For more information, visit floydcardoz.com.

Joanne Chang, an honors graduate of Harvard College with a degree in Applied Mathematics and Economics, left a career as a management consultant to enter the world of professional cooking. After working as a pastry chef in a number of restaurants in the Boston area, she opened Flour—a bakery and cafe of national acclaim—in the city's South End in 2000; there are now four branches of Flour in Boston and Cambridge. In 2007, with her husband,

Christopher Myers, Joanne opened Myers + Chang, a Chinese restaurant in the South End. Joanne is the author of four cookbooks: *Flour, Spectacular Recipes from Boston's Flour Bakery + Cafe* (Chronicle, 2010); *Flour Too, Indispensable Recipes for the Cafe's Most Loved Sweets and Savories* (Chronicle, 2013); *Baking with Less Sugar: Recipes for Desserts Using Natural Sweeteners and Little-to-No White Sugar* (Chronicle, 2015); and the upcoming *Myers + Chang at Home* (Houghton Mifflin, 2017).

Amanda Cohen is the chef and owner of Dirt Candy, the award-winning vegetable restaurant on Manhattan's Lower East Side. After graduating from New York's Natural Gourmet Cookery School Chef's Training Program, Cohen worked in some of the city's most esteemed veggie-forward restaurants, including Bobby Flay's Mesa Grill, Teany, Pure Food and Wine, and Heirloom (which won *Time Out New York's* Reader's Choice Award for Best Vegetarian Restaurant under Cohen's leadership). Amanda was the first vegetarian chef to compete on Food Network's *Iron Chef America* and her cookbook, *Dirt Candy: A Cookbook* (Clarkson Potter, 2012), is the first graphic novel cookbook to be published in North America. For more information, visit dirtcandynyc.com.

Elizabeth Karmel, a North Carolina native, is a nationally respected authority on grilling, barbecue, and Southern food. In 2014, she launched CarolinaCueToGo.com, an "online barbecue shack" specializing in North Carolina whole-hog barbecue seasoned with Elizabeth's signature Lexington-Style Vinegar Barbecue Sauce. The founding executive chef of Hill Country Barbecue Market (in New York City and Washington, D.C.) and Hill Country Chicken (in Brooklyn, New York), she also writes a bi-monthly column for the Associated Press called The American Table and is the author of three acclaimed cookbooks. Elizabeth is the founder of the long established, gender-breaking GirlsattheGrill.com.

Dave Pasternack is the James Beard Award–winning chef and co-owner of ESCA in New York City. In his three-star *New York Times* review of the restaurant, then-critic Frank Bruni aptly dubbed Dave "the fish whisperer." An avid fisherman, the Long Island, New York, native developed a love for the sea—and its creatures—at an early age. He attended Johnson & Wales University in Providence, Rhode Island, and spent 20 years working in some of New York's top restaurants, many of them French, before opening ESCA with Mario Batali and Joseph Bastianich in 2000. Even today in the restaurant, one might find Dave serving fish that he's caught that morning off the shores near his Long Island home. He is the author of *The Young Man and the Sea: Recipes & Crispy Fish Tales* (Artisan, 2007). For more information, visit esca-nyc.com.

Hiroko Shimbo is a world-renowned authority on Japanese cuisine who serves as a chef-instructor at respected culinary schools and a consulting chef to diverse food service industries. Hiroko has written three award-winning cookbooks: *The Japanese Kitchen* (Harvard Common Press, 2000), *The Sushi Experience* (Alfred Knopf, 2006), and *Hiroko's American Kitchen* (Andrews McMeel, 2013), which was IACP's Best American Cookbook for 2013. To keep up with her activities, visit hirokoskitchen.com and follow @hirokoshimo (Twitter) and HIROKOSHIMBO (Instagram).

Adam Sobel has been winning praise for the innovative vegan fare served at his Cinnamon Snail food truck since its opening in 2010. It's been called the Best Food Truck in NYC by Gothamist, one of the Ten Best Food Trucks in America by *The Huffington Post,* and won the Vegnews Veggie Award for Best Vegetarian Street Cart in 2012, 2013, and 2014. Among Adam's many Vendy Awards are the People's Choice Winner 2012, the Vendy Hero Award 2013 (for serving free meals to Hurricane Sandy victims), and finally taking the top prize Vendy Cup in 2014. Although the Cinnamon Snail no longer graces the streets of Manhattan's Chelsea neighborhood, it can be found most Sundays during the season at the Red Bank (New Jersey) Farmers' Market or at special events. Adam's first cookbook is *Street Vegan* (Clarkson Potter, 2015). For more information, visit cinnamonsnail.com.

Jacques Torres is widely acknowledged to be the authority on all things chocolate. Raised in France, he came to the United States in 1988 as the Corporate Pastry Chef for Ritz Carlton. A year later, he became Executive Pastry Chef at Le Cirque, where he gained fame for his opulent desserts and fantastic chocolate creations. The first artisan chocolatier to start from cocoa beans to make his own chocolate, Jacques opened his first chocolate factory, Jacques Torres Chocolate, in 2000, and expanded to a much larger facility in 2013. He now has retail shops across Manhattan. Jacques has hosted television series on both PBS and Food Network; his third cookbook, *A Year in Chocolate* (Stewart, Tabori and Chang) was released in 2008. Among his numerous accolades are the 1994 James Beard Pastry Chef of the Year Award and induction to the James Beard Who's Who of American Food & Beverage Award in 2003. Since 1993, Jacques has served as Dean of Pastry Arts at New York's International Culinary Center. For more about Jacques, visit mrchocolate.com.

Marc Vetri, a native Philadelphian trained in Bergamo, Italy, is renowned for bringing a contemporary sensibility to classic Italian cooking. He is the chef/founder of a critically acclaimed group of Italian restaurants in the Philadelphia area: Amis Trattoria, Osteria (Philadelphia and New Jersey), Pizzeria Vetri, Alla Spina, Vetri, and Lo Spiedo. Marc is the 2005 winner of the James Beard Award for "Best Chef Mid-Atlantic" and the author of three cookbooks: *Il Viaggio di Vetri* (Ten Speed Press, 2008), *Rustic Italian Food* (Ten Speed Press, 2011), and *Mastering Pasta* (Ten Speed Press, 2015). His Vetri Foundation for Children helps kids experience the connection between healthy eating and healthy living. Follow Marc and his restaurants at vetrifamily.com.

Jasper White is a James Beard Award–winning chef and restaurateur who is recognized as one of the leading authorities on New England food and its history, in particular seafood. Jasper is the author of four cookbooks: *Jasper White's Cooking from New England* (Harper & Row, 1989), *Lobster at Home* (Scribner, 1998), *Fifty Chowders* (Scribner, 2000), and *The Summer Shack Cookbook* (W.W. Norton & Co., 2007). Jasper has been associated with many of Boston's finest restaurants for almost 40 years, including (with Lydia Shire) the Copley Plaza, The Parker House, and The Bostonian. In 1983, he opened Jasper's Restaurant on Boston's historic waterfront, a mecca for anyone in search of fine dining and great seafood. In 2000, Jasper opened the acclaimed Jasper White's Summer Shack in Cambridge, Massachusetts, and three more soon followed, in Boston, at the Mohegan Sun resort in Connecticut, and in Dedham, Massachusetts. For more on Jasper and his restaurants, visit summershackrestaurant.com.

Grace Young, a native of San Francisco, has been called the "Stir-Fry Guru" and "Stir-Fry Master" by *The New York Times*. Her most recent cookbook, *Stir-Frying to the Sky's Edge* (Simon & Schuster, 2010) won the James Beard Award for Best International Cookbook. She is also the author of *The Breath of a Wok* (Simon & Schuster, 2004; winner of the IACP International Cookbook Award and the IACP Jane Grigson Cookbook Award for Distinguished Scholarship) and *The Wisdom of the Chinese Kitchen* (Simon & Schuster, 1999; winner of the IACP International Cookbook Award). Her online stir-fry class is available through Craftsy.com. You can find out more about Grace by visiting her website: graceyoung.com.

SOURCES

AJI AMARILLO PASTE

Kalustyan's is a legendary New York City specialty food store stocked with exotic ingredients from around the world and especially Southeast Asia. Visit kalustyans.com for aji amarillo paste, chickpea flour, Egyptian rice, garam masala, gochugaru flakes, makrut (kaffir) lime leaves, pomegranate molasses, and tamarind.

BEANS

Anson Mills grows specialty beans and heirloom grains, including polenta, in South Carolina. To order online, visit ansonmills.com.

Bob's Red Mill offers an extensive variety of beans, grains, and flours, including chickpea and other alternative flours. To find a retailer near you, or to order online, visit bobsredmill.com.

Rancho Gordo has a large selection of colorful, unusual heirloom beans, as well as dried chiles, grains, and spices, all of which can be ordered online at ranchogordo.com.

CHORIZO

Aurelia's Chorizo is made in Boerne, Texas, from an authentic Spanish recipe. Visit aureliaschorizo.com to order online.

La Tienda, located in Williamsburg, Virginia, offers the largest selection of Spanish food online, including chorizo, dried and roasted peppers, and fideo pasta. Visit tienda.com for the complete selection.

Palacios is authentic chorizo sausage imported from Spain. Visit palacioschorizo.com to order online.

DUCK

Maple Leaf Farms is a family owned and operated company that is the leader in United States duck production. Visit mapleleaffarms .com to purchase whole ducks, duck breasts, legs (natural and confit), duck fat, and other prepared duck products.

EVERYTHING BAGEL TOPPING

King Arthur Flour, founded in Boston in 1790 and now located in Norwich, Vermont, is America's oldest flour company. Visit kingarthurflour.com to order Everything Bagel Topping, Italian-Style Flour, and to find information about their Baking Education Center.

FIDEO PASTA

La Tienda (see Chorizo listing at left: tienda.com)

FLOUR

Italian 00 Flour
ditalia.com is a St. Louis, Missouri, and online marketplace for Italian food specialties, including Italian 00 flour, rice, and pasta.

igourmet.com is an online retailer of specialty foods, selling a range of international products, including Italian 00 flour, beans, grains, and Italian (Arborio and Carnaroli) and Spanish rice (Valencian) varieties.

King Arthur Flour (see Everything Bagel Topping listing above: kingarthurflour.com)

Chickpea (Garbanzo Bean) Flour

Bob's Red Mill (see Beans listing at left: bobsredmill.com)

Kalustyan's (see Aji Amarillo Paste listing at left: kalustyans.com)

FOOD SCALE

OXO Good Grips makes my favorite measuring cups, and I also like their stainless steel food grade scale with pull out display. For further details and to find a retailer near you, visit oxo.com.

GARAM MASALA

Kalustyan's (see Aji Amarillo Paste listing at left: kalustyans.com)

Penzeys Spices is a wonderful source of high-quality, fresh spices and seasonings. To find a Penzeys store near you or to order online, visit penzeys.com for garam masala, Turkish bay leaves, and many different dried chiles both whole and ground.

GOCHUJANG PASTE

Mother-in-Law's Kimchi is my favorite prepared brand. Order their gochujang paste and their kimchi (in many varieties, including vegan) at milkimchi.com.

GRAINS

Anson Mills (see Beans listing at left: ansonmills.com)

Bob's Red Mill (see Beans listing at left: bobsredmill.com)

igourmet.com (see Flour listing at left)

Rancho Gordo (see Beans listing at left: ranchogordo.com)

JAMAICAN JERK SEASONING

Walkerswood Caribbean Foods is a Jamaica-based maker of Caribbean seasonings, sauces, and condiments, including my favorite Jamaican Jerk Seasoning. For ordering information, visit walkerswood.com.

KIMCHI

Mother-in-Law's Kimchi (see Gochujang Paste listing on page 350: milkimchi.com)

LASER THERMOMETERS

Etekcity produces and sells a range of affordable, instant-read laser thermometers like the one used by Jacques Torres for tempering chocolate. For more information and to order, visit etekcity.com.

LENTILLES DU PUY

igourmet.com (see Flour listing on page 350)

MAKRUT (KAFFIR) LIME LEAVES

importfood.com is an online supermarket for Thai and other Asian food products, including makrut (kaffir) lime leaves and tamarind.

Kalustyan's (see Aji Amarillo Paste listing on page 350: kalustyans.com)

NEW ENGLAND–STYLE HOT DOG BUNS

famousfoods.com is an online source for New England foods of all types and brands, including New England–style top-sliced hot dog buns.

Pepperidge Farm makes New England–style top-sliced hot dog buns under their "Bakery Classics" label. For more information, visit pepperidgefarm.com.

OROSHIGANE GRATER

Chubo is an online purveyor of fine Japanese kitchenware, specializing in fine knives and accessories, including a selection of oroshigane graters for ginger. To order directly, visit chuboknives.com.

PARCHMENT COOKING BAGS

PaperChef makes a variety of culinary parchment products, including cooking bags. For more information and a list of retailers, visit paperchef.com.

POLYCARBONATE CHOCOLATE MOLDS

N.Y. Cake is a family-owned retailer whose Manhattan store is stocked to the ceilings with all manner of baking supplies, including polycarbonate chocolate molds like those used by Jacques Torres. To order online, visit nycake.com.

POMEGRANATE MOLASSES

Kalustyan's (see Aji Amarillo Paste listing on page 350: kalustyans.com)

RICE

Egyptian Rice
Kalustyan's (see Aji Amarillo Paste listing on page 350: kalustyans.com)

Valencia, Arborio, Carnaroli, or Vialone Nano Rice
ditalia.com (see Flour listing on page 350)

igourmet.com (see Flour listing on page 350)

SALSA

Fronterafiesta.com is the online source for the Frontera line of gourmet foods from chef Rick Bayless, including salsas, chips, marinades, and sauces.

TAMARIND

Kalustyan's (see Aji Amarillo Paste listing on page 350: kalustyans.com)

importfood.com (see Makrut [Kaffir] Lime Leaves listing at left)

TORTILLA PRESS

The Rick Bayless by Gorham Tortilla Press is available at Bed Bath & Beyond. Visit bedbathandbeyond.com to order.

TURKISH BAY LEAVES

Penzeys Spices (see Garam Masala listing on page 350: penzeys.com)

VANILLA BEAN PASTE

Nielsen-Massey Vanillas & Flavors has been creating fine vanilla products and flavor extracts since 1907. For product details and to find a retailer near you, visit nielsenmassey.com.

ZESTER

KitchenIQ's Better Zester provides the finest citrus zest I've ever seen. For product details and retail information, visit kitcheniq.com.

SEASONAL PRODUCE GUIDE

When you use fresh fruits, vegetables, and herbs, you don't have to do much to make them taste great. Although many fruits, vegetables, and herbs are available year-round, you'll get better flavor and prices when you buy what's in season. This guide helps you choose the best produce so you can create tasty meals all year long.

SPRING

Fruits
- Bananas
- Blood oranges
- Coconuts
- Grapefruit
- Kiwifruit
- Lemons
- Limes
- Mangoes
- Navel oranges
- Papayas
- Passion fruit
- Pineapples
- Strawberries
- Tangerines
- Valencia oranges

Vegetables
- Artichokes
- Arugula
- Asparagus
- Avocados
- Baby leeks
- Beets
- Belgian endive
- Broccoli
- Cauliflower
- Dandelion greens
- Fava beans
- Green onions
- Green peas
- Kale
- Lettuce
- Mushrooms
- Radishes
- Red potatoes
- Rhubarb
- Snap beans
- Snow peas
- Spinach
- Sugar snap peas
- Sweet onions
- Swiss chard

Herbs
- Chives
- Dill
- Garlic chives
- Lemongrass
- Mint
- Parsley
- Thyme

SUMMER

Fruits
Apricots
Blackberries
Blueberries
Boysenberries
Cantaloupes
Casaba melons
Cherries
Crenshaw melons
Figs
Grapes
Guava
Honeydew melons
Mangoes
Nectarines
Papayas
Peaches
Plums
Raspberries
Strawberries
Watermelons

Vegetables
Avocados
Beans: pole, shell, and snap
Beets
Bell peppers
Cabbage
Carrots
Celery
Chile peppers
Collards
Corn
Cucumbers
Eggplant
Green beans
Jicama
Lima beans
Okra
Pattypan squash
Peas
Radicchio
Radishes
Summer squash
Tomatoes

Herbs
Basil
Bay leaves
Borage
Chives
Cilantro
Dill
Lavender
Lemon balm
Marjoram
Mint
Oregano
Rosemary
Sage
Summer savory
Tarragon
Thyme

FALL

Fruits
Apples
Cranberries
Figs
Grapes
Pears
Persimmons
Pomegranates
Quinces

Vegetables
Belgian endive
Bell peppers
Broccoli
Brussels sprouts
Cabbage
Cauliflower
Eggplant
Escarole
Fennel
Frisée
Leeks
Mushrooms
Parsnips
Pumpkins
Red potatoes
Rutabagas
Shallots
Sweet potatoes
Winter squash
Yukon gold potatoes

Herbs
Basil
Bay leaves
Parsley
Rosemary
Sage
Tarragon
Thyme

WINTER

Fruits
Apples
Blood oranges
Cranberries
Grapefruit
Kiwifruit
Kumquats
Lemons
Limes
Mandarin oranges
Navel oranges
Pears
Persimmons
Pomegranates
Pomelos
Tangelos
Tangerines
Quinces

Vegetables
Baby turnips
Beets
Belgian endive
Brussels sprouts
Celery root
Escarole
Fennel
Frisée
Jerusalem artichokes
Kale
Leeks
Mushrooms
Parsnips
Potatoes
Rutabagas
Sweet potatoes
Turnips
Watercress
Winter squash

METRIC EQUIVALENTS

The information in the following charts is provided to help cooks outside the United States successfully use the recipes in this book. All equivalents are approximate.

COOKING/OVEN TEMPERATURES

	Fahrenheit	Celsius	Gas Mark
Freeze Water	32° F	0° C	
Room Temp.	68° F	20° C	
Boil Water	212° F	100° C	
Bake	325° F	160° C	3
	350° F	180° C	4
	375° F	190° C	5
	400° F	200° C	6
	425° F	220° C	7
	450° F	230° C	8
Broil			Grill

LIQUID INGREDIENTS BY VOLUME

¹/₄ tsp	=					1 ml		
¹/₂ tsp	=					2 ml		
1 tsp	=					5 ml		
3 tsp	=	1 Tbsp	=	¹/₂ fl oz	=	15 ml		
2 Tbsp	=	¹/₈ cup	=	1 fl oz	=	30 ml		
4 Tbsp	=	¹/₄ cup	=	2 fl oz	=	60 ml		
5¹/₃ Tbsp	=	¹/₃ cup	=	3 fl oz	=	80 ml		
8 Tbsp	=	¹/₂ cup	=	4 fl oz	=	120 ml		
10²/₃ Tbsp	=	²/₃ cup	=	5 fl oz	=	160 ml		
12 Tbsp	=	³/₄ cup	=	6 fl oz	=	180 ml		
16 Tbsp	=	1 cup	=	8 fl oz	=	240 ml		
1 pt	=	2 cups	=	16 fl oz	=	480 ml		
1 qt	=	4 cups	=	32 fl oz	=	960 ml		
				33 fl oz	=	1000 ml	=	1 l

DRY INGREDIENTS BY WEIGHT
(To convert ounces to grams, multiply the number of ounces by 30.)

1 oz	=	¹/₁₆ lb	=	30 g
4 oz	=	¹/₄ lb	=	120 g
8 oz	=	¹/₂ lb	=	240 g
12 oz	=	³/₄ lb	=	360 g
16 oz	=	1 lb	=	480 g

LENGTH
(To convert inches to centimeters, multiply the number of inches by 2.5.)

1 in	=					2.5 cm		
6 in	=	¹/₂ ft			=	15 cm		
12 in	=	1 ft			=	30 cm		
36 in	=	3 ft	=	1 yd	=	90 cm		
40 in	=					100 cm	=	1 m

EQUIVALENTS FOR DIFFERENT TYPES OF INGREDIENTS

Standard Cup	Fine Powder* (ex. flour)	Grain (ex. rice)	Granular (ex. sugar)	Liquid Solids (ex. butter)	Liquid (ex. milk)
1	120 g	150 g	190 g	200 g	240 ml
³/₄	90 g	113 g	143 g	150 g	180 ml
²/₃	80 g	100 g	125 g	133 g	160 ml
¹/₂	60 g	75 g	95 g	100 g	120 ml
¹/₃	40 g	50 g	63 g	67 g	80 ml
¹/₄	30 g	38 g	48 g	50 g	60 ml
¹/₈	15 g	19 g	24 g	25 g	30 ml

* Metrics based on King Arthur Flour.

RECIPE INDEX

SUBJECT INDEX

Editors: Marisa Bulzone, Rachel Quinlivan West, R.D.

Editorial Assistants: Nicole Fisher, April Smitherman

Assistant Managing Editor: Jeanne de Lathouder

Assistant Project Editor: Lauren Moriarty

Designers: Chalkley Caulderwood, Maribeth Jones

Food Stylists: Nathan Carrabba, Victoria E. Cox, Margaret Monroe Dickey, Grace Parisi, Catherine Crowell Steele

Executive Photography Director: Iain Bagwell

Photo Editor: Kellie Lindsey

Photographers: Quentin Bacon, Hélène Dujardin, Victor Protasio, Lucy Schaeffer

Photo Assistant: Biz Jones

Photo Stylists: Kay E. Clarke, Stephanie Hanes, Mindi Shapiro Levine

Hair/Makeup Stylists: Pamela Arnone, Kerri Bunn

Senior Production Manager: Greg A. Amason

Assistant Production Director: Sue Chodakiewicz

Copy Editor: Jacqueline Giovanelli

Proofreader: Deri Reed

Indexer: Mary Ann Laurens

Fellows: Laura Arnold, Jessica Baude, Dree Deacon, Loren Lorenzo, Natalie Schumann, Mallory Short, Caroline Smith

ISBN-13: 978-0-8487-4441-0

ISBN-10: 0-8487-4441-1

Library of Congress Control Number: **2015956841**

First Edition 2016
Printed in the United States of America
10 9 8 7 6 5 4 3 2 1